SECOND EDITION

ASSESSMENT IN THE CLASSROOM
A CONCISE APPROACH

PETER W. AIRASIAN
Boston College

McGraw Hill

Boston   Burr Ridge, IL   Dubuque, IA   Madison, WI   New York   San Francisco   St. Louis
Bangkok   Bogotá   Caracas   Lisbon   London   Madrid
Mexico City   Milan   New Delhi   Seoul   Singapore   Sydney   Taipei   Toronto

McGraw-Hill Higher Education

A Division of The **McGraw-Hill** *Companies*

ASSESSMENT IN THE CLASSROOM: A CONCISE APPROACH, SECOND EDITION

This book is printed on acid-free paper.

1 2 3 4 5 6 7 8 9 0 QPF/QPF 0 9 8 7 6 5 4 3 2 1 0

ISBN 0–07–228953–8

Editorial director: *Jane E. Vaicunas*
Sponsoring editor: *Beth Kaufman*
Developmental editor: *Cara Harvey*
Marketing manager: *Daniel M. Loch*
Project manager: *Susan J. Brusch*
Production supervisor: *Enboge Chong*
Coordinator of freelance design: *Michelle D. Whitaker*
Senior photo research coordinator: *Carrie K. Burger*
Senior supplement coordinator: *David A. Welsh*
Compositor: *Shepherd, Inc.*
Typeface: *10/12 Veljovic Book*
Printer: *Quebecor Printing Book Group/Fairfield, PA*

Cover designer: *Diane Beasley*
Cover image: ©*SuperStock, Inc.*
Photo research: *LouAnn K. Wilson*

CHAPTER OPENERS:
1: © *Elizabeth Crews;* **2:** © *Michael Newman/Photo Edit;* **3:** © *1987 Joel Gordon;*
4: © *Blair Seltz/Photo Researchers;* **5:** © *Cary Wolinsky/Stock Boston;* **6:** © *Elizabeth Crews;*
7: © *Arthur Grace/Stock Boston*

Library of Congress Cataloging-in-Publication Data

Airasian, Peter W.
    Assessment in the classroom: a concise approach / Peter W. Airasian.—2nd ed.
      p.   cm.
    Includes indexes.
    ISBN 0–07–228953–8
    1. Educational tests and measurements—United States.
2. Examinations—Validity—United States.   3. Grading and marking
(Students)—United States.   I. Title.
LB3051.A5626   2000
371.26—dc21   99–31296
                                                   CIP

www.mhhe.com

41326321

For Lynn, Greg, and Gwen

ABOUT THE AUTHOR

Peter W. Airasian is a Professor in the Educational Research, Measurement, and Evaluation Program at Boston College. His main teaching responsibilities are instructing pre- and in-service teachers in strategies of classroom assessment. He received his Ph.D. from the University of Chicago with a concentration in testing, evaluation, and assessment. He is a former chemistry and biology teacher. He is author or co-author of *School Effectiveness: A Reassessment of the Evidence* (1980), *The Effects of Standardized Testing* (1982), *Classroom Assessment* (1991, 1994, 1997), and *Teacher Self-Evaluation Tool Kit* (1997). He is a past Chair of the American Educational Research Association's Special Interest Group on classroom assessment. Currently he is continuing his study of classroom assessments and examining issues related to the evaluation of teachers.

CONTENTS IN BRIEF

CONTENTS

PREFACE

The ability to conduct assessment in the classroom ranks among a teacher's most essential educational tool. Ongoing formal and informal classroom assessments provide teachers with the information they need to monitor and make decisions about their pupils, teaching, learning, and grading. Increasingly, teachers must confront not only their own traditional classroom assessments, but also those required by external sources such as school districts, states, and national bodies.

In addition to the increase in assessments in the classroom, teacher education programs are changing. In many cases, the new curriculums that are emerging are streamlined versions of their predecessors, having fewer credit hours to teach a professional knowledge base that seems continually to expand. This tightening of the professional curriculum together with increased amounts of field experience has resulted both in restructured core courses and, in some places, in an array of narrower courses that give only one or two credit hours at completion. In most cases, the new courses do not map well with the large survey texts that were produced for the old curriculum.

In view of this curriculum variation, this revision of *Assessment in the Classroom: A Concise Approach* is designed to fit a variety of curriculum arrangements. Because of its modest length and price, and its emphasis on the assessment needs of regular classroom teachers, it is ideal for the following situations:

- ◆ To be the core text in either brief or full-length courses for teachers.
- ◆ To teach the assessment "unit" in educational psychology courses.
- ◆ To teach the assessment component of those integrated methods courses (course blocks) that combine formerly separate content areas and often last a full year.

The special mission of *Assessment in the Classroom: A Concise Approach* is to show how assessment principles and practices apply to the full range of teacher decision making, including assessments for: organizing a class at the start of the school year, planning and conducting instruction, grading, constructing formal assessments to determine student learning, and interpreting standardized and state-mandated tests. The goal is to show students that assessment is an everyday, ongoing part of their teaching, not some esoteric affair that is divorced from their daily routine. This edition retains the following features of the prior edition:

- ◆ *Realistic assessment* The focus throughout is on the realities of classrooms and how assessment techniques can serve these realities.
- ◆ *Validity and reliability* These central assessment concepts are introduced in Chapter 1 and then linked in later chapters to each specific type of assessment information. In this way, the particular validity and reliability problems of informal assessment, planning and delivering teaching, grading, paper-and-pencil tests, and performance assessments are identified. Practical strategies to improve the validity and reliability of various assessment techniques are also presented in each chapter.
- ◆ *Practical guidelines* A good portion of each chapter is devoted to practical guidelines to follow and common errors to avoid when using the type of assessment under discussion. The implications of ignoring the recommendations are also described.
- ◆ *Teacher thinking* Interspersed throughout the text are excerpts from interviews with real teachers that add the wisdom of practice to the text discussions.

New to This Edition

In addition to retaining the focus of the prior edition, this edition contains the following changes:

- ◆ Sizing-up assessment, assessment conducted early in the school year to organize and learn about pupils, is now a separate chapter to emphasize its importance.
- ◆ Focus on accommodating pupils with disabilities both during instruction and during formal assessments is expanded.
- ◆ Increased links between objectives and types of instructional approaches are provided.
- ◆ The chapter on performance/alternative assessment has been updated.
- ◆ Coverage of statewide standards and assessments, with examples, has been expanded.
- ◆ Over 20 web sites related to educational and classroom assessment are provided and described.
- ◆ The instructor's manual has been restructured to match the changes in this edition. In particular, the number of test items and student-centered activities has been increased.

Acknowledgments

With great appreciation I acknowledge the following reviewers whose frank and detailed suggestions guided this revision: Kathleen L. Matthew, Western Kentucky University; Eleanor Vernon Wilson, University of Virginia; and Betty Jo Simmons, Longwood College. As previously, I dedicate this book to Lynn, Greg, and Gwen, who provide support and inspiration for all my endeavors. I also wish to thank Lane Akers, who conceived this book and did a great deal to make it a reality. Beth Kaufman and Cara Harvey at McGraw-Hill were exceptionally helpful and supportive in the preparation of this revision. Susan Brusch ably guided the manuscript to production. Thanks and appreciation to Susan Gracia, my graduate assistant, who proofread the manuscript and carried out many of the necessary tasks associated with putting the revision together. Lastly, I acknowledge my mother and father, who made education an important part of my life; John Walsh, who was responsible for starting me on my career; and Ben Bloom, who provided guidance and perspectives that still influence my thought and work.

Peter W. Airasian

ASSESSMENT IN THE CLASSROOM

A CONCISE APPROACH

THE CLASSROOM AS AN ASSESSMENT ENVIRONMENT

CHAPTER OBJECTIVES

After reading this chapter, the student will be able to:

1. define basic terms: for example, assessment, measurement, test, standardized, validity, and reliability.

2. contrast the three main purposes of assessment and give examples of each.

3. describe the characteristics of various methods of collecting assessment data.

4. differentiate standardized and nonstandardized and individual and group assessments.

5. explain what validity and reliability are and how they influence the use of assessment information.

6. state examples of teachers' ethical responsibilities in collecting or using assessment information.

Today was a typical day in Ms. Lopez' classroom. In addition to preparing her room for the day's instructional activities, writing the homework assignments on the blackboard, reviewing her lesson plans, taking attendance, passing out a new textbook, and reminding pupils of next Thursday's field trip, Ms. Lopez:

♦ assigned grades to her pupils' science tests.

♦ selected Martha, not Matt, to deliver a note to Mr. Henderson, the school principal.

♦ decided on topics to cover in tomorrow's lessons.

♦ suggested ways that Robert could improve the first draft of his book report.

♦ completed the monthly school progress report on each of her pupils.

♦ referred Aaron to the Special Education Department because of his poor gross motor skills.

♦ stopped the planned language lesson halfway through the period in order to review the previous day's lesson.

♦ placed pupils who were below the accepted cutoff score on the state-mandated basic skills test into a special remedial group.

♦ rearranged the class seating plan to separate Bill from Leroy and to put Monroe in the front of the room so he could see the blackboard better.

♦ moved Jennifer from the middle to the high reading group.

♦ called on Kim twice even though her hand was not raised.

- praised Anne for her B grade, but encouraged Tim to work harder in order to improve his B grade.
- switched instruction from discussion to individual seatwork when the class became bored and unruly.
- previewed and selected a filmstrip on astronomy for next week's science unit.
- determined that she should construct her own test for the science unit on physical and chemical changes rather than using the unit test provided by the textbook publisher.
- sent Randy to the school nurse when he complained of a headache.
- corrected her pupils' projects for the unit on the three branches of American government.
- decided to spend an extra two days letting her students reread and evaluate their poetry portfolios.
- judged that Rose's constant interruptions and speaking out in class warranted a note to her parents about the problem.
- assigned homework in science but not in social studies.
- checked with the school counselor regarding possible reasons for Joshua's increasingly inattentive class behavior.
- developed a scoring rubric for assessing her students' writing portfolios.
- paired Kim, a class isolate, with Mary, a class leader, for the group project in social studies.
- sent Ralph to the school principal because he swore at a teacher and fought with a classmate.
- held an after-school parent-teacher conference with Tim's parents.
- consulted last year's standardized test scores to determine whether the class needed a review of the basic rules of capitalization.

As you can see, Ms. Lopez' day in the classroom, like those of all teachers, was filled with situations that required decisions to be made: decisions about grading, planning instruction, judging the success of instruction, providing for pupils' needs, interacting with and encouraging pupils, testing, assigning homework, and dealing with parents. Some of her decisions were about individual pupils and some about the class as a whole. Some were about instructional matters, some about classroom climate and behavior, some about pupil personalities, and some about pupil learning. Some, like the decision to change Jennifer's reading group or refer Aaron for screening, are decisions made infrequently during the school year. Others, like planning topics for instruction, calling on pupils during class, and assigning grades to pupils, are made many times each day.

Teacher decisions and the evidence that guides them are the lifeblood on which classrooms function. Taken together, all these decisions help

Teachers are constantly gathering information to make classroom decisions.

teachers to establish, organize, and monitor classroom features such as interpersonal relations, social adjustment, instructional content, lesson pace, and pupil learning (Clark & Peterson, 1986; Biddle, Good, & Goodson, 1996). Gathering evidence and making decisions are necessary and ongoing aspects of life in all classrooms. Because classroom decisions are necessary and important, they should be made on the basis of good evidence.

The decisions Ms. Lopez made were based on many different kinds of evidence that she was continually collecting. Why, for example, did Ms. Lopez praise Anne for her B grade but encourage Tim, who attained the same grade, to do better next time? How did she know that the way to settle down her bored and unruly class was to switch from discussion to seatwork? What made her decide to move Jennifer to the high reading group? Why did she finally decide that Rose's parents needed to be notified about their child's behavior? Why did she think pairing Kim with Mary for the social studies project was better than pairing Kim with Martha, Rose, or Joshua? Why did she feel that letting pupils spend two extra days reflecting on their poetry portfolios would be more beneficial than using the time to introduce some other topic? Why was Martha, but not Matt, trusted to deliver a note to the principal? All of these decisions were based upon information Ms. Lopez gathered to help her select appropriate courses of action in her classroom. This book is about the process of gathering, evaluating, and using such information to help make good classroom decisions.

PURPOSES OF ASSESSMENT

Teachers assess for many purposes because they are required to make many decisions. If we review Ms. Lopez' decisions during her classroom day, we get a sense of the many purposes teachers have for assessment. The remainder of this text focuses on assessment concerns and strategies for the following purposes: establishing classroom equilibrium, planning and conducting instruction, placing students, providing feedback and incentives, diagnosing pupil problems, and judging and grading academic learning and progress.

Establishing Classroom Equilibrium

An often overlooked purpose of assessment is to establish and maintain the classroom society.

An often overlooked purpose of assessment is to establish and maintain the social equilibrium of the classroom. Classrooms are complex social settings where people interact with one another in a multitude of ways. For classrooms to be positive social and learning environments, order, discipline, and cooperation must be present. Thus, helping pupils to learn and maintaining order in the classroom are closely related; some amount of orderliness is needed if teaching and learning are to be successful.

When Ms. Lopez selected Martha instead of Matt to deliver a note to the school principal, and when she changed the class seating plan to move Bill and Leroy farther apart, she was making decisions to preserve classroom order and stability. The fact that she allowed Randy to go alone to the school nurse indicated her trust in him. On the other hand, Rose's constant interruptions and speaking out necessitated sending a note to her parents, and Ralph's swearing and fighting led to his being removed from the classroom. Ms. Lopez' efforts to make Kim a part of the classroom society by calling on her even though her hand was not raised was another attempt to create and maintain a viable social and learning environment.

Planning and Conducting Instruction

Many of the decisions that Ms. Lopez made were focused on planning and conducting classroom instruction. This should not be surprising, since instruction is a central classroom activity. The instructional decisions that Ms. Lopez made can be divided into two types: planning decisions and process, or teaching, decisions. When Ms. Lopez selected the topics to be included in tomorrow's lessons, previewed and selected the astronomy filmstrip for next week's science unit, decided to spend two extra days on the poetry portfolios, and assigned homework in one subject but not another, she was planning future instructional activities.

In addition to planning decisions, the actual process of teaching a class requires constant assessment and decision making. At two points during the day, Ms. Lopez altered her instruction in the middle of the lesson because her pupils were confused and unruly. Once she stopped her language lesson to review the prior day's lesson because pupil responses to her questions indicated that the class did not understand its content. Another time she switched her method of instruction from discussion to seatwork when the students became bored and unruly. A great deal of teacher assessment is for the purpose of planning and conducting instruction.

Placing Pupils

Most classroom teachers must make decisions about the placement of their pupils. Whenever a teacher divides pupils into reading or math groups, organizes groups for cooperative learning, pairs or groups pupils for class projects, or recommends that a particular student be placed with a particular teacher next year, assessments for placement purposes have been made. Ms. Lopez made a placement decision when she moved Jennifer from the middle to the high reading group. She made another placement decision when she identified pupils who were below the cutoff score on the state-mandated basic skills test and placed them into a remedial group. Finally, when she paired Kim, the class isolate, with Mary in the social studies

Placement decisions are made for social as well as academic reasons.

project group, she made another placement decision. Note that Ms. Lopez' placement decisions were made for both academic and social reasons.

Providing Feedback and Incentives

Another important reason for classroom assessment is to provide feedback and incentives to pupils. For example, Ms. Lopez praised Anne for attaining a B grade but suggested that Tim could work harder and do better in the future, even though he received the same grade. She used assessment information from Robert's first-draft book report to suggest improvements. In each of these cases, information about academic performance was used to provide feedback to pupils about their performance. The term used to describe feedback intended to alter and improve students' learning while instruction is going on is **formative assessment.** In order to provide such feedback, teachers must constantly assess student learning and behavior.

Accurate feedback about academic performance is needed in order to provide students with incentive to improve.

Diagnosing Pupil Problems

Teachers are always on the lookout for pupils who are having learning, emotional, or social problems in the classroom. Having identified such problems, the teacher can sometimes carry out the remedial activities needed, but at other times the pupil must be referred for more specialized diagnosis and remediation outside of the classroom. Thus, Ms. Lopez set up her own in-class group for basic skills remediation, but she recommended that Aaron be screened by a specialist for his apparent gross motor skills deficiency. She reviewed last year's standardized test scores to determine whether her pupils needed remedial work in capitalization, but she also checked with the school counselor about possible reasons for Joshua's inattentive behavior. Much of the assessment data teachers gather is used to identify, understand, and remediate pupils' problems and learning difficulties.

Teacher assessments are used to identify and remediate pupil problems.

Judging and Grading Academic Learning and Progress

A number of Ms. Lopez' decisions had to do with judging pupils' academic learning and progress. She assigned grades to her pupils' science tests, completed a monthly progress report on each pupil, decided to construct her own test for the science unit rather than to use the test provided in her textbook, corrected pupil projects on the American government unit, and conducted a parent-teacher conference with Tim's parents. Much of a teacher's time is spent collecting information used to grade pupils or make final judgments about their academic progress. The term used to grade or

TABLE 1.1   COMPARISON OF THREE TYPES OF CLASSROOM ASSESSMENTS

	Official	Instructional	Sizing-Up
Purpose	Carry out the bureau-cratic aspects of teaching, such as grading, grouping, and placing	Plan instructional activities and monitor the progress of instruction	Provide teacher with a quick perception and practical knowledge of pupils' characteristics
Timing	Periodically during the school year	Daily throughout the school year	During the first week or two of school
Evidence-gathering method	Formal tests, papers, reports, quizzes, and assignments	Formal observation and pupil papers for planning; informal observation for monitoring	Largely informal observation
Type of evidence gathered	Mainly cognitive	Largely cognitive and affective	Cognitive, affective, and psychomotor
Record keeping	Formal records kept in teacher's mark book or school files	Written lesson plans; monitoring information not written down	Information kept in teacher's mind; few written records

make final judgments about students' learning at the end of instruction is **summative assessment.**

Types of Assessment

All of Ms. Lopez' decisions and all of the purposes of assessment just described can be grouped into three general types or areas of assessment (Airasian, 1997). Table 1.1 describes and compares these three assessment types. Some classroom assessments help teachers carry out their official responsibilities as members of the school bureaucracy. Decisions such as grading, grouping, assessing progress, interpreting test results, conferencing with parents, identifying pupils for special needs placement, and making promotion recommendations are all part of the official responsibilities a teacher assumes as an employee of a school system. These are **official assessments.** Other assessments are used to plan and deliver instruction and include decisions about what will be taught, how and when it will be taught, what materials will be used, how a lesson is progressing, and what changes in planned activities must be made. These are **instructional assessments.** A third kind of assessment is used by teachers early in the school year to learn about their pupils' social, academic, and behavioral characteristics and needs so as to enhance instruction, communication,

Teachers perform three types of assessment: official (administrative) assessment, instructional assessment, and sizing-up assessment.

Instructional assessments are used to help plan and deliver instruction.

Teachers size up their students in the first weeks of school so that they can organize their classrooms into social and learning communities.

and cooperation in the classroom. These assessments allow teachers to set up and maintain an effective classroom society. They are called **sizing-up assessments.** Succeeding chapters will describe these three general types of assessment in greater detail. At this point it is only necessary to recognize that assessment serves many classroom purposes.

SOME DEFINITIONS: TESTING, MEASUREMENT, ASSESSMENT, AND EVALUATION

Assessment is the process of collecting, synthesizing, and interpreting information to aid in decision making.

Assessment is the process of collecting, synthesizing, and interpreting information to aid in decision making. When people hear the word "assessment," many envision pupils taking paper-and-pencil tests to determine how much they have learned. While paper-and-pencil tests are important components of assessment, the preceding list of Ms. Lopez' decisions makes clear that there is much more to assessment in classrooms than administering tests to grade pupils. Assessment, as we will use the term, includes the full range of information teachers gather in their classrooms: information that helps them understand their pupils, plan and monitor their instruction, and establish a viable classroom culture, in addition to testing and grading.

There are differences among assessments, tests, measurements, and evaluations. Assessment is a general term that includes all the ways teachers gather and use information in their classrooms. A **test** is a formal, systematic, usually paper-and-pencil procedure used to gather information about pupils' performance. Tests are only one of the many types of assessment information teachers deal with, and thus, testing is only one strategy for assessment. Other important assessment strategies are observations, oral questions, projects, and portfolios.

A test is a formal, systematic, usually paper-and-pencil procedure for gathering information.

Measurement is the process of quantifying or assigning a number to performance.

Measurement is the process of quantifying or assigning a number to performance. The most common example of measurement in the classroom is when a teacher scores a quiz or test. Scoring produces a numerical description of performance: Jackie got 17 out of 20 items correct on the biology test; Dennis got a score of 65 percent on his math test; Rhonda's score on the creative essay was 85 percent. In each example, a numerical score is used to represent the individual's performance.

Evaluation is the process of judging the quality or value of a performance or a course of action.

Once assessment information is collected, teachers use it to make decisions or judgments about pupils, instruction, or classroom climate. **Evaluation** is the process of making judgments about what is good or desirable as in, for example, judging the quality of pupils' essays or the desirability of a particular instructional activity. Evaluation occurs after assessment information has been collected, synthesized, and thought about because this is when the teacher is in a position to make informed judgments.

Imagine a teacher who wishes to *assess* the mathematics readiness of a pupil in order to decide where to start instruction for him. Notice that the reason for assessing is that a decision must be made. First, the teacher gives a grade-appropriate paper-and-pencil *test* of mathematics readiness. The pupil's score on the test, 25 percent of the items correct, provides a *measurement* of his math readiness. Of course the teacher uses other forms of assessment to determine the pupil's readiness. She talks to the pupil about math, watches him while he does math exercises, and checks prior grades and test scores in his school record file. The teacher then thinks about all the assessment information she has collected. She *evaluates,* or makes a judgment about, the pupil's current stage of readiness in math. Her final decision, based on her assessment and evaluation, is to recommend a tutor for the pupil to help him catch up to the rest of the class. Table 1.2 summarizes the definitions of assessment, test, measurement, and evaluation.

While the focus of this book is teacher-centered classroom assessment, it is important to note that other types of assessment also go on in classrooms. Just as teachers constantly assess their pupils, instruction, and classroom climate, so too do pupils constantly assess their teacher, instruction, and classroom climate. Just as teachers want to know whether pupils are motivated, hardworking, academically able, and adjusted to the culture of the classroom, so too do pupils want to know if the teacher is fair, gives hard tests, enforces rigid discipline, can be swayed by a "sob story," and likes them as individuals (Jackson, 1990). Moreover, in all classrooms, pupils are being constantly assessed by their peers. The classroom is a public place and it does not take most pupils long to learn where they stand, both in the teacher's eyes and in the academic, athletic, and social pecking orders established by their peers. Assessment in the classroom is as likely to come from classmates as from the teacher. Discussion of these pupil-teacher and pupil-pupil assessments is interesting and important, but beyond the scope of this work. It is useful, however, to bear in mind the pervasiveness of assessment in classrooms and its consequences for both pupils and teachers.

In classrooms, teachers constantly assess their pupils, and pupils assess the teacher, instruction, and each other.

TABLE 1.2   DEFINITIONS OF COMMON ASSESSMENT-RELATED TERMS

Assessment: The collection, synthesis, and interpretation of information to aid the teacher in decision making.

Test: A formal, systematic, usually paper-and-pencil procedure for gathering information.

Measurement: The process of quantifying or assigning a number to performance.

Evaluation: The process of making judgments about the quality or goodness of performance or a course of action.

METHODS OF COLLECTING ASSESSMENT INFORMATION

Teachers gather most of their assessment information using paper-and pencil techniques, observation techniques, and oral questioning techniques.

Teachers use three primary methods to gather assessment information: paper-and-pencil techniques, observation techniques, and oral questioning techniques. Each technique is relied upon heavily by teachers to help them obtain the assessment information they need to make classroom decisions.

Paper-and-Pencil Techniques

Paper-and-pencil assessments involve pupils writing down their responses to questions or problems.

There are two forms of paper-and-pencil assessment: selection and supply.

Selection techniques require students to select an answer from choices that are provided; supply techniques require pupils to construct a response to a question or problem.

Paper-and-pencil techniques refer to assessment methods in which pupils write down their responses to questions or problems. When pupils take a multiple-choice test, complete a written homework assignment, turn in a written report, draw a picture, write an essay, or fill in a worksheet, they are providing paper-and-pencil evidence to the teacher. Paper-and-pencil assessment techniques are of two general forms: selection and supply. Multiple choice, true-false, and matching items are called **selection questions,** or selected response items, because as the name implies, the pupil responds to each question by selecting an answer from choices provided. **Supply items,** or production items, require the pupil to construct a response to a question. The length of the response can vary substantially. For example, an essay question necessitates the pupil's construction of a lengthy, detailed response, while a short answer or "fill in the blank" question may only require a word or phrase. Complex supply items, such as book reports, journal entries, portfolios, science experiments, and class projects, are also commonly referred to as **performance assessments.** Notice that a selection-type item provides the maximum degree of control for the question writer, since he or she specifies both the question and the answer choices. A supply-type item provides the question writer with control only over the item itself, since responsibility for constructing a response resides with the pupil.

Observation Techniques

Observation techniques are applied to student activities and to student products.

Observation is the second major method classroom teachers use to collect assessment data. As the term suggests, **observation** involves watching or listening to pupils carry out some activity (observation of process) or judging a product a pupil has produced (observation of product).Teachers are made aware of such student behaviors as mispronouncing words in oral reading, interacting in groups, speaking out in class, bullying other pupils, losing concentration, having puzzled looks on their faces, patiently waiting their turn, raising their hands in class, dressing shabbily, and failing to sit still for more than three minutes through observation. When pupils submit a science fair project, produce a still-life drawing, set up laboratory equipment, or complete a project in shop class, the teacher observes and judges the product they have produced.

Thus, Ms. Lopez observed that Monroe often squinted and decided to move him to the front of the room so he could see the blackboard better. She noticed Randy with his head on his desk and a grimace on his face and sent him to the school nurse for examination. During the language lesson she saw blank looks on her pupils' faces and got no raised hands when she asked questions, so she stopped to review the lesson from the previous day. Ms. Lopez observed Ralph swearing at another teacher and fighting with a classmate, actions that earned him a trip to the principal's office. These examples show how observations produce information that leads to classroom decisions.

In most classrooms, the teacher's desk faces the pupils' desks, and during instruction, the teacher often faces the pupils. The fact that teachers and their classes are located in a confined space, facing and interacting with one another from one to six hours per day, means that teachers can observe a great deal of their pupils' behavior, appearance, and reactions.

Some observations are formal and planned in advance, as when teachers assess pupils as they read aloud in reading group or present an oral report to the class. In such situations, the teacher wants to observe a particular set of pupil behaviors. For example, in reading aloud, the teacher might be watching and listening for clear pronunciation of words, changing voice tone to emphasize important points, periodic looking up from the book while reading, and so forth. Because such observations are planned, the teacher has time to prepare the pupils and identify in advance the particular behaviors that will be observed.

Some teacher observations are formal and planned in advance while others are informal and spontaneous.

Other teacher observations are unplanned and informal, as when the teacher sees Bill and Leroy talking when they should be working, notices the pained expression on a pupil's face when a classmate makes fun of his clothes, or observes the pupils fidgeting and looking out the window during a science lesson. Such spontaneous observations, based on what is often called "kid watching," reflect momentary unplanned happenings that the teacher observes, mentally records, and interprets. Both formal and informal teacher observations are important information gathering techniques in classrooms.

Oral Questioning Techniques

Asking oral questions is the third major method teachers use to collect assessment data. Why do you think the author ended her story that way? Explain to me in your own words what an improper fraction is. Did you call Ron a nasty name? Raise your hand if you can tell me why this answer is

Oral questioning provides a great deal of formal and informal information about pupils. Questioning is especially useful during instruction.

incorrect. Who can summarize yesterday's discussion about the water cycle? Why don't you have your homework today? These are all teacher-type questions used to assess pupils during and at the end of a lesson. Questioning students is very useful during instruction, when it can be used to review a prior topic, brainstorm a new topic, find out how the lesson is being understood by pupils, and engage a student who is not paying attention. The teacher can gather the information he or she wants without the intrusiveness of some form of paper-and-pencil assessment. Oral questioning is a common feature of all classrooms, and after lecture, it is the most used instructional activity. Oral examinations are used in subject areas such as foreign language, speech, and vocal music.

The full range of data analysis methods is needed to gather all the information required for classroom assessment.

Selection, supply, observation, and questioning techniques complement one another in the classroom. Imagine classroom decision making without being able to observe pupils' appearances, reactions, performances, answers to questions, and interactions. Now imagine what it would be like if no paper-and-pencil information could be obtained in classrooms. Now imagine what it would be like if teachers could not ask oral questions of their students. Each type of information is needed to carry out the rich and meaningful assessments that occur in classrooms. As a result, a teacher's mastery of all of these evidence gathering approaches is important.

Supplementary assessment information can be obtained from previous teachers, school staff, and parents.

In addition to the types of assessment described, helpful supplementary information can be obtained from the pupils' prior teachers, school nurses, and parents. Teachers routinely consult previous teachers to corroborate or reinforce current observations. Parents frequently volunteer information and respond to teacher queries. While useful, each of these supplementary sources of information has its limitations and should be treated with caution when making decisions.

STANDARDIZED AND NONSTANDARDIZED ASSESSMENTS

The information teachers collect and use in their classrooms comes from assessment procedures that are either standardized or nonstandardized.

Standardized Assessments

Standardized assessment procedures are those that are administered, scored, and interpreted in the same way for all test takers, regardless of where or when they are assessed. Standardized assessments are meant to be administered in many schools across the nation. Standardized assessments are intended to be given to pupils in many different classrooms, but always under identical conditions of administration, scoring, and interpretation. The main reason for standardizing assessment procedures is so fair comparisons across pupils in different schools and states can be made without the conditions of administration, scoring, and interpretation distorting the comparisons.

Standardized assessments are intended to be administered, scored, and interpreted in the same way for all test takers.

The Scholastic Assessment Test (SAT) and the ACT are examples of standardized tests. So are national achievement tests such as the Iowa Tests of Basic Skills and the Stanford, Metropolitan, California, and SRA Achievement tests. Regardless of where a pupil is taking the test, that pupil will be administered the same test, under the same conditions, with the same directions, in the same amount of time as all other students who are taking the test at that time. Moreover, the results of the test will be scored and interpreted the same way for all test takers. When Ms. Lopez identified pupils below the cutoff score on the state-mandated basic skills test and consulted the previous year's test scores to determine if the class needed a review of capitalization rules, she was examining information from standardized assessment instruments.

Nonstandardized Assessments

Few teacher-made assessments are standardized. Most are constructed for use in a single classroom with a single group of pupils. Most reflect the particular areas of instruction focused on in that single classroom. The teacher has no intent or desire to administer the same assessment to pupils in other classes for comparative purposes and so does not need to standardize conditions beyond his or her particular class.

Nonstandardized (teacher-made) assessments are developed for a single classroom with a single group of students and are not used for comparison with other groups.

When Ms. Lopez assigned grades to her pupils based upon her science test and decided to construct her own test for the science unit, she was relying upon assessment information that was nonstandardized. Many of Ms. Lopez' unplanned observations of her students' behavior also are classified as nonstandardized assessments. These fleeting, infrequently occurring, unpredictable, seldom repeated classroom observations represent a rich and important, though nonstandardized, form of assessment data. Teachers use these idiosyncratic observations to make decisions about individual pupils and the class as a group.

It is important to note that standardized assessments are not necessarily better than nonstandardized ones. Standardization is important when comparing pupils across many different classrooms and locations. If comparison beyond a single classroom is not desired, rigorous standardization is not needed, and in fact may be less appropriate for students in that classroom.

Standardization is important when pupils are compared across different locations and classrooms.

INDIVIDUAL AND GROUP ASSESSMENTS

Assessments can be administered to one pupil at a time or to a group of pupils simultaneously. The former are called individually administered assessments and the latter are termed group-administered assessments.

Individual Assessments

Individually administered assessment information is collected either under formal conditions or from teacher observation of interaction with a single pupil. Standardized tests like the Stanford-Binet Intelligence Scale or the Wechsler Intelligence Scale for Children (WISC), two commonly used school intelligence tests, are given under controlled conditions to one pupil at a time. As with most individually administered assessments, they are given orally and require that the examiner pay constant attention to the pupil, since the way the pupil interacts with and responds to the examiner provides information just as important as the score he or she attains.

One-on-one assessment provides an opportunity for clinical observation and clarification.

One major advantage of individually administered assessments is that in a one-on-one assessment situation, there are many opportunities for clinical observation of the pupil. For example, the administrator can observe the pupil's attention span, listening ability, speech, frustration level, and problem-solving strategies, as well as the specific answers the pupil provides. The administrator also has the chance to follow up on a pupil's response in order to clarify or comprehend it more completely. Most standardized individually administered assessments require the administrator to have a great deal of training and experience. Some individually administered instruments, including the Stanford-Binet and the WISC, can only be given by persons who are certified.

It is also clear that teachers focus upon, interact with, and assess their pupils as individuals. When Ms. Lopez moved Jennifer to the high reading group, she did so on the basis of assessment evidence she had gathered about Jennifer's reading performance. When Ms. Lopez selected Martha, not Matt, to deliver a note, she did so because her individual assessment of Martha's personal qualities indicated that she was a responsible pupil who could be relied upon to carry out an unsupervised task. Sending Ralph to the principal was based upon informal, unplanned observations of Ralph's behavior. When Ms. Lopez sat down with Tim's parents at a parent-teacher conference, much of the information she conveyed was based upon her assessment of Tim as an individual. Assigning grades to pupils is also an individualized assessment procedure.

Group Assessments

Group-administered assessments, whether standardized or not, are more efficient than individually administered ones because in the amount of time needed to gather information from one student, group assessments gather information from a whole class. However, the cost of this efficiency is the loss of rapport, insight, and knowledge about each pupil that individually administered assessments provide. Virtually all group-administered assessments rely on paper-and-pencil tests, since these permit many pupils to work simultaneously on a task. When the task to be assessed involves oral reading, giving a speech, or assembling equipment, group-administered procedures are not useful.

Administering group assessments saves time but provides less insight and information about individual pupils.

Informal group assessment occurs often in the classroom, primarily through teacher observation. Thus, when Ms. Lopez watched the class become bored and unruly during a lesson, she was performing group assessment. Similarly, when her pupils had difficulty answering her questions during the language lesson, she stopped what she was doing to review the previous day's lesson. This is another example of informal, group-based assessment.

In summary, assessments vary according to their purpose, method of data collection, degree of standardization, and individual or group administration. We can use these characteristics to describe different kinds of assessments. For example, a test such as the SAT or the ACT can be described as a standardized, group-administered, paper-and-pencil assessment. An assessment intended to determine how well a pupil can shoot free throws, use a hand saw, or assemble laboratory apparatus can be described as an observational, standardized, individually administered, performance assessment. Most teacher-constructed classroom tests are nonstandardized, group-administered, paper-and-pencil assessments. Finally, teacher's judgments about a pupil's ability to get along with his or her classmates in social situations is likely based upon nonstandardized, individual performance assessments.

CHARACTERISTICS OF GOOD ASSESSMENT: VALIDITY AND RELIABILITY

Assessment is the process of gathering, interpreting, and synthesizing information to aid decision making in the classroom. Whether assessment information helps teachers to make *good* decisions depends upon whether the assessment information collected is itself good. We begin our examination into the characteristics of good assessment information with an example.

Whether assessment information helps produce good decisions depends on whether the assessment information is good.

Mr. Ferris has just finished a three-week math unit on computing long division problems with remainders. During the unit, he taught his pupils the computational steps involved in doing long division problems and the concept of a remainder. He gave and reviewed both homework problems and examples from the text, and he administered a few quizzes. Now, at the end of the unit, Mr. Ferris wants to gather assessment information to find out whether his pupils have learned to do computational problems involving long division with remainders. He wants to gather this information to help him make a decision about how well his pupils have learned from his instruction so that he can assign a grade to each pupil.

To gather the information needed, Mr. Ferris decides to give a test containing items similar in content, format, and difficulty to those he has been teaching. From the millions of possible long division with remainder problems, Mr. Ferris selects 10 that are representative of his teaching. Note that if he picks 10 items that cover different content or are much harder, easier, or presented in a different format than what he taught in class, the results of the test will *not* provide good decision-making information. To assess how well his students learned from his instruction, his test items must match his instruction in content, format, and difficulty.

Mr. Ferris recognizes this potential pitfall and avoids it by writing 10 items that are similar in content, difficulty, and format to the items taught and practiced in his classroom. He assembles the items into a test, administers the test during one class period, and scores the tests on a scale of 0 to 100. Mr. Ferris then has the assessment information he needs to make a decision about each pupil's grade.

Manuela and Joe each score 100 on the test and receive an A grade for the unit. Stuart scores 30 and receives a D grade. The grades are based upon Mr. Ferris' evaluation of the quality of their performance on the 10-item test. If Mr. Ferris is asked to interpret what Manuela's and Joe's A grades mean, he will likely say that "Manuela and Joe can do long division with remainder items very well." He will also likely say that Stuart's D is "indicative of the fact that he cannot do such items well."

In making these statements, Mr. Ferris illustrates the relationship between assessment data and resulting teacher decisions. Consider carefully how Mr. Ferris describes the performance of Manuela, Joe, and Stuart. He says Manuela and Joe "can do long division with remainder items very well." He does not say "Manuela and Joe can do the 10 items I included on my test very well." He judges and describes their performance in *general* terms rather than in terms of his specific 10-item test. Similarly, Stuart is judged in general rather than in test-specific terms.

The logic that Mr. Ferris and all teachers use in making such judgments is that if a pupil can do well on the test items or performances that are actually assessed, the pupil is likely to do well on similar items and performances that are not assessed. If pupils do poorly on the 10 test items, it is likely that they also will do poorly on similar, unasked items. Hence, when asked to describe the performance of Manuela and Joe, he indicates that they do very well on long division with remainder problems in general.

Mr. Ferris' 10-item test illustrates a characteristic that is common to virtually all classroom assessments, regardless of whether they are formal or informal, paper-and-pencil, observational or oral, or standardized or non-standardized. The essence of classroom assessment is to look at a *sample* of a pupil's performance and use that sample to make a generalization or

The essence of classroom assessment is to look at some of a pupil's behavior and to use that information to make a generalization or prediction about the pupil's behavior in similar situations or on similar tasks.

prediction about the pupil's performance on similar, unobserved tasks. Mr. Ferris uses performance on 10 test items to make a generalization about his pupils' likely performance on the millions of similar items that could have been, but were not, included on his test.

This process is not confined to assessments of pupils' learning. Teachers often form lasting impressions of their pupils' personalities or motivation based a few brief observations made in the first week of school. They observe a small sample of the pupil's behavior and on the basis of this sample make general judgments such as "he is unmotivated," "she is a troublemaker," and "they are hard workers." These are informal generalizations about pupils that teachers routinely make based on only a small sample of the pupil's school behavior.

What if the behavior sample the teacher collects is irrelevant or incomplete? What if the items on Mr. Ferris' test were not typical of his classroom instruction? What if the pupil has an "off day" or the teacher's impatience does not permit a pupil to show his or her "true" performance? If these things happen, then the decision made about the pupil is likely to be wrong and probably unfair.

Validity

The single most important characteristic of good assessment is its ability to help the teacher make a correct decision. This characteristic is called **validity.** Without validity, the assessment data will not lead to correct decisions. When a teacher asks, as all teachers should, Am I collecting the right kind of information for the decision I want to make? she is asking about the validity of her assessments (Linn, 1997; Moss, 1995). For any decision, some forms of evidence are more valid than others. For example, it was more valid for Mr. Ferris to determine his pupils' achievement by giving a test that contained items similar to those he had been teaching than it would have been for him to ask pupils to write an essay about their feelings towards math. Similarly, it is more valid to determine pupils' motivation or ability by observing their classroom work over a period of time than it is to base such judgments on the performance of their older siblings or the section of the city they come from. These latter indicators are likely to be less valid for decision making than more direct classroom observation.

We shall have more to say about validity throughout this text. At this point it is sufficient to say three things about the validity of assessment information. First, validity is concerned with whether the information being gathered is really relevant and appropriate to make the desired decision. Second, validity is the most important characteristic that assessment information can possess because without it, the assessment information is of no use. Third, concerns about validity pertain to all classroom assessment, not just to those involving formal, paper-and-pencil techniques. Each of the many decisions Ms. Lopez made during the school day was based

Validity is concerned with whether the information being gathered is relevant to the decision that needs to be made.

Invalid assessment information is of no use.

Validity (relevance to decision making) is just as applicable to informal teacher observations as it is to formally gathered paper-and-pencil information.

> **TABLE 1.3   KEY ASPECTS OF ASSESSMENT VALIDITY**
>
> 1. Validity is concerned with this general question: To what extent will this assessment information help me make an appropriate decision?
> 2. Validity refers to the decisions that are made from assessment information, not the assessment approach itself. It is not appropriate to say the assessment information is valid unless the decisions or groups it is valid for are identified. Assessment information valid for one decision or group of pupils is not necessarily valid for other decisions or groups.
> 3. Validity is a matter of degree; it does not exist on an all-or-nothing basis. Think of assessment validity in terms of categories: highly valid, moderately valid, and invalid.
> 4. Validity is always determined by a judgment made by the test user.

upon some type of assessment information. It is appropriate, therefore, to ask about the validity—that is, the appropriateness—of the assessment information behind each of Ms. Lopez' many daily decisions. Table 1.3 identifies key concerns in the validity of assessments.

Reliability

Reliability refers to the stability or consistency of assessment information, i.e., whether it is typical of a pupil's behavior.

A second important characteristic of good assessment information is its consistency, or **reliability.** Would the assessment results for this person or class be similar if they were gathered at some other time? If you weighed yourself on a scale, got off it, then weighed yourself again on the same scale, you would expect the two weights to be almost identical. If they weren't, you wouldn't trust the information provided by the scale. The information it provides you is not reliable. Similarly, if assessment information does not produce stable, consistent information, a teacher should exercise caution in using that information to make a decision about a pupil or the class.

Think of a friend whom you consider to be unreliable. Is he sometimes punctual and sometimes late? When she tells you something or promises to do something, can you rely on what she says? A person who is unreliable is inconsistent. It is the same with assessment information; unreliable or inconsistent information does not help teachers make decisions that they can rely on.

Recall that Ms. Lopez observed Rose's class interruptions and Joshua's inattentive behavior over a period of time before deciding to take action. She did this to be sure that she was observing stable, consistent behavior from these students. Did they behave the same way at different times and under different circumstances? By observing them over a period of time, Ms. Lopez could have faith in the reliability of her observations. Similarly, Mr. Ferris included 10 long division with remainder questions on his test,

> ### TABLE 1.4 KEY ASPECTS OF ASSESSMENT RELIABILITY
>
> 1. Reliability refers to the stability or consistency of assessment information and is concerned with this question: How consistent or typical of the pupils' behavior is the assessment information I have gathered?
>
> 2. Reliability is not concerned with the appropriateness of the assessment information collected, only with its consistency, stability, or typicality. Appropriateness of assessment information is a validity concern.
>
> 3. Reliability does not exist on an all-or-nothing basis, but in degrees: high, moderate, or low. Some types of assessment information are more reliable than others.
>
> 4. Reliability is a necessary but insufficient condition for validity. An assessment that provides inconsistent, atypical results cannot be relied upon to provide information useful for decision making.

not just one, so that he would obtain reliable information about his pupils' achievement. He can have more confidence about pupils' learning by assessing them on 10 items than on only one or two.

Since any single assessment provides only a limited sample of a pupil's behavior, no single assessment procedure or instrument can be expected to provide perfect, error-free information (Thorndike, 1990). All assessment information contains some unreliability or inconsistency due to such factors as ambiguous test items, interruptions during testing, differences in pupils' attention spans, clarity of assessment directions, pupils' luck in guessing, changes in pupils' moods, mistakes in scoring (especially essay and observational assessments), and obtaining too small a sample of behavior to permit the pupil to show consistent, stable performance (Frisbie, 1988). These and other factors conspire to introduce some inconsistency into all assessment information. Obviously, it is important to minimize the inconsistency. Table 1.4 reviews key aspects of the reliability of assessment information.

All assessment information contains some error or inconsistency; thus validity and reliability are both a matter of degree and do not exist on an all-or-nothing basis.

One of the purposes of this text is to suggest methods that can help reduce the amount of unreliability in classroom assessment information. If a teacher cannot rely upon the stability and consistency of the information gathered during the assessment process, he or she must be careful not to base important decisions on that information. Thus, along with validity, which asks if the assessment information being gathered is relevant to the decision to be made, the classroom teacher must also be concerned with reliability, which asks if the information obtained is consistent and stable. Once again, validity is concerned with whether or not the targeted characteristic is being assessed appropriately, while reliability is concerned with the consistency of the assessment information.

Consider the following assertion regarding the relationship between validity and reliability. "Valid assessment must be reliable, but reliable assessment need not be valid." The first half of the statement is fairly straightforward. Valid decisions are not possible if the assessment data on which the decisions are based are not consistent. So, in order to have a valid assessment, there must be reliable information.

As to the second part of the statement, imagine the following scenario. Suppose you ask a pupil in your class how many brothers and sisters he has. He tells you six, and you ask him again. He tells you six. You repeat the question several times, and each time the pupil indicates six brothers and sisters. You have assessed the number of his brothers and sisters with consistency; the assessment information you have gathered from him is reliable. Suppose you then use this reliable information to make a decision about what reading group to place the pupil in: the more brothers and sisters, the higher the placement. Since the number of brothers and sisters has little relevance to the pupil's reading performance, a decision based on this information, no matter how reliable it is, is not valid. In short, assessments can be reliable, but not necessarily valid. Succeeding chapters will explore the relationship between validity and reliability in greater detail and offer suggestions for improving the validity and reliability of classroom assessment.

ETHICAL ISSUES AND RESPONSIBILITIES

Teachers' assessments have important long- and short-term consequences for students; thus teachers have an ethical responsibility to make decisions using the most valid and reliable information possible.

Thus far we have considered many technical aspects of classroom assessment. However, assessment is more than just a technical activity; it is a human activity that influences and affects many people, including pupils, parents, teachers, coaches, college admission counselors, and employers. Think about the different kinds and purposes of assessment described in this chapter, and then think about all the ways people can be affected by them. This will give you a sense of the human side of assessment.

Teaching is a profession that has both a knowledge base and a moral base. Like other professionals who have knowledge and expertise their clients do not have and whose actions and judgments affect their clients in many ways, classroom teachers are responsible for conducting themselves in an ethical manner. This responsibility is particularly important in education, because unlike most other professions, pupils have no choice about whether they will or will not attend school. Also, compared to their teachers, pupils tend to be less experienced and more impressionable. Among the ethical standards that cut across all dimensions of teaching are the need to treat each pupil as an individual, to avoid physical or emotional abuse of pupils, to respect diversity, to be intellectually honest with pupils, to avoid favoritism and harassment, to provide a balanced perspective on issues raised in instruction, and to provide the best instruction possible for all pupils (Fenstermacher, 1990; Clark, 1990; Strike and Soltis, 1991).

In simple terms, each of these ethical standards refers to some aspect of a teacher's fairness in dealing with his or her pupils. Clearly, gathering and interpreting valid and reliable data for decision making are fundamental to the fairness of teachers' assessments. Other aspects of fairness include: (1) informing students about teacher expectations and assessments before beginning teaching and assessment; (2) teaching pupils what they are to be tested on before assessment; (3) not making snap judgments and identifying pupils with emotional labels (e.g., disinterested, at-risk, slow learner) before you have spent time with them; (4) avoiding stereotyping pupils (e.g., "He's just a dumb jock," "Kids from that part of town are troublemakers," and "Pupils who dress that way have no interest in school"); (5) avoiding terms and examples that may be offensive to students of different gender, race, religion, culture, or nationality; (6) avoiding bias towards pupils with limited English or with different cultural experiences when providing instruction and constructing assessments (Airasian, 1997; McMillan, 1997). There are many dimensions to fairness in the classroom.

In addition, there are ethical considerations specifically applicable to assessment. Classroom teachers are in a position to obtain a great deal of information about their pupils' academic, personal, social, and family backgrounds. But beyond having access to such information, teachers use it to make decisions that can have important short- and long-term consequences for pupils. For example, college entrance and future employment opportunities, not to mention pupil self-esteem, often hang in the balance of teachers' assessment decisions. Consequently, there are responsibilities associated with the collection and use of assessment information. Teachers should always strive to obtain valid and reliable information before making important decisions that can influence pupils. Moreover, once assessment information is collected, teachers have a responsibility to protect its privacy, recognize its decision-making limitations, and never use it to demean or ridicule a pupil. See Appendix A for other important teacher competencies in the assessment of pupils.

Table 1.5 presents a list of ethical standards for teachers developed by the National Education Association. Note the range of ethical concerns and responsibilities that accompany teaching.

This chapter has indicated that classrooms are complex environments calling for teacher decision making in many areas. Within such an environment, teachers are not expected to be correct in every decision they make. That would be an unrealistic standard to hold anyone to, especially in fluid, decision-rich classroom settings where uncertainty abounds. However, teachers should be expected and are morally bound to provide defensible assessment evidence to support classroom decisions and actions. This is the least that can be expected in an environment where teacher actions have such vital consequences for pupils.

TABLE 1.5   ETHICAL STANDARDS FOR TEACHERS'
             RELATIONS WITH PUPILS

Commitment to the Student

The educator strives to help each student realize his or her potential as a worthy and effective member of society. The educator therefore works to stimulate the spirit of inquiry, the acquisition of knowledge and understanding, and the thoughtful formulation of worthy goals.

   In fulfillment of the obligation to the student, the educator:

1. Shall not unreasonably restrain the student from independent action in the pursuit of learning.

2. Shall not unreasonably deny the student access to varying points of view.

3. Shall not deliberately suppress or distort subject matter relevant to the student's progress.

4. Shall make reasonable effort to protect the student from conditions harmful to learning or to health and safety.

5. Shall not intentionally expose the student to embarrassment or disparagement.

6. Shall not on the basis of race, color, creed, sex, national origin, marital status, political or religious beliefs, family, social or cultural background, or sexual orientation, unfairly:
   a. Exclude any student from participation in any program
   b. Deny benefits to any student
   c. Grant any advantage to any student

7. Shall not use professional relationships with students for private advantage.

8. Shall not disclose information about students obtained in the course of professional service, unless disclosure serves a compelling professional purpose or is required by law.

SOURCE: From *NEA Handbook*, 1992–1993. Reprinted with permission of the National Education Association.

CHAPTER SUMMARY

♦ Every day in every classroom, teachers make decisions about their pupils, their instruction, and their classroom's climate. Teachers collect and interpret various sources of evidence to help them evaluate and choose suitable courses of action.

♦ There are many purposes for classroom assessment: establishing classroom equilibrium, planning and conducting instruction, placing pupils, providing feedback and incentives, diagnosing pupil problems, and judging and grading academic learning and progress.

♦ All the purposes of assessment can be divided into three general categories: official assessments, such as grades, which teachers are expected to provide as part of their role in the school bureaucracy; instructional assessment, which includes both planning and delivering instruction to pupils; and sizing-up assessment, which occurs early in the school year and is used by teachers to get to know their pupils.

◆ Assessment is the general process of collecting, synthesizing, and interpreting information to aid teachers in their decision making. A test is a formal, usually paper-and-pencil way to gather information. Measurement is describing performance numerically. Evaluation is making judgments about what is good or desirable.

◆ Many forms of assessment evidence are used by teachers, including tests, observations, interviews, comments from prior teachers, and school record folders.

◆ Standardized assessments are intended to be administered, scored, and interpreted in the same way, no matter when or where they are given. These conditions are necessary because a primary purpose of standardized assessments is to compare the performance of pupils across different classrooms. Nonstandardized assessments are typically used by classroom teachers.

◆ The goodness of assessments is determined by their validity and reliability. Validity, the most important characteristic of assessments, is concerned with the collection of information that is most relevant for making the desired decision. Reliability is concerned with the consistency or typicality of the assessment information collected.

◆ Although assessment is thought of as a technical activity, there are ethical concerns associated with the assessment process. Since teachers' decisions can influence pupils' self-perception and life opportunities, when assessing, teachers must be aware of their many ethical responsibilities.

QUESTIONS FOR DISCUSSION

1. In what ways do the three general types of classroom assessment described in this chapter influence and interact with one another? For example, how do sizing-up assessments influence instructional assessments?

2. What assessment strategies would teachers likely use to diagnose pupils' problems, plan instruction, and judge or grade pupil learning? Would the strategies be the same for each decision?

3. What kinds of learning are best assessed by observation? By selection items?

4. Do teachers' ethical responsibilities to their pupils change as pupils get older? How? Are there some ethical responsibilities that remain constant across age levels?

REFLECTION EXERCISE

This chapter described assessment as an aid to teacher decision making. Imagine that you are a teacher and have to size up a new group of pupils at the start of the school year. Reflect on what you have to do to size up your pupils. List five actions you can employ to learn about your pupils' characteristics. What are the advantages and disadvantages of each action?

ACTIVITIES

1. Interview a teacher about classroom decision making. Ask the teacher how he or she sizes up students at the start of the school year: what characteristics are considered, on what basis are decisions about pupils made, etc? Compare the teacher's responses to your own answers in the preceding Reflection Exercise. How are they the same? How are they different? Why are they different?
2. Imagine you are a first-year teacher. School starts in 3 weeks. Discuss in small groups what you must do to prepare for its start. Select the 3 most important things and explain why.

REVIEW QUESTIONS

1. What are the three main types of classroom assessment? How do they differ in purpose, timing, and the types of information most likely to be used in carrying them out?
2. Explain the difference between standardized and nonstandardized assessments; supply and selection test items; and validity and reliability.
3. How would you explain the concept of validity to a fellow teacher? What examples would you use to make your point?
4. Why are validity and reliability important concerns in classroom assessments? Why is validity more important?
5. What are three ethical responsibilities a teacher has to her or his pupils? Give an example of how each responsibility might occur in a classroom.

REFERENCES

Airasian, P. W. (1997). *Classroom assessment* 3d ed. New York: McGraw-Hill.

Biddle, B., Good, T., and Goodson, I. (1996). *The international handbook of teachers and teaching*. New York: Kluher.

Clark, C. M. (1990). The teacher and the taught: Moral transactions in the classroom. In J. Goodlad, R. Soder, and K. Sirotnik (Eds.), *The moral dimensions of teaching* (pp. 251–265). San Francisco: Jossey-Bass.

Clark, C. M., and Peterson, P. L. (1986). Teachers' thought processes. In M. C. Wittrock (Ed.), *Handbook of research on teaching* (pp. 255–296). New York: Macmillan.

Fenstermacher, G. D. (1990). Some moral considerations on teaching as a profession. In J. Goodlad, R. Soder, and K. Sirotnik (Eds.), *The moral dimensions of teaching* (pp. 130–151). San Francisco: Jossey-Bass.

Frisbie, D. A. (1988). Reliability of scores from teacher-made tests. *Educational Measurement: Issues and Practice, 7* (1), 25–35.

Jackson, P. W. (1990). *Life in classrooms*. New York: Teachers College Press.

Linn, R. L. (1997). Evaluating the validity of assessments: The consequences of use. *Educational Measurement: Issues and Practices, 16* (2), 14–16.

McMillan, J. H. (1997). *Classroom assessment.* Boston: Allyn and Bacon.

Moss, P. A. (1995). Themes and variations in validity theory. *Educational Measurement: Issues and Practices, 14* (5), 5–13.

Strike, K., and Soltis, J. (1991). *The ethics of teaching.* New York: Teachers College Press.

Thorndike, R. L. (1990). Reliability. In H. J. Walberg and G. D. Haertel (Eds.), *The international encyclopedia of educational evaluation* (pp. 260–273). Oxford: Pergamon Press.

LEARNING ABOUT PUPILS: SIZING-UP ASSESSMENT

CHAPTER OBJECTIVES

After reading this chapter, the student will be able to:

1. define basic terms: logical error, self-fulfilling prophesy, triangulation.
2. state features of classrooms that make them social environments and relate these features to teachers' classroom assessment needs.
3. explain the purpose and process of sizing-up assessment.
4. state weaknesses in the validity and reliability of information commonly used in sizing-up assessment.
5. give examples of strategies that can improve the validity and reliability of sizing-up assessments.

The first few days of school are important for both teachers and pupils. These days set the tone and lay the foundation for the rest of the school year, and it is in these days that a group of diverse individuals come together to become a class. Each new group of pupils has its own special mix of backgrounds, abilities, interests, personalities, and needs that make it unlike any other class the teacher has ever encountered. In the first few days of school, teachers try to learn about each pupil and the class as a whole in order to organize them into a classroom society that is characterized by communication, order, and learning. In this chapter we explore assessments that confront all teachers at the start of the school year: How do I get to know my new students and what do I need to know about them to provide them with an orderly, civil learning environment? We will consider sizing-up assessment, why it is necessary, how it is carried out, and threats to its validity and reliability.

The activities in the first few days of school set the stage for how well pupils will behave, attend, and learn during the school year. In the first days of school, teachers and pupils must get to know and understand one another.

To start, it is important to understand that a classroom is more than a group of pupils who happen to be in the same place at the same time. It is a complex environment, a society, in which people communicate with one another, pursue common goals, and follow rules of order. It is also an instructional setting in which teaching and learning are expected to take place. And finally, it is a place where one member, the teacher, has responsibility for other members, the pupils, thus making it a moral environment (McCaslin & Good, 1996).

Although all classrooms are simultaneously social, academic, and moral environments, the specific features of particular classrooms differ greatly from one to another. For example, the academic and socioeconomic backgrounds of pupils, as well as their mix of personalities, learning styles, languages, special needs, and interests, differ from classroom to classroom (Ladson-Billings, 1994; Delpit, 1995). From one year to the next, a teacher cannot count on having similar groups of pupils. Because of these differences, planning and delivering instruction are context-bound activities;

that is, the ways that teachers plan and teach are dependent upon the varied characteristics of their pupils. Try to imagine planning and teaching a lesson for a group of pupils you know nothing about. What will interest the pupils? How long can they pay attention? What have they learned previously? What learning needs do they have? Or, try to imagine how you will discipline students you do not know. What strategies will work with different pupils? Is a student acting out because she is bored, unable to follow the lesson, or testing the teacher? It is to answer such questions that teachers size up their pupils at the start of the school year.

However, while teachers do control many classroom features (for example, rules and routines, methods of instruction, topics covered, and grading practices) there are a number of classroom features they do not control. Table 2.1 contains descriptions of two teachers' classrooms. Imagine that these classrooms are at the same grade level and that each teacher is planning a lesson on the same topic. Notice that all of the characteristics listed in Table 2.1 are ones the teachers normally have little control over; they are the "givens" that each teacher has to work with. Which of the listed characteristics are most important, and how might they influence the way the two teachers plan instruction? Which characteristics are the most advantageous to a teacher, and which are the most disadvantageous? Are the teachers' "givens" likely to lead to identical lessons? How would pupil characteristics influence the lessons? Thinking about these questions should give you some sense of how instructional planning is always dependent on both the students and the classroom "givens."

Teaching is a context-bound activity involving many things teachers cannot control, such as the characteristics of their students and the resources available to them.

TABLE 2.1 COMPARISON OF TWO CLASSROOM CONTEXTS

Classroom A	Classroom B
22 pupils	34 pupils
Range of pupil abilities	Mainly low-ability pupils
Strong pupil self-control	Poor pupil self-control
Good prerequisite skills	Range of prerequisite skills
Intense parental interest	Moderate parental interest
10-year-old textbooks	New textbooks
Mandated district curriculum	Teacher-selected instructional topics
Poor school library	Excellent school library
Small classroom size	Large classroom size
Individual pupil desks	Pupils sit at four-person tables
Little colleague support	Strong colleague support

PUPIL CHARACTERISTICS

At the beginning of each year teachers must get to know their pupils so that they can organize them into a classroom learning community.

In order to teach well, teachers must strive to know and accommodate the needs and characteristics of their pupils. But how do teachers do this? What assessment information do they rely upon? What are some of the ways teachers commonly go about getting to know, or size up, their pupils so that they can interact with them, plan for them, instruct them, and help them function as an organized classroom society? These are important questions, not just in relation to planning and delivering instruction, but also in relation to the social interactions that characterize all classrooms.

The teacher's main focus in the first few days of school is to get to know each pupil and the group as a whole in order to organize them into a classroom society that is characterized by communication, order, and learning. Thus, an important and often overlooked form of classroom assessment that all teachers must accomplish takes place at the start of the school year and lays the foundation for classroom activities and interactions for the rest of the school year. But sizing up and identifying relevant pupil characteristics is becoming more difficult for teachers. American teachers increasingly face learners varied in ability, class, race, culture, and language. Issues of poverty, disabilities, violence, abuse, teen pregnancy, and drugs confront too many of our students and impact their school performance and success (Wiseman, Cooner, & Knight, 1999). However, in spite of this difficult reality, teachers are expected to know and teach all their students. So, during the beginning days of school, the teacher must collect a broad range of information about pupils and use this information to form an initial set of perceptions and expectations about them (McCaslin & Good, 1996). These perceptions and expectations will influence the way the teacher plans for, interacts with, and manages pupils and instruction. Teachers also recognize that some important pupil characteristics may not manifest themselves in the first few days of school. Issues such as poverty, violence, abuse, and pregnancy may not immediately be apparent to a teacher, while issues of culture, language, and physical disabilities probably will be.

While the information teachers seek about their pupils differs by grade level, all teachers need to size up their pupils to some extent. How do you think sizing-up assessment differs for elementary and high school teachers? Which pupil characteristics do you think concern both and which do you think are specific to each teaching level?

SOURCES OF INFORMATION

The information teachers use to size up their pupils comes from a variety of sources: the school grapevine, comments by other teachers, school records, performance of siblings, classroom observations, pupil comments, and a variety of formal assessments. For example, sit and listen in the teachers' room. Hear Ms. Robinson or Mr. Rutherford complain about Jim or Shaylah's continual inattentiveness or defiant behavior in class. Listen to Mr. Hobbs describe Marion's cooperation and insight. Hear Ms. Jeffry complain about Mike's interfering and demanding parents. One does not have to know Jim, Shaylah, Marion, or Mike personally to begin forming impressions of them as persons and pupils. Many pupils' reputations precede them into the classroom and teachers who have never set eyes on them often already have heard a great deal about their strengths and weaknesses.

Teachers use a variety of information to size up their students, including personal observations, school records, comments from other teachers, and formal assessments.

Several teachers tell here what information they collect to help them size up their pupils at the start of the school year.

> School records are kept in the office and are available on all pupils. I could look at these before the school year started to get information about my pupils' abilities, prior school performance, home situation, and learning problems.

> In my school, classes are assigned by level. Before classes start I know whether a class is high or low level.

> Sometimes when I compare my class list with another teacher's, the other teacher may comment on a pupil, the sibling of the pupil, or the parents of the pupil. Susie's brother was a nice, quiet boy. Sam's sister was defiant and disruptive in class. Andy is the last of the eight Rooney children, thank goodness. Be careful, Mrs. Roberts is overly protective of Peter and very concerned about grades.

> By the end of the first week of school I will know whether each child is going to work, care about school, get along with the other pupils, be responsible enough to relay messages for me, and have a pleasant personality. I know these things by observing the children in class. Whether a student volunteers an answer or comments willingly or if he needs to be called on to give an answer tells me about the pupil's type of personality. I watch how they get along with each other. The look of interest on their faces tells me about how hard they will work.

Thus, at the start of school, teachers have their antennae up, constantly searching the environment for information about their students (Garcia, 1994). Sometimes their search leads them to expected places: school record folders, prior teachers' perceptions, diagnostic or readiness tests, and the way pupils interact with them and their peers. The search also leads to some unexpected places that seem, on the surface, to have little to do with the main task of the school: the way pupils dress, their posture and body language, pupil discussions in the hallways and cafeterias, and who they "hang around" with. By the end of the first or second week of school, most teachers have sized up their pupils and classes and can provide fairly detailed descriptions of pupil characteristics.

Two features of this early sizing-up information deserve attention. First, much of it comes from informal observations. Most teachers do not rely heavily on tests or formal assessments when initially determining pupil characteristics. If they seek formal information, and many do not, they often go to the school record folders or administer subject matter

Teachers rely heavily on informal observations when initially sizing up their students.

pretests. Second, because this initial information is obtained largely by means of informal observations, teachers are exposed to only a small sample of each pupil's behavior. Since teachers can observe any given pupil only part of the time, it is inevitable that their informal observations will be incomplete and limited to what the pupils happen to be doing or saying when the teacher glances their way.

Stiggins (1997) notes that personal observations and exchanges with pupils provide a great deal of information about them. He uses the term "personal communication" to describe six common forms of teacher-pupil exchanges: questioning, conferencing, classroom discussions, oral examinations, pupil journals, and conversations with others who know the pupil or pupils. These are teacher-pupil interactions that are often used, consciously or unconsciously, to inform teachers' sizing-up assessments. What kinds of information could a teacher gather about students from each of the six forms of personal communication?

However, Stiggins also rightly points out that personal communication is a subjective classroom assessment strategy. That is, the usefulness and appropriateness of the information gathered is dependent on the interpretations of the teacher. Two problems can limit the validity and reliability of all forms of personal communications. First, because of the limits of the human mind and memory, teachers may "lose," or forget, important pieces of information about a student or class. Most of the six personal communication approaches involve dealing with many students over short time periods, thus taxing the depth and accuracy of teacher memory. If memory is faulty or incomplete, the appropriateness or validity of the personal communication information is lowered. A second problem concerns the amount of information teachers obtain to size up a student or class. Since teachers can observe any given pupil only part of the time, it is inevitable that their observations will be incomplete and limited (McCasin & Good, 1996). Personal communications are varied, often brief, and focused on a large number of pupils, thus increasing the possibility that insufficient information will be obtained to provide reliable interpretations about pupil characteristics. Thus, while all six of the personal communication approaches can help teachers obtain valuable information about pupils, teachers should also recognize the potential problems of selective memory and insufficient information.

FORMING DESCRIPTIONS OF PUPILS

Teachers synthesize their sizing-up assessments into general descriptions of pupils.

Joslyn (a fifth grader) walks into class each day with a worried and tired look on her face. Praising her work, or even the smallest positive action, will bring a smile to her face, though the impact is brief. She is inattentive, even during the exercises we do step-by-step as a class. She is shy, but sometimes will ask for help. But before she gives herself a chance, she will put her head down on her desk and close her eyes. I don't know why she lacks motivation so severely. Possibly it's a chemical imbalance or maybe problems at home. She will probably be this way all year.

David (an eighth grader) is a smooth talker, a Casanova. He is a nice dresser, a nice kid with a head on his shoulders. Unfortunately David is very unmotivated, most likely because of his background. He's street smart, loves attention, and has a good sense of humor. He is able to "dish it out" but can also take it. David is loud in class but not to the point of disruption; he knows where to draw the limit. If only he had some determination, the kid could go a long way.

These are rich and detailed descriptions of pupils. Each includes many different pupil characteristics, relies heavily on informal information, and conveys a perception about many dimensions of pupil behavior and background (Goodson, 1992). Notice that the teachers' descriptions include both academic and nonacademic factors. Notice also that they often make a prediction about how the pupil will perform during the school year. That teachers size up pupils is not in itself remarkable; people in any social system size each other up. What is important, however, is the speed at which sizing-up assessments can form impressions about almost all the pupils in the class.

Sizing-up assessments produce a set of perceptions and expectations that influence the manner in which the teacher plans for, instructs, and interacts with the pupils throughout the school year (Good & Brophy, 1997). This is, after all, the purpose of sizing-up assessment: to help the teacher get to know the pupils so he or she can organize them into a classroom society and know how to interact with, motivate, and teach them.

To get a sense of the use and importance of sizing-up assessment, imagine that it is the middle of January and you have been called in to substitute for the regular eighth grade teacher at Memorial Middle School. You have detailed plans for the subject matter you are to teach during the day. Just after the beginning bell rings and pupils are seated, a boy in the back of the room raises his hand and asks to go to his locker to get a book he has forgotten. Should you let him go? Can he be trusted to return after getting the book or will he wander the corridors for an hour? What is the classroom teacher's policy on forgotten books? A few minutes later two girls get up and start to leave the room. "We always go to the library to see Ms. Flanders for extra help at this time on Wednesday. We'll be back in about an hour." Do they? Will they? Shortly thereafter, two pupils start arguing over the last copy of a reference book. The argument grows louder and begins to disturb the class. How should you react? What strategy will pacify these particular pupils? The classroom teacher knows the answers to all these questions because she or he is a founding member of the classroom society. She or he is the person who has sized up the pupils' characteristics and established the routines. As a substitute, you are an outsider, a

Sizing-up assessments provide teachers with the kinds of practical, nitty-gritty information needed in order to make a classroom function effectively.

TABLE 2.2   CHARACTERISTICS OF SIZING-UP ASSESSMENT

1. **Sizing up is done at the start of the school year.** Most teachers can describe the personal, social, and academic characteristics of each pupil and the class as a whole after the first two weeks of school.

2. **Sizing up is pupil-centered.** Pupils and their characteristics are the focus of assessment.

3. **Informal observation is used.** Much of the information about pupil behavior and performance is collected through spontaneous, informal observations.

4. **Observations are synthesized into perceptions.** Teachers put together their observations in idiosyncratic ways to form a generalized perception of pupils.

5. **Impressions are rarely written down.** Unlike test scores or grades, which are written down in rank books or report cards, the perceptions formed from sizing-up assessments are unwritten and selectively communicated.

6. **Observations are broad and diverse.** Teachers attend to a broad range of cognitive, affective, and psychomotor characteristics when they size up their pupils.

7. **Early impressions tend to become permanent.** Teachers are very confident about the accuracy of the sizing-up assessments they do in the first days of school. Initial perceptions are very stable from the first week of school to the end of the school year.

stranger to this classroom society and thus do not know its workings, personalities, rules, and routines. Sizing-up assessments provide the classroom teacher with the kinds of practical, nitty-gritty knowledge needed to make a classroom function (Bullough, Knowles, & Crow, 1992; Solas, 1992).

Table 2.2 reviews the main characteristics of sizing-up assessment.

Bear in mind that sizing-up assessments are simply a special case of a natural tendency to observe and make judgments about people on the basis of what is seen and heard about them in everyday interactions. These assessments facilitate "knowing" or "labeling" others so that it is no longer necessary to interact with them as if they were strangers; they help bring order into social situations, including schools. They provide a frame of reference within which social interaction and meaningful instruction can take place.

FEATURES OF SIZING-UP ASSESSMENTS

Because sizing-up assessments form the basis for many important judgments made throughout the school year, teachers have an ethical responsibility to make them as valid and reliable as possible. However, an assessment process that is based upon quickly obtained, often incomplete evidence has the potential to produce incorrect, invalid, and unreliable decisions about pupils.

Consider these features of sizing-up assessments. First, teachers' initial impressions of their pupils tend to remain stable over time. Once a teacher forms an impression of a pupil, that impression is likely to stick, and teachers will act to maintain their pupil impressions, even in the face of contradictory evidence. In general, classroom teachers are fairly accurate in their beginning-of-the-year predictions of pupils' academic performance as measured by test scores. However, even the most accurate teacher is not correct about every pupil. Teachers' accuracy when sizing up pupils' personalities, interests, emotions, motivation, self-concepts, and social adjustment is less understood. Overall, teachers' perceptions of these emotional characteristics are less accurate than their academic perceptions, at least at the start of the school year.

Because initial sizing-up assessments have important consequences for pupils, teachers have an ethical responsibility to make them as valid and reliable as possible.

Second, sizing-up assessments not only influence the way teachers perceive, treat, and make decisions about pupils, they are often transmitted to pupils. Teachers often unknowingly and unintentionally communicate their sizing-up assessments, such as with offhand comments that tell individuals and the class a great deal about the teacher's perceptions: "Oh Robert, can't you even remember what we just talked about?"; "All right, Sarah, will you tell the rest of the class the answer it can't seem to come up with?"; and "Didn't Ruby read that paragraph with a lot of expression?" Sometimes perceptions are conveyed indirectly, as when a teacher waits patiently for one pupil to think through a problem but allows another only a few seconds; expresses encouragement and assurance to one pupil but says "at least try" to another; encourages one to "think" but another to "take a guess." Tone of voice, physical proximity, gestures, seating arrangements, and other signals all tell pupils how they are perceived in the classroom.

Teachers often communicate their sizing-up assessments to pupils in unintended ways, and students may live up to these teacher perceptions.

Teachers' perceptions and expectations may even create a **self-fulfilling prophesy,** in which the expectations for a pupil lead the teacher to interact with that pupil in a particular manner (Good & Brophy, 1997). The pupil, in turn, observes the way the teacher interacts with him or her and begins to behave in the way or at the level the teacher expects, whether or not the original expectation is correct. Needless to say, it is the teacher's ethical responsibility to avoid this situation by making the sizing-up assessments as fair and accurate as possible for all pupils, and not using them to demean or embarrass a pupil. This is especially so since the sizing-up process happens so quickly, is often done unconsciously, and leaves no permanent record outside the teacher's head.

To summarize, we have seen that sizing-up assessments are largely based upon information that is gathered at the start of the school year, that teachers form these assessments relatively quickly, that they use them to "know" students, and that they remain fairly stable once formed. Sizing-up assessments determine perceptions and expectations, which in turn influence teachers' interactions with pupils. Because sizing-up assessments can be so influential in setting expectations, influencing pupil-teacher interactions, and affecting pupils' performance and self-perceptions, it is important to examine more closely the dangers inherent in that process and the strategies teachers can use to improve their initial assessments.

QUALITY OF SIZING-UP ASSESSMENTS

As stated in Chapter 1, the two main criteria for good assessments are validity and reliability. Validity is concerned with the collection of *appropriate* evidence; that is, evidence that is related to the pupil characteristic under consideration: Does the evidence I have gathered tell me about the characteristic I wish to judge? Reliability pertains to collecting *enough* evidence to be relatively certain that the pupil's *typical* performance is being observed: Is the evidence gathered indicative of the pupil's typical or normal performance? Validity and reliability work hand-in-hand to ensure that the perceptions formed in sizing-up assessment are appropriate and fair, leading to good decisions about pupils.

Threats to Validity

Observer prejudgment can stem from prior knowledge, first impressions, or personal prejudices, and often interferes with fair and valid assessments.

There are two main problems that occur during sizing-up assessment that diminish the validity of the information teachers gather: prejudgment and logical error. **Prejudgment** occurs when a teacher's prior knowledge, first impressions, or personal prejudices and beliefs interfere with the ability to make a fair and valid assessment of a pupil. All of us have personal prejudices or beliefs; we prefer some things to others and some people to others. We have beliefs, interests, ideas, and expectations that differentiate us from others. However, when these likes, dislikes, beliefs, and prejudices interfere with our ability to make fair pupil assessments, there is a real problem.

Prejudging pupils results from three main sources. The first is *prior information,* information a teacher obtains before meeting a pupil. Information passed through the school grapevine or the performance of prior siblings often influences and prejudices a teacher's perceptions, even before the pupil enters the teacher's classroom: "Oh, you're Sarah's brother! I'm expecting you to do as well as she did when she was in my class."

The second is *initial impressions,* which tend to influence subsequent impressions. If the teacher judges a pupil upon how he is dressed on the first day of school or how she behaved in study hall last year, the teacher may unconsciously let this initial impression dictate subsequent observations and interpretations of the pupil's characteristics.

The third source of prejudging is teachers' *personal theories and beliefs* about particular kinds of pupils, which often lead to stereotyped perceptions. When teachers think This pupil is from Oldtown, and kids from

Oldtown are poor learners and discipline problems; Girls do poorly in math; Everyone knows that members of that group have no interest in school; or He's just another dumb jock, they are expressing their personal theories or stereotypes of what they think certain people are like and how they behave. Being labeled with such stereotypes without a fair chance to show true characteristics can injure pupils and inhibit their learning.

This is especially so with regard to teachers' racial, cultural, disability, and language prejudices or stereotypes. While the variety of pupil languages, cultures, races, and disabilities represented in American classrooms is increasing, the variety of teachers who teach these students is not increasing as quickly. When sizing up pupils, teachers who are not familiar with pupils' cultures and languages often interpret what are really cultural *differences* as cultural *deficits* (Ladson-Billings, 1994; Delpit, 1995). Similarly, teachers' stereotypes or personal beliefs can produce invalid sizing-up assessments for students who are different from the teacher. For example, many Americans, including many teachers, believe that the majority of children of color are poor, live in large cities, come from single-family homes, and live on public assistance. In fact, none of these beliefs is true regarding children of color. How might a teacher who erroneously believes these misconceptions perceive a pupil of color on the first day of school? Do you think he or she might have some prejudgments or stereotypes that could influence initial perceptions of the pupil? The dangers of prejudgment are real and consequential. Teachers must strive to recognize their personal beliefs and stereotypes and judge each individual pupil on the basis of how he or she actually performs in class. Each pupil is entitled to be judged on his or her own merits, not on the basis of stereotypes and personal beliefs. This is a teacher's ethical responsibility.

Teachers should be careful not to interpret cultural differences as cultural deficits.

Many teachers recognize that prejudgments and stereotyping can invalidate sizing-up assessments, as the following statements indicate.

> I don't like to hear anything about a student's behavior from past teachers. Every teacher is different, just like every student is different. A student may have a negative experience with one teacher, but a positive experience with another teacher. I prefer to make my own decision about every child.

> I remember the time I stereotyped three of my female students as "valley girls"—not too bright and mainly superficial—on the first day of class. This assessment came about due to their physical appearance and their shallow contributions in discussion. Yet when it came time for formal assessment, these three individuals ranked the highest in the class.

Logical error occurs when teachers select the wrong indicators to assess desired pupil characteristics, thereby invalidating their judgments. It is tempting to read a great deal into a single observation, especially at the start of the year when teachers want to quickly characterize each pupil in order to organize their classes. It would be convenient, for example, to read a whole series of inferences about motivation, attention span, interest in the subject, self-concept, and leadership from a pupil's eager hand raising. Maybe all the interpretations will prove to be correct, but it is dangerous not to recognize the difference between what is directly observed and interpretations made from an observation. When observation of one characteristic (hand raising) is used to make inferences about other, unobserved characteristics (motivation, interest), the potential for logical errors and invalid assessment is great.

> A fifth grade teacher described Katie's first day in school in this way: "I knew right away that Katie was cooperative and a hard worker. She was the first child to complete her Summer Vacation essay, and instead of wasting her free time, she offered to get the dictionary and help the other children with their spelling." Are cooperative and hard working the only interpretations of Katie's behaviors? What are some others? If Shandella, not Katie, had done the same things, would Shandella have been judged in the same way?

Teachers should be careful not to mislabel students based on observations that do not justify the label.

The labels teachers use to describe their pupils represent their interpretations of observed behaviors. Teachers do not directly observe characteristics such as motivation, intelligence, leadership, self-confidence, aggressiveness, anxiety, shyness, intolerance, and the like. Rather, teachers observe a pupil behaving in some way, interpret what the behavior signifies, and give the behavior a name. In most cases, it is the name given to the behavior that attaches to the pupil, not the specific behavior that prompted the name. Teachers remember that a pupil is a bully, self-confident, aggressive, aloof, motivated, or shy, but they rarely remember the specific observations that led them to label the pupils in that way. Because teachers' labels "stick" to pupils, it is important that the observations leading to a label are valid indicators of that label.

Threats to Reliability

Teachers should be careful not to form a permanent perception of pupils based on one or two observations that may not be typical behavior.

While validity is concerned with collecting information that is appropriate for determining a pupil's characteristics, reliability is concerned with collecting enough information to be sure that it represents typical pupil behavior. For example, was the teacher's observance of Katie's performance on that first day of school sufficient to conclude that she will be cooperative and a hard worker? Probably not. Why? Whether formal or informal, teachers' sizing-up assessments are based upon samples of their pupils' behavior. These samples are used to determine pupils' more general behavior patterns. Remember Mr. Ferris, Manuela, Joe, and Stuart? Thus, an important issue in teacher assessment is how well the observed samples represent pupils' general or typical behavior patterns. Reliable information captures consistent and stable pupil characteristics.

The nature of sizing-up assessment creates special reliability problems. As noted earlier, the spontaneity of many teacher-pupil interactions limit what teachers are able to see and what pupils are willing to show. Also, the time available to observe pupils often is brief, since attention must be distributed among many pupils and classroom activities, especially at the beginning of the school year. In short, the few, initial samples of behavior that are observed under these circumstances may not provide reliable indicators of pupils' typical behavior.

Many teachers recognize this problem, as evidenced by the following statements.

> First impressions are so important. They can either make or break a child. It all depends on how much opportunity a particular teacher gives to a student to prove himself before passing a judgment.

> The first three days are very difficult. The students will not even present their normal classroom behaviors to you in the first three days. They are somewhat intimidated and uncomfortable; they don't know you. Even kids who are badly behaved in the first three days, they're just feeling you out, they're testing, trying to see how far they can get.

> Carol breaks up with her boyfriend a week before the beginning of school, leaving her depressed and unmotivated. Does her English teacher know the reason for Carol's behavior? Is her assessment of Carol after one day of school correct?

The implication of these comments is that teachers must be sure they observe sufficient samples of pupils' behavior before they solidify their initial perceptions and use them for decision making. There are times, such as the start of the school year, when pupils' behavior may not be indicative of their typical behavior. Typical behavior cannot be determined by observing a pupil just once, especially at a time when the pupil may feel uncomfortable in new surroundings. Table 2.3 summarizes the threats to validity and reliability that have been discussed.

TABLE 2.3   THREATS TO THE VALIDITY AND RELIABILITY OF SIZING-UP ASSESSMENTS

Validity Threats

I. Observer prejudgments: Prevent teachers from making an objective assessment of the pupils.
   A. Prior information from school grapevine, siblings, or nonclassroom experiences
   B. First impressions that influence subsequent impressions
   C. Personal theories or attitudes that influence subsequent observation (e.g., girls can't do math or athletes have no interest in serious academic pursuits)

II. Logical errors: Teachers judge pupils based on the wrong characteristics (e.g., observe attention and judge learning; observe clothes and judge ability).

Reliability Threats

I. Inadequate behavior sampling: Too few observations prevent learning about pupils' typical behavior and characteristics.
   A. Basing decisions about a pupil on a single piece of information.
   B. Observing behaviors in one setting (e.g., the playground) and assuming behavior will be the same in another setting (e.g., the classroom).

IMPROVING SIZING-UP ASSESSMENTS

Following are some strategies that can be used to improve sizing-up assessments. While teachers will never be correct in all their sizing-up assessments, it is their ethical responsibility to do everything possible to minimize errors and to revise judgments when initial impressions prove to be wrong.

1. *Be aware of sizing-up assessment and its effects on pupils.* Sizing-up assessment is such a natural part of the start of the school year that many teachers are unaware that they are doing it. They do not recognize the dangers of forming incorrect impressions of pupils. As a first step, then, it is important for teachers to be aware of this type of assessment and to be sensitive to the consequences of making incorrect judgments based on incomplete or invalid observations.

Teachers should treat initial impressions as hypotheses to be confirmed or corrected by later information.

2. *Treat initial impressions as hypotheses to be confirmed or corrected by subsequent observations and information.* First impressions should be considered tentative hypotheses that need to be confirmed or disproved by subsequent observation and information. Teachers should refrain from judging and labeling pupils on the basis of hearsay, a single brief observation, or a pupil's race, culture, gender, or language. They should also gather their own evidence about pupils and confirm first impressions with subsequent observations and information. They should not be afraid to change an incorrect first impression.

When making assessments, teachers should try to use information that requires minimum interpretation.

3. *Use direct indicators to gather information about pupil characteristics.* To size up pupils, teachers must interpret the pupil observations they gather. Some observations require less interpretation than others. The closer the behavior observed is to the pupil characteristic a teacher wishes to describe, the more valid the resulting information is and the more confident the teacher can be about the pupil's true characteristic. For example, actually listening to a pupil read aloud provides more direct and valid evidence about a pupil's oral reading than the reading grades the pupil got from a prior teacher or the pupil's reported interest in reading.

In sizing-up assessments, teacher-pupil encounters are often brief, and the tendency is for the teacher to focus on superficial, indirect characteristics such as dress, facial expression, helpfulness, mood, or general appearance. Teachers then read into these superficial observations complex traits and personality factors like motivation, self-concept, trustworthiness, self-control, and interest. Such indirect generalizations are likely to be invalid. Thus, the moral is to focus evidence gathering on direct behaviors and indicators.

4. *Supplement informal observations with more formal, structured activities.* There is no rule that demands that only informal observations be used to size up pupils. In fact, complete reliance on informal observations means that the teacher does not have control over many of the behaviors that occur, especially in the first few days of school. Good teachers recognize this limitation and supplement their informal sizing-up observations with more structured activities. For example, they

- ◆ administer textbook review or diagnostic pretests to assess pupils' entering levels.
- ◆ require pupils to keep a journal during the first week of school or write an essay on What I Did Last Summer to assess pupils' experiences, writing skills, and thought processes.
- ◆ carry out group discussions or group projects to assess how pupils interact and work in groups.
- ◆ let pupils read aloud to determine reading facility.
- ◆ play classroom games based on spelling words, math facts, geographical knowledge, or current events to assess general knowledge, interest, and competitiveness.
- ◆ use games related to listening skills to assess pupils' abilities to follow directions and process auditory information.
- ◆ employ more formal observational instruments.

Because informal observations involve spontaneous behavior that may not be repeated, teachers should supplement their informal observations with more structured activities.

Some school systems collect samples of pupils' work into what are called portfolios. These portfolios often accompany the pupils as they progress from grade to grade and provide a new teacher with concrete examples of a pupil's work. Note that having actual samples of a pupil's work from previous years is quite different from the hearsay evidence teachers accumulate through the school grapevine. (Portfolios and other formal methods of assessing pupil performance are described more fully in Chapter 5.) Formal assessments provide information about pupils' interests, styles, and academic performance that is not always obtainable from informal observations. Formal assessments also often require all pupils to perform the same behavior and thereby permit comparisons of desired characteristics among pupils.

Formal assessments that require students to perform the same behavior permit comparison among pupils.

5. *Observe long enough to be fairly certain of the pupil's typical behavior.* Reliable information is that which represents the *typical* behavior of a pupil. To obtain reliable data, the teacher must look for *patterns* of behavior, not single, one-time behaviors. The greater the consequences that an assessment is likely to have for pupils, the more the teacher should strive to gather reliable information. A good rule of thumb to follow is See it at least twice, thus making sure the behavior being observed is typical.

Reliable assessments usually require multiple observations in order to identify typical student behavior.

6. *Determine whether different kinds of information confirm each other.* Teachers can have more confidence in their pupil perceptions if they are based upon two or more kinds of supporting evidence. For example, Are test scores supported by classroom performance? Are classroom observations of a pupil's needs consistent with those identified by last year's teacher and the pupil's parents? Do classroom behavior patterns persist in the lunchroom and on the playground?

Whenever possible, teachers should base their decisions on different kinds of information that support one another.

> **TABLE 2.4   STRATEGIES TO IMPROVE SIZING-UP ASSESSMENT**
>
> **1.** Recognize that sizing-up assessment is going on; without this awareness, it is difficult to improve the process.
>
> **2.** Let first impressions represent initial hypotheses to be confirmed or rejected by additional information; see behaviors at least twice before judging pupils.
>
> **3.** Observe important pupil behaviors directly rather than inferring them from ancillary behaviors and characteristics.
>
> **4.** Supplement informal observation with more formal, structured assessments such as pretests and games.
>
> **5.** Pick one pupil characteristic per day and structure classroom activities to permit pupils to demonstrate that characteristic.
>
> **6.** Determine whether different types and sources of information (e.g., informal observation, formal observation, tests, or other teachers' comments) provide similar information about pupil characteristics.

These questions suggest the use of multiple sources of information to corroborate the teacher's perception of a pupil. However, note that it is better if the present teacher forms his or her own impressions of the pupil *before* obtaining corroborative information from other sources. By doing this, the teacher's perceptions will not be influenced or prejudiced by the perceptions of others. Table 2.4 summarizes the strategies for improving the validity and reliability of sizing-up assessments.

CHAPTER SUMMARY

- ◆ In the first few days of school teachers must learn about their pupils and organize them into a classroom society characterized by communication, order, and learning.

- ◆ Information for sizing up pupils comes from a variety of sources, including the school grapevine, comments by other teachers, school records, classroom discussion and observation, pupil comments, pretests, body language, and pupil dress, among others.

- ◆ Sizing-up assessments are a natural part of social interactions. In classrooms they lead teachers to form and often communicate expectations to pupils. Moreover, teachers' first impressions of pupils tend to remain stable, although they are not always accurate. As a consequence, teachers must consider carefully when sizing up and labeling pupils at the start of the school year.

- ◆ Two main problems affect the validity of sizing-up assessments: prejudgment and logical error. Prejudgments occur when a teacher's prior knowledge, first impression, or personal beliefs interfere with his or her ability to make a fair and objective assessment of a pupil. This is of special concern when teachers know little about the racial, cultural, handicapping, and language characteristics of their pupils. Teachers who are not familiar with pupils' varied cultures and languages often interpret what are really cultural differences as cultural deficits when they judge pupils who are different from themselves. Logical error occurs when teachers use the wrong kind of information to judge pupil characteristics, as, for example, when they judge interest by where a pupil sits in a class.

◆ Reliability is a special problem in sizing-up assessment because the process takes place so quickly and is based upon many fleeting observations; thus, it is difficult to assess pupils' typical or consistent performance. However, reliability is important in sizing-up assessments, and teachers should not label pupils based on only a few observations.

◆ Six suggestions for improving sizing-up assessments are (1) be aware of sizing up and its potential effects on students; (2) treat initial impressions as hypotheses to be confirmed or corrected by subsequent observation and information; (3) use direct, low inference indicators to gather information about pupil characteristics; (4) supplement informal observations with more formal, structured activities; (5) observe students long enough to be fairly certain of the pupil's typical behavior; and (6) determine whether different kinds of information confirm one another.

QUESTIONS FOR DISCUSSION

1. How does the fact that a classroom is a social setting influence planning, teaching, grading, managing, and interacting with pupils?

2. What are the advantages and disadvantages of examining a pupil's school (cumulative) record folder before the start of class? Under what circumstances would you examine a pupil's record folder?

3. How much must teachers really know about a pupil's home and family background? What home and background information is absolutely essential for teachers to know? Why? What information does a teacher have no right to know about a pupil's home or background?

4. Why do teachers rely so heavily on informal observation when sizing up pupils? Should teachers use sizing-up assessment to label pupils?

REFLECTION EXERCISES

◆ Did you ever have a teacher who liked or disliked you? who trusted or did not trust you? who thought you were smart or dumb? who had a perception about your ability, character, motivation, or effort? How could you tell the teacher felt that way about you? What did the teacher do or say to communicate that perception to you? How do you know you were reading the teacher's message correctly? What can you do to control the messages you send to pupils?

◆ What are the three most common ways teachers transmit their feelings and attitudes about a student to the student?

ACTIVITIES

1. Table 2.1 shows the resources available in two different classrooms. In small groups, compare the two classrooms. How do the resources in each classroom influence planning and instructing pupils? Give specific examples.

2. Interview a classroom teacher. Find out the answers to such questions as What information does the teacher have about pupils before the first day of class? What are the sources of that information? How much does the teacher rely upon the comments of other teachers when getting to know a new class? If the teacher could know only two specific characteristics of each pupil at the end of the first day of class, what would these be? Why? What information is most useful for managing pupils in the classroom? Add three questions of your own to this list. Why did you select those three questions?

REVIEW QUESTIONS

1. What factors make a classroom a social setting or society? How do these factors influence a teacher's assessment responsibilities?

2. What is sizing-up assessment? How is it done? How does it differ from other types of classroom assessments? What are three dangers that can reduce the validity and reliability of sizing-up assessment? What are three strategies a teacher can use to improve sizing-up assessments?

3. What are the main problems of validity and reliability in sizing-up assessment and assessments for planning and delivering instruction?

4. Why are sizing-up assessments important? What do they help teachers accomplish?

5. What are some differences between formal and informal observation?

REFERENCES

Bullough, R. V., Knowles, J. G., and Crow, N. A. (1992). *Emerging as a teacher.* New York: Routledge.

Delpit, L. (1995). *Other people's children: Cultural conflict in the classroom.* New York: The New Press.

Garcia, E. (1994). *Understanding and meeting the challenge of student cultural diversity.* Boston, MA: Houghton Mifflin.

Good, T. L., and Brophy, J. E. (1997). *Looking in classrooms.* New York: Longman.

Goodson, I. (1992). Studying teachers' lives: Problems and possibilities. In I. Goodson (Ed.), *Studying teachers' lives* (pp. 234–249). New York: Teachers College Press.

Ladson-Billings, G. (1994). *The dreamkeepers.* San Franciso: Jossey-Bass.

McCaslin, M., and Good, T. (1996). *Listening to students.* New York: Harper-Collins.

Solas, J. (1992). Investigating teacher and student thinking about the process of teaching and learning using autobiography and repertory grid. *Review of Educational Research, 622,* 205–225.

Stiggins, R. J. (1997). *Student-centered classroom assessment.* Columbus, OH: Prentice Hall.

Wiseman, D. L., Cooner, D. D., and Knight, S. L. (1999). *Becoming a teacher in a field-based setting.* Belmont, CA: Wadsworth.

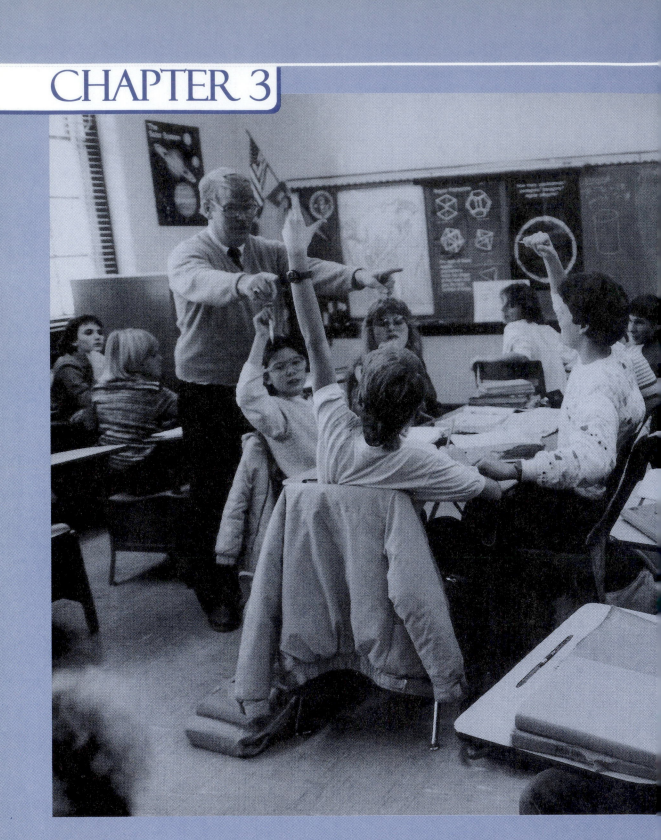

CHAPTER 3

ASSESSMENT IN PLANNING AND DELIVERING INSTRUCTION

CHAPTER OBJECTIVES

After reading this chapter, the student will be able to:

1. define basic terms: for example, curriculum, instruction, achievement, ability, and educational objective.

2. describe characteristics considered in planning leasons.

3. write a lesson plan that communicates purpose, process, and assessment strategy.

4. state educational objectives, differentiate well-stated from poorly stated objectives, and distinguish between and write higher level and lower level educational objectives.

5. critique textbook objectives and lesson plans in terms of clarity, completeness, and appropriateness.

6. identify instructional accommodations for pupils with disabilities.

7. cite common errors in planning instruction.

8. compare features of assessment used for planning and delivering instruction.

9. suggest ways to improve the validity and reliability of assessment during instruction.

10. explain the purposes and strategies of oral questioning.

Education is the process of helping to change students' knowledge and behavior in desired ways.

The purpose of schools is to educate pupils, but what does it mean to educate? Under what circumstances can a teacher claim credit for helping to educate a pupil? To **educate** means to help pupils change, to help them learn and do new things. When teachers have helped pupils to read, identify parts of speech in a sentence, use the scientific method, or write a cohesive paragraph, they have educated these students. Many experts describe education as a process intended to help pupils change in important and desirable ways (Airasian, in press). This view leads to a fundamental question all teachers have to ask themselves: What do I want my pupils to know or be able to do following instruction that they did not know or do at the start of instruction? Education is the process of fostering these important and desired pupil changes.

It is important to point out, however, that this view of education is not the only possible one. Thoughtful critics (Perkinson, 1993) suggest that education conceived solely as a process of preplanned pupil behavior change can lead to a preoccupation with narrow outcomes and afford the pupil virtually no role in the creation of his or her own educational program. Critics recognize the importance of a teacher's ability to artistically build upon a pupil's prior experience and to seek multiple, not necessarily predefined, outcomes from instruction. Despite the merits of alternative views, for most teachers, education is conceived, practiced, and assessed with the primary function of helping to change learners in desired ways.

A **curriculum** describes the skills, performances, knowledge, and attitudes pupils are expected to learn in school. The curriculum contains statements of desired pupil learning and descriptions of the methods and materials that will be used to help pupils attain this. The methods and processes actually used to change pupils' behavior are called **instruction.** Lectures, discussions, worksheets, cooperative projects, and homework are but a few of the instructional techniques used to help pupils learn.

A curriculum describes the knowledge, skills, performances, and attitudes pupils are expected to learn in school, while instruction refers to the methods of teaching the curriculum.

Pupils undergo many changes during their school years, and many sources beside the school contribute to these changes: maturation, peer groups, family, reading, and TV, among others. The term **achievement** is used to describe school-based learning, while terms like **ability** and **aptitude** are used to describe broader learning that stems from nonschool sources. Since the focus of schooling is to help pupils attain particular behaviors, understandings, and processes, almost all of the formal tests that pupils take in school are intended to assess their achievement. The Friday spelling test, the unit test on chemical equations, the math test on the Pythagorean theorem, the delivery of an oral speech, the autobiography, and midterm and final examinations all should focus on assessing pupil achievement, that is, what they have learned of the things that were taught in school.

Achievement refers to school-based learning, while ability and aptitude refer to broader learning acquired mostly through nonschool sources such as parents and peer groups.

To summarize, we have seen that the purpose of schools is to educate, and that the mainstream view of education is that it helps pupils learn and do new and desired things. The school curriculum identifies these planned outcomes and the general guidelines for bringing them about. Instruction includes the methods that are used to produce the desired pupil changes. Pupil achievements are those occurring as a result of school-based instruction.

THE INSTRUCTIONAL PROCESS

The instructional process comprises three basic steps. The first is *planning instruction,* which includes identifying desired pupil learning outcomes, selecting materials to foster these outcomes, and organizing learning experiences into a coherent, reinforcing sequence. The second step involves *delivering the planned instruction* to pupils, that is, teaching them. The third step involves determining whether or not pupils have learned or achieved the desired outcomes, or *assessing pupil outcomes.* Notice that to carry out the instructional process the three steps should be aligned with one another. That is, the planned instruction should be logically related to the actual instruction and the assessments should relate to the plans and instruction.

The instructional process involves three interdependent steps: planning, delivering, and assessing.

Figure 3.1 shows these three steps and the relationships among them. Notice that the diagram is presented as a triangle rather than as a straight

FIGURE 3.1
Steps in the
Instructional Process

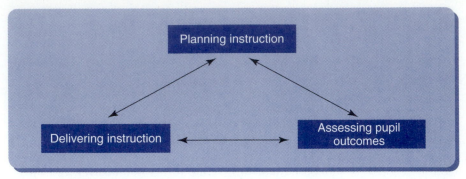

All three steps in the
instructional process
involve assessment and
teacher decision making.

line. This indicates that the three steps are interrelated in a more complicated way than a simple one-two-three sequence. For example, in planning instruction (step 1), the teacher considers the characteristics of pupils and the resources and materials available to help attain desired changes (step 2). Similarly, the information gained at the time of pupil assessment (step 3) is useful in assessing the appropriateness of the learning experiences provided pupils (step 2) and the suitability of intended pupil outcomes (step 1). Thus, the three steps are interdependent pieces in the instructional process that can be aligned in different orders.

All three steps in the instructional process involve teacher decision making and assessment. Obviously step 3, assessing pupil outcomes, involves the collection and synthesis of formal information about how well pupils are learning or have learned. But the other two steps in the instructional process are also dependent upon a teacher's assessment activities. For example, a teacher's planning decisions incorporate information about pupil readiness, appropriate methods, available instructional resources, materials, pupil culture, language, and other important characteristics obtained from sizing-up assessments. Similarly, during instruction the teacher is constantly "reading" the class to obtain information to help make decisions about lesson pace, reinforcement, interest, and comprehension. Thus, the entire instructional process, not just the formal assessment step, depends upon decisions that rely on assessment evidence of various kinds.

The processes of planning and providing instruction are important activities for classroom teachers. Not only do they occupy a substantial amount of their time, but teachers define their teaching rewards in terms of their pupils' instructional successes. Teachers like to work with pupils, make a difference in their lives, and experience the joy of a pupil "getting it" (Louis Harris & Associates, 1995). Teachers feel rewarded when they know that their instruction has reached their pupils. Since the classroom is where pride in teaching is forged, it is not surprising to find that teachers guard their classroom instructional time jealously. They want few interruptions to distract them from their pupils, teaching responsibilities, and rewards.

Teachers define their
own success and
rewards in terms of their
students' learning.

Purpose of Planning Instruction

Teachers plan in order to modify the curriculum to fit the unique characteristics of their particular pupils. When teachers plan, they decide what the pupils should learn from instruction, which topics to cover, whether to add or delete textbook sections, the special needs of their pupils, the time to allocate to instruction, the specific activities to expose pupils to, the sequence and pace in which to present these activities, the homework to assign, and the techniques to use in assessing pupil learning. Thinking through all of these planning activities helps teachers feel comfortable and prepared for instruction; it gives them a sense of command and personal ownership over the teaching act.

Teachers plan to order to fit the curriculum to the unique characteristics of their particular class.

The most important plans teachers develop are unit or chapter plans, followed by weekly and daily lesson plans. Unit or chapter plans provide an overview of a sufficiently large block of material so that weekly and daily plans can be developed. Planning only daily lessons does not provide the generalization and continuity needed for successful instruction. Thus, teachers tend to plan in manageable chunks like units or chapters and use the cohesiveness of these chunks to provide a structure for daily planning.

Most teachers feel that unit or chapter plans are the most important followed by weekly and daily plans.

Planning is important because, as we have seen, classrooms are complex environments. The uncertainties, complexities, and variety of pupils' needs and characteristics require some structure, order, and control, especially when teachers carry out formal instruction. In such an environment, some form of planning and organization is needed to impose structure and attend to varied pupil needs.

Planning in advance of teaching helps teachers in three ways. First, it helps reduce uncertainty and anxiety about instruction by providing teachers with a sense of purpose and subject matter focus. Second, it affords teachers an opportunity to review and become familiar with the subject matter and activities before actually teaching. Third, it includes ways to get instruction started, activities to pursue, and a framework to use during the actual delivery of instruction.

Planning helps teachers bring needed structure into the complex and fast-paced classroom environment.

CHARACTERISTICS CONSIDERED IN PLANNING INSTRUCTION

Having sized up pupils, the teacher is ready to plan meaningful and appropriate lessons. The following sections describe the many factors teachers must consider when planning instruction.

Pupil Characteristics

An initial and extremely important consideration is the present status and needs of pupils. What are they developmentally ready to learn? What topics have they mastered thus far in the subject area? How complex are the instructional materials they can handle? How well do they work in groups? Are they independent learners? Do they have special needs? What accommodations must be made for pupils with handicaps of various kinds? The answers to such questions provide needed perspective and valuable insights about how and what to teach. The importance of valid and reliable sizing-up assessment becomes apparent when teachers plan their lessons.

Instructional planning tends to be more complex in elementary schools because students usually are more differentiated and because teachers must plan in many subject areas.

Instructional planning in elementary schools is generally more complex than in high schools because the pupil characteristics that need to be considered are more numerous and differentiated at this level. For example, in addition to lesson content, the teacher must take into account pupil readiness, attention span, learning styles, and how a lesson will fit with other lessons of the day. While all teachers should attend to these planning factors, they are more often employed by elementary teachers than those teaching higher grades. Moreover, the elementary teacher often works with differentiated pupil groupings, and instructional materials vary with the level of the group. Plans for each group differ according to the readiness, needs, and socialization levels of the group. Further, most elementary schoolteachers are responsible for planning instruction in all subjects, not just one or two as is typical at the high school level.

It is obvious that such pupil characteristics as ability, readiness, needs, independence, attention span, disabilities, and self-control should be taken into account in planning instructional activities. Not to do so would be irrational. However, it is very important to recognize that much of the information used to plan comes to teachers from the initial sizing-up assessments made early in the school year. Consequently, it is crucial that teachers strive to make their initial sizing-up assessments as valid and reliable as possible.

Teacher Characteristics

Most beginning teachers do not take their own characteristics into account when planning instruction. However, subject matter knowledge, personality, and physical limitations are important factors in planning and delivering instruction. It is impossible for teachers to know everything about all the topics they teach. Nor can they be expected to keep abreast of all advances in subject matter knowledge or pedagogy. Consequently, the topics teachers choose to cover, the accuracy and up-to-dateness of their topical coverage, and their teaching methods all are influenced by their own knowledge limitations. Moreover, teachers' personalities often lead them to favor certain instructional techniques over others. While individual preferences are to be expected among teachers, it is important to understand that when carried to the extreme, they can result in an overly narrow repertoire of teaching methods. This has the potential to limit learning opportunities for those pupils who could learn better from other instructional techniques. Finally, since teaching is a rigorous, fatiguing activity, teachers should consider their own physical limitations when planning instruction. This caution is especially appropriate for beginning teachers, whose enthusiasm and lack of experience often lead them to overestimate what they can physically accomplish in the classroom. A common complaint heard from college students during their first full-time classroom practicum is how mentally and physically draining a day in the classroom can be.

Instructional Resources

The instructional resources available to a teacher influence not only the nature of instruction but also the learning outcomes that are possible. The term *resources* is used here in its broadest sense to include available supplies, equipment, space, aids or volunteers, texts, and time. Each of these resources influences the nature of instruction and therefore the pupil achievements that can be pursued.

When planning instruction, teachers should take their own characteristics and knowledge into account along with their pupils' characteristics and the time and resources available.

A biology teacher may wish his or her class to learn about the internal organs of a frog by having each pupil perform a frog dissection. However, if the school has no biology laboratory and no dissecting equipment, the teacher must forgo this objective. Classroom aids or volunteers who read to pupils, work with small groups, or serve as "microscope moms" during a unit on the microscope can free the classroom teacher to plan and pursue enrichment activities that might not have been possible otherwise. Resources of all kinds are important to consider when planning instruction.

Time is another important, though often overlooked, resource that greatly influences planning. Implicitly, each teacher's decisions about what content to stress or omit is based upon the instructional time available. While teachers make decisions about the allocation of instructional time on a daily basis, it is in the last few weeks of the school year that these decisions become most apparent: "We must cover subtraction of fractions before the end of the year, but we can omit rate, time, and distance word problems;" "If I don't finish parts of speech this year, next year's teacher will be upset, so I'll take some time from the poetry unit." Time is a limited resource, and thus has important consequences for planning instruction.

A final resource that greatly influences what is planned, taught, and learned in classrooms is the textbook. More than any other single resource, the textbook determines instructional plans in many classrooms. A large part of students' learning time and a large part of the teacher's instructional time are focused on textbook use (Woodward & Elliott, 1990).

The teacher's edition of most textbooks contains many resources to help teachers plan, deliver, and assess instruction. However, teachers should not abdicate their planning, teaching, and assessment decision-making responsibilities to the textbook. To do so reduces the classroom teacher from a professional decision maker to a mindless technician carrying out the instructional program and plans of others. It is incumbent upon all teachers to assess the status and needs of *their* pupils, the curriculum requirements of *their* state or community, and the resources available in *their* classrooms when planning instruction for *their* pupils. In the end, decisions about what to emphasize rest with the individual classroom teacher, who knows her pupils better than anyone else and who is in the best position to plan and carry out instruction that is suited to their needs.

To slavishly follow the lessons in a textbook is to abdicate instructional decision making.

LESSON PLANS

Once relevant information about the pupils, the teacher, and the instructional resources are identified, the teacher's task is to synthesize it into a set of instructional plans. When planning, teachers try to visualize themselves teaching, mentally viewing and rehearsing the learning activities they contemplate using in the classroom. This mental dress rehearsal provides instructional direction for both pupils and teacher.

There are many different instructional approaches that teachers can and do use when planning instruction, such as Madeline Hunter's lesson design cycle model (Hunter, 1982), cooperative learning models (Slavin, 1995), and more recently, the work of Howard Gardner on multiple intelligence (Gardner, 1995). Gardner's approach divides intellectual or thinking abilities into seven distinct kinds of intelligence: linguistic (using words), logical/mathematical (using reasoning), spatial (using images and pictures), musical (using rhythms), interpersonal (using interpersonal interactions), intrapersonal (using meditation or planning), and body/kinesthetic (using physical activities). Employing Gardner's approach to multiple intelligence—or any other approach to learning—has implications for classroom instruction. For example, Gardner would argue that his approach demands that teachers teach a broader range of outcomes using a broader range of styles that engage pupils in different multiple intelligences. While simultaneously implementing the seven multiple intelligences in classrooms may be very difficult, Gardner's theory reminds teachers that there is more than one way for all pupils to learn and be assessed. How might instruction and assessment based on a cooperative learning approach differ from instruction and assessment in a multiple-intelligence approach? Different methods often lead to different instructional strategies and different outcomes (Wiggins & McTighe, 1998).

Different methods of instruction lead to different forms of instruction and assessment. Teachers must be able to teach pupils in more than one way.

For example, consider three different approaches to planning lessons that are commonly used by beginning teachers: *direct instruction, informal presentation,* and *structured discovery* (Price & Nelson, 1999). Direct instruction, also called supervised practice, is teacher directed. In essence, it can be characterized as "I do it, we do it, and you do it"; that is, the teacher demonstrates, the pupils and teacher do it together, and the students do it alone. This approach is useful for factual or procedural outcomes. Informal presentation involves the teacher dispensing information to students. It is a classical lecture format in which the teacher tells students what they are to learn, the students listen to what the teacher tells them and then listen to the teacher again telling them what they were to have learned. While direct instruction focuses on doing, informal presentation focuses on knowing. Structured discovery involves the pupils "discovering" teacher-planned information or concepts. The teacher knows in advance what the pupils are to discover and structures activities, explorations, and examples so that the pupils actually do discover the intended information or concept. This format can be conducted with pupils cooperatively or individually. There are many additional approaches to lesson planning and teaching (Arends, 1997; Borich, 1996). The important points to recognize are that different instructional approaches lead to different teaching and assessment and that no teacher can survive using a single approach to teaching.

While the specific steps and activities suggested by different instructional models often vary, usually all include four basic lesson planning elements: educational objectives, needed materials, teaching/learning strategies, and assessment procedures. Table 3.1 describes what is usually included in each of these elements.

Most experienced teachers' lesson plans are less detailed than the general planning model shown in Table 3.1. Typically, experienced teachers'

TABLE 3.1 COMPONENTS OF A LESSON PLAN

Educational objectives. Description of the things pupils are to learn from instruction; what pupils should be able to do after instruction (e.g., the pupils can write a summary of a story; the pupils can differentiate adverbs from adjectives in a given passage)

Materials. Description of the resources, materials, and apparatus needed to carry out the lesson (e.g., overhead projector, clay, map of United States, Bunsen burners, video on the Civil Rights Movement, etc.)

Teaching activities and strategies. Description of the things that will take place during instruction; often includes factors such as determining pupil readiness, identifying how the lesson will start, reviewing prior lessons, providing advance organizers, specific instructional techniques to be used (e.g., discussion, lecture, silent reading, demonstration, seatwork, game, cooperative activities, etc.), sequence of techniques, providing pupils with practice, and ending the lesson

Assessment. Description of how pupil learning from the lesson will be assessed (e.g., homework assignment, oral questions, writing an essay, etc.)

plans consist of a list of activities to be performed during instruction, a list that directs the teacher and/or pupil to do this, say this, write this, ask this, or show this. In planning, one advantage experienced teachers have over beginning teachers is a mental notepad filled with past experiences that can be called up from memory by a brief list of phrases and activities (Leinhardt, 1989). When experienced teachers prepare lesson plans, they typically think mainly about what they and the students will be doing during instruction. While such plans describe both pupil and teacher activities, they rarely indicate what pupils are to learn from the activities (educational objectives) or how the teachers will determine the success of their instruction (assessment). This is unfortunate, since it focuses planning on activities, which are merely the means, not the ends, of instruction. To help keep the real purpose of instruction in mind, it is recommended that all teachers include statements of objectives in their lesson plans to indicate what they want the pupils to learn from instruction.

EDUCATIONAL OBJECTIVES

Objectives are statements that describe what pupils are expected to learn from instruction. They tell where the instruction is going. Other names for educational objectives include instructional objectives, learning objectives, performance objectives, behavioral objectives, curriculum objectives, learning targets, and pupil outcomes. Whatever their label, objectives should be included in lesson plans to identify important learning outcomes, guide instructional approaches towards these outcomes, and identify appropriate assessment of learning. Objectives are logically and closely tied to instruction and assessment.

The use of educational objectives helps teachers focus not just on what students are to learn but on the instructional activities used to promote that learning.

Behavior Domains

Classroom assessments cover cognitive, affective, and psychomotor behaviors.

Classroom objectives, instruction, and assessments differ in terms of three general types of human behavior: the cognitive, affective, and psychomotor domains.

Cognitive Domain

Cognitive assessments involve intellectual activities such as memorizing, interpreting, applying, problem solving, reasoning, analyzing, and thinking critically.

The most commonly taught and assessed educational objectives are those in the cognitive domain. **Cognitive behaviors** include intellectual activities such as memorizing, interpreting, applying, problem solving, reasoning, analyzing, and thinking critically. Virtually all the tests that pupils take in school are intended to measure one or more of these cognitive activities. Teachers' instruction is usually focused on helping pupils attain cognitive mastery of some content or subject area. A weekly spelling test, a unit test in history, a worksheet on proper use of *lie* and *lay,* an essay on supply and demand, and an oral recitation of a poem all require cognitive behaviors. The Scholastic Assessment Test (SAT), the ACT, the written part of a state driver's test, an ability test, and standardized achievement tests such as the Iowa Test of Basic Skills and the Stanford, Metropolitan, SRA, and California Achievement tests also are intended to assess pupils' cognitive behaviors.

In Chapter 1, Ms. Lopez was relying primarily upon cognitive information about her pupils when she made the following decisions: assigned grades, moved Jennifer from the middle to the high reading group, planned instruction, suggested that Robert spend extra time working on his report, identified pupils for remedial work in basic skills, graded pupils' American government projects, and consulted last year's standardized test scores to find out whether she needed to review the rules of capitalization for the class. In each case, Ms. Lopez was assessing her pupils' thinking, reasoning, memory, or general intellectual behaviors.

The many behaviors in the cognitive domain have been organized into six general categories. This organization is called the *Taxonomy of Educational Objectives: Cognitive Domain* (Bloom, Englehart, Furst, Hill, & Krathwohl, 1956), but it is most frequently referred to as Bloom's Taxonomy or the Cognitive Taxonomy. Bloom's Taxonomy is widely accepted and used in describing different types of cognitive behavior.

A taxonomy is a system of classification. Bloom's Taxonomy is organized into six levels, with each level representing a more complex type of cognitive thinking or behavior. Starting with the simplest and moving to the most complex, the six levels are knowledge, comprehension, application, analysis, synthesis, and evaluation. The type of cognitive behavior exemplified by each level of the taxonomy is illustrated in the following listing.

1. **Knowledge.** Memorization behaviors; for example, remembering formulas, poems, spelling words, state capitals.

2. **Comprehension.** Understanding behaviors; for example, summarizing what has been read or explaining an idea.

3. **Application.** Using prior information to solve unfamiliar problems; for example, predicting the outcome of actions.

4. **Analysis.** Breaking a large body of information into smaller parts; for example, analyzing the tone, style, form, and meaning of a poem.

5. **Synthesis.** Combining smaller bits of information into a generalization or conclusion; for example, formulating a general principle based upon a series of laboratory observations.

6. **Evaluation.** Judging the merit or worth of a person, object, or idea; for example, weighing the pros and cons of a course of action and deciding what to do.

Although taxonomies can differ in the particular levels or categories they include, their most important function is to remind teachers of the

Lower level cognitive behaviors involve rote memorization and recall; cognitive behaviors that involve more than rote memorization or recall are termed higher level cognitive behaviors.

distinction between higher and lower level thinking behaviors. In general, any cognitive behavior that involves more than rote memorization or recall is considered to be a **higher level cognitive behavior.** Thus, the knowledge level of Bloom's Taxonomy represents **lower level cognitive behavior,** since the focus is upon memorization and recall. All succeeding levels in these taxonomies represent higher level behaviors that call for pupils to carry out thinking and reasoning processes more complex than memorization. There is a growing emphasis in classroom instruction and assessment to focus upon teaching pupils higher order thinking skills (HOTS) that go beyond rote memorization.

Affective Domain

Affective assessments involve feelings, attitudes, interests, preferences, values, and emotions.

Teachers rarely make formal affective assessments but are constantly making them informally.

A second behavior domain is the affective domain. **Affective behaviors** involve feelings, attitudes, interests, preferences, values, and emotions. Emotional stability, motivation, trustworthiness, self-control, and personality are all examples of affective characteristics. Although affective behaviors are rarely assessed formally in schools and classrooms, teachers constantly assess affective behaviors informally, especially when sizing up pupils. Teachers need to know who can be trusted to work unsupervised and who cannot, who can maintain self-control when the teacher has to leave the classroom and who cannot, who needs to be encouraged to speak in class and who does not, who is interested in science but not in social studies, and who needs to be prodded to start class work and who does not. Most classroom teachers can describe their pupils' affective characteristics based on their informal observations and interactions with the pupils.

Ms. Lopez was relying mainly upon her assessment of pupils' affective behaviors when she selected Martha, not Matt, to deliver a note to the school principal and when she changed the class seating plan to separate Bill and Leroy, who were unable to control themselves when seated together. When she switched instruction from discussion to seatwork to avoid unruliness, decided to send a note home to Rose's parents about her interruptions in class, paired Kim with Mary in the hopes of overcoming Kim's shyness and reticence, and kept Ralph in from recess for swearing and fighting, she also was making decisions based upon the affective characteristics of her pupils.

In contrast to the cognitive domain, there is no single, widely accepted taxonomy of affective behaviors, although the taxonomy prepared by Krathwohl and associates (Krathwohl, Bloom, & Masia, 1964) is the most commonly referred to and used. In general, affective taxonomies are all based upon the degree of a person's involvement in an activity or idea. The lower levels of affective taxonomies contain low-involvement behaviors such as paying attention, while the higher levels contain high-involvement behavior characterized by strong interest, commitment, and valuing.

Psychomotor Domain

A third behavior domain is the psychomotor domain. **Psychomotor be-haviors** include physical and manipulative activities. Shooting a basket-ball, setting up laboratory equipment, building a bookcase, typing, holding a pencil, buttoning a jacket, brushing teeth, and playing a musical instru-ment are examples of activities that involve psychomotor behaviors. Al-though psychomotor behaviors are present and important at all levels of schooling, they are especially stressed in the preschool and elementary grades, where tasks like holding a pencil, opening a locker, and buttoning or zippering clothing are important to master. (How would you like to but-ton the jackets of 24 pupils?) Similarly, with certain special-needs pupils, a major part of education involves so-called "self-help" skills such as getting dressed, attending to personal hygiene, and preparing food, all of which are psychomotor accomplishments.

Psychomotor assessments involve physical and manipulative behaviors.

Psychomotor assessments are particularly important with very young or some special-needs students.

There are a number of psychomotor behavior domain taxonomies (Hannah & Michaels, 1977; Harrow, 1972; Simpson, 1972). Like the affec-tive domain, however, no single taxonomy has become widely accepted and used by the majority of teachers and schools. The organization of psy-chomotor taxonomies typically ranges from a pupil showing a readiness to perform a psychomotor task, to the pupil using trial and error to learn a task, to the pupil actually carrying out the task on his or her own.

Ms. Lopez was concerned with her pupils' psychomotor behavior when she moved Monroe to the front of the room so that he could see the black-board better, sent Randy to the school nurse because he felt ill, and re-ferred Aaron to the special-education department because he continued to exhibit poor gross motor skills. In each case, Ms. Lopez' decision was based upon assessment evidence that pertained to some aspect of a pupil's physical or motor behavior.

As noted previously, sizing-up assessments encompass the cognitive, af-fective, and psychomotor domains because teachers are interested in knowing about their pupils' intellectual, attitudinal, and physical character-istics. Notice, however, that different assessment approaches characterize the different behavior domains. For example, the cognitive domain is most likely to be assessed using paper-and-pencil tests or various kinds of oral questioning. Behaviors in the affective domain are most likely to be as-sessed by observation or questionnaires: for example, Which subject do you prefer, English or chemistry? Do you believe that teachers should be accountable for their pupils' learning? Psychomotor behaviors are gener-ally assessed by observing pupils carrying out the desired physical activity.

Stating Educational Objectives

There are many ways to state objectives, but not all of them convey clearly what pupils are to learn from instruction. There are three general levels of objectives (Airasian, in press). The broadest objectives are called

goals and define comprehensive, visionary objectives that may take many years to accomplish. Examples of such goals are: The pupil will become a lifelong learner, or The pupil will become mathematically literate. The next, more specific objectives are called **educational objectives** and are used for planning a unit of instruction. Examples of educational objectives are: The pupil will interpret various forms of statistical data, or The pupil can read musical scores. The most specific objectives are called **instructional objectives** and are used to plan daily lessons. Examples of instructional objectives are: The pupil can cite three causes of World War II, or The pupil can subtract two-digit numbers. Thus, a teacher usually has many instructional objectives, fewer educational objectives, and very few goals. In their lesson planning, teachers typically focus on educational and instructional objectives, depending on whether they are planning a unit or daily instruction. For simplicity, here the term *objective* represents both educational and instructional objectives. The issues addressed in the following discussion pertain to both types.

Examine the sample objectives in Table 3.2 and consider their usefulness in helping a teacher plan and guide instruction and assessment. Remember, the intent of an objective is to clearly identify what pupils are to learn in order to (1) communicate to others the purpose of instruction, (2) to help teachers select appropriate instructional methods and materials, and (3) to help plan assessments that will indicate whether or not pupils have learned what they were taught.

In Table 3.2, objectives 1, 2, and 3 all have the same deficiency. Each describes a body of content that will be covered in instruction, but each omits information about what the pupils will be expected to do with that content. Will they be expected to identify causes of the war, match generals to battles, cite strengths and weaknesses of the two sides, or explain in their own words why Gettysburg was the turning point of the war? What should pupils know or understand about American government and the laws of motion? Without including information about what pupils are to

---

TABLE 3.2   SAMPLE STATEMENTS OF POOR EDUCATIONAL OBJECTIVES

1. The Civil War
2. American government
3. The laws of motion
4. Analyze
5. Understand
6. Appreciate
7. Worthy use of leisure time
8. Pursue lifelong learning
9. Become a good citizen

know or do about the Civil War, American government, or laws of motion, it is hard to select appropriate instructional materials, activities, and assessment techniques. For example, it will make a difference in instruction and assessment if pupils have to match generals to battles (teach recall and assess with a matching item) or explain in their own words why Gettysburg was the turning point of the war (teach interpretation and assess with an open-ended question). Clarity and consistency between what is taught and what is assessed is necessary for valid assessment results.

Objectives 4, 5, and 6—analyze, understand, and appreciate—provide no reference to content matter. These statements prompt the question Analyze, understand, and appreciate what? Just as a content description by itself lacks clarity because it does not include a desired pupil performance, so too does a behavior by itself lack clarity if there is no reference to a targeted body of content.

There is an additional problem in objectives 4, 5, and 6. Words like *analyze, understand,* and *appreciate* are themselves nonspecific. They can be interpreted in many different ways and hence do not clearly convey what pupils will learn. For example, one teacher might interpret the objective Understanding the basic features of a society to mean the pupils will be able to explain the features in their own words. Another teacher might interpret the same objective to mean the pupils will give a real-life example of the social features studied. A third teacher might want pupils to distinguish between correct and incorrect applications of features. Although each teacher taught "Understanding the basic features of society," each would teach and assess completely different outcomes. Such misunderstandings can be avoided if teachers describe their educational objectives in terms of the actual behaviors they expect their pupils to perform after instruction. For example, pupils can *explain* features in their own words, *give real-life examples* of the features, or *distinguish correct from incorrect* applications of the features. This level of specificity distinguishes clearly the different interpretations of *understand.*

Well-written educational objectives should clearly specify what students are to learn and how they are to demonstrate that learning.

In stating educational objectives, it is better to clearly describe the behavior the pupil will perform than to use more general, ambiguous terms that are open to many different interpretations. Thus, it is better to say *explains* the importance of conserving natural resources than to say *realizes* the importance of conserving natural resources; better to say *translates* Spanish sentences into English than to say *understands* Spanish sentences; better to say Can *differentiate* subjects and predicates than to say *knows* about subjects and predicates; better to say *states* three differences between good and bad art than to say *appreciates* art. In each example, the first statement describes a pupil behavior that can be observed, instructed, and assessed, while the second uses less clear, unobservable, and ambiguous terms. Clear descriptions foster alignment among objectives, instruction, and assessment, thus producing valid assessment results.

Objectives 7, 8, and 9 are too general and complicated to be achieved by pupils in a single subject area or grade level. They are, as noted previously, goals. These outcomes not only take years to develop, their generality provides the classroom teacher with little guidance regarding the activities and materials that could be used to attain them. Broad goals such as these must be narrowed by the classroom teacher before they can be used to instruct and assess pupils.

In summary, the basic requirements for well-stated educational objectives are that they (1) describe a *pupil* behavior that should result from instruction; (2) state the behavior in *terms that can be observed* and assessed; and (3) *indicate the content* on which the behavior will be performed. A simple model for preparing educational objectives is The pupils can (*observable behavior*) (*content*). Here are examples of appropriately stated educational objectives. Other useful and varied examples are provided by Gronlund (1995).

- ♦ The pupils can list three causes of the Civil War.
- ♦ The pupils can solve word problems requiring the sum of two numbers.
- ♦ The pupils can write a correctly formatted and punctuated business letter.
- ♦ The pupils can translate a French paragraph into English.
- ♦ The pupils can count to 20 aloud.
- ♦ The pupils can list three differences in the climates of Canada and Mexico.
- ♦ The pupils can write balanced chemical equations.
- ♦ The pupils can state the main idea of short stories.
- ♦ The pupils can explain the water cycle in their own words.

Notice how these objectives help focus the intended student learning and thus help the teacher identify suitable instructional activities, materials, and assessments.

Other information can be added to elaborate an objective. For example, some teachers wish to include information in their objectives about the conditions of pupil performance and about how well the pupil must perform the objective in order to master it. Such extended objectives would be written as follows:

- ♦ Given ten word problems requiring the sum of two numbers, the pupils can solve at least eight correctly.
- ♦ Given a diagram of the water cycle, the pupils can explain in their own words what the water cycle is with fewer than two errors.
- ♦ Given a French paragraph of less than 20 lines and a dictionary, the pupils can translate the paragraph into English in 5 minutes with fewer than six errors.

Extended objectives provide additional details about the conditions under which pupils must demonstrate their learning and the level of performance they must show.

Extended objectives provide more details about the conditions under which the behavior must be performed and the level of performance the pupil must show. Extended objectives take more time to prepare than their simpler counterparts and are sometimes difficult to state prior to the start of instruction. Consequently, the simpler model suffices in most instructional situations.

Questions about Educational Objectives

Educational objectives are usually the starting point in the instructional process because they identify the desired outcomes of instruction in terms of pupil behaviors. Some have called stating objectives a backward approach to planning because it starts by defining the intended result of teaching (Wiggins & McTighe, 1998). Because they are important, a few common issues and questions about educational objectives require attention.

Educational objectives are the starting point in the instructional process because they identify desired pupil outcomes.

1. *Is it necessary to write down objectives?* Beginning teachers and students in a teaching practicum usually are required to write lesson objectives. Even if you are an experienced teacher, listing your objectives reminds you to focus on what pupils are expected to get out of instruction, not just what your teaching activities will be. Annual assessment of existing objectives is an important part of *any* teacher's classroom assessment responsibilities, because each year pupils and curriculum change.

2. *What are higher level objectives?* Cognitive behaviors can be divided into lower level ones such as memorizing and remembering and higher level ones requiring more complex thinking behaviors. Higher level behaviors, or higher order thinking skills (HOTS), include activities such as analyzing information, applying information and rules to solve new problems, comparing and contrasting objects or ideas, and synthesizing disparate pieces of information into a single, organized idea. In the following examples, the lower level objective calls only for memorization, while the higher level objective calls for a more complex behavior.

Lower level: The pupil can write a definition of each vocabulary word.

Higher level: The pupil can write sentences using each vocabulary word correctly.

Higher level objectives include cognitive activities such as analysis, application, synthesis, and evaluation. These take longer to teach and evaluate than lower level objectives involving rote memorization.

Lower level: The pupil can match quotes from a short story to the characters who said them.

Higher level: The pupil can contrast the motives of the protagonist and the antagonist in a short story.

Lower level: The pupil can write the formula for the Pythagorean theorem.

Higher level: The pupil can use the Pythagorean theorem to solve new word problems involving the length of ladders needed by the fire department.

All teachers should be aware of the difference between lower and higher level thinking skills and should strive to incorporate some higher level objectives in their plans and instruction.

3. *How many objectives should I state in a subject area?* The answer to this question depends in part upon the time frame being considered and the specificity of the objectives: the longer the period of instruction and the more specific the objectives, the more objectives that can be stated with expectation for pupils to attain. In general, there may be many instructional objectives and fewer educational objectives. Also, higher level objectives usually take longer to teach and learn, so fewer of them can be taught in a given instructional period; it takes longer to teach pupils to interpret graphs than to memorize a formula. Teachers who have hundreds of objectives for the year's instruction either are expecting too much of themselves and their pupils or are stating their objectives too narrowly. On the other hand, teachers who have only five objectives for the school year are either underestimating their pupils or stating their objectives much too broadly.

4. *Are there any cautions I should keep in mind regarding objectives?* Objectives are usually stated before instruction actually begins and are meant to guide both instruction and assessment. However, objectives are not meant to be followed slavishly when circumstances suggest the need for adjustments. Because objectives are written *before* instruction starts and because it is difficult to anticipate the flow of classroom activities during instruction, teachers must exercise discretion regarding how closely they will follow the objectives they stated prior to the start of actual instruction.

Because educational objectives are written before instruction begins, teachers must be ready to deviate from them when necessary.

TEXTBOOK OBJECTIVES AND LESSON PLANS

Modern textbooks and their accompanying teacher aids provide a great number of resources to help teachers plan, deliver, and assess their instruction. The richest and most used source of information is the teacher's edition of the textbook. Figure 3.2 shows the range of resources found in most teacher's editions. While not every teacher's textbook provides each one of the resources listed in Figure 3.2, most provide a majority of them. More instructional aids are generally found in elementary school texts and instructional packages than in high school ones, but this disparity is diminishing.

Figure 3.3 presents two pages from a teacher's edition of a third-grade mathematics textbook. The top-middle section of the table shows what the pupil's textbook looks like for Lesson 4. The rest of the table shows the resources provided to carry out instruction. The lesson objective is in the upper-left corner. Beneath the objective are the relevant National Council of Teachers of Mathematics standards, a list of needed manipulatives, and lesson resources (provided with the text). Problem of the Day and Math Minute exercises are warm-ups for students. The bottom of the figure shows the three steps for teaching the lesson: introduce, teach, and wrap

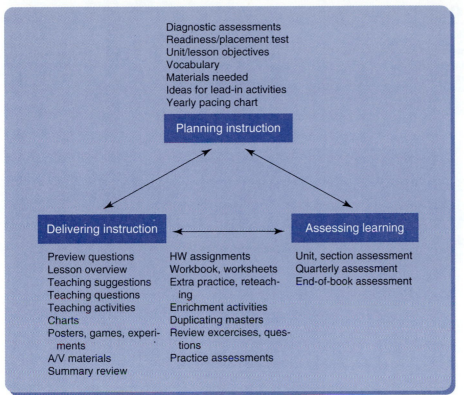

FIGURE 3.2
Instructional Resources in Teacher's Editions of Textbooks

up. Suggestions for instruction are provided (with appropriate answers) and higher level instruction such as analysis are suggested. Two brief items serve to assess understanding and to provide a challenging example. The right side of the figure shows practice, reteaching, and extended examples for students to attempt. There is a common error alert for the teacher to focus on during instruction and a section on meeting individual needs. In addition to these resources, the text also provides answer keys, assessment guides, a practice workbook, a daily review book, overhead transparencies, a test generator, a manipulative kit, and an English-Spanish glossary.

The arrangement of the teacher's edition shown in Figure 3.3 is similar to ones used in many teacher's texts. Examine some teacher's editions of textbooks in the subject area and grade level you plan to teach to get a sense of how much support textbook authors provide for you in planning instruction. Especially read the introductory sections of the teacher's edition, which describe all the resources and materials provided to help teachers plan, instruct, and assess.

The objectives, teaching strategies, worksheets, assessment items, and other resources that accompany teacher's editions can be very useful to the classroom teacher and can tempt the teacher to rely exclusively upon them. To do so, however, is to abdicate instructional and

It is the teacher's responsibility to adapt textbook materials to the specific needs of his or her students.

Lesson Organizer

Objective: Use base-ten blocks to add.

- **NCTM Standards:** 3, 6, 8, 13
- **Manipulatives:** base-ten blocks
- **Lesson Resources:**
  Chapter File Folder
     Practice, Reteach, Extend 3-4
     Teaching Tools 22, 44
  Daily Review 3-4

Problem of the Day   3-4

Sela has a dollar. Item A costs $0.32, item B costs $0.49, and item C costs $0.31. About how much more does she need to buy all 3 items? **About $0.10 more**

Add.

10 + 8 *(18)*	40 + 50 *(90)*
20 + 8 *(28)*	70 + 30 *(100)*
30 + 20 *(50)*	

Math Minute

 EXPLORE: Regrouping in Addition

Lots of Blocks

You can use base-ten blocks to add numbers.

Learning About It

Work with your group.

Use base-ten blocks to add 356 + 67.

What You Need

For each group: base-ten blocks

Step 1 Show 356 and 67 with hundreds, tens, and ones blocks.

356
67

Step 2 Look at the ones. Regroup 10 ones as 1 ten.

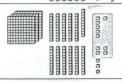

Step 3 Look at the tens. Regroup 10 tens as 1 hundred.

Step 4 Look at the hundreds. There are not enough hundreds to regroup.

Count the blocks you have. What is the sum of 356 + 67? **423**

 86

---

1 Introduce

Visual
Whole Class Activity

WHOLE CLASS	5–10 MINUTES

Materials: Overhead Base-Ten Blocks

1. A volunteer shows 1 hundred, 9 tens, and 10 ones using the overhead blocks.
   - Ask: **How many tens can you regroup the ones for?** *(1)*
2. A volunteer regroups 10 ones for 1 ten.
   - Ask: **How many hundreds can you regroup the tens for?** *(1)*
3. Then 10 tens are regrouped for 1 hundred.
   - Ask: **How many hundreds in all?** *(2)*

2 Teach   Pages 86–87

Discuss regrouping using base-ten blocks.

When regrouping 356 + 67, ask: **Will the sum have at least 1 thousand? Explain your answer.** *(No; there are not enough hundreds to regroup as 1 thousand.)*

Critical Thinking ANALYSIS

After Think and Discuss, ask: **Can you have an addition problem in which you have to regroup more than ten ones?** *(No, if you add only two addends; yes, if you add more than two addends)*

Assess Understanding

Before Practice, ask: **To find 29 + 57, do you need to regroup? Explain.** *(Yes; you need to regroup 10 ones as 1 ten.)*

★ CHALLENGE

Model 48 + 127 + 283 using base-ten blocks and find the sum. *(458)*

FIGURE 3.3
Mathematics, Teacher Guide, Grade 3.
SOURCE: Reprinted by permission of Silver Burdett Ginn, Inc.

Step 5 Record your work in a chart like this.

Addition Sentence	Did I regroup 10 ones for 1 ten?	Did I regroup 10 tens for 1 hundred?	Did I regroup 10 hundreds for 1 thousand?
356 + 67 = 423	yes	yes	no

Step 6 Repeat Steps 1 to 5 four or more times. Take turns picking different numbers each time. Regroup when you can.

Think and Discuss How can you know just by looking at an exercise whether or not you need to regroup? If you have more than 9 ones, 9 tens, or 9 hundreds, you need to regroup.

Practice

1. Ann and Sal's blocks looked like this after they put them together. What regrouping can they do? They can regroup 10 ones for 1 ten and 10 tens for 1 hundred.

2. Manolo looked at the problem 347 + 158. He said he needs to regroup 10 tens for 1 hundred. Is he right? Explain your answer. Yes; 7 ones + 8 ones = 15 ones, which are regrouped for 1 ten 5 ones. Then there will be 10 tens, since 4 tens + 5 tens + 1 ten = 10 tens.

3. Karen and Teri showed the numbers 621 and 238 with blocks. Will they need to regroup when they add their numbers together? Explain your answer. No; the sum of the ones is less than 10, the sum of the tens is less than 10, and the sum of the hundreds is less than 10.

(87)

3 Wrap-up

Describe the regrouping for 462 + 539. (Regroup 10 ones as 1 ten; 10 tens for 1 hundred; 10 hundreds as 1 thousand.)

Journal Idea List the times you add in a week. Why were you adding and did you regroup?

Common Error Alert

Watch for students who miscount and regroup 9 or 11 ones as 1 ten. Tell students to count carefully.

Meeting Individual Needs

Kinesthetic Activity For Extra Help

SMALL GROUPS — 5–10 MINUTES

Materials: coin set

- One student models 16 cents using all pennies.
- The group exchanges pennies for dimes if possible. *(10 pennies for 1 dime)*
- Students switch roles and repeat the activity, first using 27 pennies and then using 32 pennies.

LESSON 4 87

FIGURE 3.3
Continued

TABLE 3.3   BASIC FACTORS TO CONSIDER WHEN EXAMINING TEXTBOOK OBJECTIVES AND LESSON PLANS

Textbook Objectives

1. **Clarity.** Are objectives clearly stated, especially the behavior pupils are to perform after instruction?
2. **Comprehensiveness.** Do the objectives include most learner outcomes for this topic?
3. **Level.** Do the objectives include both higher and lower level thinking behaviors?
4. **Prerequisites.** Do pupils have the prerequisite skills needed to master the objectives?
5. **Time.** Can pupils reasonably be expected to master the objectives in the time available for instruction?

Textbook Lesson Plans

1. **Pertinence.** Do plans help foster the stated objectives?
2. **Level.** Do plans include activities for fostering both higher and lower level objectives?
3. **Realism.** Are plans realistic, given pupil ability, learning style, reading level, attention span, and so on?
4. **Resources.** Are the resources and materials needed to implement plans and activities available?
5. **Follow up.** Are follow-up materials (e.g., worksheets, enrichment exercises, and reviews) related to the objectives and do they reinforce lesson plans and activities?

TABLE 3.4   ADVANTAGES AND DISADVANTAGES OF TEXTBOOK OBJECTIVES AND LESSON PLANS

Advantages	Disadvantages
Convenient, readily available objectives and plans	Designed for teachers and pupils in general, not necessarily for a given teacher or class
Can save valuable time in planning	
Provides an integrated set of objectives, plans, activities, and assessments	Heavy emphasis on lower level objectives and activities
Contains many ancillary materials for planning, instructing, and assessing	Lesson activities tend to be didactic and teacher led
	If accepted uncritically, can lead to inappropriate instruction for pupils

assessment decision-making responsibilities. Textbook authors cannot possibly tailor objectives, plans, resources, and assessments to every teacher or pupil. They cannot take the status, needs, and readiness of all pupils into account, so they offer resources that they think *most* teachers would accept for their pupils.

Adoption of unexamined textbook resources can affect the validity and reliability of instructional and official assessments. The pupils' needs and disabilities may not be attended to in the teacher's text materials. The objectives and topics the teacher chooses to emphasize may not match what is in the teacher's text. The teacher's style of teaching may not fit that of the text. Further, teacher's text assessment exercises tend to be multiple choice and matching, which usually means a heavy focus on rote learning. One study of elementary teacher's edition texts indicated that about 90 percent of the texts' test items were at the recall, memorization level (Frisbie, Miranda, & Baker, 1993). The researchers also found that the typical number of assessment items in each chapter of the teacher's texts was 21. If a chapter has seven objectives and they are evenly spread across 21 items, each objective is assessed by only three items. This small number of assessment items per objective raises concern about the reliability of the textbook assessments.

It is the responsibility of all classroom teachers to assess their textbook's suitability for their own particular situation. Blindly following what is in the textbook undermines the classroom teacher's responsibility to determine outcomes, instructional activities, and assessment strategies that are well matched to the level and needs of pupils. Table 3.3 provides specific questions that teachers should ask when reviewing the appropriateness of textbook objectives, lesson plans, and assessments.

Every teacher should ask three important general questions about objectives in the teacher's text: (1) Do the objectives and lesson plans contain a clear description of what the pupils will learn and will the instructional activities foster the intended learning? (2) Are the objectives and plans appropriate for the particular pupils in my class? and (3) Does the textbook include all the important outcomes and appropriate assessments that pupils should attain? If only a portion of the materials in the teacher's text are appropriate, the teachers may have to supplement the text with some of their own objectives, activities, and assessments.

Since most textbooks focus on lower level objectives, teachers may be forced to supply their own higher level objectives.

Table 3.4 lists the advantages and disadvantages of textbook objectives and lesson plans.

IMPROVING PLANNING ASSESSMENTS

In planning instruction, there are a few common guidelines that teachers can follow to strengthen the effectiveness of their planning.

1. *Perform complete sizing-up assessments of pupils' needs and characteristics.* Since the purpose of instruction is to help pupils do things they were unable to do before, planning responsive lessons requires consideration of the needs and characteristics of pupils. Knowledge of pupils' readiness, abilities, and attention spans helps the classroom teacher to correctly plan how long to make lessons, whether they should involve whole-class or small-group activities, and whether they should be teacher led or pupil directed. The more valid and reliable pupil and class sizing-up assessments are, the more appropriate the lesson plans are likely to be.

In planning instruction, good sizing-up assessments provide an important starting point.

2. *Use sizing-up assessment information when planning.* A teacher may have done an exceptional job of sizing up pupils, but if he or she does not use that information when planning lessons, it is useless. Planning involves fitting instruction to pupil needs and characteristics, and it is the teacher's responsibility to plan accordingly.

3. *Do not rely entirely and uncritically on textbooks and their accompanying aids when planning.* As we have seen, teacher's edition textbooks can provide much of the information needed to plan, carry out, and assess instruction, but usually not all. It is important to match textbook plans and assessments with pupil characteristics and needs. Teacher's guides should be assessed, adapted, and supplemented to provide the best possible instruction to each teacher's class.

Good lesson plans should include a mix of higher and lower level objectives.

4. *Include a combination of lower level and higher level objectives.* The instructional activities offered in most teacher's editions are heavily weighted towards whole-class practices such as recitation, teacher presentation, and seatwork. Such practices normally emphasize lower level objectives. It is important, therefore, that lesson plans and activities (whether textbook or teacher made) include *both* lower and higher level objectives.

5. *Include a wide range of instructional activities and strategies to fit the pupils' instructional needs.* Teachers who use the same strategy (e.g., lecture, seatwork, or board work) every day with little change or variety create two problems. First, they risk boring pupils and reducing their motivation to attend to the repetitive activity. Second, by limiting their teaching repertoire to a single or very few strategies, they may not be reaching pupils whose learning styles, handicaps, or language are best suited to some other method (e.g., small-group instruction, learning games, hands-on materials). It is important to include varied teaching strategies and activities in lesson plans.

Effective instruction is keyed to lesson objectives.

6. *Align objectives, teaching strategies, and planned assessments.* Objectives describe the desired results of instruction. Teaching strategies and activities represent the means to achieve those results. Assessment is a measure of the success of the objectives and instruction. In order to reach the desired ends, the means must be relevant and appropriate. Without ends clearly in mind, it is difficult to judge the adequacy of an instructional plan or the quality of the assessment. Table 3.5 shows the relationship between statements of means (teaching activities) and ends (objectives).

> ### TABLE 3.5   EXAMPLES OF INSTRUCTIONAL MEANS AND ENDS
>
> **Means.** Read a short story silently.
>
> **End.** The pupils can summarize a short story in their own words.
>
> **Means.** Show a film on the computer.
>
> **End.** The pupils can differentiate between computer hardware and software.
>
> **Means.** Do seatwork on pp. 47–48 in math book.
>
> **End.** The pupils can calculate the area of squares and triangles.
>
> **Means.** Discuss the organization of the periodic table.
>
> **End.** The pupils can place an element in its periodic group when given a description of the element's properties.

7. *Recognize one's own knowledge and pedagogical limitations.* Teachers assess many things when planning instruction, but one often-neglected area is assessment of themselves. Content knowledge limitations may lead a teacher to omit an important topic, teach it in a perfunctory, superficial manner, or provide pupils with incorrect information. Likewise, preferences for one or two teaching methods may deprive pupils of exposure to other methods or activities that would enhance their learning. When a teacher's knowledge limitations and pedagogical preferences outweigh pupil considerations in determining what is or is not done in classrooms, serious questions can be raised about the adequacy of the teacher's instructional plans.

8. *Include assessment strategies in instructional plans.* The object of planning and conducting instruction is to help pupils learn new content and understandings. Consequently, lesson plans should include some formal measure or measures to determine whether pupils have learned the desired objectives and to identify areas of misunderstanding or confusion. While informal assessments based on pupil enthusiasm and participation can be useful, they are not substitutes for more formal assessments such as follow-up seatwork, homework, quizzes, or oral questioning.

Table 3.6 summarizes the guidelines to follow in planning lessons.

ADDRESSING PUPIL ACCOMMODATIONS

As noted, an important aspect of planning and delivering instruction is accommodating pupils' needs and disabilities. (We will consider assessment accommodations later, in Chapter 4). Clearly, pupil needs and disabilities span a very broad range, from pupils with severe cognitive, affective, and/or psychomotor disabilities to pupils with mild attention problems (Cegelka & Berdine, 1995; Cartwright, Cartwright, & Ward, 1995). While it

---

TABLE 3.6   GUIDELINES IN PLANNING INSTRUCTION

♦ Perform complete sizing-up assessments of pupils' needs and characteristics.

♦ Use sizing-up assessments when planning.

♦ Do not rely entirely and uncritically on textbooks and their accompanying aids when planning.

♦ Include a combination of lower and higher level objectives.

♦ Include a range of instructional activities and strategies.

♦ Create a match between educational objectives and teaching strategies and activities.

♦ Recognize one's own knowledge and pedagogical limitations and preferences.

♦ Include assessment strategies in instructional plans

A variety of strategies to accommodate pupils with disabilities are available to help teachers provide appropriate instruction for all.

is not possible to address all available accommodation strategies for instruction here, a sample of useful strategies to illustrate the breadth of such strategies are reviewed. The following examples, organized in terms of different aspects of lesson planning, are from Price and Nelson, who have developed an in-depth survey of strategies to accommodate varied pupil needs and disabilities (Price & Nelson, 1999, Chap. 6). Accommodations when planning content:

♦ If students have fallen behind in the curriculum, teach what is most generalizable.

♦ Teach learning strategies along with teaching content area.

♦ Select content based on student interests; for example, allow them to read the sports page to practice reading skills.

Accommodations when planning objectives:

♦ Pretest before teaching to make sure the objective is appropriate for the students.

♦ Determine whether the objective can be altered for some students; for example, Can pupils who have poor writing skills demonstrate their knowledge orally?

Accommodations when deciding on instructional methods:

♦ Recognize that pupils with some learning and behavior disabilities often need very explicit directions.

♦ Evaluate the level of structure pupils need to be successful; do not assume that all students learn best with unstructured approaches.

♦ If pupils have fallen behind in the curriculum use time-efficient methods.

♦ Be sure pupils have the necessary skills to be successful in the instructional method being used.

Accommodations when planning the lesson body:

♦ Provide directions, procedures, and rules; describe them orally and in writing.

♦ Follow up by asking questions or by having pupils repeat or paraphrase what they are to do.

♦ Repeat key words often, using the same wording.

♦ Ask for frequent active responses.

♦ Break up information; teach a couple of steps, practice, teach a couple of more steps, practice. Keep reminding pupils of the whole task. Stop often to summarize.

♦ Point to steps on a written list as each is demonstrated.

In addition to the preceding accommodations, there are strategies for pupils with specific needs. For example, for pupils who have difficulty maintaining attention, provide a seat near an adult or quiet peers; seat them away from high-traffic areas; seat them at a single desk, not a table; provide more breaks or task changes; and use more active participation activities. For pupils having difficulty beginning a task, provide a cue card of steps on the desk that the pupil can check off as steps are completed; go to the pupil quickly at the start of the task and help him or her get started (indicate that you will return to check progress); and provide a peer helper. For pupils having difficulty organizing, list assignments and materials needed on the board or transparency; have students use notebooks with pocket dividers; use color-coding materials needed for various subjects; and provide time to gather books and materials at the start and end of the school day (Price & Nelson, 1999).

These accommodations represent only a few of the ways lessons can be planned to help pupils get the most out of instruction. Based on the knowledge gained from sizing-up assessment and the teaching of initial lessons, teachers should begin to identify needs and appropriate accommodations for pupils. With this knowledge, accommodations can be planned and implemented for students who need them to learn most effectively, thus improving the validity of their instruction and assessments.

ASSESSMENT DURING INSTRUCTION

The assessment activities that teachers carry out when planning instruction are very different from those they carry out when delivering it. The most obvious difference between the two is the time at which assessment occurs. Planning assessments take place before or after instruction, while instructional assessments take place during instruction. Planning assessments are focused on identifying appropriate objectives, content topics, activities, accommodations, and assessments, while assessments during instruction are focused upon making instantaneous decisions about what to do, say, or ask to keep instruction flowing smoothly. It is during instruction that lesson plans are put to the ultimate test.

Instructional assessment refers to those assessments made during instruction that indicate how well the lesson is going.

Although discussed separately in this chapter, it is important to understand that planning and delivering instruction are integrally related. The instructional process constantly cycles from planning instruction to delivering instruction to revising planning to delivering more instruction and so on. There is a logical, ongoing, and natural link between the two processes.

Teachers' Tasks during Instruction

Once instruction begins, teachers carry on two tasks: they deliver the instruction that they have planned and they constantly assess the progress and success of their instruction in order to modify it if necessary. For many reasons, things do not always go as planned. Interruptions, misjudgments about pupil readiness and attention, shifts in pupil interest, and various spontaneous events (e.g., fire drills, assemblies, squawk box interruptions) all alter planned instruction. As a result, the teacher must constantly sense the mood and learning of the class to make decisions about what to do next. Thus, once the teacher initiates instruction, he or she engages in an ongoing process of assessing its progress and deciding about pupils' reactions to it.

Doing this, of course, is a complicated task, since instruction, assessment, and decision making are taking place almost simultaneously. For example, during class discussion

> . . . a teacher must listen to student answers, watch other students for signs of comprehension or confusion, formulate the next question, and scan the class for possible misbehavior. At the same time, the teacher must attend to the pace of the discussion, the sequence of selecting students to answer, the relevance and quality of the answers, and the logical development of the content. When the class is divided into small groups, the number of simultaneous events increases, and the teacher must monitor and regulate several different activities at once (Doyle, 1986, 384).

Certainly, many decisions are required during instruction, and these decisions, in turn, are informed by assessments that teachers make as part of the instructional process.

Figure 3.4 illustrates this process of ongoing assessment. Once *teaching* begins, the teacher constantly *assesses* its progress by observing pupil reactions and asking them questions. On the basis of these reactions and

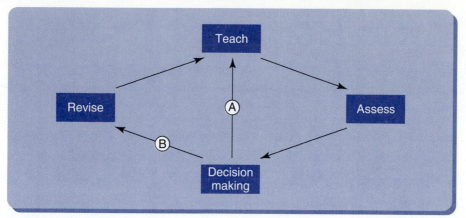

FIGURE 3.4
*Steps in Instructional
Assessment*

responses, the teacher makes a *decision* about how instruction is going. If the teacher decides that the lesson is progressing satisfactorily, the teacher continues teaching as planned (path A). If the teacher senses a problem, such as lack of pupil understanding or interest, the teacher *revises* the planned instructional activity to alleviate the problem and initiates another teaching activity or strategy (path B). This cycle is repeated many times in the course of a single lesson.

Teachers' Thinking during Instruction

A large proportion of teachers' thinking during instruction concerns the adequacy of their instruction. Teachers described much of their thinking in terms such as these:

♦ I was thinking about the fact that they needed another example of this concept.
♦ I was trying to get him to see the relationship between the Treaty of Versailles and Hitler's rise to power without actually telling him.
♦ I was thinking about a worksheet that would reinforce the idea.
♦ I decided that it was necessary to review yesterday's lesson.

Teachers' thoughts are particularly concerned with the *effect* of instruction on pupils; that is, how much they are attending to and profiting from instruction. This form of teacher thinking is closest to the concept of reading the audience and is expressed through thoughts such as

Teachers tend to look more for signs of student engagement than of student learning.

♦ I realized that they didn't understand the concept at all.
♦ I thought, at least everyone is concentrating on the topic.
♦ I figured I'd better call on Larry, just to make sure he was with us.

◆ I asked Mike to explain it because I thought he would know it and could explain it in a way many pupils could understand.

Note that when planning instruction, the focus is on pupil characteristics, readiness, subject matter objectives, and learning activities. Once instruction actually begins, the focus shifts to more action-oriented concerns, especially on how pupils are reacting to the instructional process. This shift is logical, of course, the result of being caught up in the here and now of a complex teaching process. During instruction, teachers collect assessment data to help monitor factors such as

- Interest level of individual pupils and the class as a whole
- Apparent or potential behavior problems
- Appropriateness of the instructional technique or activity being used
- Most appropriate pupil to call on next
- Adequacy of a pupil's answer
- Pace of instruction
- Usefulness and consequences of pupils' questions
- Smoothness of transitions from one concept to another and from one activity to another
- Usefulness of examples used to explain concepts
- Degree of comprehension on the part of individual pupils and the class as a whole
- Desirability of starting or ending a particular activity

Assessing these factors leads teachers to decisions about instructional activities. For example, depending upon the appropriateness of the answer one pupil gives, the teacher may try to (1) draw out a better answer from the pupil, (2) seek another pupil to provide a more complete answer, or (3) ask the next logical question in the content sequence. In short, the need to respond to a variety of immediate classroom needs allows teachers little time to reflect on what they are doing or the motives for their actions. Nonetheless, most teachers feel that they have a good sense of their instructional success, which implies that they do assess many environmental cues.

Assessment Indicators

Given the pace and complexity of instructional activities and the need to keep instruction flowing smoothly, it is no surprise that teachers rely much more heavily on informal than formal assessment evidence to monitor their instruction. They rely on behavioral cues from the students, such as attention or facial expressions, rather than more formal paper-and-pencil assessments. The latter could break the flow of the lesson and pupil involvement.

To determine what types of indicators teachers use to monitor and judge the success of their instruction, they were asked how they knew when their instruction was successful. Their responses included the following:

> It is easy to tell when things are not running as planned. Children get impatient, facial expressions become contorted, their body language, voice level, and eyes tell the story of their reaction to instruction.

> If my class is daydreaming—looking blankly out the window and unresponsive— that tells me something. At times like these I have to decide what to do, since I don't want the pupils to think that by acting disinterested they always can make me change my plans.

> Some examples of a good lesson are when the pupils are eager to be called on, raise their hands, give enthusiastic answers, look straight at me, scream out answers, show excitement in their eyes. During a bad lesson, the kids have their heads on the desk, look around the room, play with little objects at their desks, talk to their neighbor, or go to the bathroom in droves.

To summarize, the direction, flow, and pace of instruction are dictated by the chemistry of the classroom at any given time. The teacher's assessment task during instruction is to monitor the progress and success of the instruction. In most classrooms, monitoring boils down to assessing the appropriateness of the instructional procedures and the pupils' reaction to them. Decisions that teachers make during instruction are prompted by (1) unusual pupil behavior that requires a response or reaction from the teacher and (2) typical issues that arise during instruction, such as responding to a pupil's question, deciding whom to call on next, and deciding whether to move on to the next topic. The assessment information that teachers gather when they monitor their instruction comes mostly from informal observations of the pupils. These cues, plus the teacher's knowledge of the class, support the quick assessments and decisions that teachers make during classroom instruction.

The assessment information that teachers gather during instruction comes mostly from informal observation of their pupils.

THE QUALITY OF INSTRUCTIONAL ASSESSMENTS

Because there is little time for a teacher to reflect on what is observed or to collect additional information during instruction, teachers must make decisions and act on the basis of incomplete and uncertain evidence. Even so, good teachers are quite successful in overcoming these difficulties and do carry out informative instructional assessments. In spite of the success of some teachers, however, it would be naive and inappropriate to overlook validity and reliability problems associated with instructional assessment.

Problems That Affect Validity

Validity relates to collecting evidence that will help the teacher correctly interpret observed pupil performance and make appropriate decisions about pupils' attention, comprehension, and learning as well as the pace and suitability of the instructional activities. As mentioned previously, during instruction, teachers assess these areas mainly by observing pupil attentiveness and by the verbal reactions and responses of their pupils. An important validity question is Do these pupil indicators provide the information teachers need to make appropriate decisions about instructional success? Two potential threats to validity are (1) the lack of objectivity by teachers when judging their own instruction and (2) the incompleteness of the evidence used to make decisions about instruction and pupil learning.

Objectivity of the Teacher/Observer

Being a participant in the instructional process can make it difficult for the teacher to be a dispassionate, detached observer who can make unbiased judgments about his or her own instruction. Teachers have a stake in the success of instruction and derive their primary rewards from it; they have a strong personal and professional investment in the instructional process. Every time the teacher makes a favorable judgment about instruction or pupil learning, the teacher is also rewarding him- or herself. Because teachers rely heavily on their observations to assess instruction, it can be asked whether teachers see only what they want to see, that is, only those things that will give them reinforcement. If so, the evidence they use to assess their instruction is potentially invalid.

Because teachers want to feel good about their instruction, there is the danger that they will look only for positive student reactions.

Evidence of invalid assessments of instruction is not hard to find. For example, the types of questions teachers ask can influence their sense of personal effectiveness. Simple, factual questions are likely to produce more correct pupil responses than open-ended, complex ones. Concentration on lower level, rote skills and information, rather than on higher level skills and processes, can ensure more pupil participation and mastery. Teacher comments, such as This topic is too hard for my pupils, so I'll skip over it, may be a realistic appraisal of pupil readiness or it may simply be a way for teachers to avoid instructional disappointments. In short, the desire to achieve teaching satisfaction may bias the teacher's observations and produce invalid conclusions about the success of instruction, with harmful consequences for pupils.

Teachers sometimes ask easy, low-level questions in order to get correct answers that make them feel good about their instruction.

Incompleteness of Instructional Indicators

The primary indicators that teachers use to monitor instruction are those that are most readily available, most quickly surveyed, and least intrusive: reactions from students such as facial expressions, posture, participation, questions, and attending. Using such indicators, teachers "read" a pupil or the class and judge the success of their teaching. But the real criterion of teachers' instructional success is *pupil achievement.* Although the *process* of instruction (its flow, pace, and student reactions) is important and should be assessed, it does not provide direct evidence of pupil learning. It deals only with intermediate events that may or may not lead to a more important outcome, namely, learning.

Being attentive and involved in instruction is desirable, but does not necessarily mean that learning is taking place. Thus, valid assessment of instruction should include appropriate information about *both* pupil involvement and pupil learning. If it does not, if it focuses only on pupil interest and facial expressions, judgments about the ultimate goal, how well pupils are learning, may be invalid.

Instructional assessment should focus on student learning as well as student involvement.

Problems That Affect Reliability

Inadequate Sampling of Pupils

Reliability is concerned with the stability or consistency of the assessment data that are collected. However, one of the features of teaching is the fast-changing nature of instruction. If the message a teacher gets from his or her observations changes each time new evidence is gathered, the teacher cannot rely upon that evidence to help in decision making. Since teachers obtain most of their information about the success of instruction by observing their pupils, the broader the group of pupils observed, the more reliable the information.

Instructional assessment that involves feedback from a broad range of students is more reliable than assessments based on the reactions of one or two students.

Often because of seating arrangements or an unconscious preference for certain pupils, teachers tend to use an overly narrow sample of pupils when assessing the success of instruction. This, of course, reduces the reliability of their assessment. It must be understood, however, that problems of narrow sampling during instruction result as much from the rapidity of classroom events as from the teacher's inattention to particular class members.

Table 3.7 summarizes validity and reliability problems in instructional assessment.

IMPROVING ASSESSMENTS DURING INSTRUCTION

Oftentimes in basketball, a player is said to have a shooting "touch." Beyond the mechanics of knowing how to shoot a basketball, the player has an intangible ability to put the ball into the basket with unusual success. Equally amazing is an actor's ability to "read" an audience and react to it. This ability also goes beyond the technical aspects of acting; it involves a

TABLE 3.7 VALIDITY AND RELIABILITY PROBLEMS IN INSTRUCTIONAL ASSESSMENT

Validity Problems

1. Lack of objectivity by classroom teacher-observer

2. Concentrating instruction on objectives and assessments that provide the teacher maximum reinforcement but narrow instruction for pupils

3. Focusing on instructional process indicators (e.g., facial expressions, posture, or participation) without also considering instructional outcome indicators (e.g., pupil learning)

Reliability Problems

1. Fast pace of classroom activities and decision making inhibit the opportunity to collect corroborative evidence

2. Focusing on a limited number of pupils to obtain information about the process of instruction and pupil learning

---

Good teachers can sense the success or failure of their instruction just as a skillful actor can sense the reaction of an audience.

special sensitivity to the audience. Just as the basketball player has touch and the actor can read an audience, so too does successful instructional assessment depend upon a teacher's feel for the instructional process and climate. This feel is dependent in large measure upon the teacher's sizing-up knowledge of the pupils' characteristics and typical behavior.

Assessments made during instruction depend in some measure on an intangible, unarticulated process. To try to describe the instructional assessment process by spelling out a detailed list of rules and procedures corrupts the natural flow of classroom events and likely destroys the process altogether. Teachers will always have to rely in part upon their feel for the classroom situation when gathering assessment information and making decisions during the fast pace of instruction. This fact, however, does not mean that the process cannot be made more valid and reliable. Remembering the following recommendations during instruction will improve the validity and reliability of instructional assessments.

1. *Include a broad sample of pupils when assessing instruction.* As stated earlier, teachers evaluate themselves largely in terms of pupil involvement and attention during instruction. Consequently, they may observe or call only on those pupils whose behaviors or answers are likely to reinforce their perception of instructional success. Likewise they may be tempted to focus on lower level or simple instructional activities, those in which pupils are more likely to succeed. To avoid these pitfalls, an effort must be made to observe and question a wide range of pupils in the class. Unless the teacher attends to a range of pupils, evidence about the progress and success of instruction may be both inappropriate and unreliable.

2. *Supplement informal assessment information with more formal informa-tion about pupil learning.* In order to get a more complete and reliable picture of instructional success, teachers should supplement their informal observa-tions during instruction with more formal types of evidence such as home-work papers, chapter and lesson review exercises, quizzes, worksheets, and tests. Each of these is a valuable source of assessment information.

3. *Use appropriate questioning techniques and strategies to assess pupil learning.* To gather needed information about pupil learning during in-struction, teachers rely heavily on oral questions. Questioning is a major instructional assessment technique for most classroom teachers, with some teachers asking as many as three hundred to four hundred ques-tions per day.

Purposes of Questioning

During instruction, teachers ask questions for many reasons (Morgan & Saxton, 1991; McMillan, 1997; Stein, Grover, & Henningsen, 1996), includ-ing the following:

1. *To capture attention.* Questioning is a way to keep pupils' attention during a lesson, a way to engage them actively in the process of learning.
2. *To prompt deeper processing.* Questioning lets pupils verbalize their thoughts and ideas, thereby promoting thinking and reasoning that can lead to deeper processing and understanding.
3. *To foster peer teaching and learning.* Questioning allows pupils to hear their peers' interpretations and explanations of ideas, processes, and issues. Often other pupils explain things in ways that are more in tune with and helpful to their peers.
4. *To provide reinforcement.* Teachers use questioning to reinforce im-portant points and ideas. The questions teachers ask cue pupils about what and how they should be learning.
5. *To maintain pace and control.* Questions that elicit brief, correct an-swers keep pupils engaged in learning and require them to pay con-tinuous attention. Questions that are more general and open ended slow the pace of instruction so pupils can reflect upon and frame their answers and explanations.
6. *To assess learning.* Questioning provides the teacher with informa-tion about pupil and class learning. Teachers' questions supplement their informal observations of pupil learning in the least disruptive way. Also, for group or cooperative learning activities, questioning of group members after completion of their task is a useful way to assess the success of the group.

Teachers should supplement their informal assessments of instruction with formal feedback such as homework, worksheets, and lesson reviews.

Oral questioning is the most common form of instructional assessment.

Teachers ask questions in order to reinforce important points, to diagnose problems, to keep students' attention, and to promote deeper processing of information.

Types of Questions

Convergent questions are those that have a single correct answer, whereas divergent questions may have several appropriate answers.

Not all teacher questions are alike. There are higher and lower level questions and convergent and divergent questions. Convergent questions have a single correct answer: What is the capital of Brazil? Who is credited with the discovery of radium? How many corners does a cube have? Divergent questions may have many appropriate answers: What are the benefits of a good education? Describe some differences between the American and French systems of government; What kinds of jobs do people in your neighborhood have? Both types are important to use during instruction (Wiggins & McTighe, 1998).

Questions also can be categorized in terms of whether they require higher or lower levels of pupil thinking. Lower level, factual questions typically begin with words such as *who, when, what,* and *how many.* Examples of such questions are When did the U.S. Civil War take place? What is the definition of *taxonomy?* In what country is the city of Bejing located? Such information is important because solving more complex, higher level problems often depends upon retrieving and manipulating factual knowledge.

Lower level, factual questions generally begin with words such as who, what, and when, whereas higher level questions begin with action words such as explain, predict, distinguish, and solve.

Teachers also want their pupils to apply, analyze, and synthesize factual knowledge in order to solve new problems. Higher level questions typically start with such words as *explain, predict, relate, distinguish, solve, contrast, judge,* and *produce.* Examples of such questions are Explain in your own words the main idea of the story; Predict what will happen to the price of oil if the supply increases but the demand remains the same; and Distinguish between statements that are facts and statements that are opinions in the passage we have just read. Questions such as these set tasks that require pupils to go beyond factual recall. Note, however, that if the answers to these questions had been specifically taught to pupils during instruction, they would not be higher level questions, since pupils could answer them from memory, rather than having to construct an answer for themselves.

Table 3.8 provides examples of questions at different levels of Bloom's Taxonomy. While the taxonomy provides a useful model, it is less important to ask questions at specific taxonomic levels than it is to focus generally on asking a range of questions that stimulate both memory and reflection.

Questioning Strategies

The following strategies can be used to increase the effectiveness of oral questioning.

1. *Ask questions related to important objectives.* Questions communicate to the pupils what topics are important and in what ways these topics should be learned, so there should be consistency among objectives, instruction, questioning, and assessment. It is especially useful to prepare a few higher level questions before instruction begins and to incorporate them into the lesson plan.

TABLE 3.8 EXAMPLES OF QUESTIONS FOR THE LEVELS OF BLOOM'S COGNITIVE TAXONOMY

Knowledge (remembering)	What is the definition of a noun?
	How many planets are in our solar system?
	In what year did the Boston Tea Party occur?
Comprehension (understanding)	Summarize the story in your own words.
	Explain what $E = MC^2$ means.
	Paraphrase the author's intent.
Application (using information to solve new problems)	What is a real-world example of that principle?
	Predict what would happen if the steps in the process were reversed.
	How could the Pythagorean theorem be used to measure the height of a tree?
Analysis (reasoning, breaking apart)	Which of these statements are facts, and which are opinions?
	How did the main character change after her scary nightmare?
	Explain the unstated assumption that underlies this argument.
Synthesis (constructing, integrating)	What do all these pictures have in common?
	Describe a generalization that follows from these data.
	State a conclusion supported by these facts.
Evaluation (judging)	What was the most important moment in the story and why?
	What is your opinion of the school policy for grades and extracurricular participation?

2. *Avoid global, overly general questions.* Do not ask Does everyone understand this? because many pupils will be too embarrassed to admit they do not and others will think they understand what has been taught when in reality they do not. Ask questions that probe pupils' comprehension of what is being taught. Similarly, avoid questions that can be answered with a simple yes or no unless the pupils are also expected to explain their answers.

3. *Be aware of patterns in distributing questions among pupils.* Try to involve the entire class in the questioning process. Some teachers call on high-achieving pupils more frequently than low achievers, on girls more than boys, or on those in the front rows more than those in the back. Other teachers do the opposite. Be sensitive to such questioning patterns and strive to give all pupils an equal opportunity to respond.

Teachers should be aware of their questioning patterns to avoid distributing questions unfairly among different groups of students.

4. *Allow sufficient "wait time" after asking a question.* Permitting pupils time to think about and frame a response produces more complete, thoughtful responses. Pupils need time to process their thoughts, especially when the question is a higher level one. Remember, silence immediately after a question is asked is good, because it means the pupils are thinking. Three to 5 seconds is a suitable wait time that permits most pupils, even the slower ones, to think about an answer to the question. Giving pupils time to think also leads to improved answers.

5. *State questions clearly and directly in order to avoid confusion.* Avoid vague questions or prompts like What about the story? or Talk to me about this experiment. Also, avoid questions that take 5 minutes to ask. If pupils are to think in desired ways, the teacher must be able to state questions in ways that focus and produce that type of thinking. Clarity focuses thinking and improves the quality of answers. Again, preparing key questions before teaching a lesson is a useful practice. When questions are vague, tricky, or too abstract, pupils may answer incorrectly and feel failure. They may be hesitant to participate in future questioning and have a poor attitude towards learning.

6. *Probe pupil responses with follow-up questions.* Using such probing questions as Why? Explain how you arrived at that conclusion, and Can you give me another example? indicates to pupils that the whys, or logic, behind a response is as important as the response itself. This also encourages pupils to articulate their reasoning.

7. *Some pupils are shy and difficult to engage in the questioning process.* If possible, allow private questioning time for shy pupils, perhaps during seatwork or study time. Then, as they become more confident in their private responses, gradually work them into public discussions, first with small groups and then with the whole class. If you do call on them for an answer in class, be sure that they are likely to answer correctly. Initial success encourages increased participation.

8. *Remember that oral questioning is a social process involving interaction between teacher and pupils in a public setting.* Consequently, all pupils should be treated with encouragement and respect. Incorrect, incomplete, or even unreasonable answers should not evoke demeaning, sarcastic, or angry teacher responses. Be honest with pupils; do not lie to or try to bluff them if they pose a question that *you* cannot answer. Find the answer and report it to pupils the next day.

CHAPTER SUMMARY

- ◆ Education is the process of helping pupils acquire new skills and behaviors. A curriculum is the statement of what pupils are expected to learn in school or in a course. Instruction includes the methods used to help pupils acquire the desired skills and behaviors. Changes in pupil behavior brought about through formal instruction are called achievements.

- ◆ The instructional process comprises three steps: identifying desirable objectives for pupils to learn, selecting materials and providing instruction to help pupils learn, and assessing whether pupils have learned. Each step requires teacher decision making and assessment.

- ◆ Planning instruction involves understanding and modifying the curriculum and instruction to fit the needs and characteristics of pupils. Planning helps teachers reduce anxiety and uncertainty about their instruction, review and become familiar with subject matter before teaching, and select ways to get the lessons started.

- ◆ Planning is dependent upon the context in which instruction takes place and must take into account both classroom characteristics teachers control and those they do not. In order to organize the classroom and plan appropriate instruction, teachers must carry out good sizing-up assessments to learn their pupils' needs and characteristics.

- ◆ Most instructional approaches rely on four basic elements that teachers should include in their lesson plans: objectives, materials needed, teaching activities and accommodations, and assessment procedures. Lesson plans should be written down in advance of instruction.

- ◆ Objectives describe the behaviors pupils are expected to perform after instruction is completed. They help in selecting appropriate instructional methods and resources, communicating the purposes of instruction to others, and planning appropriate pupil assessment.

- ◆ Well-stated objectives include a clear description of the content matter and the behavior or process to be applied to the content.

- ◆ Higher level objectives are those that require pupils to do more than just memorize facts and rules. Higher level objectives involve behaviors that require application, analysis, synthesis, and evaluation.

- ◆ Planning instruction is greatly aided by modern textbooks and their accompanying aids and resources. However, teachers must remember that every class is different and that they must assess the textbook and its resources in light of the unique needs, readiness, and learning styles of their students.

♦ Planning lessons can be improved by knowing pupils' learning needs and characteristics; addressing pupil needs and characteristics when planning; critically examining the textbook and its accompanying aids for appropriateness; emphasizing both lower and higher level objectives; using a range of instructional strategies, accommodations, and activities; recognizing the relationship between objectives and teaching activities; understanding one's own content and teaching strategy weaknesses; and including assessment activities in plans.

♦ During instruction, teachers must accomplish two tasks simultaneously: deliver instruction to pupils and constantly assess the progress and success of that instruction.

♦ Assessments during instruction are more spontaneous and informal, focusing on indicators such as body language, participation, facial expressions, and questions asked.

♦ Because of its informal, spontaneous nature, assessment during instruction must overcome validity problems such as the lack of teacher objectivity regarding the success of instruction and the tendency to judge instructional success by facial expressions and participation, not by actual pupil achievement.

♦ Reliability problems during instructional assessment center on the difficulty of observing pupils in detail because of the fast pace of instruction and the fact that teachers often observe or call on only some pupils in the class.

♦ Questioning is the most useful strategy a teacher can use to assess the progress of instruction while it is going on. It provides information to the teacher about pupil learning, lets pupils articulate their own thoughts, reinforces important concepts and behaviors, and influences the pace of instruction.

♦ Good questioning technique includes asking both higher and lower level questions; keeping questions related to the objectives of instruction; involving the whole class in the process; allowing sufficient "wait time" for pupils to think about their responses; probing responses with follow-up questions that have the pupils defend or explain why they chose their answer; and never demeaning or embarrassing a pupil for a wrong or unreasonable answer.

QUESTIONS FOR DISCUSSION

1. What pupil characteristics are most important to take into account when planning instruction? How realistic is it to expect a teacher to plan instruction that takes into account the important needs of all her or his pupils?

2. In what ways can teacher's editions of textbooks both enhance and detract from good instruction?

3. Educational objectives usually describe what all pupils in a class are expected to learn. Do you think it is a good idea to expect all pupils to master the same objectives? Why or why not?

4. What factors should determine the proper balance between higher and lower level objectives in a learning unit?

5. How might the fact that a teacher is the planner and deliverer of instruction *and* the assessor of its success negatively influence the ways the teacher plans and delivers instruction?

6. In what ways can teacher's editions of textbooks both enhance and detract from good instruction?

REFLECTION EXERCISES

♦ List as many factors as you can (at least 20) that can affect a pupil's learning and behavior in school. Put an X beside the three factors you think are the most important for pupil learning. Put a Y beside all the factors you think a teacher would know about from sizing-up assessment. Put a Z beside all the factors that the teacher has very little control over.

♦ Review your responses and pick the three factors that a teacher is likely to know about and be able to influence in the classroom. What are some of the ways you think the lesson plans of an experienced teacher differ from those of an inexperienced teacher? What do you think accounts for the differences?

ACTIVITIES

1. Using the model shown in Table 3.1, develop a lesson plan for a topic you would like to teach to a class. Your plan should address the following areas.

   Educational objectives: Describe the things pupils are to learn from instruction; what should they be able to do after instruction that they could not do before instruction? Write at least one lower level and one higher level objective for your plan.

   Materials: Describe the materials and resources you will need to carry out the lesson.

   Teaching activities: Describe the things that will be going on during the lesson. What will you be doing and what will the pupils be doing? What is the sequence of planned activities?

   Assessment: Describe how you will determine whether pupils learned from the lesson.

2. With a partner select a recent (1995 or later) teacher's edition of a textbook in a subject matter and grade level you are interested in teaching. Select a chapter or unit. Using the criteria shown in Table 3.3, write a two- to three-page critique of this chapter or unit. What are its strong and weak points? Are the various parts of the lesson integrated and reinforcing?

3. Working in small groups, select a unit or chapter in a textbook. Using the content of the unit or chapter, write one question that assesses each of the six levels of Bloom's Taxonomy (*see* Table 3.8).

REVIEW QUESTIONS

1. Explain the differences among education, achievement, instruction, and curriculum.

2. How does sizing-up assessment contribute to planning and delivering good instruction to pupils?

3. What are the advantages and disadvantages of teacher's editions of classroom textbooks? What cautions should teachers exercise when using them?

4. What common errors are made in planning instruction, and how can they be overcome?

5. How do decisions about educational objectives influence decisions about instruction and assessment? What are the features of a well-stated educational objective?

6. What are some accommodations that can be made to help pupils with disabilities during instruction?

7. What strategies of oral questioning can a teacher use to make assessments during instruction more valid and reliable?

8. How does the assessment process differ for planning instruction and delivering instruction?

9. What areas and behaviors do teachers assess while they are delivering instruction?

REFERENCES

Airasian, P. W. (in press). Types, uses, and critiques of objectives. In D. R. Krathwohl and L. Anderson (Eds.), *A taxonomy of teaching and learning.* New York: Addison Wesley Longman.

Arends, R. I. (1997). *Classroom instruction and management.* New York: McGraw-Hill.

Bloom, B. S., Englehart, M. D., Furst, E. J., Hill, W. H., and Krathwohl, D. R. (1956). *Taxonomy of educational objectives. Handbook I: Cognitive domain.* New York: McKay Publishing.

Borich, G. (1996). *Effective teaching methods.* Englewood Cliffs, NJ: Merrill.

Cartwright, P. G., Cartwright, C. A., and Ward, M. E. (1995). *Educating special learners.* Boston: Wadsworth Publishing.

Cegelka, P. T., and Berdine, W. H. (1995). *Effective instruction for students with learning difficulties.* Needham Heights, MA: Allyn and Bacon.

Doyle, W. (1986). Classroom organization and management. In M. C. Wittrock (Ed.), *Handbook of research on teaching* (pp. 392–431). New York: Macmillan.

Frisbie, D. A., Miranda, D. U., and Baker, K. K. (1993). An evaluation of elementary textbook tests as classroom assessment tools. *Applied Measurement in Education, 6* (1), 21–36.

Gardner, H. (1995). *Frames of mind: The theory of multiple intelligence.* New York: Basic Books.

Gronlund, N. (1995). *How to write and use instructional objectives.* Englewood Cliffs, NJ: Prentice Hall.

Hannah, L. S., and Michaels, J. U. (1977). *A comprehensive framework for instructional objectives: A guide to systematic planning and evaluation.* Reading, MA: Addison-Wesley.

Harrow, A. J. (1972). *A taxonomy of the psychomotor domain.* New York: McKay.

Hunter, M. (1982). *Mastery teaching.* El Segundo, CA: TIP Publications.

Krathwohl, D. R., Bloom, B. S., and Masia, B. B. (1964). *Taxonomy of educational objectives. Handbook II: Affective domain.* New York: David McKay Publishing.

Leinhardt, G. (1989). Math lessons: A contrast of novice and expert competence. *Journal for Research in Mathematics Education, 20,* 52–75.

Louis Harris & Associates. (1995). *Metropolitan Life survey of the American teacher, 1984–1995: Old problems, new challenges.* New York: Louis Harris & Associates, Inc.

McMillan, J. H. (1997). *Classroom assessment.* Needham Heights, MA: Allyn and Bacon.

Morgan, N., and Saxton, J. (1991). *Teaching, questioning, and learning.* New York: Routledge.

Perkinson, H. (1993). *Teachers without goals, students without purposes.* New York: McGraw-Hill.

Price, K. M., and Nelson, K. L. (1999). *Daily planning for today's classroom.* Belmont, CA: Wadsworth Publishing.

Simpson, E. J. (1972). *The psychomotor domain.* Washington, D.C.: Gryphon House.

Slavin, R. E. (1995). *Cooperative learning: Theory, research, and practice.* Needham Heights, MA: Allyn and Bacon.

Stein, M. K., Grover, B. W., and Henningsen, M. (1996). Building student capacity for mathematical thinking and reasoning: An analysis of mathematical tasks used in reform classrooms. *American Educational Research Journal, 33* (2), 455–488.

Wiggins, G., and McTighe, J. (1998). *Understanding by design.* Alexandria, VA: Association for Supervision and Curriculum Development.

Woodward, A., and Elliott, D. L. (1990). Textbooks: Consensus and controversy. In D. L. Elliott and A. Woodward (Eds.), *Textbooks and schooling in the United States. The eighty-ninth yearbook of the National Society for the Study of Education. Part I* (pp. 146–161). Chicago: University of Chicago Press.

CHAPTER 4

FORMAL ASSESSMENT: TEACHER-MADE AND TEXTBOOK TESTS

CHAPTER OBJECTIVES

After reading this chapter, the student will be able to:

1. define basic item writing terms: for example, selection item, supply item, stem, specific determiner, and measurement.

2. explain the basic purpose and steps in classroom achievement testing.

3. state characteristics that should be examined before using a textbook test.

4. write correct higher and lower level supply-and-selection items for given objectives; identify and correct faults in poorly written test items.

5. explain the concept of achievement test validity and describe the factors that contribute to it.

6. state basic principles for assembling and administering tests; identify strategies in formal assessments that accommodate pupils with disabilities.

7. distinguish between objective and subjective scoring.

8. identify methods to improve the objectivity of essay test scoring.

T hus far we have seen that assessment plays an important role in classrooms and that teachers use it to help them make decisions about

♦ getting to know pupils early in the school year.

♦ establishing the classroom as a learning community with rules and order.

♦ selecting appropriate educational objectives for pupils.

♦ developing lesson plans that accommodate pupils' strengths and needs.

♦ selecting and critiquing instructional materials and activities.

♦ monitoring the instructional process and pupil learning during instruction.

Much of the evidence that supports these decisions comes from informal observations and perceptions. Rarely written down, they are used mainly to guide teachers' moment-to-moment decisions about solving pupil problems, controlling the class, conducting a lesson, and judging pupils' reactions to instruction. These assessments are used to form or improve ongoing classroom processes and so are called formative assessments; they provide information when it is still possible to influence the everyday processes that are at the heart of teaching.

Formative assessments are used to alter or improve instruction while it is still going on.

Although critical to teachers' decision making, informal assessments should be supplemented by more formal kinds of evidence. Such formal assessments usually come at the end of instruction when it is difficult to alter or rectify what has already occurred. Called summative assessments,

TABLE 4.1   COMPARISON OF FORMATIVE AND SUMMATIVE ASSESSMENTS

	Formative	Summative
Purpose	To monitor and guide a process while it is still in progress	To judge the success of a process at its completion
Time of assessment	During the process	At the end of the process
Type of assessment technique	Informal observation, quizzes, homework, pupil questions, and worksheets	Formal tests, projects, and term papers
Use of assessment information	Improve and change a process while it is still going on	Judge the overall success of a process; grade, place, promote

they are used to evaluate, or sum up, the outcomes of instruction and are exemplified by end-of-chapter tests, projects, term papers, and final examinations. Table 4.1 compares formative and summative assessments.

Summative assessments represent a third type of classroom assessment called official assessments. Official assessments are more formal and systematic than either sizing-up or instructional assessments. They help teachers to make the decisions the school bureaucracy requires of them: testing and grading pupils, recommending whether pupils should be promoted or placed in an honors section, and referring pupils to special-education services if they have special needs. These decisions stem from official assessments.

Unlike sizing-up and instructional assessments, official assessments are usually made public in report cards, record folders, and reading or ability group designations. Further, most official assessments inform decisions about individual pupils rather than groups or classes; individuals are graded, promoted, honored, and placed, not groups. Because they are public, have important consequences for pupils, and often must be defended, official assessments are usually based upon formal evidence like tests, projects, or reports.

Teachers have mixed emotions about official assessments, as the following comments show.

Summative assessments are used to evaluate the outcomes of instruction and take the form of tests, projects, term papers, and final exams.

Official assessments are needed by the school bureaucracy for purposes such as pupil testing, grading, and placement.

I hate giving tests. I find the testing situation to be one where tests become public expressions of what I already knew about the kid and what the kid already knew about the subject matter. In other words, I knew who would get A's and who would get F's because I taught the class.

Each test gives me some feedback on what I'm doing right and what I'm not, as well as what the class is learning best. I like to give a large number of tests to get this feedback.

My tests are helpful in that they offer concrete evidence to show parents if the student is deficient in an area. I'll tell a parent that Johnny can't add and they'll sometimes respond "I know he can add when he wants to." Then I show them a classroom test that shows Johnny's deficiency. One drawback to the tests, especially in the early grades, is that a child sometimes will become upset during testing.

Official assessments can have important consequences for students and should be taken quite seriously by teachers.

Although teachers differ in their views of official assessment, it is clear that no matter how they feel about them, they use them in their classrooms. Despite their lukewarm endorsement by many teachers, it is a grave mistake to underestimate the importance of official assessments. Pupils, their parents, and the public at large consider them to be very important and take them quite seriously. The grading, placement, promotion, and other decisions that result from official assessments influence pupils' lives both in and out of school. They are the public record of a pupil's school accomplishments and are often the sole information a parent has of how a child is doing in school. Thus, although official assessment occurs infrequently compared to other types of assessment, its perceived importance makes it a central part of any classroom's activities.

THE LOGIC OF FORMAL ASSESSMENT

Good teaching refers to what teachers do during instruction, while effective teaching refers to the outcomes of instruction.

There is an important difference between good teaching and effective teaching. Good teaching refers to the *process* of instruction (Were pupils taught well?), while effective teaching refers to the *outcomes* of instruction (Did pupils learn?). A good teacher is one who, among other things, provides a review at the start of a new lesson, states appropriate objectives, maintains an appropriate level of lesson difficulty, engages pupils in the learning process, emphasizes important points during instruction, gives pupils practice doing what they are expected to learn, and maintains an orderly classroom.

Effective teaching goes one step beyond good teaching to focus upon whether pupils actually learn from instruction. An effective teacher is one whose pupils learn what they have been taught. Clearly there is a relationship between good and effective teaching: the better the teaching, the more likely that it will be effective. Teachers who misjudge the level of their pupils' ability, fail to review or point out important concepts to pupils, and permit disciplinary problems to distract instruction have a poorer chance of producing learning than good teachers.

Sizing-up and instructional assessments focus attention primarily on the instructional process, while official assessments focus attention primarily on pupil achievement at the completion of instruction. In short, official assessments seek to obtain evidence about teaching effectiveness, so they should be linked to the objectives, activities, and instruction provided pupils. It is impossible to evaluate pupils' achievement if the things assessed do not match the things pupils were taught.

Always remember that the primary aim in assessing pupil achievement is to *provide pupils a fair opportunity to demonstrate what they have learned from the instruction provided.* It is not to trick pupils into doing poorly, entertain them, or insure that most of them get A's. It is not to determine the total knowledge pupils have accumulated as a result of their learning experiences, both in and out of school. It is simply to let pupils show what they have learned from the things they have been taught in their classroom.

The primary aim of assessing achievement is to provide pupils an opportunity to demonstrate what they have learned from the instruction provided.

PREPARING FOR ASSESSMENT

At the time for formal achievement testing, usually at the completion of instruction on a unit or chapter, the teacher must decide the following:

1. What should be tested?
2. What type of assessment items should be used?
3. How long should the assessment take?
4. Should a teacher-made or textbook assessment be used?

An Example of Preparing for Official Assessment

Mr. Wysocki is a seventh grade English teacher who was teaching his class about descriptive paragraphs. Based upon his sizing-up assessments, the pupils' previous English curriculum, the textbook, and other instructional resources available to him, Mr. Wysocki decided that the unit would focus upon the following objectives:

- The pupil can name the three stages of the writing process (i.e., prewriting, writing, and editing).
- The pupil can explain in his or her own words the purposes of the three stages of the writing process.
- The pupil can select the topic sentences in given descriptive paragraphs.
- The pupil can write a topic sentence for a given descriptive writing topic.
- The pupil can write a descriptive paragraph with a topic sentence, descriptive detail, and a concluding statement.

Table of Specifications

To organize his objectives, Mr. Wysocki developed a table of specifications that identified the cognitive processes pupils were to demonstrate, the content on which they were to demonstrate these processes, and the

TABLE 4.2   TABLE OF SPECIFICATIONS

| | Process Dimension | | | | | |
Content Dimension	Knowledge	Comprehension	Apply	Analyze	Synthesize	Evaluate
Stages of writing	X (L)	X (M)				
Topic sentences			X (M)	X (L)		
Writing essay					X (H)	

amount of emphasis each objective would receive in instruction. Table 4.2 shows Mr. Wysocki's table of specifications.

The table of specifications has two dimensions, content and process. The content dimension includes the main topics of instruction and assessment. The process dimension, which you will recognize as the six categories of Bloom's Taxonomy, lists the cognitive processes related to each content topic. In Mr. Wysocki's table, for example, the intersection of knowledge (process dimension) and stages of writing (content dimension), represented by the X, referred to the objective The pupil can name the three stages of the writing process (i.e., prewriting, writing, and editing); that is, the pupil will remember the names of the three writing stages. The L after the X referred to the amount of time allotted to this objective. Since it was a simple memorization task, a low (L) amount of time was spent teaching it. The intersection of comprehension (process dimension) and stages of writing (content dimension) referred to the objective The pupil can explain in his or her own words the purposes of the three stages of the writing process. Notice that stages of writing related to two different objectives, because there were two processes Mr. Wysocki was concerned with, remembering and explaining. Notice also that Mr. Wysocki placed more emphasis on pupils' own explanation of the three stages (M) than on their remembering the stages (L). Note that he could also have stated the planned number of test items to be used with each intersection of content and process instead of using L, M, and H.

Mr. Wysocki's third and fourth objectives indicated that he wanted his pupils to both select and write their own topic sentences. Selecting called for an analysis that differentiates topic sentences from other types of sentences. Writing a topic sentence called for application of a procedure. Writing an essay, the final objective, called for a correct synthesis of the three stages of descriptive writing. The writing objective was the most important and complex outcome, so more time was allotted to it than to the other four objectives.

Once his objectives were identified and organized, Mr. Wysocki developed lesson plans for them. In selecting activities, he considered the ability levels of his pupils, their attention spans, the suggestions made in the textbook, and the additional resources that were available to supplement and reinforce the textbook. He also planned activities that would give pupils practice in each objective. One of the benefits of a table of specifications is that it emphasizes the different processes that intersect with the content. Thus, the table reminded Mr. Wysocki that he needed both remembering and explaining activities to attain his first two objectives.

With the objectives and the planned activities identified, Mr. Wysocki commenced instruction. First, he introduced pupils to the three steps in the writing process: (1) prewriting (identifying the intended audience, purpose, and initial ideas); (2) writing; and (3) editing what has been written. He told pupils they would be expected to memorize the names of the three stages. Next, he gave pupils topics and had them describe how they would go through the three steps. He had them give reasons why each step is necessary for good writing. He then introduced them to the concept of a paragraph, and they read descriptive paragraphs to find a common structure. He noted that a paragraph is made up of a topic sentence, detail sentences, and a concluding sentence. Then he had the pupils select the topic sentences in several paragraphs. Later, he had them write their own topic sentences.

Instruction seemed to go along fairly well except that pupils had a hard time finding the common structure in paragraphs. Mr. Wysocki had to give additional explanation to the class. Also, even after instruction, his end-of-lesson assessments indicated that many pupils had the mistaken idea that the topic sentence always came first in a paragraph, so he devised a worksheet in which many of the topic sentences were not at the start of the paragraph.

Finally, Mr. Wysocki had pupils write descriptive paragraphs. First he had them all write on the same topics so they could compare topic sentences and the amount of detail in each other's paragraphs. He thought this strategy might be useful because pupils could learn from one another's efforts. Homework assignments were returned to pupils with suggestions for improvement, and pupils were required to edit and rewrite their paragraphs. Later, pupils were allowed to construct descriptive paragraphs on topics of their choice.

Not all teachers would have instructed their pupils in this fashion; different teachers have different pupils, resources, and styles. But Mr. Wysocki did what he judged was best for his particular class. He instituted instructional procedures that gave pupils practice on the behaviors they were expected to learn, provided feedback on pupil performance during instruction, and revised his plans based upon his observations during instruction. He demonstrated the characteristics of a good teacher.

Mr. Wysocki felt that he had a fair sense of how well the class had mastered the objectives. Although he knew something about the achievement of each pupil, he was not sure about each one's achievement of all five objectives. He felt a formal, end-of-unit assessment would provide information about each pupil's mastery of all he had taught. Then he would not have to rely upon incomplete, informal perceptions when grading his pupils. However, in order to develop the assessment, he had to make some decisions about the nature of the test he would administer, including the following.

A fair and valid test covers information and skills similar to those covered during instruction.

1. *What should I test?* The first important decision when preparing to assess pupil achievement is to identify the information, processes, and skills that will be tested. A valid achievement test is one that provides pupils a fair opportunity to show what they have learned from instruction. Therefore, in deciding what to test, it was necessary for Mr. Wysocki to focus attention upon both his objectives and the actual instruction that took place. Usually the two are very similar, but sometimes it is necessary to add or omit an objective once teaching begins. In the final analysis, the things that are actually presented during instruction are the most important to assess.

Mr. Wysocki knew, then, that he had to gather information about how well pupils could memorize and explain in their own words the three stages of the writing process, select topic sentences in a paragraph, write suitable topic sentences, and compose a descriptive paragraph with a topic sentence, descriptive detail, and summarizing statement. But what about other important skills such as taking notes on a topic or knowing the difference between a descriptive and an expository paragraph? These are also useful so should they be on Mr. Wysocki's test?

The answer to this question is NO! There will always be more objectives to teach than there is time to teach them. There will always be useful topics and skills that have to be omitted from tests because they cannot be taught. This is why thoughtfully planning instruction in terms of pupils' needs and resources is so important. Including untaught skills on an achievement test diminishes its validity, making it less than a true and fair assessment of what pupils have learned from classroom instruction.

By confining his test questions to what he actually taught, Mr. Wysocki could say to himself I decided what the important objectives were for pupils, "I provided instruction on those objectives, I gave pupils practice performing the objectives, and I gave a test that asked pupils to do things similar to those I taught. The results of the test should fairly reflect how much the pupils have achieved in this unit and permit me to grade fairly."

The type of assessment procedure chosen depends on the nature of the objective being assessed.

2. *What type of assessment should be given?* The key to gathering appropriate information about learning is found in the objectives and the instruction provided. Each objective contains a target process or behavior that pupils are taught and expected to learn. The processes in Mr. Wysocki's objectives are remember (memorize), comprehend (explain in one's own words), analyze (select a topic sentence), apply (write a topic sentence), and synthesize (integrate and write an essay). Three of these processes, explain in one's own words, write, and integrate and write, are best assessed by **supply questions.** These require the pupil to produce (supply) an answer or product. The objective calling for selecting topic sentences is best assessed by selection questions. These require the pupil to choose (select) the correct answer from given options. The objective requiring memorization of the three stages of writing can be appropriately assessed by a supply question (list or orally state the three stages) or a selection question (circle the three stages). Thus, the nature of the process stated in an objective determines the format used to assess learning.

Many teachers feel that only essay tests are good. Others use multiple-choice items as much as possible, and still others believe that tests should contain a variety of question types. When teachers are asked about the kinds of questions they use in their tests, the responses are similar to the following.

> I always give the kids essay tests because that's the only way I can see how well they think.

> Multiple-choice items are easy and fast to score, so I use them most of the time to test pupils' achievement. Besides, most standardized tests like the SAT are made up of multiple-choice questions, so my tests give the pupils practice with this kind of item.

> I make sure that every test I make up has some multiple-choice questions, some fill-in questions, and at least one essay question. I believe that variety in the kinds of questions keeps students interested and gives all students a chance to show what they know in the way that's best for them.

Each of these teachers states a reason for following a particular classroom testing strategy. The reasons are neither wrong nor inappropriate, but they are secondary to the main purpose of official achievement testing, which is *to permit pupils to show how well they have learned the behaviors or processes they were taught.* Thus, no single type of assessment item is applicable all the time. What makes a particular procedure useful is whether it matches the objectives and instruction provided.

Factors such as the age of the students, the subject being tested, and the length of the class period all impact the length of a test.

3. *How long should the test take?* Since time for testing is limited, choices must be made in deciding the length of a test. Usually, practical matters such as the age of the pupils or the length of a class period are most influential. Since the stamina and attention span of young pupils is less than that of older ones, a useful strategy to follow with elementary school pupils is to test them fairly often using short tests that assess only a few objectives. Because of their typical attention spans, 15- to 30-minute tests, depending on the grade and group, are suggested for elementary pupils.

Curricula for some school subjects such as history, social studies, and English are composed of relatively discrete, self-contained units. In other subjects such as mathematics, foreign language, and science, knowledge must be built up in a hierarchical sequence. Whereas topics in history may stand on their own, topics in mathematics or Spanish usually cannot be understood unless prior math and Spanish lessons have been mastered. Consequently, when teaching in a hierarchical subject area, it is useful to give more frequent tests to keep pupils on task in their studying and to make sure they grasp the early ideas that provide the foundation for subsequent, more complex ideas. Testing in middle, junior, and high schools is usually restricted by the length of the class period. Most teachers at these levels plan their tests to last almost one complete class period.

Mr. Wysocki's class periods are 50 minutes long. He wanted a test that would take about 40 minutes for most pupils to complete. A 40-minute test would allow time for distribution and collection of the tests, as well as a few minutes for those pupils who always want "one more minute" before handing in their test.

The number of test questions per objective depends on the instructional time spent on each objective and its importance.

In deciding how many questions to ask for each objective, Mr. Wysocki tried to balance two factors: (1) the instructional time spent on each objective and (2) its importance. Usually there are some objectives that are more important than others. These objectives tend to be the more general ones, that call for the integration of several narrower objectives. Even though a great deal of instructional time was spent on writing and identifying topic sentences, Mr. Wysocki values this skill less for it own sake than for its contribution to the more general objective of constructing a descriptive paragraph. Thus, the number of test questions dealing with writing and identifying topic sentences was not proportional to the instructional time he spent on it. It is not necessary to include an equal number of questions for each objective, but all objectives should be assessed by some items. On the basis of these factors and the instruction he had provided, Mr. Wysocki felt that a test with the following format would be fair to pupils and would provide a valid and reliable assessment of their learning.

- ◆ The pupil can *name* the three stages of writing. Use one supply question: list the three names.
- ◆ The pupils can *explain* in their own words the three stages of the writing process (i.e., prewriting, writing, and editing). Use a short essay question.
- ◆ The pupils can *select* the topic sentence in a given descriptive paragraph. Use three multiple-choice questions, each consisting of a paragraph and a list of possible topic sentences from which the pupil has to select the correct one.
- ◆ The pupils can *write* a topic sentence for a given descriptive topic. Use three short-answer questions that give the pupils a topic area and require them to write a topic sentence for each area.
- ◆ The pupils can write a descriptive paragraph using a topic sentence, descriptive detail, and a concluding statement. Use an essay question in which each pupil writes a descriptive paragraph on a topic of his or her choice. The paragraph cannot be on a topic the pupil used previously during instruction or practice.

4. *Should a teacher-made or a textbook test be used?* Teachers are inevitably confronted with the question of whether to use the textbook test or to construct their own. The very availability of textbook tests is seductive and causes many teachers to think: After all, the test comes with the textbook, seems to measure what is in the chapter I'm teaching, looks attractive, and is readily available, so why shouldn't I use it? Mr. Wysocki asked himself the same question.

Notice that the decision about using a textbook test or constructing one cannot be answered until *after* the teacher has reflected on what was taught and has identified the topics and behaviors to be tested. The usefulness of any achievement test cannot be judged without reference to the planned objectives and actual instruction.

Textbook tests furnish a ready-made instrument for assessing the objectives stressed in the textbook and can save classroom teachers much time. Test formats vary across textbook publishers in terms of length, layout, and question type. Look through the teacher's edition of some textbooks to see the range of tests available.

Before using these tests, teachers should consider the criteria that permit a teacher to use a textbook or teacher-made test with confidence. The basic concern is whether the items on the test match the instruction provided pupils. Table 4.3 identifies important points to consider when deciding about whether or not to use a textbook test.

Regardless of whether a teacher is constructing his or her own test or judging the adequacy of a textbook test, he or she must consider the same basic validity issue: Do the items on the test match the instruction provided pupils? The more a teacher alters and reshapes the textbook curriculum, the less valid its accompanying tests become. As one teacher put it, "The textbook tests look good and can be time-savers, but they often don't test exactly what I've been doing in the classroom. Every time I change what I do from what the text suggests I do, and every time I leave out a lesson or section of the text from my instruction, I have to look at the text test carefully to make sure it's fair for my pupils."

The main consideration in judging the adequacy of a textbook test is the match between its questions and what pupils were actually taught in class.

TABLE 4.3   KEY POINTS TO CONSIDER IN JUDGING TEXTBOOK TESTS

1. The decision to use a textbook test must come *after* a teacher identifies the objectives that he or she has taught and now wants to assess.

2. Textbook tests are designed for the typical classroom, but since few classrooms are typical, most teachers deviate somewhat from the text in order to accommodate their pupils' needs.

3. The more classroom instruction deviates from the textbook objectives and lesson plans, the less valid the textbook tests are likely to be.

4. The main consideration in judging the adequacy of a textbook test is the match between its test questions and what pupils were taught in their classes:
   a. Are questions similar to the teacher's objectives and instructional emphases?
   b. Do questions require pupils to perform the behaviors they were taught?
   c. Do questions cover all or most of the important objectives taught?
   d. Is the language level and terminology appropriate for pupils?
   e. Does the number of items for each objective provide a sufficient sample of pupil performance?

TABLE 4.4   COMMON PROBLEMS IN DEVELOPING OR SELECTING
TESTS TO ASSESS PUPIL ACHIEVEMENT

1. Failure to consider objectives and instructional emphases when planning a test

2. Failure to assess all of the important objectives and instructional topics

3. Failure to select item types that permit pupils to demonstrate the desired behavior

4. Adopting a test without reviewing it for its relevance to the instruction provided

5. Including topics or objectives not taught to pupils

6. Including too few items to assess the consistency of pupil performance

7. Using tests to punish pupils for inattentiveness or acting out

To summarize, both textbook and teacher-made tests should (1) assess the objectives and instruction provided and (2) include sufficient questions to measure all or most of those objectives. That way, the test provides a valid sample of pupil learning. Table 4.4 summarizes the problems teachers encounter in addressing these two important aspects.

PREPARING PUPILS FOR FORMAL ACHIEVEMENT TESTING

Fair and valid assessment involves preparing appropriate objectives, providing good instruction on these objectives, and determining how these objectives are best assessed.

Mr. Wysocki's actions point out that fair and valid assessment includes a number of steps: determining appropriate educational objectives, providing good instruction on the objectives, and determining how the objectives are best assessed. With these decisions made, Mr. Wysocki could then determine whether a textbook or a teacher-made test was more appropriate (he chose to construct his own). After these initial decisions, others arise, including preparing pupils for testing.

Issues of Test Preparation

Tests and other assessments help in making decisions about pupils' learning in some area. Performance on a test or assessment is meant to represent pupils' mastery of a broader body of knowledge and skills than just the specific examples used in class. As noted in Chapter 1 (remember Manuela and Joe), tests gather *samples* of a pupil's behavior and this information is used to generalize how the pupil will perform on similar tasks or items. For example, the performance of a pupil who scores 90 percent on a test of poetry analysis, chemical equation balancing, or capitalization rules is used as an indication that the pupil has mastered about 90 percent of the general content he was taught and tested on. The specific tasks or test items are selected to represent a larger group of similar tasks or items.

Throughout this chapter, two points have been stressed. First, assessment of achievement should provide a fair and representative indication of how well pupils have learned what they were taught. Second, in order to do this, test questions must ask pupils to respond to items similar to those they were taught during instruction. The important word here is *similar*.

There is an important ethical difference between teaching to the test and teaching the test itself. Teaching to the test involves teaching pupils the general skills, knowledge, and behaviors they need to answer the questions on the test. This is an appropriate and desirable practice; it is what good teaching and testing are all about. But teaching the test itself, that is, teaching pupils the answers to the specific questions that will appear on the test, is neither appropriate nor ethical. It produces a distorted, invalid picture of pupil achievement. Such a test gives information about how well pupils can remember the specific items they were taught, but it will not tell how well they can do on questions that are similar, but not identical, to the ones they have been taught. Teachers have an educational and ethical responsibility not to corrupt the meaning of pupils' achievement test performances by literally teaching them the test.

Tests are intended to gather valid and reliable samples of student behavior that can be used to make generalizations about student learning.

Achievement tests should give information about how well a student can answer questions similar but not identical to those taught in class.

Provide Good Instruction

The single most important thing a teacher can do to prepare pupils for formal classroom achievement tests is to provide them with good instruction. A primary ethical responsibility of teaching is to offer the best instruction possible, without corrupting the achievement test in the ways described previously. In the absence of good instruction, little else is important.

Good instruction is the most important preparation for formal achievement testing.

Review before Testing

While teaching a unit or chapter, many objectives are introduced, some early and others at the end of instruction. Because the topics best remembered tend to be those most recently taught, it is good practice to review material with students prior to formal testing. The review can take many forms: a question-and-answer session, a written or oral summary of main ideas, a review test, or the chapter or unit reviews found in textbooks. The review reminds pupils of objectives taught early in the unit, provides one last chance to practice important behaviors and skills, and affords an opportunity to ask questions about things that are unclear. Often, the review exercise itself provokes questions that help pupils grasp partially understood ideas.

Test reviews often provoke questions that help students grasp partially understood ideas.

Many teachers fail to conduct a review because they feel it might tip pupils off to the material on the test. This is faulty reasoning. The purpose of a review is to indicate to pupils that "These are examples of the ideas, behaviors, and skills that I expect you to have learned. See how well you have learned them. Practice them before the test that counts towards your grade. If you have questions or difficulties, we'll go over them before the test. After that, you're on your own." A pertinent review prior to the test helps pupils do their best.

Notice that the review exercises or questions should be *similar* but not identical to the exercises or questions that make up the final test. If they are the actual test questions, a valid assessment of pupil learning cannot be obtained because the test has been reduced to a short-term memory exercise rather than a measure of long-term mastery of general learning objectives.

Familiarity with Question Formats

If students are not familiar with the types of questions used on a test, the test does not produce a valid assessment of what they have learned.

If the test contains questions in an unfamiliar format, pupils should be given practice on that format prior to testing. The need for such practice is especially important in the elementary grades, where pupils first encounter matching, multiple-choice, true-false, short-answer, and essay questions. To do their best and to provide a valid indication of their learning, pupils must know how to respond to each type of question. Clearly, an opportune place to teach these things is during the review exercises prior to the chapter or unit test.

In addition to familiarizing pupils with new types of questions and new response formats, there are some test-taking guidelines that can help pupils do their best, including the following (Ebel & Frisbie, 1991):

- ♦ Read and follow the test directions.
- ♦ Find out how questions will be scored. Will all questions count equally? Will points be taken off for spelling, grammar, or neatness?
- ♦ Pace yourself so that you can complete all the questions.
- ♦ Plan and organize essay questions before responding.
- ♦ When using a separate answer sheet, check often to make certain that you are marking your responses in the correct places.
- ♦ Be in good physical and mental condition at the time of testing by avoiding late-night cram sessions.

Test wiseness skills help pupils identify errors in test questions. These errors provide clues to correct answers. For example, when responding to multiple-choice questions, the testwise pupil knows the following:

- ♦ If the words *some, often,* or other vague words are in one of the options, it is likely to be the correct answer.

- ◆ The option that is longest or most precisely stated is likely to be the correct one.
- ◆ Any choice that has grammatical or spelling errors is not likely to be the correct one.
- ◆ Choices that do not attach smoothly to the stem of the question are not likely to be correct.

To be testwise is to be able to identify unintended clues to the correct answers.

There are many other testwise strategies that pupils use to overcome a lack of content knowledge; more detailed descriptions of these are found in the references. It is best to make pupils aware of such general test-taking skills and then to concentrate on writing fair, appropriate, and error-free test questions.

Scheduling the Test

It has already been recommended that teachers administer an achievement test after pupils have had the opportunity to review, study, and reflect on the instruction. There are other considerations, however, about the times when pupils are most likely to show their best performance. For example, if a teacher tests pupils the day of the school's championship football game, the period after an assembly or lunch, or on the first day after a long school vacation, it is likely that pupils will give a subpar test performance. Likewise, should a teacher schedule a test on a day that he or she will be away so that the substitute teacher will have something to keep the pupils busy? The answer is no, because the substitute may not be able to answer pupils' questions about either the test or the meaning of particular questions. Further, if an elementary classroom is involved, the presence of a stranger may make the pupils uncomfortable and unable to do their best. While no teacher has complete control over scheduling tests, it is useful to bear in mind that there are some times when pupils are better able to perform than others.

Giving Pupils Information about the Test

Usually a chapter or unit review alerts pupils to the fact that a formal assessment for grading purposes is coming. It is a good idea, however, to tell the pupils when a test will be given, what will be on it, what kinds of questions it will contain, how many questions there will be, how much it counts, and how long it will be. By providing this information, the teacher helps reduce some of the anxiety that inevitably accompanies the announcement of a test.

Of course, unless a teacher has thought about the nature of the test to be given, it is impossible to provide the pretest information pupils need to prepare for the test. The specifics of test content, types of questions, and

Hastily planned tests too often focus on memory items and fail to cover a representative sample of the instruction provided.

test length need to be considered well before the test is given. Hastily planned tests too often focus on memorization skills and fail to cover a representative sample of the instruction provided pupils. In order to inform pupils about test characteristics, therefore, a teacher should not put off planning the test until the last minute.

PAPER-AND-PENCIL TEST QUESTIONS

As described, a good assessment plan takes many things into consideration: identifying important objectives, selecting question formats that match these objectives, deciding whether to construct a test or use one from the textbook, and providing good instruction, review, and information about the test. The success of these important preparatory steps can be undone, however, if the actual test questions are faulty or confusing. Poorly constructed or unclear questions do not give pupils a fair chance to show what they have learned and consequently do not provide a valid foundation for decision making.

Tests comprise a series of short communications called questions, or **items.** Each item must be brief and set a clear problem for the pupil to solve.

Types of Test Items

Multiple-choice, true-false, and matching questions are examples of selection items. Supply items are those in which the student constructs his or her own answer.

There are two basic types of paper-and-pencil test questions: selection items and supply items. As their names suggest, selection items require the pupil to select the correct answer from among a number of choices, while supply items require the pupil to supply or construct his or her own answer.

Selection Items

Within the general category of selection items are multiple-choice, true-false, and matching questions.

Multiple-Choice Items

Multiple-choice items consist of a stem, which presents the problem or question, and a set of options from which the pupil selects an answer.

Multiple-choice items consist of a **stem,** which presents the problem or question to the pupil, and a set of **options,** or choices, from which the pupil selects an answer. The multiple-choice format is widely used in achievement tests of all types, primarily to assess learning outcomes at the factual knowledge and comprehension levels. However, with suitable introductory material, this format can also be used to assess higher level thinking involving application, analysis, and synthesis. (Item 3 from the following examples is a multiple-choice item that assesses higher level thinking.) The main limitations of the multiple-choice format are that it does not allow pupils to construct, organize, and present their own answers, and it is susceptible to guessing.

Here are examples of multiple-choice items.

1. You use me to cover rips and tears. I am made of cloth. What am I?

    A. perch   B. scratch   C. patch   D. knot

2. The basic purpose of the Marshall Plan was to

    A. provide military defense for Western Europe.
    B. develop industry in African nations.
    C. help American farmers during the Great Depression.
    D. rebuild business and industry in Western Europe.

3. Read the following passage.

    (1) For what men say is that, if I am really just and am not also thought just, profit there is none, but the pain and the loss on the
    (3) other hand is unmistakable. But if, though unjust, I acquire the reputation of justice, a heavenly life is promised to me. Since then
    (5) appearance tyrannizes over truth and is lord of happiness, to appearance I must devote myself. I will describe around me a
    (7) picture and shadow of virtue to be the vestibule and exterior of my house; behind I will trail the subtle and crafty fox.

    Which one of the following states the major premise of the passage?

    A. For what men say (line 1)
    B. if I am really just (line 1)
    C. profit there is none, but the pain and the loss (line 2)
    D. appearance tyrannizes over truth and is the lord of happiness (lines 5-6)
    E. a picture and shadow of virtue to be the vestibule and exterior of my house (lines 7–8)

True-False Items

The true-false format requires pupils to classify a statement into one of two categories: true or false; yes or no; correct or incorrect; fact or opinion. True-false items are used mainly to assess factual knowledge and comprehension behaviors, although they also can be used to assess higher level ones. The main limitation of true-false questions is their susceptibility to guessing.

The main limitation of true-false questions is their susceptibility to guessing.

Although primarily used to assess knowledge and comprehension, both multiple-choice and true-false items can be used to assess higher level thinking.

The following are typical true-false items.

1. The chemical symbol for calcium is Cl.   T   F

2. In the equation $E = mc^2$, when m increases E also increases.   T   F

3. Read the statement. Circle T if true and F if false. If the statement is false, rewrite it to make it true by <u>changing only the underlined part of the statement</u>.

    The level of the cognitive taxonomy that describes recall and memory behaviors is called the <u>synthesis</u> level.   T   F

Matching Items

Matching items consist of a column of premises, a column of responses, and directions for matching the two. They assess mainly lower level thinking.

Matching items consist of a column of **premises,** a column of **responses,** and directions for matching the two. The matching exercise is similar to a set of multiple-choice items, except that in a matching question, the same set of options or responses is used for all the premises. Its main disadvantage is that it is limited to assessing mainly lower level behaviors. The following is an example of a matching exercise.

On the line to the left of each invention in Column A, write the *letter* of the person in Column B who invented it. Each name in Column B may be used only once or not at all.

Column A

_____ (1) telephone
_____ (2) cotton gin
_____ (3) assembly line
_____ (4) polio vaccine

Column B

A. Eli Whitney
B. Henry Ford
C. Jonas Salk
D. Henry McCormick
E. Alexander Graham Bell

Supply Items

Supply items consist of short-answer and completion (also called fill-in-the-blank) items and essay questions.

Short-Answer and Completion Items

Short-answer items use a direct question to present a problem; completion items use an incomplete sentence. Both tend to assess mainly factual knowledge and comprehension.

Short-answer and completion items are very similar. Each presents the pupil with a question to answer. The short-answer format presents the problem with a direct question (e.g., What is the name of the first president of the United States?), while the completion format presents the problem as an incomplete sentence (e.g., The name of the first president of the United States is _____). In each case, the pupil must supply his or her own answer. Typically, the pupil is asked to reply with a word, phrase, number, or sentence, rather than with a more extended response. Short-answer questions are fairly easy to construct and diminish the likelihood that pupils will guess answers. However, they tend to assess mainly factual knowledge or comprehension.

The following are examples of completion and short-answer items.

1. Scientists who specialize in the study of plants are called _____.

Next to each state write the name of its capital city.
2. Michigan   _____
3. Massachusetts   _____
4. South Carolina   _____
5. In a single sentence, state one way that inflation lowers consumers' purchasing power.

Essay Items

Essay questions give pupils the greatest opportunity to construct their own responses, making them the most useful for assessing higher level thinking processes like analyzing, synthesizing, and evaluating. The essay question is also the primary way teachers assess pupils' ability to organize, express, and defend ideas. The main limitations of essays are that they are time-consuming to answer and score, permit testing only of a limited amount of pupils' learning, and place a premium on writing ability.

Essay questions are most useful for assessing higher level thinking skills but are time-consuming to answer and score and favor the student with writing ability.

Here are some examples of essay questions.

1. What is the value of studying science? Give your answer in complete, correct sentences. Write at least five sentences.

2. "In order for revolutionary governments to build and maintain their power, they must control the educational system." Discuss this statement using your knowledge of the American, French, and Russian revolutions. Do you agree with the statement as it applies to the revolutionary governments in the three countries? Include specific examples to support your conclusion. Your answer will be judged on the basis of the similarities and differences you identify in the three revolutions and the extent to which your conclusion is supported by specific examples. You will have 40 minutes to complete your essay.

Table 4.5 compares selection and supply questions across a number of characteristics. It shows that supply questions are much more useful than selection questions in assessing pupils' ability to organize thoughts, present logical arguments, defend positions, and integrate ideas. Selection questions, on the other hand, are more useful when assessing application and problem-solving skills. Given these differences, it is not surprising that knowing the kind of item that will be on a test can influence the way pupils prepare for the test. In general, supply items encourage global, integrative study, while selection items encourage a more detailed, specific focus.

Supply questions are most useful for assessing students' ability to organize and present their thoughts, defend positions, and integrate ideas.

Table 4.5 also shows that while supply and selection items consume approximately the same amount of time to construct and score, each format allocates its time differently. Selection items are time-consuming to construct, but can be scored quickly. Supply items are less time-consuming to construct, but are more time-consuming to score.

Selection items are most useful when application and problem-solving skills are assessed.

Higher Level Test Items

There is a growing emphasis on teaching and assessing pupils' higher level thinking. As the following quotes show, teachers recognize the importance of pupils learning how to manipulate and apply their knowledge. They know that knowledge takes on added meaning when it can be used in real-life situations.

TABLE 4.5 COMPARISON OF SELECTION AND SUPPLY TEST ITEMS

	Selection Tests	Supply Tests
Types of items	Multiple-choice, true-false, matching, interpretive exercise	Short-answer, essay, completion
Behaviors assessed	Factual knowledge and comprehension; thinking and reasoning behaviors like application and analysis when using interpretive exercises	Factual knowledge and comprehension; thinking and reasoning behaviors like organizing ideas, defending positions, and integrating points
Major advantages	1. Items can be answered quickly so a broad sample of instructional topics can be surveyed on a test. 2. Items are easy and objective to score. 3. Test constructor has complete control over the stem and options so the effect of writing ability is controlled.	1. Preparation of items is relatively easy; only a few questions are needed. 2. Affords pupils a chance to construct their own answers; only way to test behaviors such as organizing and expressing information. 3. Lessens chance that pupils can guess the correct answer to items.
Major disadvantages	1. Time-consuming to construct; most time spent constructing items. 2. Many items must be constructed. 3. Guessing is a problem.	1. Time-consuming to score; most time spent scoring items. 2. Covers small sample of instructional topics. 3. Bluffing is a problem.

The kids need to go beyond the facts and rote learning. You can't survive in society unless you can think, reason, and apply what you know.

It would be so boring to only teach facts. Some memorization is needed, of course, but day after day of memorization work would be demeaning to me and the pupils. I have to make room for thinking and reasoning skills.

What is more exciting for a pupil and her teacher than that moment when the pupil's eyes light up with recognition that he or she can solve a new problem or apply a new idea. That excitement doesn't come very often when instruction is focused on rote, memorization behaviors.

Any test question that demands more from a pupil than memory is a higher level item.

Many people believe that essay questions are the only way to test higher level thinking, but that is not the case. Any test question that demands more than memory from a pupil is a higher level item. Thus, any true-false, short-answer, or multiple-choice item that requires the pupil to solve a problem, interpret a chart, or identify the relationship between two phenomena qualifies as a higher level thinking item. Similarly, any assessment that requires pupils to demonstrate their ability to carry out an activity (e.g., give an oral talk, construct a mobile, or read an unfamiliar foreign language passage aloud) also qualifies as a higher level performance.

Interpretive Exercise

The interpretive exercise is a common form of multiple-choice item that can assess higher level thinking. An interpretive exercise gives pupils some information or data and then asks a series of selection-type questions based on that information. Item number 3 on page 109 is an example of an interpretive exercise. Generally, multiple-choice items that ask for interpretations of graphs, charts, reading passages, pictures, or tables (e.g., What is the best title for this story? According to the chart, which year had the largest decline?) are classified as interpretive exercises. Such exercises can assess higher level behaviors like recognizing the relevance of information, identifying warranted and unwarranted generalizations, recognizing assumptions, interpreting experimental findings, and explaining pictorial materials.

Interpretive exercises assess higher level skills because the pupils must interpret or apply given information.

To answer the questions posed, pupils have to interpret, comprehend, analyze, apply, or synthesize the information presented. Interpretive exercises assess higher level skills because they contain all the information needed to answer the questions posed. Thus, if a pupil answers incorrectly, it is because he or she cannot do the thinking or reasoning required by the question, not because the pupil failed to memorize background information.

The principle of testing pupils' higher level skills by providing them with necessary information and then asking questions that require them to use that information can be applied beyond the realm of interpretive exercises. Compare what might be tested in these two versions of the same question.

Version 1
In one or two sentences, describe what Henry Wadsworth Longfellow is telling the reader in the first two verses of his poem "A Psalm of Life," which we read in class but did not discuss.

Version 2
In one or two sentences describe what Henry Wadsworth Longfellow is telling the reader in these lines of his poem "A Psalm of Life."

> Tell me not, in mournful numbers,
>   Life is but an empty dream! —
> For the soul is dead that slumbers,
>   And things are not what they seem.
> Life is real! Life is earnest!
>   And the grave is not its goal;
> Dust thou art, to dust returnest,
>   Was not spoken of the soul.

If a pupil does poorly on the first version, the teacher does not know whether the pupil failed to remember the poem or, remembering the poem, could not interpret what Longfellow was trying to say. In the second version, memory is made irrelevant by providing the needed

TABLE 4.6   ADVANTAGES AND DISADVANTAGES OF TYPES OF TEST ITEMS

Test Type	Advantages	Disadvantages
Multiple-Choice Items	1. Large number of items can be given in a short period 2. Higher and lower level objectives can be assessed 3. Scoring is usually quick and objective 4. Less influenced by guessing	1. Takes substantial time to construct items 2. Not useful when "show your work" is required 3. Often hard to find suitable options 4. Reading ability can influence pupil performance
True-False Items	1. A large number of items can be given in a short time 2. Scoring is usually quick and objective	1. Guessing correct answer is a problem 2. Difficult to find statements that are clearly true or false 3. Items tend to stress recall
Matching Items	1. An efficient way to obtain a great deal of information 2. Easy to construct 3. Scoring is usually quick and objective	1. Focus is mainly on lower level outcomes 2. Homogeneous topics are required
Short-Answer Items	1. Guessing is reduced; pupil must construct an answer 2. Easy to write items 3. Broad range of knowledge can be assessed	1. Scoring can be time-consuming 2. Not useful for complex or extended outcomes
Essay Items	1. Directly assesses complex higher level outcomes 2. Takes less time to construct than other item types 3. Assesses integrative, holistic outcomes	1. Difficult and time-consuming to score 2. Provides a deep but small sample of pupils' performance 3. Bluffing and the quality of writing can influence scores
Interpretive Exercise Items	1. Assesses integrative and interpretive outcomes 2. Assesses higher level outcomes 3. Scoring is usually quick and objective	1. Heavily dependent on pupils' reading ability 2. Difficult to construct items

verses, and inability to interpret the poem's message is the most plausible explanation for a pupil's poor performance. Eliminating memorization in order to answer a higher level thinking question gives a purer assessment of the higher level behavior of interest. However, this approach is only useful when memorization is not the focus of a test. If a teacher wants pupils to memorize poems, formulas, rules, and the like, it makes no sense to provide them on the test.

Like the essay question, the interpretive exercise is a useful way to assess higher level behaviors. However, unlike the essay question, interpretive exercises cannot show how pupils organize their ideas when solving a problem or how well they can produce their own answers to questions.

Table 4.6 summarizes advantages and disadvantages of six test item types.

GENERAL GUIDELINES FOR WRITING AND CRITIQUING TEST ITEMS

Whether writing test items or selecting those prepared by others, there are three general guidelines that help insure good tests: (1) cover important objectives; (2) write clearly and simply; and (3) review items before testing. This section discusses and illustrates these guidelines.

Cover Important Objectives

Test items should reflect important topics and skills emphasized during instruction, should be stated briefly and clearly, and should be self-contained.

One important guideline to keep in mind when preparing tests is not to focus exclusively on trivial knowledge and skills. Studies that examined the nature of the test items written by classroom teachers have found that the vast majority assessed memory-level behaviors (Marso & Pigge, 1989, 1991). From elementary school to the university, items that stress recall and memory are much more extensively used than items that assess higher level thinking and reasoning, mainly because it is much easier to write short-answer or multiple-choice questions. In far too many instances the richness of instruction is undermined by the use of test items that trivialize the breadth and depth of the concepts and skills taught.

Each example that follows states the objective taught, the test item used to assess it, and an alternative item that would have provided a more suitable assessment of the objective. Note that the poor items trivialized higher level objectives by assessing them with a memory item.

1. **Objective:** Given a description of a literary form, the pupils can classify the form as fable, mystery, folktale, or fantasy.
   Poor item: What kind of stories did Aesop tell? _____
   A. fables   B. mysteries   C. folktales   D. fantasies
   Better item: A story tells about the year A.D. 2020 and the adventures of a young Martian named Zik, who traveled to other worlds to capture strange creatures for the zoo at Martian City. This story is best classified as a

   _____.
   A. fable   B. mystery   C. folktale   D. fantasy

2. **Objective:** The pupils can describe similarities and differences in chemical compounds and elements.
   Poor item: Chlorine and bromine are both members of a chemical group called the _____.
   Better item: Chlorine and bromine are both halogens. What similarities do they possess that make them halogens? What are two differences in their chemical properties?

3. **Objective:** The pupils can explain how life was changed for the Sioux Indians when they moved from the forests to the grasslands.
   Poor item: What animal did the Sioux hunt on the grasslands?
   Better item: What are three changes in the life of the Sioux that happened when they moved from the forests to the grasslands?

Test items that do not reflect the important topics of instruction are not valid indicators of student achievement.

There are two main reasons for insuring that the questions in an achievement test align with the important topics and skills that were emphasized during instruction. First, if there is not a good alignment between instruction and the test questions, performance on the test will be a poor indication of actual learning. Pupils may have learned what was taught but were stymied by an invalid test. Low grades usually accompany such invalid tests and can diminish pupils' effort and confidence.

Second, tests that do not align with instruction have little positive influence on motivating and focusing pupil study. If pupils find little relationship between instruction and test content, they will undervalue instruction. Each of you can remember instances when you prepared well for a test based on the teacher's instruction and review only to find that the test contained many questions that focused either on picky, isolated details or on types of problems that were not discussed in class. Recall how you felt when you tried to prepare for the next test given by that teacher.

The problem of mismatch between tests and instruction can be overcome to a large degree by thinking about testing earlier than the day before the test is to be given. With relatively little advance planning, tests that assess the important aspects of instruction can be prepared.

Write Clearly and Simply: Six Rules

If test questions use ambiguous words or sentence structure, include inappropriate vocabulary, or contain clues to the correct answers, the test will not be a valid indicator of pupil achievement. The most important skill in writing or selecting good test items is the ability to express oneself clearly and succinctly. Test items should be (1) briefly stated so pupils do not spend a disproportionate amount of time reading, (2) clearly expressed so pupils understand their task, and (3) capable of standing alone since each item provides a separate measurement.

The following paragraphs describe six rules for writing sound test items. Each is illustrated by some confusing test items prepared by teachers who knew the content they wanted to test but who were unable to clearly state their intent. A better version of the same items is also shown for comparison.

Rule 1: Avoid ambiguous and confusing wording and sentence structure. Pupils must understand test questions. If the wording or sentence structure is confusing and prevents pupils from figuring out what they are being asked, pupils cannot demonstrate their learning. Consider the following test items.

1. All but one of the following is not an element. Which one is not?
   A. carbon   B. salt   C. sugar   D. plastic

2. Maine is not the only state that does not have a border with a neighboring state.   T F

In these examples, the wording and sentence construction are awkward and confusing. The pupil has to sort through multiple negatives to figure out what is being asked. It is better, therefore, to phrase questions briefly, directly, and in the positive voice, as shown in these edited versions.

1. Which one of these is an element?
   A. carbon   B. salt   C. sugar   D. plastic

2. Maine borders another state.   T F

Other items, such as examples 3 and 4, are more than just confusing, they are virtually incomprehensible.

3. What is the relative length of the shortest distance between Chicago and Detroit and Sacramento? _____

4. The _____ produced by the _____ is used by the green _____ to change _____ and _____ into _____. This process is known as _____.

What is a reasonable answer to each? Taken individually, the words in example 3 are not overly difficult, but their sequencing makes their intent altogether unclear. Example 4 is so mutilated with blank spaces that a pupil has to be a mind reader just to figure out what is being asked. No pupil should be confronted by such a question. Pupils will answer items like examples 3 and 4 incorrectly regardless of how well they have mastered the information and skills taught them. The following changes overcome the problems in these two examples.

Test items should be brief, clearly written, and free of ambiguous words so that comprehension is not an issue.

3. Which is closer to Sacramento, Chicago or Detroit? _____

4. The process in which green plants use the sun's energy to turn water and carbon dioxide into food is called _____ .

If a pupil answers the revised items incorrectly, it is because he or she does not know the desired answer. That is acceptable. Remember, the purpose of a test item is not to guarantee correct answers, but to give pupils a *fair* chance to show how much they know about the things they were taught. To do this, test items must be readily comprehended.

Another factor that prevents pupils from being able to focus quickly and clearly on the question being posed is the use of ambiguous words or phrases. Read examples 5, 6, and 7 and try to identify a problem in each that could cause pupils difficulty in deciding how to answer.

5. Shakespeare was the world's greatest playwright.　　　　T　F

6. The most important city in the Southeast is _____.
   A. Atlanta　　B. Miami　　C. New Orleans　　D. Tuscaloosa

7. Write an essay in which you consider the future of atomic energy.

Each example contains an ambiguous term that could be puzzling to pupils and make their choice of an answer difficult. The true-false example contains the undefined word *greatest*. Did the teacher mean that Shakespeare wrote more plays than any other playwright? that more of his plays are still being performed than those of any other playwright? that his plays are required reading in more American classrooms than any other playwright's? Until pupils know what the teacher means by *greatest,* they will have difficulty responding. Example 6 has the same fault. What does the phrase *most important* mean? Each of these cities is important in many ways. Words like *greatest, most important, best,* and similar ambiguous words should be replaced by more specific language, regardless of the type of test item used.

Note the rewritten versions of examples 5 and 6.

5. More of William Shakespeare's plays are required reading in American classrooms than those of any other playwright.　　　　T　F

6. The main transportation center for train and airplane traffic in the Southeast is _____.
   A. Atlanta　　B. Miami　　C. New Orleans　　D. Tuscaloosa

In example 7 the teacher wants the pupils to consider the future of atomic energy. Does the teacher mean compare and contrast atomic energy to fossil fuel; discuss the relative merits of fission versus fusion as a means of generating energy; or explain the positive and negative consequences of increased use of atomic energy? It is not clear. The item needs to be more specific for the pupils to respond in the way the teacher desires as shown in this revised version.

7. Describe the advantages and disadvantages of increased use of atomic energy in the automobile manufacturing process.

In most cases, the teachers who wrote the preceding examples knew what they wanted to ask pupils but were unable to write items that clearly conveyed their intent. Teachers must say precisely what they mean, not assume or hope that their pupils will interpret their test items in the ways intended.

Rule 2: Use appropriate vocabulary. The difficulty level of test questions can be influenced dramatically by vocabulary. If pupils cannot understand the vocabulary used in test questions, their test scores will reflect their vocabulary deficiencies rather than how much they have learned from instruction. Based on sizing-up assessment, every teacher should take into account the vocabulary level of his or her pupils when writing or selecting the items for achievement tests. Note the difference in the following two ways of writing a true-false question to assess pupils' understanding of capillary action, a principle that explains how liquids rise in narrow passages.

The postulation of capillary effectuation promotes elucidation of how pliant substances ascend in incommodious veins.   T F

The principle of capillary action helps explain how liquids rise in small passages.   T F

Clearly, vocabulary level can affect pupils' ability to understand what is being asked in a test question.

Rule 3: Keep questions short and to the point. Items should quickly focus pupils on the question being asked. Examine these questions.

Questions should be short, specific, and written at pupils' vocabulary level.

8. Switzerland
   A. is located in Asia.
   B. produces large quantities of gold.
   C. has no direct access to the ocean.
   D. is a flat, arid plain.

9. Billy's mother wanted to bake an apple pie for his aunt and uncle, who were coming for a visit. Billy had not seen them for many months. When Billy's mother saw that she had no apples in the house, she sent Billy to the store to buy some. Her recipe called for 8 apples to make a pie. If apples at the store cost 30 cents for two, how much money will Billy need to buy eight apples?
   A. $.30   B. $.90   C. $1.20   D. $2.40

In example 8, the stem does not clearly set a problem for the pupil, that is, after pupils read the item stem Switzerland, they still have no idea of the question being asked. Only after reading the stem *and* all the options does the point of the item begin to become clear. The item could be more directly stated as follows.

8. Which of the following statements about the geography of Switzerland is true?

 A. It is located in Asia.
 B. It is a flat, arid plain.
 C. It has no direct access to the ocean.
 D. It has a tropical climate.

Example 9 is intended to determine whether the pupil can correctly calculate the cost of some apples. The information about the aunt and uncle's visit, how long it had been since Billy last saw them, or the lack of apples in the house is not important, can be distracting, and takes time away from relevant items. A better way to state the item is shown here.

9. To make an apple pie Billy's mother needed 8 apples. If apples cost 30 cents for two, how much will 8 apples cost?

 A. $.30 **B.** $.90 **C.** $1.20 **D.** $2.40

In short-answer or completion items, the blanks should come at the end of the sentence so pupils know what kind of a response is required. Compare these two items and notice how placing the blank at the end helps convey what the item is about.

 _____ and _____ are the names of two rivers that meet in Pittsburgh.

 The names of two rivers that meet in Pittsburgh are _____ and _____.

Matching items can also be written to help pupils focus more quickly on the questions being asked. Look over example 10 and suggest a change that would focus pupils more clearly on the questions they have to answer.

10. Draw a line to match the president in Column A with his accomplishment in Column B.

Column A	Column B
G. Washington	signed the Emancipation Proclamation
T. Jefferson	president during the New Deal
U. Grant	first president of the United States
F. Roosevelt	head of Northern troops in Civil War
	main author of the Declaration of Independence

Most matching items can be improved by placing the column with the lengthier descriptions on the left and the column with the shorter descriptions on the right, as shown next.

10. Draw a line to match the president in Column B with his accomplishment in Column A. One accomplishment will not be used.

Column A
signed the Emancipation Proclamation
president during the New Deal
first president of the United States
head of Northern troops in Civil War
main author of the Declaration of Independence

Column B
G. Washington
T. Jefferson
U. Grant
F. Roosevelt

Rule 4: Write items that have one correct answer. With the exception of essay questions, most paper-and-pencil test items are designed to have pupils select or supply one best answer. With this goal in mind, read examples 11, 12, and 13. See how many correct answers you can provide for each item.

With the exception of essays, most test items should have only one correct answer.

11. Who was George Washington? _____.

12. Ernest Hemingway wrote _____.

13. Where is Dublin?
   A. south of Scotland   **B.** near England
   C. in Ireland   **D.** in the Irish Sea

Each of these items has more than one correct answer. George Washington was the first president of the United States, but he also was a member of the Continental Congress, commander of the Continental Army, a Virginian, a surveyor, a slave owner, and a man with false teeth. Faced with such an item, pupils ask themselves Which of the many things I know about George Washington should I answer? Similarly, Ernest Hemingway wrote short stories, letters, in Spain, and in pencil, as well as famous novels such as *The Old Man and the Sea.*

Examples 11, 12, and 13 can be restated so that pupils know precisely what is being asked. Notice how each question asks for something specific—a name or a country—thus indicating to pupils the nature of the expected answer.

11. What is the name of the first president of the United States? _____.

12. The name of the author of *The Old Man and the Sea* is _____.

13. In what country is Dublin located?
   A. England   **B.** France   **C.** Germany   **D.** Ireland   **E.** Spain

Items with more than one correct answer occur much more often in short-answer and completion items than in selection items. Unless short-answer or completion items are stated specifically and narrowly, the teacher can expect many different responses. The dilemma for the teacher then becomes whether to give credit for answers that are technically correct but not the desired one.

Rule 5: Give information about the nature of the desired answer. While the failure to properly focus pupils is common to all types of test items, it is most often seen in essay items. Despite pupils' freedom to structure their own responses, essay questions should still require pupils to demonstrate mastery of key ideas, principles, or concepts that were taught. An essay, like any other type of test item, should be constructed to find out how well pupils have learned the things they were taught.

Here are a few typical essay questions written by classroom teachers.

14. Compare and contrast the North and South in the Civil War. Support your views.

15. Describe what happened to art during the Renaissance.

16. Why should you study science?

In each of these questions, the pupil's task is not clearly defined. When pupils encounter global questions such as these they may have little idea of what the teacher is looking for and may end up with a poor grade because they incorrectly guessed the teacher's intent. This practice is unfair to pupils and produces test results that do not reflect their achievement.

Essay questions should focus students' answers on the major points covered by instruction.

In order to determine whether pupils have learned what was taught, essay questions should be narrowed to focus pupils on the areas of interest. Pupils should be informed about the nature and scope of the expected answer. While essay questions should provide the pupil freedom to select, organize, state, and defend positions, they should not give pupils total freedom to write whatever they want. Obviously, to develop a well-focused essay question the teacher must give considerable thought to the purpose and scope of the question before actually writing it.

Examples 14, 15, and 16 have been rewritten to more precisely reflect the teacher's intent. Notice how the vague and ambiguous directions (support your views; describe) are made clearer to pupils in the revised questions.

14. What forces led to the outbreak of the Civil War? Indicate in your discussion economic conditions, foreign policies, and social conditions in both the North and the South before the war. Which two factors were most influential in the start of the Civil War? Give two reasons to support your choice of each factor. Your answer will be graded on your discussion of the differences between the North and South at the start of the war and the strength of the arguments you advance to support your choice of the two factors most influential in the start of the war (30 minutes).

15. Compare art during the Renaissance to art prior to the movement in terms of the portrayal of the human figure, use of color, and emphasis on religious themes. Your essay will be judged in terms of the distinctions

you identify between the two periods and the explanations you provide to account for the differences.

16. Give two reasons a third grade pupil should study science. What are some things that studying science teaches us? What are some jobs that use science? Write your answer in at least five complete sentences.

Certainly these are not the only ways that these essay items could have been rewritten, but these revisions point out the need for focus in essay questions. When pupils approach these revised items, they have a clear sense of what is expected of them; they no longer have to guess what the scope and direction of their answers should be. Note also that it is much more difficult for the pupil to bluff an answer to the revised items than it is to the initial, broadly stated items. The revised items call for answers that are specifically related to instruction, and therefore test what was taught and make scoring easier. In order to write such items, however, the teacher must have a clear sense of what he or she is trying to assess before administering the essay.

To summarize, regardless of the particular type of test item used, pupils should be given a clear idea of what their task is. In the case of multiple-choice items this may mean elaborating a stem in order to clarify the options. In matching items it may involve putting the longer options in the left column. In short-answer or completion items it may mean placing the blank at the end of the statement or specifying precisely the nature of the desired answer. In essay questions it may mean elaborating to include information about the scope, direction, and scoring criteria for a desired answer. In all cases, the intent is to allow the pupil to respond validly and efficiently to the items.

For all types of test items, pupils should have a clear sense of what is expected of them.

Rule 6: Do not provide clues to the correct answer. The item-writing rules discussed thus far have all been aimed at problems that inhibited pupils from doing their best. However, the opposite problem arises when test items contain clues that help pupils answer questions correctly even though they have not learned the content being tested. Many types of clues may appear in items: grammatical clues, implausible option clues, and specific determiner clues. Try to identify the clue in examples 17 and 18.

Test item writers should take care not to provide grammatical clues, implausible option clues, or specific determiner clues.

17. A figure that has eight sides is called an _____.
   A. pentagon   B. quadrilateral   C. octagon   D. ogive

18. As compared to autos of the 1960s, autos in the 1980s _____.
   A. more horsepower.
   B. to use more fuel.
   C. contain more safety features.
   D. was less often constructed in foreign countries.

These examples contain grammatical clues. As in example 17, using the article *a* or *an* at the end of the question or stem indicates to pupils what letter will begin the next word. The *an* before the blank tells the pupil that the next word must begin with a vowel, so the options pentagon and quadrilateral cannot be correct. There are two ways to correct this problem: replace the single article with the combined *a(n)* or get rid of the article altogether by writing the question in the plural form.

17. Figures that have eight sides are called _____.

    A. pentagons   **B.** quadrilaterals   **C.** octagons   **D.** ogives

In example 18, only option C grammatically fits the stem. Regardless of pupils' knowledge, they can select the correct answer because of the grammatical clue. The corrected item might read

18. As compared to autos of the 1960s, autos in the 1980s

    A. have more horsepower.
    B. use more fuel.
    C. contain more safety features.
    D. are always constructed in foreign countries.

Now try to find the clues in examples 19 and 20.

19. Which of the following best describes an electron?

    A. negative particle
    B. neutral particle
    C. positive particle
    D. a voting machine

20. Match the correct phrase in Column A with the term in Column B. Write the *letter* of the term in Column B on the line in front of the correct phrase in Column A.

Column A	Column B
_____ 1. type of flower	A. cobra
_____ 2. poisonous snake	B. fission
_____ 3. how amoebae reproduce	C. green
_____ 4. color of chlorophyll	D. hydrogen
_____ 5. chemical element	E. rose

A distractor is a reasonable but incorrect option in a multiple-choice item.

Example 19 contains a clue that is less obvious than those in examples 17 and 18, but which is quite common in multiple-choice items. One of the options is inappropriate or implausible and therefore is immediately dismissed by the pupils. Choice D, a voting machine, is dismissed as an unlikely answer by all but the most careless readers. As much as possible, options in test questions should be realistic and reasonable choices. A useful rule of thumb is to have at least three incorrect (but reasonable) options, or **distractors,** in each multiple-choice item.

The more choices pupils have, the less likely it is that they can guess the correct answer. Understanding this, teachers sometimes write three or four good options for an item and then add a fourth or fifth, such as none of the above or all of the above. It is usually better to avoid such general options.

Example 20 is a very easy question; the topics are so different from one another that many of the options in Column B are implausible matches to the statements in Column A. The item does not test one homogeneous subject area.

Consider the following matching item, that tests pupils' knowledge of a single, homogeneous topic. Note the difficulty in answering this item compared to example 20.

A matching item should test the students' knowledge of a single homogeneous topic.

20. Match the names of the animals in Column A to their correct classification in Column B. Write the *letter* of the correct classification on the line in front of each animal name. The choices in Column B may be used more than once.

Column A

_____ 1. alligator
_____ 2. condor
_____ 3. frog
_____ 4. porpoise
_____ 5. snake
_____ 6. salamander

Column B

A. amphibian
B. bird
C. fish
D. mammal
E. reptile

The revised item is a better test of pupils' knowledge in two ways. First, it does not include the obvious matches and mismatches that occur when many unrelated topics are contained in the same matching item. The revised version focuses on a single topic, classification of animals into groups. Second, unlike example 20, the revised item has an unequal number of entries in Columns A and B. Unequal entries in the two columns of a matching item prevent pupils from getting the last match correct by the process of elimination.

Look for the clues in examples 21 and 22.

21. Some people think the moon is made of green cheese.   T F

22. One should never phrase a test item in the negative.   T F

These items contain clues that are called **specific determiners.** In true-false questions, words such as *always, never, all,* and *none* tend to appear in statements that are false, and testwise pupils tend to answer accordingly. Conversely, words like *some, sometimes,* and *may* tend to appear in statements that are true. Thus, in example 21, it is reasonable to assume that *some* people think the moon is made of green cheese, so T should be marked. On the other hand, example 22 must be marked F if there is even a single situation in which a test item can reasonably be stated in the negative (e.g., Which one of these is *not* an example of democracy?).

Table 4.7 provides a list of useful item-writing rules for each of the various types discussed in this chapter (Gallagher, 1998; Gronlund, 1998). These rules supplement the more general item-writing principles just considered.

TABLE 4.7 SUGGESTIONS FOR PREPARING TEST ITEMS

Multiple-Choice Items
- ♦ Set pupils' task in the item stem.
- ♦ Include repeated words in the stem.
- ♦ Avoid grammatical clues.
- ♦ Use positive wording if possible.
- ♦ Include only plausible options.
- ♦ Avoid using *all of the above* or *none of above.*

True-False Items
- ♦ Make statements clearly true or false.
- ♦ Avoid specific determiners.
- ♦ Do not arrange responses in a pattern.
- ♦ Do not select textbook sentences.

Matching Items
- ♦ Use a homogeneous topic.
- ♦ Put longer options in left column.
- ♦ Provide clear direction.
- ♦ Use unequal numbers of entries in the two columns.

Completion and Short-Answer Items
- ♦ Provide a clear focus for the desired answer.
- ♦ Avoid grammatical clues.
- ♦ Put blanks at the end of the item.
- ♦ Do not select textbook sentences.

Essay Items
- ♦ Use several short-essay questions rather than one long one.
- ♦ Provide a clear focus in questions.
- ♦ Indicate scoring criteria to pupils.

Review Items before Testing

Is it helpful to have a colleague or friend critique test items before the test is administered to students.

The best advice that can be given to improve most classroom tests is to review them before reproducing and administering them to pupils. Having written or selected the items for a chapter or unit test, it is recommended that a teacher wait one day and then reread them. The teacher should also ask a colleague, spouse, or friend to review the items critically.

Most of the links in the chain of achievement testing—the importance of providing pupils with good instruction, the decisions that must be made in planning achievement tests, the instructional review that should precede testing, and the construction or selection of test items that give pupils a fair chance to demonstrate their learning—have all been examined. Two final links that influence the adequacy of achievement tests are (1) assembling and administering the test and (2) scoring the test.

ASSEMBLING THE TEST

Once items have been reviewed and revised, they must be arranged into a test. If a textbook test is used, the items are already arranged and ready for copying. In a teacher-made test, similar types of items should be grouped together and kept separate from other item types. Grouping items by type avoids the necessity of pupils shifting from one response mode to another as they move from item to item. Also, a single set of directions can be used for all of the items in that test section, making scoring easier.

When a test is assembled, test items of the same type should be grouped together.

Another important consideration in assembling the test is the order in which the item types are presented to pupils. Selection items should be first and supply items last. Within the supply section, short-answer or completion questions should be placed before essay questions. Finally, in arranging items on the test, remember these common-sense practices.

When a test is assembled, supply items should be placed last.

1. Little pupils write big, so leave enough space, especially on essay tests, for young pupils to write their answers.
2. Do not split a multiple-choice or matching item across two different pages of the test.
3. Place multiple-choice options on a new line below the stem.
4. Number test items, especially if pupils must record answers on a separate answer sheet or in a special place on the test.

Each section of the test should have directions that focus pupils on what to do, how to respond, and where to place their answer. For older pupils, it is also helpful to indicate the number of points that will be given to each test section so they can make decisions about how to allocate their time. Lack of directions is one of the most common faults in teachers' tests. Here are some sample directions, ones that give specific guidance to students.

Each section of the test should have directions telling students what to do, how to respond, and where to place their answer.

- ◆ Items 1 to 15 are multiple-choice items. Read each item carefully and write the *letter* of your answer on the line in front of the question number.
- ◆ Answer each question by writing the correct answer in the space below the question. No answer should be longer than one sentence.
- ◆ Mark each statement true or false. *Circle* the letter (T or F) of your choice.

Enough copies should be reproduced so that each pupil has his or her own copy. Writing the test questions on the blackboard can be time-consuming, create problems for pupils with poor vision, and encourage pupils to look around the room during the test. Oral tests place a premium on listening ability and prevent pupils from working at their own pace.

They also put pupils with hearing or limited English-speaking ability at a severe disadvantage. For these reasons, oral tests should be avoided unless listening skills are being assessed.

The more items on a test the higher its reliability, because the teacher can look at a larger sample of pupil performance.

Tests that promote valid decisions also need to be reliable. The main factors in attaining reliable achievement tests are the number and representativeness of the items included on the test and the objectivity of scoring. In general, the more items on the test the higher its reliability, because the test allows a teacher to view a larger sample of pupil performance. Which of the following spelling tests do you think would produce the more stable and consistent information about a pupil's spelling achievement? Test 1, which consists of a single word selected from a 100-word list, or Test 2, which contains a sample of 15 words selected from the same 100-word list?

Table 4.8 summarizes guidelines for assembling tests.

TABLE 4.8   GUIDELINES FOR ASSEMBLING A TEST

◆ Organize the test by item type: selection before supply, essay last.

◆ Allow sufficient space for written responses, especially for young children's essay items.

◆ Don't split multiple-choice or matching items across two pages; separate stem from options in multiple-choice questions.

◆ Number test items.

◆ Provide clear directions for each section of the test; for older pupils, indicate value of each section or question.

◆ Provide enough questions to assure reliability.

ADMINISTERING THE TEST

Test administration is concerned with the physical and psychological setting in which pupils take the test. The aim is to establish both a physical and psychological setting that permits pupils to maximize their test performance.

Physical Setting

One way to minimize interruptions is to post a sign on the door indicating testing is occurring.

Pupils should have a quiet, comfortable environment in which to take the test. Interruptions should be minimized by posting a sign on the door indicating testing is going on. When an interruption does occur, the teacher must make a judgment about whether it is fair for pupils to continue with the test. Obviously a 1-minute interruption is less disruptive than a

15-minute fire drill, which gives pupils an opportunity to talk to one another about the test. If it is judged that an interruption is sufficiently disruptive to diminish pupils' ability to provide a fair and representative indication of their achievement, testing should be terminated.

Occasionally typographical errors or problems with items are not detected until testing has begun, usually when a pupil points out a problem. In such situations, an announcement should be made to the whole class informing them of the problem (e.g., Please correct item 17 in the following way or Option B in item 29 should be changed to . . .). The decision of whether and how to answer pupil questions during testing rests with the individual teacher. This is appropriate as long as the teacher is consistent in responding to all pupils who ask questions.

Psychological Setting

Establishing a productive psychological setting that reduces pupil anxiety and sets a proper atmosphere for testing is as important as providing a comfortable physical environment. Giving pupils advance notice about the test, giving them an opportunity to prepare for it, and providing a good chapter or unit review will help diminish test anxiety. Even so, it is probably impossible to completely allay all pupils' test anxiety.

Test anxiety is diminished by giving students advance notice of the test, an opportunity to prepare for it, and by conducting a test review.

The line between overemphasizing the importance of the test, thereby heightening pupil anxiety, and underemphasizing the test, thereby diminishing pupil motivation, is hard to define. Tests should be taken seriously by pupils and they should be encouraged to do their best. The appropriate middle ground between over- and underemphasizing the importance varies with the age and characteristics of pupils. Each teacher must find this middle ground for his or her class, knowing that whatever preparations are chosen, there will usually be some pupils who will be very anxious about their performance and some who will not care.

Accommodations for Student Testing

Test accommodations for pupils with disabilities are of two types: those in test administration and those in the test itself. The most common accommodations of each type are listed.

Accommodations in test administration are as follows:

- ◆ Read directions and/or questions out loud to pupil
- ◆ Have pupil repeat directions to ensure understanding
- ◆ Tape record pupil's answers
- ◆ Provide extra time or make the test untimed
- ◆ Divide the test into separate sections to be administered at different times

- ◆ Change the setting of the test to cut down distractions
- ◆ Allow pupil to use notes or definitions
- ◆ Give pupil math and science formulas to decrease reliance on memory

Accommodations in testing are as follows:

- ◆ Divide the test into sections for better pupil focus
- ◆ Spread items out on the page; leave enough space for answers
- ◆ Arrange items from concrete to abstract
- ◆ Present directions or a sequence of steps the pupil should follow
- ◆ Ease reading problems by putting each sentence on a single line
- ◆ Provide a sample of each item type
- ◆ Include definitions and formulas in the items
- ◆ Provide the test in Braille, large print, native language, or on tape, as needed

Cheating

Teachers can discourage cheating with seating arrangements, careful proctoring, and swift punishment of those who do cheat.

Unfortunately, cheating on tests is a fairly common occurrence that has a variety of motives. Pupils may experience external pressure from teachers or parents to do well; they may fail to prepare for tests and rely upon cheating to get them through; they may be in an intensively competitive classroom where the teacher's policy is one of grading on the curve; or they may be confused about what is acceptable behavior in a classroom where "everybody else does it."

The forms of cheating vary from looking at another's paper, to bringing crib sheets to an exam, to hiring someone to take a test . No matter how or why it is done, cheating is dishonest and unacceptable behavior. It is the teacher's responsibility to discourage cheating with seating arrangements, careful proctoring, and other activities (Slavin, 1994). Table 4.9 presents suggestions to control cheating, both before and during testing.

If some pupils do cheat, those who do not are unfairly penalized for their appropriate and ethical behavior. Teachers should discourage cheating and penalize pupils caught doing it, because it is both an immoral activity and provides a distorted, invalid picture of a pupil's achievement. It is, however, important to have strong evidence to support charges of cheating, since pupils have certain due-process rights when accused.

Table 4.10 summarizes important concerns in test administration.

TABLE 4.9   STRATEGIES TO PREVENT CHEATING

Strategies Prior to Testing
♦ Teach well; be sensitive to pupils' instructional needs and misunderstandings.
♦ Announce the test ahead of time; give pupils ample opportunity to prepare.
♦ Describe for pupils the general nature and content of the test.
♦ Identify for pupils what constitutes cheating and explain the consequences if caught.

Strategies During Testing
♦ Have pupils remove all unneeded materials from their desktop.
♦ Space pupils about the room; have them sit in alternating seats.
♦ Watch students during testing; move about the room quietly.
♦ Forbid sharing of materials like erasers, calculators, and charts.
♦ Prepare different test forms or arrange pages in varying orders.
♦ Enforce established cheating rules.

TABLE 4.10   GUIDELINES FOR ADMINISTERING A TEST

♦ Provide a quiet, comfortable setting.
♦ Try to anticipate and avoid questions with good directions.
♦ Provide a good psychological setting; provide advance notice, review, and encouragement for pupils to do their best.
♦ Discourage cheating through seating arrangements, circulating the room, and enforcement of rules and penalties.
♦ Help pupils keep track of time.

SCORING TESTS

After administering a test, the teacher has a stack of papers to score. The process of scoring a test involves measurement, that is, representing each pupil's performance with a number using the same criteria. After scoring, as we will see in Chapter 6, scores are converted to pupil grades.

Measurement is the process of representing an individual's performance level with a number.

Of course, when pupil achievement is scored, each pupil should be scored in the same way. Whatever rules are used for scoring one pupil should also be applied to all other pupils. It would be unfair to give Jessy

5 points for getting an item correct and Nita or Arthur only 2 points for their equally correct answer to the same item. Thus, good measurement requires that common rules be used when assigning scores.

Scoring Selection Items

Selection items can be scored objectively because they are usually brief and have only one correct answer.

Selection items are the easiest to score, short-answer and completion items next easiest, and essays most difficult. Pupils respond to selection items by writing, circling, or marking the letter of their response. Scoring selection items is essentially a clerical task that involves comparing each pupil's answers to a **key,** which lists the correct answers. The number of matches indicates the pupil's score on the test. Scoring selection test items is usually quite objective. An objective score is one in which independent scorers will arrive at the same or very similar scores. Selection items can be scored objectively mainly because the responses are brief and there is usually one clearly correct answer to each item.

Subjective test scores are those where independent scorers have difficulty arriving at the same or similar scores.

To instill confidence in a test score, it is important that the score is as objective as possible.

As pupils' responses to items become more lengthy and complex, and as the clarity of what is a correct or incorrect answer blurs, scoring becomes more subjective and time-consuming. A **subjective score** is one that independent scorers will score differently. If a test is subjective, a pupil's performance depends as much on *who* scores the test as on the pupil's answers. It has long been known that even when the same person scores the same essay test twice, there is no guarantee that the scores will be the same or similar (Starch & Elliott, 1912; Starch & Elliott, 1913). To have confidence in a test score it is important that the score is objective.

Scoring Short-Answer and Completion Items

As long as short-answer, completion, and other open-ended supply items are clearly written, focus pupils on their task, and call for a short response such as a word, phrase, date, or number, scoring is not difficult and can be quite objective. However, as items require lengthier pupil responses, subjectivity of scoring increases because there is greater interpretation of pupils' responses. No matter how well a teacher has prepared and reviewed test items of any kind, he or she never knows how an item will work until *after* it is administered to pupils. Inevitably, especially with supply items, there are occasions when pupils come up with correct answers that the teacher did not expect. The pupils' answers are correct given their interpretation, but incorrect given the teacher's intention. How should such occurrences be handled in scoring?

In scoring unexpected responses, teachers must decide if wrong answers are the result of faulty test items or a lack of student learning.

How a teacher interprets such unexpected interpretations and responses influences pupils' test scores and ultimately their grades. For example, suppose that one item in a 10-item achievement test reveals many unexpected but correct responses. If the teacher simply marks these responses wrong because they do not match the answer key, he or she may be penalizing pupils for his or her own faulty test item. This 10 percent deduction could make a big difference in a pupil's eventual grade. In reviewing unexpected responses, the teacher must decide if wrong answers are the result of faulty items or a lack of pupil learning. Test scores should not automatically be raised simply because many pupils got an item wrong, but the teacher must make a judgment about the likely source of the problem and how it will be rectified, if at all.

In the end, scoring decisions rest with the teacher. Teachers must decide who is at fault when pupils misinterpret an item and whether pupils should lose credit for wrong answers on items that were not discussed in class. Two principles should be considered in making such decisions. First, since the test scores should reflect pupils' achievement on the chapter or unit, the scores should deal only with topics that were taught and with items that were clearly written. If points are deducted for things not taught or for misinterpreting ambiguous questions, the score does not reflect true achievement. Second, whatever decision is made regarding the scoring of poor or untaught items, it should be applied uniformly to all pupils.

Three guidelines can help to overcome problems of scoring open-ended supply items.

Test scores that reflect ambiguous or untaught items are less-valid indicators of student achievement.

1. **Prepare an answer key** before scoring. Determine what is being sought in pupil responses *before* scoring.
2. **Determine how factors** such as spelling, grammar, and punctuation, which are usually ancillary to the main focus of the response, will be handled in scoring. Should points be taken off for such factors? Decide before scoring and inform pupils before testing.
3. **If pupils' responses are correct** but not initially considered in guideline 1, give credit to each unexpected but correct response.

Scoring Essay Items

Essay questions represent the ultimate in scoring complexity because they permit pupils to construct their own lengthy responses to questions. As a result, interpretation of essay responses is necessary. Further, essay responses are presented in a form that contributes to subjective scoring.

Think of an essay answer you have written. Remember what it looked like spread out over the page. Keep in mind that the purpose of the question was to determine how well you understood and could manipulate information you had been taught. However, the person who scored your essay was probably influenced by many of the following characteristics:

- ◆ your handwriting
- ◆ your writing style, including sentence structure and flow
- ◆ your spelling and grammar

♦ your neatness
♦ the teacher's fatigue
♦ the teacher's knowledge of your identity
♦ the location of your test in the pile of essays

Each of these factors can influence a teacher's reaction to an essay answer, although none of them has anything to do with the actual content of a response. For example, penmanship that is so poor it forces the teacher to figure out what each scribbled word means will frustrate the teacher and divert attention away from the content of the answer. The essay likely will get a lower score than that of a pupil who provides the same answer but in more legible handwriting. A pupil whose answer flows smoothly and interestingly from point to point likely will get a higher score than a pupil who states the same points but in a string of simple, declarative sentences. Poor grammar and misspelled words create a negative impression and may also divert a teacher's attention from the content of the pupil's response.

Scoring essays is also a time-consuming and tiring task, and scores may be influenced by how alert the teacher is when the essays are read. For example, after a teacher has read the same general essay response 15 or so times, boredom and fatigue can set in and the next pupil who provides essentially the same answer may get a score different from those whose essays were read earlier.

In almost all essay questions there is at least one point when the reader must interpret what the pupil meant to say because the pupil expressed his or her thoughts ambiguously. Knowledge of the author's identity often influences the teacher's interpretation. For example, Roger and Alicia each answered an essay question and included some statements that were ambiguous. The teacher knows that Roger is an interested, able pupil who always does well on tests and in class discussions. The teacher reasons that although Roger didn't make this point clearly, he probably knew the answer even though it didn't come out right. And Roger will get the credit. The teacher also knows that Alicia generally does poorly in school and remembers her indifference during a recent class discussion. The teacher thinks since Alicia is a poor student and doesn't care about this subject, she probably had no idea of what was correct here. And Alicia will not get credit. One way to avoid such biased scoring is to identify papers by number or to have pupils put their names on the last page of a test.

Lastly, consider the following situation. At the end of an essay exam the teacher allows a student to put her test paper anywhere in the pile of pupil papers he will grade. The instructor tells her that he will start with the top paper and work down through the pile in order. Where should the student place hers? Where would you place your test paper? Could the choice within the stack make a difference in the score? If you think it could, what does this say about the potential subjectivity of essay tests?

If essay scores are to validly represent pupils' achievement and be used as a basis for grading or making other decisions about pupils, it is important for the teacher to have confidence that the scores are as objective as possible. This confidence is influenced by the scoring approach the teacher employs, either holistic scoring or analytic scoring.

Holistic versus Analytic Scoring

Teachers typically use two approaches to scoring essay questions: holistic or analytic. **Holistic scoring** reflects the teacher's *overall impression* of the essay by providing a single score or grade. **Analytic scoring,** on the other hand, views the essay as being made up of many components and provides *separate scores* for each one. Thus, an essay that is scored analytically might result in separate scores for accuracy, organization, supporting arguments, and grammar and spelling. Analytic scoring provides more detailed feedback that pupils can use to improve their essays. Consequently, it is especially useful when judging initial drafts of essays. However, attempting to score more than three or four separate features often makes scoring confusing and time-consuming. In both holistic and analytic scoring, helpful or encouraging suggestions written on pupils' tests are recommended.

Holistic scoring provides a single, overall impression of the complete essay. Analytic scoring provides a separate score for each component of the essay.

Steps to Ensure Objectivity

Whether the teacher's approach to scoring is holistic or analytic, there are steps he or she can take to improve objectivity and reduce, if not eliminate, subjectivity in essay scoring. Certain steps should be followed to ensure that pupils' essays are scored objectively. Although the following suggestions are time-consuming, they are necessary if scores are to be valid for decision making.

1. *Define what constitutes a good answer before administering an essay question.* The less focused an essay question is, the broader the range of pupil responses and the more difficult to apply uniform scoring criteria. Including information about the pupils' specific task, the scope of the essay, and the scoring criteria in the essay directions has numerous benefits. First, it helps pupils respond to a precise set of teacher expectations. This, in turn, diminishes scoring subjectivity. Second, by writing questions that clearly indicate the characteristics of a good answer, the teacher automatically has to confront the issue of scoring. The criteria that focus pupils' responses are also the basic criteria used in scoring the pupils' answers.

A well-focused essay item includes scoring criteria and specific information about the pupils' task.

2. *Decide and tell pupils how handwriting, punctuation, spelling, organization, and spelling will be scored.*

3. *If possible, score pupils anonymously.* This will help keep the scoring objective by eliminating knowledge and accompanying perceptions of the pupil's effort, ability, interest, and past performance. Each pupil should be scored on the basis of present performance, not in terms of teacher perceptions or past performance.

TABLE 4.11   GUIDELINES FOR SCORING A TEST

♦ Test scores should be based upon topics that were taught and items that are clearly written.

♦ Make sure the same rules are used to score all pupils.

♦ Be alert for the following distractors that may affect the objectivity of essay scores: writing style, grammar and spelling, neatness, scorer fatigue, prior performance, and carryover effects.

♦ Define what constitutes a good answer before administering an essay question.

♦ Score all answers to the first essay question before moving on to score the succeeding question.

♦ Read essay questions a second time after initial scoring.

♦ Carry out posttest review in order to locate faulty test items and when necessary to make scoring adjustments.

4. *In tests with multiple essays, score all pupils' answers to the first question before moving to the second question.* If it is difficult to score a single essay question objectively, it is more difficult to score two or three different essay questions in succession. Scoring all the answers to a single essay question at one time guards against the carryover effect, or the tendency to let the reaction to a pupil's initial essay influence the perception of succeeding essays written by that same pupil.

Before scores of essay items are finalized, the teacher should check for objectivity by rereading and, if necessary, rescoring a sample of essays.

5. *Read essay answers a second time after initial scoring.* The best way to check for objectivity in essay scoring is to have a second individual read and score pupils' essays using the same criteria the teacher used. Since this is usually impractical, except when making very important decisions (e.g., awarding a scholarship, selecting for an honor society), an acceptable procedure is for the teacher to reread and, if necessary, rescore a sample of papers. Two scorings by the same person, even if done quickly and on only a sample of papers, are better than a single scoring and lead to more objective decision making.

Essay questions permit the assessment of many thought processes that can be evaluated in no other way. When such thought processes are part of the instructional objectives and are actively taught to pupils, they should be assessed to obtain a representative picture of pupil learning. Nevertheless, when using essay questions, the difficulty inherent in scoring them and the dangers of scoring them improperly must be realized. A teacher should use essay questions if they are the best way to assess what has been taught, but time should be set aside to score them objectively so that their results can be used with confidence.

Table 4.11 summarizes guidelines to follow when scoring tests.

DISCUSSING TEST RESULTS WITH PUPILS

Pupils want information about their test performance. Teachers can provide this information through comments written on papers, tests, or projects that indicate to pupils what they did well and how they might improve. It also is helpful to go over the results of a test with pupils. This is especially useful when the pupils have their marked tests in front of them during the review. The teacher should pay special attention to items that a large number of students got wrong in order to clear up misconceptions and to indicate the nature of the desired answer. For older pupils it also is helpful to explain how the tests were scored and graded. Finally, opportunity should be provided for shy pupils to discuss the test in private with the teacher.

Going over test results when pupils have the graded test in front of them is useful.

CHAPTER SUMMARY

♦ Official assessments help teachers make summative decisions such as assigning grades, recommending pupils for promotion, placing pupils in groups, and referring pupils to special-education services.

♦ Official assessments are taken very seriously by pupils, parents, school administrators, and the public at large because they are public and can have tangible consequences for pupils. The primary aim in assessing pupil achievement is to provide a fair opportunity for students to show what they have learned from the instruction provided.

♦ The methods used to assess pupil learning depend on the objectives and instruction provided. Methods that permit the pupils to show the behaviors taught are essential for valid assessment. Multiple-choice, matching, or true-false questions are used when pupils are taught to choose or select answers; short-answer or essay questions are used when pupils are taught to explain, construct, or defend answers; and actual performances are used when pupils are taught to demonstrate or show answers. The most basic requirement for official assessments is that they assess what pupils were taught.

♦ The decision whether to construct a test or use a textbook test depends upon how closely instruction followed the lead of the textbook. The more a teacher supplements or omits from the textbook, the less likely the textbook test will be a valid indication of pupils' learning.

♦ Preparing pupils for official assessments requires careful teacher thought and planning. First and foremost, teachers should provide the best instruction possible prior to assessment. Good instruction should be followed up by a review, which gives pupils a chance to ask questions and practice important behaviors and skills that will be tested. Pupils, especially those in early elementary grades, should be given practice with unfamiliar item formats before testing. Pupils should be informed in advance of the time, nature, coverage, and format of the test.

♦ In preparing pupils for testing, teachers should discuss items and examples similar but not identical to the actual test items.

♦ Paper-and-pencil tests can be composed of two types of questions: selection (multiple-choice, true-false, and matching) and supply (short-answer, completion, and essay). Both types of questions can assess higher and lower level thinking.

♦ Selection items can be answered quickly, cover a broad sample of instructional topics, and can be scored objectively. However, they are time-consuming to construct and guessing is a problem. Supply items can be prepared easily, afford pupils opportunity to construct their own answers, and discourage guessing. However they are difficult and time-consuming to score and tend to cover a limited number of instructional topics.

♦ Teachers should try to include higher level thinking questions in both their instruction and formal assessments. The interpretive exercise is a useful way to incorporate higher level skills into paper-and-pencil assessments.

♦ When writing or selecting paper-and-pencil test questions, three general guidelines should be followed: cover important topics and behaviors, write clearly and simply, and review items before testing.

♦ Most of the items in teacher-made and textbook tests are at the recall or memory level of thinking because such items are easiest to write. However, if tests are to be valid, they should reflect all the content and behaviors taught, both lower and higher level.

♦ Six rules that guide item writing are (1) avoid wording that is ambiguous and confusing; (2) use appropriate vocabulary and sentence structure for pupils; (3) keep questions short and to the point; (4) write items that have one correct answer; (5) give pupils information about the desired answer; and (6) do not provide clues to the correct answer.

♦ In assembling items into a test, the various item types should be grouped together. Selection items should be placed at the start of the test, and supply items at the end. Short-answer items should be placed before essay items.

♦ Each section of the test should have directions that tell pupils what to do, how to respond, and where to place their answers. Older pupils may also be helped by knowing how much each item is worth. Each pupil should have his or her own copy of the test.

♦ Making pupils comfortable, providing advance notice of a test, reviewing important objectives, and encouraging pupils to do their best without exerting undo pressure will help set a suitable physical and psychological climate in which pupils can perform their best.

♦ Accommodations for pupils can be made in constructing the test and in administering the test.

♦ Cheating is an unacceptable, dishonest testing behavior. It is the teacher's responsibility to establish conditions that reduce cheating such as pupil seating arrangements, constantly circulating around the classroom, forbidding pupils to share materials, and enforcing cheating rules and penalties.

♦ An objective test item is one that independent scorers will score the same or similarly. A subjective item is one that independent scorers will not score the same. Factors that contribute to subjectivity include handwriting, writing style, grammar, and knowledge of the pupil's identity.

♦ Selection items are usually easy to score objectively because they involve comparing a pupil's response to an answer key. Supply items become increasingly subjective as pupils are given more freedom to construct their own answers. Essay items are the most subjective type of item.

◆ The two principal methods of scoring essay tests are holistic scoring, which produces a single overall score for an essay, and analytic scoring, which produces a number of scores corresponding to particular features of the essay (e.g., organization and style).

◆ Essay tests are the most difficult to score objectively. In order to make essay scoring objective, a teacher should decide what constitutes a good answer before scoring; decide how punctuation and grammar will be scored; score essays anonymously if possible; read all responses to a single essay question before reading other questions; and reread essays to corroborate initial scores.

◆ After a test is scored, items that show unusual answers or response patterns should be reviewed to see if faulty items or pupil learning is responsible. If faulty items are judged to be responsible, a scoring adjustment may be in order.

QUESTIONS FOR DISCUSSION

1. What are some things a teacher can do to help prepare students for classroom testing? What are some dangers of test preparation that must be avoided?

2. What are the criteria for judging the goodness of a classroom achievement test? What would you need to know besides what is on the test to judge goodness?

3. What are some objectives that are best assessed by supply items, and what are some objectives that are best assessed by selection items?

4. How are sizing-up assessment, lesson plans, and actual instruction related to formal assessments of pupils' learning?

5. What harm could result if a teacher's achievement test produced invalid information about pupil learning?

6. Why are higher level objectives harder to teach and assess than lower level ones?

7. How can a teacher reduce pupils' test anxiety while maintaining their motivation to do well on the test?

8. What are some of the many ways pupils cheat on tests? How should a teacher respond to cheating? Should all forms of cheating be treated the same way? What cautions should a teacher keep in mind before accusing a pupil of cheating?

9. How would you make learning accommodations in your classroom for pupils with physical disabilities? Give some examples.

REFLECTION EXERCISES

◆ As a pupil, how could you tell whether a teacher had planned and delivered a lesson that took your learning needs into account?

◆ Think back over the recent paper-and-pencil tests you have taken. Which was the best? What characteristics made it the best? Which was the worst? What made it the worst? Consider not just the test itself, but also the instruction that preceded it, the information you were given about the test, the conditions of administration, the way the test was scored, and the grade you received.

ACTIVITIES

1. In a small group, select a chapter from a teacher's edition of a textbook. Read the chapter and examine the aids and resources provided for the teacher in planning, delivering, and assessing instruction. Compare the objectives of the chapter to the suggestions for instruction provided by the textbook author. Will the suggested instructional experiences help pupils attain the objectives? Is there a match between objectives and instructional experiences? Examine the end-of-chapter test. Is it a good test in terms of the chapter's objectives and the instructional suggestions? Does the type of item used match the objectives? What is the proportion of higher to lower level items in the test?

2. Each of the following eight test items has at least one fault. In small groups read each item, identify the fault(s), and rewrite the item to correct the fault(s). When you have finished rewriting the items, organize them into a test. Include directions for items, and group items of a similar type together.

1. What do you consider to be the most important objective in education?
   A. The student can read with comprehension.
   B. The student can correctly perform basic computations.
   C. The student gets along well with his or her peers.
   D. The student upholds democratic ideals in her or his actions.

2. Minor differences among organisms of the same kind are known as _____ .
   A. heredity   B. variations   C. adaptation   D. natural selection

3. The recall of factual information can best be assessed with a _____ item.
   A. matching   B. objective   C. essay   D. short-answer

4. Although experimental research completed, particularly that by Hansmocker, must be considered too equivocal and the assumptions viewed as too restrictive, most testing experts would recommend that the easiest method of significantly improving paper-and-pencil achievement test reliability is to _____ .
   A. increase the size of the group
   B. increase the weighting of items
   C. increase the number of items
   D. increase the amount of testing time

5. F. Scott Fitzgerald wrote _____.

6. Boston is the most important city in the Northeast.   T   F

7. An electric transformer can be used
   A. for storing up electricity.
   B. to increase the voltage of alternating current (correct answer).
   C. it converts electrical energy into direct current.
   D. alternating current is changed to direct current.

8. The only way to improve a skill is through practice.   T   F

3. Rewrite the following essay question to make it more focused for pupils. Then state the criteria you would use to judge the quality of your pupils' answers.

Essay Question: Compare the Democratic and Republican parties.

REVIEW QUESTIONS

1. What is the fundamental purpose of assessing pupils' achievement? What decisions must a teacher make when he or she is preparing to assess pupils' achievement?

2. How should the validity of an achievement test be determined?

3. What factors should be considered in determining whether to use a textbook test or to construct one?

4. In what way are assessments of pupil learning dependent on the teacher's objectives and the instruction provided?

5. What are the characteristics of a good official assessment?

6. What are some differences between selection and supply items? What are the advantages and disadvantages of each?

7. What are the differences between higher and lower level test items?

8. Three guidelines for constructing paper-and-pencil test questions are (1) cover important topics, (2) write clearly and simply, and (3) review items before testing. How does each of these guidelines lead to improved test questions?

9. What are examples of clues to be avoided in multiple-choice, true-false, completion, and matching items?

10. What is the difference between objective and subjective scoring? What factors make it difficult to score essay questions objectively? What steps can a teacher take to make essay scoring more objective? How do holistic and analytic scoring differ? When should each be used?

11. What is the difference between teaching the test and teaching to the test?

12. What guidelines should be followed in arranging the items in a test?

13. What are some strategies that can be used to defeat cheating on tests?

REFERENCES

Airasian, P. W. (1997). *Classroom assessment.* New York: McGraw Hill.

Ebel, R. E., and Frisbie, D. A. (1991). *Essentials of educational measurement.* Englewood Cliffs, NJ: Prentice Hall.

Gallagher, J. D. (1998). *Classroom assessment for teachers.* Columbus, OH: Merrill/Prentice Hall.

Gronlund, N. E. (1998). *Assessment of student achievement.* New York: Allyn and Bacon.

Marso, R. N., and Pigge, F. L. (1989). Elementary classroom teachers' testing needs and proficiencies: multiple assessments and in-service training priorities. *Educational Review, 13,* 1–17.

———. (1991). The analysis of teacher-made tests: Testing practices, cognitive demands, and item construction errors. *Contemporary Educational Psychology, 16,* 179–286.

Slavin, R. E. (1994). *Educational psychology: Theory and practice.* Boston, MA: Allyn and Bacon.

Starch, D., and Elliot, E. (1912). Reliability of the grading of high-school work in English. *School Review, 20,* 442–457.

Starch, D., and Elliott, E. (1913). Reliability of grading work in mathematics. *School Review, 21,* 254–259.

PERFORMANCE ASSESSMENT

CHAPTER OBJECTIVES

After reading this chapter, the student will be able to:

1. define basic terms: for example, checklist, rating scale, scoring rubric, portfolio, and performance criteria.
2. contrast performance assessment with other types of assessment.
3. state performance criteria for a given process or performance.
4. describe varied approaches to scoring performance assessments.
5. construct a scoring rubric.
6. define a portfolio and give an example of how it is used in assessment.
7. suggest strategies for scoring portfolios.
8. identify limitations in the validity and reliability of performance assessments.

There are many classroom assessment situations that require pupils to demonstrate their understanding by creating an answer, carrying out a performance, or producing a product. Typically, these forms of assessment cannot be carried out using selection-type items. They require more complex performances or products. The following situations describe common classroom assessment practices.

♦ Ms. Landers taught her ninth grade science class a unit on microscopes. She taught them how to set up, focus, and use the instrument. Each pupil identified and drew pictures of three or four objects viewed through the microscope. At the end of the unit, she tested the pupils by giving a paper-and-pencil test that asked them to label parts of a diagrammed microscope and answer multiple-choice questions about the history of the microscope.

♦ In Mr. Cleaver's third grade class, oral reading skills are strongly emphasized. He devotes a great deal of energy to helping pupils use proper phrasing, expression, and pronunciation when they read aloud. All of the tests that Mr. Cleaver uses to grade his pupils' reading achievement are paper-and-pencil tests that assess their paragraph comprehension and word recognition.

♦ Mrs. Wilkes included a unit on cardiopulmonary resuscitation (CPR) in her eleventh grade health class. Pupils were introduced to CPR and shown a movie on how to perform it. An emergency medical technician from the local fire department came to class and instructed each pupil in the technique using a practice dummy as an imaginary victim. Mrs. Wilkes tested her pupils' achievement on the unit with a 25-item true-false test on CPR technique.

These examples illustrate an important limitation of paper-and-pencil tests: they do not allow teachers to assess all kinds of important school learning. In each of these classrooms, the teacher relied solely on paper-and-pencil tests that measured *knowledge of performance,* not the ability to actually *carry out the performance.*

There are many classroom assessment situations in which valid assessment requires the teacher to gather formal information about pupils' products or performances, including such products as stories, paintings, lab reports, and science fair projects and such performances as giving a speech, holding a pencil, typing, and cooperating in groups. Generally, products give tangible outcomes—things you can hold in your hand—while performances are things you observe or listen to. Table 5.1 contrasts the selection and supply items discussed in Chapter 4 with typical examples of performance and product assessments.

Assessments in which pupils carry out an activity or produce a product in order to demonstrate their knowledge and skill are called performance assessments. Performance assessments permit pupils to show what they can do in a real situation (Wiggins, 1992). The distinction between being able to describe how a skill should be performed (knowledge, often lower level) and being able to actually perform it (performance, usually higher level) is important in classroom assessment (Wolf, Bixby, Glen, & Gardner, 1991). Teachers recognize this distinction, as the following comments illustrate.

> I want my pupils to learn to do math for its own intrinsic value, but also because math is so essential for everyday life. Making change, balancing checkbooks, doing a budget, and many other practical, real-world activities require that pupils know how to use their math knowledge.

> The kids need to learn to get along in groups, be respectful of others' property, and wait their turns. I don't want kids to be able to recite classroom rules, I

Most paper-and-pencil tests measure knowledge of performance, not performance itself.

Performance assessments allow pupils to demonstrate what they know and can do in a real situation.

TABLE 5.1 A FRAMEWORK OF ASSESSMENT APPROACHES

Selection	Supply	Product	Performance
Multiple-choice	Completion	Essay, story, or poem	Musical, dance, or dramatic performance
True-false	Label a diagram	Research report	Science lab demonstration
Matching	Short answer	Writing portfolio	Typing test
	Concept map	Diary or journal	Athletic competition Debate
		Science fair project	Oral presentation
		Art exhibit or portfolio	Cooperation in groups

want them to practice them. These behaviors are just as important for kids to learn in school as reading, writing, and math.

Some types of paper-and-pencil test items can be used to provide information about the thinking processes that underlie pupils' performance. For example, a math problem in which pupils have to show their work provides insight into the mental processes used to solve the problem. An essay question shows pupils' organizational skills, thought processes, and application of capitalization and punctuation rules. These two forms of paper-and-pencil test items can assess what pupils can *do,* as opposed to the majority of paper-and-pencil test questions that reveal what pupils *know.* With

Some paper-and-pencil assessments such as essays and reports are also performance assessments.

most selection and some supply questions, the teacher observes the *result* of the pupil's response, but not the thinking that produced the result. If the pupil gets a multiple-choice, true-false, matching, or completion item correct, the teacher assumes that the pupil followed the correct process, but there is little direct evidence to support this assumption. The only evidence of the pupil's thought process is a letter circled or a single word written. On the other hand, essays and other extended-response items provide a product that shows how pupils think about and construct their responses, permitting the teacher to see the logic of arguments, the manner in which the response is organized, and the conclusions drawn by the pupil. Thus, paper-and-pencil assessments like essays, stories, reports, or show-your-work problems are also performance assessments. Table 5.2 shows some of the differences among objective test items, essay questions, oral questions, and performance assessments.

Chapters 2 and 3 discussed how teachers observe their pupils' performance in order to size them up and obtain information about the moment-to-moment success of their instruction. Such observations are primarily informal and spontaneous. In this chapter, the focus is assessment of more formal, structured performances and products—those the teacher plans in advance, helps each pupil to perform, and then formally assesses. The assessment can take place during normal classroom instruction (e.g., oral reading activities, setting up laboratory equipment) or in some special situation set up to elicit a performance (e.g., giving a speech in an auditorium, demonstrating CPR on a dummy). In either case, the activity is formally structured; the teacher arranges the conditions in which the performance or product occurs and is judged. Such assessments permit each

Formal performance assessments permit each pupil to show mastery of the same process or task.

pupil to show his or her mastery of the same process or task, something that is impossible during informal observation of spontaneous classroom events.

This chapter describes performance assessment. It discusses the development of performances and outlines the pros and cons of performance assessment. It examines the use and assessment of portfolios and the many scoring approaches available to teachers. Threats to the validity and reliability of performance assessments are identified, and practical suggestions that lead to valid and reliable classroom performance assessment are described.

TABLE 5.2 COMPARISON OF VARIOUS TYPES OF ASSESSMENTS

	Objective Test	Essay Test	Oral Question	Performance Assessment
Purpose	Sample knowledge with maximum efficiency and reliability	Assess thinking skills and/or mastery of how a body of knowledge is structured	Assess knowledge during instruction	Assess ability to translate knowledge and understanding into action
Pupil's response	Read, evaluate, select	Organize, compose	Oral answer	Plan, construct, and deliver an original response
Major advantage	Efficiency—can administer many items per unit of testing time	Can measure complex cognitive outcomes	Joins assessment and instruction	Provides rich evidence of performance skills
Influence on learning	Overemphasis on recall encourages memorization; can encourage thinking skills if properly constructed	Encourages thinking and development of writing skills	Stimulates participation in instruction, provides teacher immediate feedback on effectiveness of teaching	Emphasizes use of available skill and knowledge in relevant problem contexts

SOURCE: Adapted from R. J. Stiggins, "Design and Development of Performance Assessments," *Educational Measurement: Issues and Practice,* 1987, *6*(3) p. 35. Copyright 1987 by the National Council on Measurement in Education. Used by permission of AERA.

PERFORMANCE ASSESSMENT IN SCHOOLS AND CLASSROOMS

Recently, a great deal of attention has been focused on the use of performance assessment in schools. The amount of attention suggests that performance assessment is new and untried in classrooms and that it can solve all the problems of classroom assessment. Neither of these beliefs is true. Performance assessment has been used extensively in classrooms for as long as there have been classrooms. Table 5.3 provides examples of common performance assessments that have long been used in schools.

Three factors account for the popularity of performance assessments. First, they are now being proposed or mandated as part of formal

TABLE 5.3   FIVE COMMON DOMAINS OF PERFORMANCE ASSESSMENT

Communication Skills	Psychomotor Skills	Athletic Activities	Concept Acquisition	Affective Skills
Writing an essay	Holding a pencil	Shooting free throws	Constructing open and closed circuits	Sharing toys
Giving a speech	Setting up lab equipment	Catching a ball	Selecting proper tools for shop tasks	Working in cooperative groups
Pronouncing a foreign language	Using scissors	Hopping	Identifying unknown chemical substances	Obeying school rules
Following spoken directions	Dissecting a frog	Swimming the crawl	Generalizing from experimental data	Maintaining self-control

Performance assessments reflect the recent emphasis on real-world problem solving.

statewide assessment programs (see Chapter 7). Thirty-six states currently assess pupils' writing performance, while 26 states assess such things as speaking and listening skills (*Education Week,* 1999). Second, problem solving, higher order thinking, and real-world reasoning strategies have been emphasized recently, and performance and product assessments are the most appropriate ways to demonstrate such outcomes. Third, it is felt that performance assessments give pupils who do poorly on selection-type tests an opportunity to show their achievement in alternative ways.

Performance-Oriented Subjects

All schools expect pupils to demonstrate communication skills, so reading, writing, and speaking are perhaps the areas most often subjected to classroom performance assessment. Likewise, simple psychomotor skills such as being able to sit in a chair or hold a pencil, as well as more sophisticated skills such as setting up laboratory equipment or using tools to build a birdhouse, are a fundamental part of school life, especially in the preschool and primary years. Closely related are the athletic performances that are taught in physical education classes.

Assessing students' understanding of concepts through hands-on demonstrations is becoming more common.

There also is a growing emphasis on using performance assessment to evaluate pupils' acquisition of conceptual knowledge. The rationale is that if pupils really grasp a concept, they should be able to *use* it to solve real-life problems. For example, after teaching pupils about money and making change, the teacher may assess learning by having them count out the money needed to purchase objects from the classroom store or act as storekeeper and make change for other pupils' purchases. Rather than giving a multiple-choice test on the chemical reactions that help identify unknown substances, the teacher could give each pupil an unknown substance and have him or her go through the process of identifying it. These kinds of hands-on demonstrations of concept mastery are growing in popularity.

Teachers are also constantly assessing their pupils' feelings, values, attitudes, and emotions. The satisfactory rating under the category works hard or obeys school rules that the teacher marks on a pupil's report card is based on observations of the pupil's performance. Teachers rely upon observations of pupils' performance to collect evidence about important behaviors such as getting along with peers, working independently, following rules, and self-control.

Most teachers recognize the importance of balancing supply and selection assessments with performance and product assessments, as indicated in the following comments.

It is important for teachers to balance supply and selection assessments with performance and product assessments.

It's not reasonable to grade reading without including the pupil's oral reading skills. I always spend some time when it's grading time listening to and rating my pupils' oral reading quality.

My kids know that a large part of their grade depends on how well they follow safety procedures and take proper care of the tools they use. They know I'm always on the lookout for times when they don't do these things and that it will count against them if I see them.

I wouldn't want anyone to assess my teaching competence solely on the basis of my students' paper-and-pencil test scores. I would want to be seen interacting with the kids, teaching them, and attending to their needs. So why should I confine my assessments of my pupils solely to paper-and-pencil methods?

Early Childhood and Special-Needs Pupils

While performance assessment cuts across subject areas and grade levels, it is heavily used in early childhood and special education. Because preschool, kindergarten, and primary school pupils often have limited communication ability or are still in the process of being socialized into the school culture, much information is obtained by observing their performances. Instruction at this age is focused upon gross and fine motor development, verbal and auditory acuity, and visual development, as well as social acclimation behaviors. Table 5.4 illustrates some of the important early childhood behaviors that teachers assess by performance-based means. There are many other behaviors that fit within these five domains (McLoughlin & Lewis, 1990), but these examples provide a sense of how heavily the early childhood curriculum is weighted toward performance outcomes.

Early education teachers rely heavily on performance-based assessments because of their students' limited communication skills.

Special-needs pupils, especially those who exhibit multiple disabilities, are often taught important processes to help them function independently. For example, pupils who are severely limited in their cognitive, affective and/or psychomotor development are taught so-called self-help

> **TABLE 5.4   EARLY CHILDHOOD BEHAVIOR AREAS**
>
> **Gross motor development.** Roll over, sit erect without toppling over, walk a straight line, throw a ball, jump on one or two feet, and skip
>
> **Fine motor development.** Cut with scissors, trace an object, color in the lines, draw geometric forms (circles, squares, triangles, etc.), penmanship, left-to-right progression in reading and writing, and eye-hand coordination
>
> **Verbal and auditory acuity.** Identify sounds, listen to certain sounds and ignore others (tune out distractions), discriminate between sounds and words that sound alike (e.g., fix–fish), remember numbers in sequence, follow directions, remember the correct order of events, and pronounce words and letters
>
> **Visual development.** Find a letter, number, or object similar to one shown by the teacher, copy a shape, identify shapes and embedded figures, reproduce a design given by the teacher, and differentiate objects by size, color, and shape
>
> **Social acclimation.** Listen to the teacher, follow a time schedule, share, wait one's turn, and respect the property of others

skills such as getting dressed, brushing teeth, making a sandwich, and operating a vacuum cleaner. Pupils are taught to carry out these performances through many, many repetitions. Observation of pupils as they perform these activities is the main assessment technique special education teachers use to identify performance mastery or areas needing further work.

Performance assessments are especially useful in performance-oriented subjects like art, music, shop, and foreign languages.

To summarize, performance assessment gathers evidence about pupil learning by observing and rating pupils' performances or products. Although appropriate at all grade levels, it is especially useful in subjects such as art, music, public speaking, shop, foreign languages, and physical education, all of which emphasize observable performances of some kind. It is also very useful with early childhood and special-needs pupils, whose lack of basic communication, psychomotor, and social skills forces the teacher to rely upon pupil performances to assess instructional success. Given the range of examples of performance assessment, it is evident that they are used in the cognitive, affective, and psychomotor domains, especially the higher levels of Bloom's Taxonomy.

DEVELOPING PERFORMANCE ASSESSMENTS

A diving competition is an instructive example of a skill that is best demonstrated by a performance. Submitting a written essay describing how to perform various dives or answering a multiple-choice test question about diving rules is hardly an appropriate way to assess diving *performance*. Rather, a valid assessment of diving performance requires seeing the diver actually perform and to make the assessment reliable, the observer must see a series of dives, not just one.

Diving judges rate dives using a scale that has 21 possible numerical scores (e.g., 0.0, 0.5, 1.0, . . . 5.5, 6.0, 6.5, . . . 9.0, 9.5, 10.0). They observe a very complicated performance made up of many body movements that together take about two seconds to complete. They do not have the benefit of slow motion or instant replay to review the performance and they cannot discuss the dive with one another. If their attention strays for even a second, they miss a large portion of the performance. Yet when the scores are flashed on the scoreboard, the judges inevitably are in very close agreement. Rarely do all judges give a dive the exact same score, but rarely is there more than a one-point difference between any two judges' scores. This is amazing agreement among observers for such a short, complicated performance.

With this example in mind, the four essential features of all formal performance assessments are now considered. The features are the same, whether for a diving competition, an oral speech, a book report, a typing exercise, or a science fair project. This overview is followed by a more extensive discussion of each feature. Briefly, performance assessments should

- *have a clear purpose* that identifies the decision to be made about the performance assessment.
- *identify observable aspects* to judge the pupil's performance or product.
- *provide an appropriate setting* for eliciting and judging the performance or product.
- *provide a judgment or score to describe performance.*

Define the Purpose of Assessment

In a diving competition, the *purpose* of the assessment is to rank the divers' performances in order to identify the best competitors. Each dive receives a score, and the diver with the highest total score wins the competition. Suppose, however, that dives were being performed during practice prior to a competition. The diver's coach would be the judge. In this case, the coach's concern would be less with the overall score of a dive than with the individual performance criteria the judges use to score during a competition. Consequently, the coach would score the practice dive not with a single overall judgment, but formatively, with a separate judgment about each part of the dive. Thus, a dive would produce not one judgment, but a series of judgments corresponding to each of the many specific performances it involves. Those areas in which the diver was weak would likely be emphasized in practice.

Teachers indicate that they use performance assessment for many purposes: grading pupils, constructing portfolios of pupils' work, diagnosing pupil learning, helping pupils recognize the important steps in a process or the important characteristics of a product, and providing concrete examples of pupils' work for parent conferences. Performance assessments are particularly suited to *diagnosis* because they provide information about how a pupil performs each of the specific criteria that make up a more general performance or product. This criterion-by-criterion assessment makes it easy to identify the strong and weak points of a pupil's performance. When the performance criteria are stated in terms of observable pupil behaviors or product characteristics, as they should be, remediation is easy. Each suggestion for improvement can be described in specific terms: report to group project area on time, wait your turn to speak, or do your share of the group work, for example. Whatever the purpose of performance assessment, it should be specified at the beginning of the assessment process so that proper kinds of performance criteria and scoring procedures can be established.

Recognizing a specific purpose for performance assessment is necessary so that proper criteria and scoring procedures can be established.

Identify Performance Criteria

Performance criteria are the specific behaviors a pupil should perform to properly carry out a performance or produce a product. They are at the heart of successful performance assessment, yet they are the area in which most problems occur.

Performances and products are normally broken down into specific, observable criteria, each of which can be judged independently.

When teachers first think about assessing performance, they tend to think in terms of global performances such as oral reading, giving a speech, safety in the laboratory, penmanship, producing a book report, organizing ideas, fingering a keyboard, or getting along with peers. In reality, such performances cannot be assessed until they are broken down into the narrower behaviors or characteristics of which they are composed. These narrower behaviors and characteristics are the performance criteria that are observed and judged by the teacher.

Performance assessments are particularly suited to diagnosis because they provide information about how pupils perform each specific criterion in a general performance.

Table 5.5 shows two sets of criteria for assessing pupils' performance when (1) working in cooperative groups and (2) playing the piano. These criteria focus and define what teachers hope to observe in the pupil's performance or product, just as the diving judges use criteria to judge diving performance. Well-stated performance criteria are essential to successful efforts at performance assessment.

In order to define performance criteria, a teacher must first decide whether a process or a product will be observed. Will processes such as typing or oral reading be assessed, or will products such as a typed letter or book report be assessed? In the former case, criteria are needed to judge the pupil's actual performance as it goes on, while in the latter, criteria are needed to judge the end product. In some cases, both process and product can be assessed. For example, a first grade teacher assessed both process and product when she (1) observed a pupil writing to determine how the

> **TABLE 5.5   EXAMPLES OF PERFORMANCE CRITERIA FOR WORKING IN GROUPS AND PIANO PLAYING**
>
> | **Working in Groups** | **Piano Playing** |
> |---|---|
> | _____ Reports to group project area on time | _____ Sits upright with feet on floor (or pedal, when necessary) |
> | _____ Starts work on own | |
> | _____ Shares information | _____ Arches fingers on keys |
> | _____ Contributes ideas | _____ Plays without pauses or interruptions |
> | _____ Listens to others | _____ Maintains even tempo |
> | _____ Waits turn to speak | _____ Plays correct notes |
> | _____ Follows instructions | _____ Holds all note values for indicated duration |
> | _____ Courteous to other group members | _____ Follows score dynamics (forte, crescendo, descrescendo) |
> | _____ Helps to solve group problems | _____ Melody can be heard above other harmonization |
> | _____ Considers viewpoints of others | |
> | _____ Carries out share of group-determined activities | _____ Phrases according to score (staccato and legato) |
> | _____ Completes assigned tasks on time | _____ Follows score pedal markings |

pupil held the pencil, positioned the paper, and manipulated the pencil and (2) judged the finished, handwritten product to assess how well the pupil formed his letters. Notice that the teacher observed different things according to whether she was interested in the pupil's handwriting _process_ or handwriting _product_. It is for this reason that teachers must know what they want to observe before performance criteria can be identified (Marzano, Pickering, & McTighe, 1993).

Performance criteria can focus on processes, products, or both.

The key to identifying performance criteria is to break down the overall performance or product into its component parts. It is these parts that are observed and judged. Consider, for example, a product assessment consisting of eighth graders' written paragraphs. The purpose of the assessment is to judge pupils' ability to write a 6- to 10-sentence paragraph on a topic of their choice. In preparing for the assessment, the teacher listed the following performance criteria for a well-organized paragraph.

- ◆ first sentence
- ◆ appropriate topic sentence
- ◆ good supporting ideas
- ◆ good vocabulary
- ◆ complete sentences
- ◆ capitalization
- ◆ spelling
- ◆ conclusion
- ◆ handwriting

Performance criteria should be specific, observable, and clearly stated.

These performance criteria identify important areas of a written paragraph, but the areas are vague and poorly stated. What, for example, is meant by first sentence? What is an appropriate topic sentence or good vocabulary? What should be examined in judging capitalization, spelling, and handwriting? If a teacher cannot answer these questions for him- or herself, how can he or she provide suitable examples or instruct pupils on the proper way to construct a well-organized paragraph? Performance criteria need to be specific enough to focus the teacher and pupils on well-defined characteristics of the performance or product. They must also be specific enough to permit the teacher to convey to pupils, in terms they can understand, the specific features that make up a well-written paragraph. Once defined, the criteria permit consistent teacher assessment of performance and consistent communication with pupils about their learning.

Clearly stated performance criteria can be used by other teachers.

In general, performance criteria are clearly stated if another teacher at the same grade level can use the performance criteria without the author's being there to explain them. The following list shows a revised version of the performance criteria for the eighth graders' paragraphs. Note the difference in clarity and how the revised version focuses the teacher and students on very specific features of the paragraph, those that are important and will be assessed. Before assigning the task, the teacher wisely decided to tell the pupils what he would be looking at in their paragraphs; that is, he told them what his criteria are.

- ♦ indents first sentence
- ♦ topic sentence sets main idea of paragraph
- ♦ following sentences support main idea
- ♦ sentences arranged in logical order
- ♦ uses age-appropriate vocabulary
- ♦ writes in complete sentences
- ♦ capitalizes proper nouns and first words in sentences
- ♦ makes no more than three spelling errors
- ♦ conclusion follows logically from prior sentences
- ♦ handwriting is legible

Cautions in Developing Performance Criteria

A few words of caution are appropriate here. First, it is important to recognize that the preceding list of performance criteria is not the only one that describes the characteristics of a well-written paragraph. Different teachers might identify other criteria that they feel are more or less important than some of the ones shown. Thus, emphasis should not be upon identifying the best or only set of criteria for a performance or product, but rather upon stating criteria that are meaningful, important, and understood by the pupils.

Second, it is possible to break down most school performances and products into many very specific steps, behaviors, or characteristics. However, a too lengthy list of performance criteria is ineffective because teachers rarely have the time to observe a large number of detailed performance criteria for each pupil. Too many criteria make the observation process intrusive, with the teacher hovering over the pupil, rapidly checking off behaviors, and often interfering with a pupil's performance.

Very long lists of performance criteria (over 15) become unmanageable and intrusive.

Numerous detailed performance criteria are useful only when the observer has the time to carry out in-depth observation of a single pupil's performance or product. Thus, it is counterproductive to spend great amounts of time listing performance criteria that cannot be reasonably observed and assessed. For classroom performance assessment to be manageable and meaningful, a balance must be established between specificity and practicality. The key to attaining this balance is to identify the *essential* criteria associated with a performance or product. About 10 to 15 performance criteria is usually a manageable number for most classroom teachers to use.

Third, the process of identifying performance criteria is an ongoing one that is rarely completed on the first attempt. As with most writing assignments, initial performance criteria will need to be revised and clarified in order to provide the focus required for valid and reliable assessment. To aid this process, teachers should think about the performance or product they wish to observe and reflect on its key aspects. They also can examine a few actual products or performances as a basis for revising their initial list of criteria.

The following list shows the initial set of performance criteria a teacher wrote to assess fourth grade pupils' oral reports.

- ♦ speaks clearly and slowly
- ♦ pronounces correctly
- ♦ makes eye contact
- ♦ exhibits good posture when presenting
- ♦ exhibits good effort
- ♦ presents with feeling
- ♦ understands the topic
- ♦ exhibits enthusiastic attitude
- ♦ organizes

Note the lack of specificity in many of the criteria: slowly, correctly, good, understands, and enthusiastic attitude. These criteria hide more than they reveal about what to observe, making it difficult to explain to pupils precisely what is expected of them and leading to assessments that are invalid and unreliable. After reflecting on and observing a few oral presentations, the teacher revised and clarified the performance criteria

Like other writing assignments, good performance criteria need to be revised and clarified over time.

as shown next. Note that the teacher first divided the general performance into three areas (physical expression, vocal expression, and verbal expression) and then identified a few important performance criteria within each of these areas. It is not essential to divide the performance into separate areas, but sometimes it is useful in focusing the teacher and pupils.

I. Physical Expression
- Stands straight and faces audience
- Changes facial expression with changes in tone of the presentation
- Maintains eye contact with audience

II. Vocal Expression
- Speaks in a steady, clear voice
- Varies tone to emphasize points
- Speaks loudly enough to be heard by audience
- Paces words in an even flow
- Enunciates each word

III. Verbal Expression
- Chooses precise words to convey meaning
- Avoids unnecessary repetition
- States sentences with complete thoughts or ideas
- Organizes information logically
- Summarizes main points at conclusion

Developing Observable Performance Criteria

The value of performance assessments depends on identifying performance criteria that can be observed and judged.

The value and richness of performance and product assessments depend heavily on identifying performance criteria that can be observed and judged. The following guidelines are useful for this purpose.

1. *Select the performance or product to be assessed and either perform it yourself or imagine yourself performing it.* Think to yourself, What would I have to do in order to complete this task? What steps would I have to follow? You may also observe pupils performing the task and identify the important elements in their performance. Finally, you can actually carry out the performance yourself, recording and studying your performance or product.

2. *List the important aspects of the performance or product.* What specific behaviors or attributes are most important to the successful completion of the task? What behaviors have been emphasized in instruction? The specific behaviors or attributes identified will become the performance criteria that guide instruction, observation, and assessment.

3. *Try to limit the number of performance criteria to those that can reasonably be assessed.* This is less important when assessing a product, but even then, it is better to assess a limited number of key criteria than a large number that vary widely in their importance. Remember, you will have to observe and judge performance on each of the criteria identified. A good rule of thumb is to limit the number of performance criteria to about 10 to 15.

4. *If possible, have groups of teachers think through the important criteria that characterize a task.* Since all first grade teachers assess oral reading in their classrooms and since the criteria for successful oral reading do not differ much from one first grade classroom to another, a group effort to define performance criteria will likely save time and produce a more complete set of criteria than that produced by any single teacher. Similar group efforts are useful for other common performances or products such as book reports and science fair projects. It is useful and reinforcing for pupils when teachers within and across grades in a school utilize similar criteria in assessing performances and projects.

When teachers within a school develop similar performance criteria across grade levels, it is reinforcing to pupils.

5. *Express the performance criteria in terms of observable pupil behaviors or product characteristics.* The performance criteria should direct attention to things the pupil is doing or characteristics of a product that the pupil has produced. Be specific when stating the performance criteria. Do not write "The child works"; write instead, "The child remains focused on the task for at least four minutes." Do not write "Organization"; write instead "Information is presented in a logical sequence." Note how each performance criterion is expressed in terms of an observable pupil behavior in the revised lists on pages 154 and 156.

6. *Do not use ambiguous words that cloud the meaning of the performance criteria.* The worst offenders in this regard are adverbs that end in *ly*. Other words to avoid are *good* and *appropriate*. Thus, criteria such as *appropriate* organization, speaks correct*ly*, writes neat*ly*, and performs grateful*ly* are ambiguous and will be interpreted in different ways at different times, diminishing the fairness and usefulness of the assessment. Instead of "organizes adequately," substitute "has an identifiable beginning, middle, and end" or "presents ideas in a logical order." Instead of "speaks correctly," substitute "enunciates each word," "can be heard in all parts of the room," or "does not run sentences together." The particular criteria depend upon the teacher and his or her instruction, but they should be stated in terms of observable behaviors and product characteristics, preferably ones that pupils and other teachers can understand. Review and revise criteria as necessary based upon experience using them.

7. *Arrange the performance criteria in the order in which they are likely to be observed.* This will save time when observing and maintain focus on the performance.

8. *Check for existing performance criteria before constructing your own.* The performance criteria associated with giving an oral speech, reading aloud, using a microscope, writing a persuasive paragraph, cutting with scissors, and the like have been thought about and listed by many

TABLE 5.6   GUIDELINES FOR STATING PERFORMANCE CRITERIA

1. Identify the steps or features of the performance or task to be assessed by imagining yourself performing it, observing pupils performing it, or inspecting finished products.

2. List the important criteria of the performance or product.

3. Try to keep the number of performance criteria small enough so that they can be reasonably observed and judged. Ten to 15 criteria is a good range to use.

4. Have teachers think through the criteria as a group.

5. Express the criteria in terms of observable pupil behaviors or product characteristics.

6. Avoid vague and ambiguous words like *correctly, appropriately,* and *good.*

7. Arrange the performance criteria in order.

8. Check for existing performance assessment instruments to use or modify before constructing them.

people. No one who reads this book will be the first to try to assess these and other common school performances. The moral here is the wheel does not need to be reinvented every time a wheel is needed. Many texts contain examples of performance criteria for many school skills, and these should be used as needed.

Table 5.6 summarizes the foregoing guidelines.

Regardless of the particular performance or product assessed, clearly stated performance criteria are critical to the success of both instruction and assessment. The criteria define the important aspects of a performance or product, guide what pupils should be taught, and produce a focus for both the teacher and pupil when assessing performance. Although performance and product assessments are widely used in most classrooms, they are frequently used in the absence of well-articulated performance criteria. If the teacher does not know what makes a good essay response or a good science fair project, how are pupils to be guided during instruction and how are they to be assessed fairly? Clear performance criteria are needed.

Provide a Setting to Elicit and Observe the Performance

Once the performance criteria are defined, a setting in which to observe the performance or product must be selected or established. Depending on the nature of the performance or product, the teacher may observe behaviors as they naturally occur in the classroom or set up a specific situation in which the pupils must perform. There are two considerations in deciding whether to observe naturally occurring behaviors or to set up a more controlled exercise: (1) the frequency with which the performance naturally occurs in the classroom and (2) the seriousness of the decision to be made.

If the performance occurs infrequently during normal classroom activity, it may be more efficient to structure a situation in which pupils must perform the desired behaviors. For example, in the normal flow of classroom activities, pupils rarely have the opportunity to give a planned 5-minute speech, so the teacher should set up an exercise in which each pupil must develop and give a 5-minute speech. Oral reading, on the other hand, occurs frequently enough in many elementary classrooms that pupils' performance can be observed as part of the normal flow of reading instruction.

The importance of the decision to be made from a performance assessment also influences the context in which observation takes place. In general, the more important the decision, the more structured the assessment environment should be. A course grade, for example, represents an important decision about a pupil. If performance assessments contribute to grading, evidence should be gathered under structured, formal circumstances so that every pupil has a fair and equal chance to exhibit his or her achievement. The validity of the assessments is likely to be improved when the setting is similar and familiar to all pupils.

Regardless of the nature of the assessment, evidence obtained from a single assessment describes only one example of a pupil's performance. For a variety of reasons, such as illness, home problems, or other distractions, a pupil's performance at a single time may not provide a reliable indication of the pupil's true achievement. To be certain of an accurate indication of what a pupil can and cannot do, multiple observations are useful. If the different observations produce similar performances, a teacher can have confidence in the evidence and use it in decision making. If different observations contradict one another, more information should be obtained.

Teachers may observe and assess naturally occurring classroom behaviors or set up situations in which they assess carefully structured performances.

Formally structured performance assessments are needed when teachers are dealing with low-frequency behaviors and making important decisions.

Multiple observations of pupil performances provide more reliable and accurate information.

Score or Rate Performance

The final step in performance assessment is to score the pupil's performance. As in previous steps, the nature of the decision to be made influences the scoring procedure. Scoring a performance assessment can be holistic or analytic, just like scoring an essay question. When decisions such as group placement, selection, or grading are to be made, holistic scoring is most useful. To make a holistic decision, a teacher determines a single, overall score for the pupil. On the other hand, if the assessment purpose is to diagnose pupil difficulties or score pupil mastery of each individual performance criterion, then analytic scoring, with a separate score on each performance criterion, is appropriate. In either case, the performance criteria dictate the scoring or rating approach that is adopted.

Holistic scoring (a single overall score) is good for such things as group placement or grading; analytic scoring (scoring individual criteria) is useful in diagnosing student difficulties.

Anecdotal records such as checklists, rating scales, and portfolios are options available to record and collect observations of pupils.

In most classrooms, the teacher is both the observer and scorer. In situations where an important decision is to be made, additional observers and/or scorers may be added. It is common for performance assessments in athletic, music, debate, and art competitions to have more than a single judge in order to make scoring more fair.

A number of options exist for collecting and recording observations of pupil performance: anecdotal records, checklists, rating scales, rubrics, and portfolios.

Anecdotal Records

Anecdotal records are written accounts of significant events and behaviors the teacher has observed in a pupil.

Anecdotal records are written accounts of significant events and behaviors the teacher has observed concerning individual pupils. Only those observations that have special significance and cannot be obtained from other classroom assessment methods should be included in an anecdotal record. Figure 5.1 shows an example of an anecdotal record. Notice that it provides information about the learner, date of observation, name of teacher observing, and a factual description of the event.

Most teachers have difficulty identifying particular events or behaviors that merit inclusion in an anecdotal record. What is significant and important in the life of a pupil is not always apparent at the time an event or behavior occurs. From the hundreds of observations made each day, how is a teacher to select the one that might be important enough to write down? It may take many observations over many days to recognize which events really are significant. Moreover, anecdotal records are time-consuming to prepare and need to be written up soon after the event or behavior is observed, while it is fresh in the teacher's mind. This is not always possible. For these reasons, anecdotal records are not extensively used by teachers. This does not mean that teachers do not observe and judge classroom events; of course they do. It simply means that they seldom write down descriptions of these events.

FIGURE 5.1
Anecdotal Record for Lynn Gregory

PUPIL *Lynn Gregory*   DATE *12/3/98*

OBSERVER *J. Ricketts*

All term Lynn has been quiet and passive, rarely interacting w/classmates in class or on the playground. Today Lynn suddenly "opened up" and wanted continual interaction w/classmates. She could not settle down, kept circulating around the room until she became bothersome to me and her classmates. I tried to settle her down, but was unsuccessful.

Checklists

A **checklist** is a written list of performance criteria. As a performance is observed or a product judged, the scorer determines whether the student's performance or product meets each specified criterion. If it does, a check-mark is placed next to that criterion, indicating that it was observed; if it does not, the checkmark is omitted. Figure 5.2 shows a completed check-list for Rick Gray's oral presentation. The performance criteria for this checklist were presented on page 156.

Checklists are diagnostic, reusable, and capable of charting pupil progress. They provide a detailed record of pupils' performances, one that can and should be shown to pupils to help them see where improvement

A checklist, which is a written list of performance criteria, can be used repeatedly over time to diagnose strengths, weaknesses, and changes in performances.

FIGURE 5.2
Checklist Results for an Oral Presentation

NAME *Rick Gray*   DATE *Nov. 11, 1998*

   I. Physical Expression

      ✓ A. Stands straight and faces audience

      _____ B. Changes facial expression with changes in tone of the presentation

      ✓ C. Maintains eye contact with audience

  II. Vocal Expression

      ✓ A. Speaks in a steady, clear voice

      ✓ B. Varies tone to emphasize points

      _____ C. Speaks loudly enough to be heard by audience

      ✓ D. Paces words in an even flow

      _____ E. Enunciates each word

 III. Verbal Expression

      _____ A. Chooses precise words to convey meaning

      ✓ B. Avoids unnecessary repetition

      ✓ C. States sentences with complete thoughts or ideas

      ✓ D. Organizes information logically

      ✓ E. Summarizes main points at conclusion

is needed. Rick Gray's teacher could sit down with him after his presentation and point out both the criteria he performed well and the ones he needs to improve. Because it focuses on the specific criteria that make up a performance or product, a checklist provides truly diagnostic information. The same checklist can be reused, with different pupils or with the same pupil, over time. In fact, using the same checklist more than once is an easy way to obtain information about a pupil's improvement.

There are, however, disadvantages associated with checklists. One important disadvantage is that they give the teacher only two choices when scoring each criterion: performed or not performed; yes or no. A checklist provides no middle ground for scoring. Suppose that Rick Gray stood straight and faced the audience most of the time during his oral presentation, or paced his words evenly except in one brief part of the speech when he spoke too quickly and ran his words together. How should his teacher score him on these performance criteria? Should Rick receive a check because he did them most of the time, or should he not receive a check because his performance was slightly flawed? Sometimes this is not an easy choice. A checklist forces the teacher to make an absolute decision for each performance criterion, even though a pupil's performance is somewhere between these extremes.

Checklists cannot record gradations in performances.

A second disadvantage of checklists is the difficulty of summarizing a pupil's performance into a single score. Checklists can be used to diagnose pupils' strengths and weaknesses, but what if a teacher wants to summarize performance across all the criteria to determine a single score for grading purposes?

One way to summarize Rick's performance into a single score is to translate the number of performance criteria he successfully demonstrated into a percentage. For example, there were 13 performance criteria on the oral presentation checklist and Rick demonstrated nine of them during his presentation. Assuming each criterion is equally important, Rick's performance translates into a score of 69 percent ($9/13 \times 100 = 69\%$). Thus, Rick demonstrated 69 percent of the desired performance criteria. (Chapter 6 discusses the way scores like Rick's 69 percent are turned into grades.)

Summarizing performances from a checklist can be done by setting up rating standards or by calculating the percentage of criteria accomplished.

A second way to summarize performance is for the teacher to set up standards for rating pupils' performance. Suppose Rick's teacher set up the following standards:

Excellent	12 or 13 performance criteria shown
Good	9 to 11 performance criteria shown
Fair	5 to 8 performance criteria shown
Poor	4 or less performance criteria shown

These standards allow the teacher to summarize performance on a scale that goes from excellent to poor. The scale could also involve letter grades A, B, C, or D or any other descriptions of the different levels of pupil performance. However, the same standards must be used to summarize each pupil's performance, so it is advisable to keep the summarizing rules as simple as possible. Rick performed 9 of the 13 criteria, and the teacher's standard indicates that his performance should be classified as good, or B.

Rating Scales

Rating scales are similar to checklists except that they allow the observer to judge performance along a continuum rather than as a dichotomy. Both checklists and rating scales are based upon a set of performance criteria, as are all performance assessments. It is not unusual for the same set of performance criteria to be used in both a rating scale and a checklist. However, a checklist gives the observer only two categories for judging, while a rating scale gives more than two.

Three of the most common types of rating scales are the numerical, graphic, and descriptive scales. Figure 5.3 shows an example of each of these scales as applied to two specific performance criteria for giving an oral presentation. In numerical scales, a number stands for a point on the rating scale. Thus, in the example, 1 corresponds to the pupil's *always* performing the behavior, 2 to the pupil's *usually* performing the behavior, and so on. Graphic scales require the rater to mark a position on a line divided into sections based upon a scale. The rater marks an X at that point on the line that best describes the pupil's performance. Scoring rubrics, also called **descriptive rating scales,** require the rater to choose among different descriptions of actual performance (Wiggins & McTighe, 1998; Goodrich, 1997). In descriptive rating scales, different descriptions are used to represent different levels of pupil performance. To score, the teacher selects the description that comes closest to the pupil's actual performance.

The three most common types of rating scales are numerical, graphic, and descriptive (also called scoring rubrics).

Descriptive rating scales, or scoring rubrics, require the rater to choose among different descriptions of actual performance.

Regardless of the type of rating scale chosen, two general rules can improve their use. The first rule is limit the number of rating categories. There is a tendency to think that the greater the number of rating categories, the better the rating scale. In practice, this is not the case. Few observers can make reliable discriminations in pupils' performance across more than five rating categories, and more categories are likely to make the ratings unreliable. Three to five well-defined and distinct rating scale points, as shown in Figure 5.4, are sufficient.

The second rule is strive to use the same rating scale for each performance criterion. This is not usually possible in descriptive rating scales, where the descriptions vary with each performance criterion. However, for numerical and graphic scales, it is best to select a single rating scale and to use it for all performance criteria. Using many different rating categories requires the observer to change focus frequently and decreases rating accuracy by distracting the rater's attention from the performance.

Having too many scales tends to distract the rater from the performance, making the ratings unreliable.

Numerical Rating Scale

Directions: Indicate how often the pupil performs each of these behaviors while giving an oral presentation. For each behavior circle **1** if the pupil **always** performs the behavior, **2** if the pupil **usually** performs the behavior, **3** if the pupil **seldom** performs the behavior, and **4** if the pupil **never** performs the behavior.

Physical Expression

A. Stands straight and faces audience

 1   2   3   4

B. Changes facial expression with changes in tone of the presentation

 1   2   3   4

Graphic Rating Scale

Directions: Place an **X** on the line which shows how often the pupil did each of the behaviors listed while giving an oral presentation.

Physical Expression

A. Stands straight and faces audience

| always | usually | seldom | never |

B. Changes facial expression with changes in tone of the presentation

| always | usually | seldom | never |

Descriptive Rating Scale

Directions: Place an **X** on the line at the place which best describes the pupil's performance on each behavior.

Physical Expression

A. Stands straight and faces audience

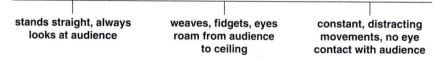

| **stands straight, always looks at audience** | **weaves, fidgets, eyes roam from audience to ceiling** | **constant, distracting movements, no eye contact with audience** |

B. Changes facial expression with changes in tone of the presentation

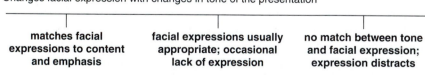

| **matches facial expressions to content and emphasis** | **facial expressions usually appropriate; occasional lack of expression** | **no match between tone and facial expression; expression distracts** |

FIGURE 5.3
Types of Rating Scales

NAME   *Sarah Jackson*   DATE   *Nov. 11, 1999*

Directions: Indicate how often the pupil performs each of these behaviors while giving an oral presentation. For each behavior **circle 4** if the pupil **always** performs the behavior, **3** if the pupil **usually** performs the behavior, **2** if the pupil **seldom** performs the behavior, and **1** if the pupil **never** performs the behavior.

I. Physical Expression

    (4) 3 2 1   A. Stands straight and faces audience

    4 3 (2) 1   B. Changes facial expression with changes in tone of the presentation

    4 (3) 2 1   C. Maintains eye contact with audience

II. Vocal Expression

    (4) 3 2 1   A. Speaks in a steady, clear voice

    4 (3) 2 1   B. Varies tone to emphasize points

    4 3 (2) 1   C. Speaks loudly enough to be heard by audience

    4 (3) 2 1   D. Paces words in an even flow

    4 3 (2) 1   E. Enunciates each word

III. Verbal Expression

    4 3 (2) 1   A. Chooses precise words to convey meaning

    4 (3) 2 1   B. Avoids unnecessary repetition

    (4) 3 2 1   C. States sentences with complete thoughts or ideas

    (4) 3 2 1   D. Organizes information logically

    4 (3) 2 1   E. Summarizes main points at conclusion

FIGURE 5.4
Rating Scale Results for an Oral Presentation

Whereas checklists measure only the presence or absence of some performance, a rating scale measures the degree to which the performance matches the criteria.

Figure 5.4 shows Sarah Jackson's completed numerical rating performance for her oral presentation. Note that the performance criteria for the rating scale shown in Figure 5.4 are identical to the checklist shown in Figure 5.2. The only difference between the checklist and the rating scale is in the way performance is scored.

While rating scales provide more categories for assessing a pupil's performance, thereby providing detailed diagnostic information, the multiple rating categories complicate the process of summarizing performance across criteria to arrive at an overall pupil score. With a checklist, summarization is reduced to giving credit only for criteria checked. This cannot be done with a rating scale because performance is judged in terms of *degree,* not presence or absence. A teacher must treat ratings of always, usually, seldom, and never differently or there is no point to having the different rating categories.

Numerical summarization is the most straightforward and commonly used approach to summarizing performance on rating scales. It assigns a point value to each category in the scale and sums the points across the performance criteria. For example, consider Sarah Jackson's ratings in Figure 5.4. To obtain a summary score for Sarah's performance, 4 points are assigned to a rating of always, 3 points to a rating of usually, 2 points to a rating of seldom, and 1 point to a rating of never. The numbers 4, 3, 2, and 1 match the four possible ratings for each performance criterion, with 4 representing the most desirable response and 1 the least desirable. Thus, high scores indicate high performance. Note that before summarizing Sarah's performance into a single score, it is important for the teacher to identify areas of weakness so that Sarah can be guided to improve her oral presentations.

Sarah's total score, 39, was determined by adding the circled numbers. The highest possible score on the rating scale is 52; if a pupil is rated always on each performance criterion, the pupil's total score is 52 (4 points × 13 performance criteria). Thus, Sarah got a score of 39 out of a possible 52 points. In this manner, a total score can be determined for each pupil rated. This score can be turned into a percentage by dividing it by 52, the total number of points available (39/52 × 100 = 75%).

Rubrics or **descriptive summarization** are a way to score performance on checklists, rating scales, and portfolios. A rubric is a set of clear expectations or criteria used to help teachers and students focus on what is valued in a subject, topic, or activity. Scoring rubrics are brief written descriptions of different levels of pupil performance based on the performance criteria. Rubrics can be used to score both performances and products. They are constructed by combining performance criteria into different levels of performance and ordering them in descriptive terms. Different descriptions represent different levels of performance.

Rubrics are used to provide an indication of the overall level at which a pupil performs.

The following rubric was used to summarize performance on Sarah Jackson's oral presentation. Notice that this rubric summarizes the performance criteria into four levels of performance. Each level describes performance in terms of the performance criteria. In this example, the teacher labeled the four descriptions as excellent, good, fair, and poor. Other teachers might have used other labels. In looking at Sarah Jackson's numerical ratings and trying to describe her overall performance in terms of the scoring rubric, it is clear that Sarah's performance was neither excellent nor poor; it was either good or fair. Her teacher has to make a judgment as to which of these two categories best describes Sarah's performance. The fact that Sarah had more 4's and 3's than 2's and 1's will probably lead Sarah's teacher to place her performance in the good category.

Excellent   Pupil consistently faces audience, stands straight and maintains eye contact; voice projects well and clearly; pacing and tone variation appropriate; well-organized, points logically and completely presented; brief summary at end.

Good   Pupil usually faces audience, stands straight and makes eye contact; voice projection good, but pace and clarity vary during talk; well-organized but repetitive; occasional poor choice of words; incomplete summary.

Fair   Pupil fidgety; some eye contact and facial expression change; uneven voice projection, not heard by all in room, some words slurred; loosely organized, repetitive, contains many incomplete thoughts; little summarization.

Poor   Pupil's body movements distracting; little eye contact or voice change; words slurred, speaks in monotone, does not project voice beyond first few rows, no consistent or logical pacing; rambling presentation, little organization with no differentiation between major and minor points; no summary.

Rubrics provide a set of guidelines that can help pupils to monitor and evaluate their own and peers' work. They can focus teachers on teaching and assessing what is important and valued in student work. They are a tool that reduces the scoring subjectivity that often accompanies scoring performance assessments.

Here is another set of criteria used by a fifth grade teacher to assess pupils' response to their journal writings.

◆ Writes complete answers
◆ Answers accurately
◆ Supports answers with specifics
◆ Includes quotes
◆ Varies sentence structure
◆ Shows correct grammar and mechanics

Figure 5.5 shows the scoring rubric the teacher developed to assess the pupils' journal writing performance. The rubric describes four levels of performance: excellent, good, needs improvement, and poor. A teacher selects the names of the rubric levels in terms of what is most useful for his or her scoring and for the pupils' understanding. Again, notice how each of the rubric levels uses the criteria to indicate the quality of the performance.

Note the difference between checklists or rating scales, which provide specific diagnostic information about pupils' strengths and weaknesses, and scoring rubrics, which summarize performance in a general way and

FIGURE 5.5
Rubric for Fifth Grade Journal Responses

Used with Permission of Gwen Airasian

SCORING RUBRIC FOR RESPONSE JOURNAL QUESTIONS

3 - Excellent   Answers are very complete and accurate. Most answers are supported with specific information from the reading, including direct quotations. Sentence structure is varied and detailed. Mechanics are generally accurate, including spelling, use of capitals, and appropriate punctuation.

2 - Good   Answers are usually complete and accurate. These answers are supported with specific information from the reading. Sentence structure is varied. Mechanics are generally accurate, including spelling, use of capitals, and appropriate punctuation.

1 - Needs Improvement   Answers are partially to fully accurate. These answers may need to be supported with more specific information from the reading. Sentence structure is varied, with some use of sentence fragments. Mechanics may need improvement, including spelling, use of capitals, and appropriate punctuation.

0 - Poor Answers are inaccurate or not attempted at all. Sentence structure is frequently incomplete. Mechanics need significant improvement.

Rubrics summarize performance in a general way, whereas checklists and rating scales provide specific diagnostic information about pupil strengths and weaknesses.

provide much less-specific diagnostic information. Rubrics are especially useful for setting pupil achievement targets and for obtaining a summative, single-score representation of pupil performance.

The use of rubrics may be new to both teacher and students. Because rubrics differ from most other assessment scores, it often takes some time for both teacher and students to become comfortable with their use. To facilitate the initial use of rubrics, five steps can be taken. First, teachers should develop simple rubrics based on a limited number of criteria (four to six) and three or four performance score levels. Second, the use and meaning of the criteria used to develop the rubric should be explained to the pupils before they are used in instruction and assessment. Remember, both teacher and students may be new to rubrics and both will need time and practice to feel comfortable with their use. Third, a rubric is a scoring tool, and valid classroom scoring tools of any kind should be linked to instruction. Fourth, using the defined criteria, students should be taught so as to master the criteria; then the rubric-based assessment provides a valid indication of learning and performance. The integration of performance criteria and rubrics is a powerful and useful combination for linking instruction and assessment. Fifth, all should recognize that rubrics are works in progress and should be revised as needed.

USES OF PERFORMANCE ASSESSMENTS

The preceding sections described the steps in developing and scoring performance and product assessments and emphasized the importance of clearly stated performance criteria. In this section, some of the different ways performance criteria and assessments are being used in schools are examined. The examples that follow do not exhaust all the rich and creative ways teachers are implementing performance assessments, but they do suggest the possibilities. In reviewing these examples, note especially how critical the identification of suitable performance criteria is to their success.

Figure 5.6 shows a book knowledge survey for use with beginning readers. Although laid out in a format different from those shown previously, this instrument is essentially a checklist. It is meant to chart each pupil's progress towards acquiring skills needed for reading and provides a section for teacher comments on pupil performance.

Self-Assessment and Peer Review

Many teachers include both the definition and the criterion being rated in their performance assessments as a means of (1) reminding themselves of the areas being assessed and (2) helping pupils critique their own and others' work. Figure 5.7 is a rating scale intended to assess high school pupils' creative writing. After the pupils have completed a creative writing assignment, the teacher may use the rating scale to rate the assignment him- or herself or ask each pupil to make a **self-assessment** of his or her assignment using the scale (Porter & Cleveland, 1995). Often, reviewing one's work with the performance criteria as a guide helps identify weaknesses in the work.

Self-assessments and peer reviews help pupils understand the performance criteria and can become the basis for class discussion and analysis.

Teachers may also engage the pupils in **peer review,** during which pupils exchange assignments and discuss and rate each other's assignment using the creative writing rating instrument (Lambdin & Walker, 1994). This process allows a pupil to see, judge, and potentially learn about another pupil's work based on the performance criteria. Often this approach helps a pupil doing peer reviews to thoroughly learn the performance criteria. It also provides them with a model against which to compare his or her own work. Peer review, based on the performance criteria, can focus class discussion and analysis of pupils' work by basing discussion on the task's performance criteria, rather than unsupported pupil opinion. The teacher may then allow the pupils an extra day to revise their assignment according to the self- or peer assessments.

BOOK KNOWLEDGE SURVEY

Student: _____

Date: _____   # of Questions Correct:

Grade: _____

Assessor: _____   # of Survey Questions: 17

Text: _____

Directions: * The book should have illustrations and 1–2+ sentences per page.

               * Ask the questions listed below as they relate to the text.

               * If the student has previously displayed mastery of a line item, the "Previously Demonstrated" column may be checked without repeating the "Survey Question."

Previously Demon.	Survey Questions	Answered Correctly	Comments
	Give student book upside down & backward. Say: "Show me the front cover."		
	"Show me the title."		
	"What is an author?"		
	"What is an illustrator?"		
	"Show me the title page."		
	On a page with both text and illustrations, ask: "Where do we read the story from?"		
	"Point to the words as I read them."		
	When text is written on both left & right pages, ask: "Which page should we read first?"		
	"Find the word _____ ."		
	"Find the capital letter _____ ."		
	"Find the lowercase letter _____ ."		
	"Show me the first letter of a word."		
	"Show me the last letter of a word."		
	Point to a period. Ask: "What is this called?" "What is it for?"		
	Point to a comma. Ask: "What is this called?" "What is it for?"		
	Point to an exclamation mark. Ask: "What is this called?" "What is it for?"		
	Point to quotation marks. Ask: "What are these called?" "What are they for?"		

FIGURE 5.6

Book Knowledge Survey

SOURCE: L. Bushnell and M. Leschen, Westwood Public Schools, Westwood, MA.

This rating scale is to help you and me assess your creative writing. Each work of creative writing you produce will be assessed in terms of the criteria in this scale. Sometimes I will assess your work and other times you or a classmate will be asked to assess your work.

Criteria
VOICE: Voice refers to the ability to express words and images in a distinct, individual manner.

The voice of the student in this piece is distinct and clear, and gives an impression of the kind of person doing the writing.
     always   sometimes   rarely   never

TONE: Tone refers to the attitude and feeling the author conveys regarding her or his subject. If the subject is a tragic one, does the author convey a tone of despair or sadness? If the subject is a joyful one, is a sense of happiness conveyed?

The tone of the piece is clear; it is obvious what type of feeling the author is trying to convey.
     always   sometimes   rarely   never

FOCUS: Focus refers to the writer's ability to concentrate on a particular situation, conflict, or character without introducing unnecessary material that serves to distract the reader.

The focus of the piece is maintained; the author brings the reader into his or her world and retains the reader's attention.
     always   sometimes   rarely   never

DEVELOPMENT: Development refers to the progression of a piece of writing. A piece should have a clear beginning, middle, and end. The characters should also be developed to give the reader a sense of how they think, act, and respond to situations.

The story line and characters are convincingly developed as the piece progresses.
     always   sometimes   rarely   never

MECHANICS: Mechanics refer to the technical aspects of writing, like grammar, spelling, sentence structure, and usage.

The piece is free from mechanical errors.
     always   sometimes   rarely   never

FIGURE 5.7
Creative Writing Rating Scale
SOURCE: Adapted from Creative Writing Rating Form, Mason Miller, Boston College, 1994. Used with permission.

Linking Assessment and Instruction

Note that self- or peer review brings assessment and instruction very close to one another. In fact, it is often difficult to tell whether assessment or instruction is taking place. When students are using the performance criteria to review their own or another pupil's writing, they are neither solely assessing nor solely learning, they are using assessment as a means of learning. Also note that this kind of self- or peer review and the learning that comes from it would not be possible with most types of paper-and-pencil test items.

Involving students in developing performance criteria helps them understand what is important about a performance or product.

Performance assessment can also link instruction and assessment in other ways. For example, rather than having the teacher tell pupils what the important criteria for a performance or product are, the teacher can involve the pupils in the process of identifying the important criteria associated with an instructional task or product. This can be accomplished through class discussion or by providing pupils with good and poor examples of the performance or product and having pupils identify the characteristics that make the examples good or poor. The identified characteristics then become the performance criteria. Involving pupils in this way gives them ownership of the criteria and provides them with concrete examples of what are good and poor performances or products. Of course, to carry out this approach, the teacher must have an idea of what the important criteria are in order to select useful examples to show the pupils.

Teachers often include performance criteria in assignments or exercises to remind the pupils of what is expected of them. In Chapter 4, the way essay questions can be made clearer by including the criteria used to score pupils' answers was examined. To focus and clarify pupils' laboratory reports a science teacher included the following performance criteria in the laboratory directions: state the basic problem the lab focuses on; list steps needed to investigate the problem; produce and list reasonable estimates of data values; apply formulas related to the problem; state a conclusion based on the data gathered and analyzed. Informing the pupils of the criteria of a good product or performance in the assignment itself helps focus pupils on the desired criteria when completing the assignment.

Grading

What are essentially scoring rubrics are now widely used as report cards, especially in the early elementary grades. Figure 5.8 illustrates a rubric first grade teachers in the Ann Arbor, Michigan Public Schools use to assign grades to pupils. The entire report card is five pages long and contains simplified versions of rubrics such as the one shown in Figure 5.8, as well as a cover page sent home to explain the report form to parents. The outcomes reported to parents are the language arts and mathematics outcomes the district has identified as most crucial for teachers to monitor

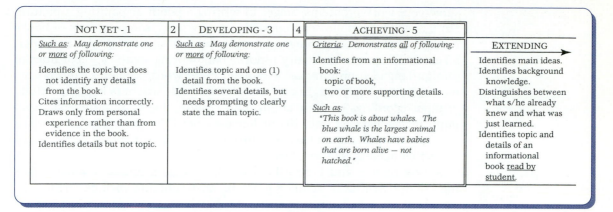

NOT YET - 1	2	DEVELOPING - 3	4	ACHIEVING - 5	EXTENDING →

Such as: May demonstrate one or *more* of following:
 	
Identifies the topic but does not identify any details from the book.
Cites information incorrectly.
Draws only from personal experience rather than from evidence in the book.
Identifies details but not topic.
		Such as: May demonstrate one or *more* of following:
		
		Identifies topic and one (1) detail from the book.
		Identifies several details, but needs prompting to clearly state the main topic.
				Criteria: Demonstrates *all* of following:
				
				Identifies from an informational book:
				  topic of book,
				  two or more supporting details.
				
				Such as:
				"This book is about whales. The blue whale is the largest animal on earth. Whales have babies that are born alive — not hatched."
					Identifies main ideas.
					Identifies background knowledge.
					Distinguishes between what s/he already knew and what was just learned.
					Identifies topic and details of an informational book <u>read by student</u>.

FIGURE 5.8

Scoring Rubric Used in First Grade Report Reprinted by permission of the Ann Arbor Public Schools.

and for students to achieve. Notice that each desired outcome is defined by specific performances or products at each of the three rubric levels: not yet, developing learner, and achieving learner.

PORTFOLIO ASSESSMENT

An important addition to the growing uses of performance assessment is portfolio assessment (Grace, 1992; O'Neil, 1993; Office of Technology Assessment, 1992). A **portfolio** is a purposeful collection of student work that can be used to describe pupils' efforts, progress, or achievement in a subject area. Students participate in selecting portfolio content, which includes guidelines for selection of pieces, criteria for judging learning, and student reflections (Arter & Spandel, 1992). The term derives from an artist's portfolio, which is a collection of the artist's work designed to show his or her creative style and range. As used in classrooms, portfolios have the same basic purpose: to collect pieces of pupil performances or products that show the pupil's accomplishments or improvement over time. Portfolios are more than folders that hold all of a pupil's work. They contain a consciously selected sample of a pupil's work that is intended to show growth and development towards some important curriculum goals. The basic aim of collecting pupils' work into portfolios is to support instruction and learning. Without a link to instruction and learning, portfolios are fruitless.

A portfolio can incorporate items from many different sources. For example, portfolios can assemble materials from various media (videos, audiotapes, pictures, computer programs, etc.); student reflections (plans, journals, self-evaluations, etc.); individual work (tests, papers, logs, homework, etc.); group work (projects, cooperative learning situations, lab partners, group performances, etc.); and processes (rough and final drafts,

Portfolios are carefully selected collections of a student's performances or products that show accomplishments or improvements over time.

show-your-work problems, stages of writing a poem or painting a picture, etc.). Specific portfolios can be made up of writing samples, lists of books read, journal entries, photographs, videotapes of musical or dramatic performances, science laboratory reports, handwriting samples, recordings of foreign language pronunciation, solved math word problems, and poems memorized or analyzed. In one school, first grade teachers kept a portfolio of tape recordings of their pupils' oral reading. Every three weeks, each pupil read a passage onto his or her own portfolio tape. The tapes were shared with parents and used with pupils to identify improvement and areas that needed additional work.

At the middle and high school levels, teachers typically have pupils maintain a writing or science portfolio that contains various writing assignments or laboratory experiments that have been done. Often these portfolios contain both rough drafts and finished products to show pupils and the teacher the progression of the work.

As the preceding examples show, portfolios can be used for many purposes. Whatever their use, it is important that they are guided by a specific purpose or purposes that limit the information collected and how it is used. Too often, teachers defer the question What should I do with all this information? until *after* they have collected large amounts of pupil work into portfolios. The purpose and focus of the portfolio should be identified before beginning to collect pieces. Table 5.7 shows the most common purposes for pupil portfolios.

Portfolios allow students to revisit and reflect upon their performances and products.

Perhaps the greatest contribution of portfolios is to give pupils a chance to revisit and reflect on their products and performances over time. For most pupils, life in school is an ongoing sequence of papers, performances, assignments, and productions. Each day a new batch of these is produced and the previous day's productions are tossed away, both mentally and physically. Collecting pupils' work in a portfolio retains it for

---

TABLE 5.7   COMMON PURPOSES FOR PUPIL PORTFOLIOS

- Makes pupils part of the assessment process by requiring them to revisit, reflect on, and judge their own work
- Gives teachers, parents, and pupils information about pupil progress over time
- Reinforces the importance of performances and products, not just selection assessments
- Provides concrete examples of pupils' work for parent conferences
- Permits diagnosis of pupils' performances and products
- Encourages pupils to think about what constitutes good performance in a subject area
- Grades pupils
- Gives pupils a chance to reflect on and assess prior work

subsequent pupil review and reflection. With suitable guidance, pupils can be encouraged to think about and compare their work over time, an opportunity rarely provided without portfolios. Pupils might be asked which of the portfolio items show the most improvement; which he or she enjoyed most and why; from which he or she learned the most; and in what areas he or she has made the most progress over the year. Pupils can see their progress and judge their work from the perspective of time and personal development.

Unfortunately, many teachers view portfolio assessment simply as the collection of pupils' every performance or product. There is, however, a great deal more to successful portfolio assessment than simply collecting pupils' work. The following suggestions can help in getting started with portfolios.

- ◆ Start with a manageable portfolio exercise, one that is focused on a single specific performance or product that will not take more than a month to complete and will produce relatively few portfolio entries.
- ◆ Before starting, think through the entire portfolio process of explaining, collecting, maintaining, reviewing, and assessing.
- ◆ Determine how pupils will be involved in the selection and review of their work. If pupils have no chance to revisit and examine their portfolios, one of the major benefits of portfolio assessment is lost.
- ◆ Determine what the pupils are to get out of the portfolio and devise instruction and assessment to reflect that purpose.
- ◆ Remember that both the teacher and the students will be moving into new, uncomfortable, and uncertain territory; educate the pupils on constructing portfolios.
- ◆ Change what does not work. Learning about portfolio assessment is an iterative process of trial and error.

Portfolio assessment involves the same four steps as other forms of performance assessment: a clear purpose, appropriate performance criteria, a suitable setting, and rating or scoring criteria.

Portfolio assessment is dependent upon the same four steps as all other types of performance assessment: (1) a clear purpose, (2) appropriate performance criteria, (3) a suitable setting, and (4) rating or scoring criteria. A discussion of each follows.

Purpose of Portfolios

The items that go into a portfolio, the criteria used to judge the items, and the frequency with which items are added or deleted from the portfolio all depend on its purpose. Thus, if the purpose of a portfolio is to showcase a pupil's typical work across subjects for a parent, its contents will likely be more wide-ranging than if its purpose is to assess the pupil's improvement in a single area such as written composition or oral reading over a single marking period. In the latter case, written compositions or tape recordings of oral readings will have to be obtained periodically

It is important to determine the purpose and guidelines for a portfolio's content before compiling it. Is it to grade, group, instruct, or diagnose pupils?

throughout the marking period, while in the former, a collection of pupil papers from one day's or week's schoolwork will suffice. If a portfolio is intended to show a pupil's best performance in an area, the contents of the portfolio will change as more samples of performance become available; if the purpose is to show improvement, earlier performances will have to be retained as the portfolio grows. If the purpose is to have pupils reflect on their work, the teacher will need to prepare prompts or questions that focus the pupils' reflections. Purpose is a crucial issue to consider in carrying out portfolio assessment, and it is important to determine the purpose and general guidelines for the pieces that go into the portfolio *before* compiling it.

Allowing students to help determine what goes into their portfolios gives them a sense of ownership.

In order to promote pupil ownership of their portfolios, it is important to allow pupils to make at least some of the choices of what pieces go into their portfolio. Some teachers develop portfolios that contain two types of pieces, those required by the teacher and those selected by the pupil. However, all pupil selections ought to be accompanied by an explanation of why the pupil feels that piece belongs in his or her portfolio. This latter information requires the pupil to reflect on the characteristics of the piece and why it belongs in the portfolio. Also, it is useful to require students to reflect on what they have learned or areas in which they have improved based on portfolio contents.

Performance Criteria

Performance criteria are needed to evaluate each of the individual pieces within a portfolio.

Performance criteria are needed to assess the individual pieces that make up a portfolio. Without such criteria, assessment cannot be consistent within and across portfolios. The nature and process of formulating such criteria is the same as those for formulating checklists and rating scales. In fact, the individual pieces in the portfolio will probably be judged using a checklist or rating scale similar to ones discussed earlier. Thus, depending upon the type of performance contained in a portfolio, many of the performance criteria discussed earlier in this chapter could be used to assess individual portfolio pieces.

If portfolios in a targeted subject area are to be kept by all teachers in a school or are to be passed from one teacher to the next as a pupil progresses through the grades, it is advisable that all the affected teachers cooperate in formulating a common set of performance criteria. Cooperative practice is useful because it involves groups of teachers in identifying important performance criteria, helps them provide common instructional emphasis within and between grades, and fosters discussion and sharing of materials among the teachers (Herbert, 1992). It is also reassuring for pupils to have some consistency in both instruction and teacher expectations as they pass through the grade levels.

As with individual checklists and rating scales, it is valuable for teachers and pupils to jointly identify the portfolio performance criteria. This gives pupils a sense of ownership over their performance and helps them think through the portfolio pieces they will produce. Beginning a lesson with joint discussion of what makes a good book report, oral reading, science lab, or sonnet is useful because it gets pupils thinking about the characteristics of the performance or product. Such discussions illustrate how performance assessments can serve both an instructional and assessment function.

There is another, very important reason why performance criteria are needed for portfolio assessment. The performances or products that make up a portfolio should, like all forms of assessment, reflect the instruction provided to pupils. Performance criteria are like a teacher's instructional objectives, identifying the important performances or criteria pupils need to learn. Without explicit criteria, instruction may not provide all the learning experiences necessary for pupils to learn the desired performance or product. This reduces the validity of the portfolio assessment. Of course, once stated, performance criteria can be amended and extended. Often, after examining the first few pieces in pupils' portfolios, the need to add, delete, or modify criteria becomes clear.

The performance criteria used in evaluating portfolios should align with a teacher's instructional objectives.

Setting

In addition to a clear purpose and performance criteria, portfolio assessments must take into account the setting in which pupils' performances are gathered and maintained. Many portfolio pieces are produced as a result of normal classroom activities. This is especially so for written work of all kinds. However, when portfolios include oral or physical performances, science experiments, artistic productions, and the like, special equipment or arrangements may be needed to properly collect the desired pupil performance, especially those that must be gathered one at a time from pupils. A concern is that many teachers underestimate the time it takes to collect the performances and products that make up portfolios, as well as the management and record keeping needed to maintain them. In lower grades teachers face basic issues such as where portfolios will be stored; when pupils can access them; and how a checking system to make sure the needed pieces are in a pupil's portfolio. In higher grades, pupils can be responsible for their own portfolios, with periodic teacher checks. This is more difficult to do in lower grades.

Scoring and Judging

It is important to note that scoring portfolios is a time-consuming task, since not only individual pieces have to be judged, but also the summarized pieces. Moreover, the complexity of the performances and products that make up the portfolio (e.g., written stories, tape recordings,

Scoring portfolios is a time-consuming process that involves judging each individual piece and the portfolio as a whole.

Individual portfolio pieces are normally judged using performance criteria that have been assembled into some form of checklist, rating scale, or rubric.

Allowing students to self-assess their portfolio encourages pupil reflection and learning.

Performance criteria used to assess an entire portfolio are different from those used to assess individual portfolio items.

laboratory write-ups) requires considerable attention to detail, which further increases scoring time. Performance criteria are especially helpful under these conditions.

When the purpose of a portfolio is only to provide descriptive information about pupil performance to next year's teacher or to parents at a parent-teacher night, no formal scoring or summarization is necessary. The parent or next year's teacher can examine the contents themselves to obtain the desired descriptive information. However, when the purpose of a portfolio is to diagnose, chart improvement, judge the success of instruction, encourage pupils to reflect on their work, or grade pupils, some form of scoring is required. For example, the fifth grade rubric for journal entries (Fig. 5.5) could be used to judge each journal entry in the portfolio.

The teacher does not always have to be the one who assesses a portfolio piece. It is desirable and instructive to allow the pupil to self-assess and reflect on some pieces in order to provide practice in critiquing and conceptualizing his or her work in terms of the performance criteria. Figure 5.9 shows a self-assessment exercise a teacher used to encourage fourth grade pupils to reflect on their work, revise it, and self-assess the revision. Notice how the teacher let the pupil select the piece to be rewritten, but asked the pupil to describe why she choose this particular piece from her writing portfolio and what its strong and weak points are. Then, after rewriting the piece, the pupil was provided performance criteria in the form of a series of rubrics to rate the revised piece.

Consider how much more involved in the writing process this pupil is than when an assignment is given, passed in to the teacher, graded, returned to the pupil, and soon forgotten. Note also the way that this kind of assessment encourages pupil reflection and learning. Even without a formal instrument, it is useful for teachers to develop questions that will focus pupils' reflection on their portfolio pieces: Which piece was most difficult and why? Which shows your best work and why? Which are you most proud of and why?

Scoring and judging entire portfolios can be a varied and difficult undertaking. There are a number of approaches to summarize the results of an entire portfolio. Most are time-consuming and rely heavily on the teacher's effort and interpretations. Thus, in planning for portfolio assessment, especially when there has been little prior experience with portfolios, it is advised to focus on only one form of portfolio entries (e.g., all journal reports, all poems, all solved math problems) rather than mixing different forms in the portfolio. Also, it is wise to include relatively few entries (five to eight) for initial attempts at portfolio assessment.

While individual teachers identify the summarization and scoring for their pupils' portfolios, there are four approaches that can provide ideas for them. First, as noted previously, there are some portfolios that do not need to be scored; their function is to provide examples of pupil work for parent-teacher night or for next year's teacher.

Second, if the main purpose of the portfolio is to examine pupil growth or improvement, earlier portfolio entries can be compared to later entries. For example, if the portfolio consists of pupils' written paragraphs, the

FIGURE 5.9
Self-Assessment
Exercise

Choose a story from your writing folder that you wish to rewrite. Answer the following questions.

I chose this story because

The best feature of this story is

The things that need improvement in this story are

Rewrite the story, making the improvements you believe are needed. Do your best work. After you have finished rewriting, judge what you have written. Circle the number that describes your story.

Spelling, grammar, punctuation
   1 = few capitals, many misspellings, incorrect punctuation
   2 = some errors in spelling, grammar, and punctuation
   3 = almost no errors in spelling, grammar, and punctuation

Organization
   1 = story switches topics, contains unneeded ideas, and is hard to follow
   2 = story usually stays focused on a single topic or idea
   3 = story is focused on a single topic or idea and is easy to follow

Word Usage
   1 = mostly simple words used, few descriptive words included
   2 = some imaginative and descriptive words used, but only in some parts
   3 = imaginative and descriptive words used throughout

Language and Details
   1 = simple sentence structure used throughout; few details included
   2 = mix of sentence structures in some places; details in some parts
   3 = varied sentence structures and details provided throughout

Story Line
   1 = no central problem or goal; little action or plot development
   2 = story problem or goal stated; story lacks action and development
   3 = story problem or goal stated; plot developed; keeps readers' interest

teacher might compare the pupils' earlier to later entries in spelling, clarity of topic sentences, capitalization and punctuation, and summarizing for main ideas. Note that identifying these areas to assess is equivalent to identifying performance criteria for scoring.

Third, if the purpose of the portfolio is to gain understanding in some subject area such as science, social studies, or math, the teacher could require that each portfolio entry be accompanied by the pupil's reflection of the importance and relation of the new entry to the prior entries. The teacher could gauge understanding in the subject area by reading and analyzing the student's reflections. A simple rubric could be constructed to grade students.

FIGURE 5.10
Narrative Description of Pupil's Writing Portfolio

Date	Genre	Topic	Reason	Length	Drafts
9/??	Self-Reflection	Thinking About Your Writing	Requested	1 page	1 draft
10/17	Narrative/Dramatic	Personal Monologue	Important	1 page	2 drafts
1/16	Response to Literature	On *The Lord of the Flies*	Unsatisfying	1 page	4 drafts
2/??	Self-Reflection	Response to Parent Comments	Requested	1 page	1 draft
2/28	Narrative/Dramatic	"The Tell-Tale Heart"	Free Pick	3 pages	2 drafts
5/22	Response to Literature	On *Animal Farm*	Satisfying	5 pages	2 drafts
6/??	Self-Reflection	Final Reflection	Requested	2 pages	1 draft

As a writer, Barry shows substantial growth from the beginning of the year in his first personal monologue to his last piece, a response to *Animal Farm*. Initially, Barry seems to have little control over the flow and transition of his ideas. His points are not tied together, he jumps around in his thinking, and he lacks specificity in his ideas. By January, when Barry writes his response to *The Lord of the Flies*, he begins a coherent argument about the differences between Ralph's group and Jack's tribe, although he ends with the unsupported assertions that he would have preferred to be "marooned on a desert island" with Ralph. Barry includes three reasons for his comparison, hinges his reasons with transition words, but more impressively, connects his introductory paragraph with a transition sentence to the body of his essay. In the revisions of this essay, Barry makes primarily word and sentence level changes, adds paragraph formatting, and generally improves the local coherence of the piece.

By the end of February when he writes his narrative response to Poe's "The Tell-Tale Heart," Barry displays a concern for making his writing interesting. "I like the idea that there are so many twists in the story that I really think makes it interesting." He makes surface level spelling changes, deletes a sentence, and replaces details, although not always successfully (e.g., "fine satin sheets and brass bed," is replaced with the summary description "extravagant furniture"). Overall, it is an effective piece of writing showing Barry's understanding of narrative form and his ability to manipulate twists of plot in order to create an engaging story.

Barry's last selection in his portfolio is an exceptional five-page, typed essay on Orwell's *Animal Farm*. The writing is highly organized around the theme of scapegoating. Using supporting details from the novel and contemporary examples from politics and sports, Barry creates a compelling and believable argument. The effective intertextuality and the multiple perspectives Barry brings to this essay result largely from an exceptional revision process. Not only does he attempt to correct his standard conventions and improve his word choices, he also revises successfully to the point of moving around whole clumps of text and adding sections that significantly reshape the piece. This pattern of revision shows the control Barry has gained over his writing.

In Barry's final reflection he describes his development, showing an awareness of such issues as organizing and connecting ideas, choosing appropriate words and details, and making his writing accessible to his readers. "I had many gaps in my writing. One problem was that I would skip from one idea to the next and it would not be clear what was gong on in the piece. . . . Now, I have put in more details so you don't have to think as much as you would. I also perfect my transitions and my paragraph form. . . . My reading . . . has improved my vocabulary and it helped me organize my writing so it sounds its best and makes the most sense possible. . . .There are many mistakes I have made throughout the year, but I have at least learned from all of them." I agree with him.

SOURCE: P. A. Moss, et al., "Portfolios, Accountability, and an Interpretive Approach to Validity," *Educational Measurement: Issues and Practice,* 1992, *11*(3), p. 18. Copyright 1992 by the National Council on Measurement in Education. Used by permission of AERA.

Finally, the contents of a portfolio can also be reported in terms of a summarizing narrative, as illustrated in Figure 5.10. The top portion of the narrative shows the portfolio's contents: a history of the pupil's writing productions, including the date produced, the literary genre, the topic addressed, the reason the piece was written, its length, and the number of drafts produced. The bottom part of the narrative shows the teacher's summary of the pupil's performance, including both descriptions and supporting illustrations. Such narratives are useful in describing a pupil's portfolio, but they are quite time-consuming to produce.

Different portfolios with different purposes require different summarizing criteria. For example, how would you summarize a portfolio containing a number of tape recordings of a pupil's Spanish pronunciation? What indicators would you use to judge *overall* progress or performance?

To summarize, assessments of performances, products, and portfolios broaden considerably the information teachers can gather about pupil achievement. They also involve pupils in their own learning in a deeper, more reflective manner than most paper-and-pencil assessments. Consequently they blur the line between instruction and assessment. Table 5.8

TABLE 5.8   ADVANTAGES AND DISADVANTAGES
OF PERFORMANCE, PRODUCT,
AND PORTFOLIO ASSESSMENTS

Advantages
- Chart pupil performance over time
- Conduct pupil self-assessment of products and performances
- Conduct peer review of products and performances
- Provide diagnostic information about performances and products
- Integrate assessment and instruction
- Promote learning through assessment activities
- Give pupils ownership over their learning and productions
- Clarify lesson, assignment, and test expectations
- Report performance to parents in clear, descriptive terms
- Permit pupil reflection and analysis of work
- Provide concrete examples for parent conferences
- Assemble cumulative evidence of performance
- Reinforce importance of pupil performances

Disadvantages
Most disadvantages associated with performance, product, and especially portfolio assessments involve the time they require
- To prepare materials, performance criteria, and scoring formats
- To manage, organize, and record keep
- For teachers and pupils to become comfortable with the use of performance assessments and the change in teaching and learning roles they involve
- To score and provide feedback to pupils

summarizes their main advantages and disadvantages. Because of the time they consume, teachers should begin implementing performance assessments slowly, focusing initially on only one or two particular performances, until everyone becomes comfortable with the demands of these kinds of assessment.

VALIDITY AND RELIABILITY OF PERFORMANCE ASSESSMENTS

Since formal performance assessments are used to make decisions about pupils, it is important for them to be valid and reliable. This section describes steps that can be taken to obtain high-quality performance assessments. Three general areas are considered: clarity of purpose, pupil preparation, and improving validity and reliability.

The purpose of performance assessment, like all classroom assessment, is to determine how much pupils have learned from instruction.

Chapter 4 discussed ways teachers use to get their pupils ready for assessment. First and foremost, they provide good instruction on whatever objectives or criteria their pupils are expected to learn and demonstrate. Pupils learn to set up and focus microscopes, build bookcases, write book reports, give oral speeches, measure with a ruler, perform musical selections, and speak French the same way they learn to solve simultaneous equations, find countries on a map, write a topic sentence, or balance a chemical equation. They are given instruction and practice. Achievement depends upon their being taught the things on which they are being assessed. One of the advantages of performance assessments is their explicit criteria, which focus instruction and assessment.

Unless students are informed about the performance criteria upon which they will be judged, they may not perform up to their abilities.

In preparing pupils for performance assessment, the teacher should inform and explain the criteria on which they will be judged (Mehrens, Popham, & Ryan, 1998). In many classrooms, teachers and pupils jointly discuss and define criteria for a desired performance or product (Herbert, 1992). This helps them to understand what is expected of them by identifying the important dimensions of the performance or product. Another, less-interactive way to do this is for the teacher to give pupils a copy of the checklist or rating form that will be used during their assessment. If performance criteria are not made clear to pupils, they may perform poorly, not because they are incapable, but because they were not aware of the teacher's expectations and the criteria for a good performance. In such cases, the performance ratings do not reflect the pupil's true achievement, and the grade received could lead to invalid decisions about the pupil's learning.

Improving Performance Assessments

Scoring performance assessments is a difficult and often time-consuming activity. The limits and difficulties described for scoring essay questions in Chapter 4 are applicable also to performance assessments. The product or process is complex and often lengthy. Unlike selection items, teachers' interpretation and judgment are necessary for scoring performances and products. Each student produces or constructs a performance or product that is different from other students. This makes scoring difficult; the more criteria to address and the more variation in the products or performances students produce, the more time-consuming, fatiguing, and potentially invalid (Linn, Baker, & Dunbar, 1991).

Scoring performance assessments is a difficult, time-consuming activity.

Further, like essays, performance assessments are subject to many ancillary aspects that may not be relevant to scoring but may influence the teacher's judgment of the performance assessments. For example, teachers' scoring of products such as essays or reports are often influenced by the quality of a pupil's handwriting, neatness, knowledge of the pupil being scored, and sentence structure and flow. These and similar factors are not key aspects of the product, but they often weigh heavily in scoring. Similarly, when teachers observe pupil performances, they cannot help but see how their pupils look, watch what they do, and hear what they say. They respond to such observations. They are pleased or annoyed by the pupil's appearance, performance, and attention to the task; they feel sympathy for the pupil who is trying very hard but cannot seem to pull off a successful performance. Teachers can rarely be completely unbiased observers of what their pupils do, because they know their pupils too well and have a set of built-in predispositions for each one. In each case, there are many irrelevant and distracting factors that can influence the teacher's judgments and the validity and reliability of performance assessments, as well.

Distractions and personal feelings can introduce error into either the observation or judging process, thereby reducing the validity and reliability of the assessment.

The key to improving rating or scoring skills is to try to eliminate the distracting factors so that the assessment more closely reflects the pupil's actual performance. In performance assessments, the main source of error is the observer, who judges both what is happening during a performance and the quality of the performance. Any distractions or subjectivity that arise during the observation or judging process can introduce error into the assessment, thereby reducing its validity and reliability.

Validity

Validity is concerned with whether the information obtained from an assessment permits the teacher to make a correct decision about a pupil's learning. As discussed previously, either failure to instruct pupils on desired performances or the inability to control personal expectations can produce invalid information and decision making. Another factor that can reduce the validity of formal performance assessment is **bias.** When some factor such as race, native language, prior experience, gender, or disability differentiates the scores of one group from those of another (e.g., English speaking and Spanish speaking, prior experience and inexperience, hearing disability and no hearing disability) we say the scores are biased. That is, judgments regarding the performance of one group of pupils are influenced by the inclusion of irrelevant, subjective criteria.

When irrelevant, subjective factors differentiate the scores of one group of pupils from another, the scores are said to be biased.

Suppose that oral reading performance was being assessed in a second grade classroom. Suppose also that in the classroom there was a group of pupils whose first language is Spanish. The oral reading assessment involved reading aloud from a storybook written in English. When the teacher reviewed her notes on the pupils' performances, she noticed that the Spanish-speaking pupils as a group did very poorly. Would the teacher be correct in saying that the Spanish-speaking pupils have poor oral reading skills? Would this be a valid conclusion to draw from the assessment evidence?

A more reasonable interpretation would be that the oral reading assessment was measuring the Spanish-speaking pupils' familiarity with the English language rather than their oral reading performance. How might the English-speaking pupils have performed if the assessment required reading in the Spanish language? In essence, the assessment provided different information about the two groups (oral reading proficiency versus knowledge of English language). It would be a misinterpretation of the evidence to conclude that the Spanish-speaking pupils had poorer oral reading skills without taking into account the fact that they were required to read and pronounce unfamiliar English words. The results of the assessment were not valid for the teacher's desired decision about oral reading for the Spanish-speaking pupils.

Teachers should select performance criteria and settings that do not give an unfair advantage to any group of students.

Teachers should write down performance assessments at the time they are observed in order to avoid memory error.

Assessing pupils on the basis of their personal characteristics rather than on their performance lowers the validity of the assessment.

When an assessment instrument provides information that is irrelevant to the decisions it was intended to help make, it is invalid. Thus, in all forms of assessment, but especially performance assessment, a teacher must select and use procedures, performance criteria, and settings that do not give an unfair advantage to some pupils because of cultural background, language, disability, or gender. Other sources of error that commonly affect the validity of performance assessments are teachers' reliance on mental rather than written record keeping and their being influenced by prior sizing-up perceptions of a pupil. The longer the interval between an observation and the written scoring, the more likely the teacher is to forget important features of pupils' performance.

Often, teachers' prior knowledge of their pupils influences the objectivity of their performance ratings. Factors such as personality, effort, work habits, cooperativeness, and the like are all part of a teacher's perception of the pupils in his or her class. Often, these prior perceptions influence the rating a pupil is given: the likable, cooperative pupil with the pleasant personality may receive a higher rating than the standoffish, belligerent pupil, even though they performed similarly. Assessing pupils on the basis of their personal characteristics rather than their performance lowers the validity of the assessment. Each of these concerns threatens the validity of teacher interpretations and scores. Note that these concerns are particularly difficult to overcome because of the complexity of performance assessment.

Reliability

Reliability is concerned with the stability and consistency of assessments. Hence, the logical way to obtain information about the reliability of pupil performance is to observe and score two or more performances or products of the same kind. Doing this, however, is not reasonable in most school settings; once a formal assessment is made, instruction turns to a new topic. Few teachers can afford the class time necessary to obtain multiple assessments on a given topic. This reality raises an important problem with the reliability of performance assessments: they may lack generalization (Popham, 1995). As noted, performances, products, and portfolios are more complex and fewer in number than selection or short-answer assessments. There are more math items on a multiple-choice test than there are on a performance assessment that requires pupils to show their math work. More short-answer items about factors that led to the Civil War can be asked than can be obtained by a single essay on the same topic. Because of such discrepancies in the quantity of information obtained from particular assessments, the teacher who employs performance assessments sees fewer examples of pupil mastery than when more narrow assessment approaches are used. The teacher's question then becomes How reliable is the limited information I have obtained from pupils? Does a single essay, a few show-your-work problems, or a portfolio provide enough evidence that students will perform similarly on other essays, show-your-work problems, or portfolios?

Teachers are put on the horns of a dilemma. Because they want their pupils to learn more than facts and narrow topics, they employ performance assessments to ensure deeper, richer learning. However, by employing an approach that is in-depth and time-consuming, they often diminish the reliability of the assessment. This is a dilemma faced by classroom teachers' own assessments and the more general, statewide pupil assessments (Koretz et al., 1992). There are few easy ways to overcome the dilemma, so teachers must acknowledge this limitation but also recognize the importance of providing pupils with performance assessments that assess higher level learning outcomes. It is better to use evidence from some imperfect performance assessments than it is to make uninformed decisions about pupil achievement of important school outcomes.

Reliability is also affected when performance criteria or rating categories are vague and unclear. This forces the teacher to interpret them, and because interpretations often vary with time and situation, this introduces inconsistency into the assessment. One way to eliminate much of

Observing a performance more than once increases the reliability of the assessment but is time-consuming.

An important concern in interpreting performance assessments is the often low generalizability of pupils' performances, products, or portfolios.

Unclear or vague performance criteria increase teacher interpretation, which introduces inconsistency into the assessment.

Having more than one person observe and rate a performance increases the objectivity of the assessment.

this inconsistency is to be explicit about the purpose of a performance assessment and to state the performance criteria and rubrics in terms of observable pupil behaviors. The objectivity of an observation can be enhanced by having several individuals independently observe and rate a pupil's performance. In situations where a group of teachers cooperate in developing criteria for a pupil performance, product, or portfolio, it is not difficult to have more than one teacher observe or examine a few pupils' products or performances in order to see whether scores are similar across teachers. This is a practice followed in performance assessments such as the College Board English Achievement Essay and in most statewide writing assessments.

The following guidelines can improve the validity and reliability of performance, product, and portfolio assessments:

♦ Know the purpose of the assessment from the beginning.

♦ Teach and give pupils practice in the performance criteria.

♦ State the performance criteria in terms of observable behaviors and avoid using adverbs such as *appropriately, correctly,* or *well* because their interpretation may shift from pupil to pupil. Use overt, well-described behaviors that can be seen by an observer and therefore are less subject to interpretation. Inform pupils of these criteria and focus instruction on them.

Performance criteria should be realistic in terms of the students' developmental level.

♦ Select performance criteria that are at an appropriate level of difficulty for the pupils. The criteria used to judge the oral speaking performance of third-year debate pupils should be more detailed than those to judge first-year debate pupils.

♦ Limit the number of performance criteria to a manageable number. A large number of criteria makes observation difficult and causes errors that reduce the validity of the assessment information.

♦ Maintain a written record of pupil performance. Checklists, rating scales, and rubrics are the easiest methods of recording pupil performance on important criteria, although more descriptive narratives are often desirable and informative. Tape recordings or videotapes may be used to provide a record of performance, so long as their use does not upset or distract the pupils. If a formal instrument cannot be used to record judgments of pupil performance, then informal notes of its strong and weak points should be taken.

♦ Be sure the performance assessment is fair to all pupils.

Performance assessment is no different from the other assessment techniques that have been discussed. In all cases, problems can be reduced by following suggested practices.

CHAPTER SUMMARY

◆ Performance assessments require pupils to demonstrate their knowledge by creating an answer, carrying out a process, or producing a product, rather than by selecting an answer. Performance assessments complement paper-and-pencil tests in classroom assessments.

◆ Performance assessments are useful for determining pupil learning in performance-oriented areas such as communication skills (oral reading, writing, and speaking); psychomotor skills (tracing, cutting with scissors, dissecting); athletic activities (jumping, throwing a ball, swimming); concept acquisition (demonstrating knowledge of concepts by using them to solve real problems); and affective characteristics (cooperation in groups, following rules, self-control).

◆ Performance assessments have many uses. They can chart pupil performance over time, provide diagnostic information about pupil learning, give pupils ownership of their learning, integrate the instructional and assessment processes, foster pupils' self-assessment of their work, and assemble into portfolios both cumulative evidence of performance and concrete examples of pupils' work. The main disadvantage of performance assessments is the time it takes to prepare for, implement, and score them.

◆ Successful performance assessment requires the following: a well-defined purpose for assessment; clear, observable performance criteria; an appropriate setting in which to elicit performance; and a scoring or rating method.

◆ The specific behaviors a pupil should display when carrying out a performance or the characteristics a pupil product should possess are called performance criteria. These criteria define the aspects of a good performance or product. They should be shared with pupils and used as the basis for instruction.

◆ The key to identifying performance criteria is to break down a performance or product into its component parts, since it is these parts that are observed and judged. It is often useful to involve pupils in identifying the criteria of products or performances. This provides them with a sense of involvement in learning and introduces them to important components of the desired performance.

◆ The number of performance criteria should be small, between 10 and 15, in order to focus on the most important aspects of performance and simplify the observation process. Teacher collaboration on common assessment areas or performances is advisable.

◆ Ambiguous words that cloud the meaning of performance criteria (e.g., *adequately, correctly, appropriate*) should be avoided; what is being looked for in the performance or product should be stated specifically. In fact, criteria should be stated so explicitly that another teacher could use them independently.

◆ Performance assessments may be scored and summarized either qualitatively or quantitatively. Anecdotal records and teacher narratives are qualitative descriptions of pupil characteristics and performances. Checklists, rating scales, and scoring rubrics are quantitative assessments of performance. Portfolios may include either qualitative, quantitative, or both kinds of information about pupil performance.

◆ Checklists and rating scales are developed from the performance criteria for a performance or product. Checklists give the observer only two choices in judging each performance criterion: present or absent. Rating scales provide the observer with more than two choices in judging: for example, always, sometimes, never or excellent, good, fair, poor, failure. Rating scales may be numerical, graphic, or descriptive. Performance can be summarized across performance criteria numerically or with a scoring rubric.

◆ Portfolios are collections of pupils' work in an area that show change and progress over time. Portfolios may contain pupil products (essays, paintings, lab reports) or pupil performances (reading aloud, foreign language pronunciation, using a microscope).

◆ Portfolios have many uses: focusing instruction on important performance activities; reinforcing the point that performances are important school outcomes; providing parents, pupils, and teachers with a perspective on pupil improvement; diagnosing weaknesses; allowing pupils to revisit, reflect on, and assess their work over time; grading pupils; and integrating instruction with assessment.

◆ Portfolio assessment is a form of performance assessment, and thus involves these four factors: definition of purpose, identification of clear performance criteria, establishment of a setting for performance, and construction of a scoring or rating scheme. In addition to performance criteria for each individual portfolio piece, it is often necessary to develop a set of performance criteria to assess or summarize the entire portfolio.

◆ To insure valid performance assessment, pupils should be instructed on the desired performance criteria before being assessed.

◆ The validity of performance assessments can be improved by stating performance criteria in observable terms; setting performance criteria at an appropriate difficulty level for pupils; limiting the number of performance criteria; maintaining a written record of pupil performance; and checking to determine whether extraneous factors (native language, cultural experience) influenced a pupil's performance.

◆ Reliability can be improved by multiple observations of performance or by checking for agreement among observers viewing the same performance, product, or portfolio and using the same assessment criteria.

QUESTIONS FOR DISCUSSION

1. What types of objectives are most suitably assessed using performance assessment?

2. How do formal and informal performance assessments differ in terms of pupil characteristics, validity and reliability of information, and usefulness for teacher decision making?

3. What are the advantages and disadvantages of performance assessments for teachers? for pupils?

4. How should a teacher determine the validity of a performance assessment?

5. How might instruction differ when a teacher desires to assess pupils' performances and products rather than their responses to selection-type tests?

6. What are some examples of how performance assessment can be closely linked to instruction? For example, how can performance assessment be used to involve pupils in the instructional process?

REFLECTION EXERCISES

♦ Suppose you have to construct a teaching portfolio that will show a prospective employer your qualifications for a teaching position. What performance or product evidence will you include in your portfolio? Why?

♦ Think back over the last three years of your schooling. During that time, what types of performance or product assessments have you been required to complete? In what subject areas? What proportion of all the assessments you have taken do you estimate to be nonselection assessments? What weaknesses can you recall in the way the performances or products were presented, explained, or graded? How could they have been improved?

ACTIVITIES

1. Select a subject area you might like to teach and identify one objective in that subject matter that cannot be assessed by selection or essay questions. Construct a performance or product assessment instrument for this objective. Provide the following information: (a) the objective and a brief description of the behavior or product you will assess and the grade level at which it will be taught; (b) a set of at least 10 observable performance criteria for judging the performance or product; (c) a method to score pupil performance; and (d) a method to summarize performance into a single score. The assessment procedure used may be in the form of a checklist or a rating scale. A two- to three-page document should adequately provide the needed information. Be sure to focus on the clarity and specificity of the performance criteria and on the clarity and practicality of the scoring procedure.

2. Rewrite in clearer form the following performance criteria for assessing a pupil's poem. Remember, what you are trying to do is write performance criteria that most people will understand and interpret the same way.

   ♦ poem is original
   ♦ meaningfulness
   ♦ contains rhymes
   ♦ proper length
   ♦ well-focused
   ♦ good title
   ♦ appropriate vocabulary level

REVIEW QUESTIONS

1. How do performance assessments differ from other types of assessment? What are the benefits of using performance assessment?

2. What four steps have to be attended to in carrying out performance assessment? What happens at each of these steps?

3. Why are performance criteria so important to performance assessment? How do they help the assessor not only with judging pupils' performance and products but also with planning and conducting instruction?

4. What are the differences among checklists, rating scales, and rubrics? How is each used to assess performance and products?

5. What are the main threats to the validity of performance assessments? How can validity be improved?

6. What are the major disadvantages of performance assessment?

7. In what ways are scoring performance assessments similar to scoring essay questions?

REFERENCES

Arter, J., and Spandel, V. (1992). Using portfolios of student work in instruction and assessment. *Educational Measurement: Issues and Practice, 11,* 36–44.

Goodrich, H. (1997). Understanding rubrics. *Educational Leadership, 54* (4), 14–17.

Grace, C. (1992). The portfolio and its use: Developmentally appropriate assessment of young children. *ERIC Digest.* ERIC Clearinghouse.

Herbert, E. A. (1992). Portfolios invite reflection—from both students and staff. *Educational Leadership, 49* (8), 58–61.

Koretz, D., McCaffrey, D., Klein, S., Bell, R., and Stecher, B. (1992). *Reliability of scores from the 1992 Vermont portfolio assessment program* (CSE Technical Report 355). Los Angeles: RAND Institute on Education and Training/CRESST.

Lambdin, D. V., and Walker, V. L. (1994). Planning for classroom portfolio assessment. *The Arithmetic Teacher, 41,* 318–324.

Linn, R., Baker, E., and Dunbar, S. (1991). Complex performance based assessment: Expectations and validation criteria. *Educational Researcher, 20* (8), 15–21.

Marzano, R. J., Pickering, D., and McTighe, J. (1993). *Assessing student outcomes: Performance assessment using the dimensions of learning model.* Alexandria, VA: Association for Supervision and Curriculum Development.

McLoughlin, J. A., and Lewis, R. B. (1990). *Assessing special students.* Columbus, OH: Merrill Publishing Co.

Mehrens, W. A., Popham, W. J., and Ryan, J. M. (1998). How to prepare students for performance assessments. *Educational Measurement: Issues and Practice, 17* (1), 18–22.

Office of Technology Assessment, U.S. Congress. (1992). *Testing in American schools—asking the right questions.* Washington, D.C.: U.S. Government Printing Office.

O'Neil, J. (1993). The promise of portfolios. *ASCD Update, 35* (7), 1–5.

Popham, W. J. (1995). *Classroom assessment.* Boston, MA: Allyn and Bacon.

Porter, C., and Cleveland, J. (1995). *The portfolio as a learning strategy.* Portsmouth, NH: Boynton/Cook.

Quality counts '99: Rewarding results, punishing failure. Education Week (January 11, 1999).

Wiggins, G. (1992). Creating tests worth taking. *Educational Leadership, 49* (8), 26–33.

Wiggins, G., and McTighe, J. (1998). *Understanding by design.* Alexandria, VA: Association for Supervision and Curriculum Development.

Wolf, D. P., Bixby, J., Glen, J., and Gardner, H. (1991). To use their minds well: Investigating new forms of student assessment. In G. Grant (Ed.), *Review of Research in Education, 17* (pp. 31–74). Washington, D.C.: American Educational Research Association.

CHAPTER 6

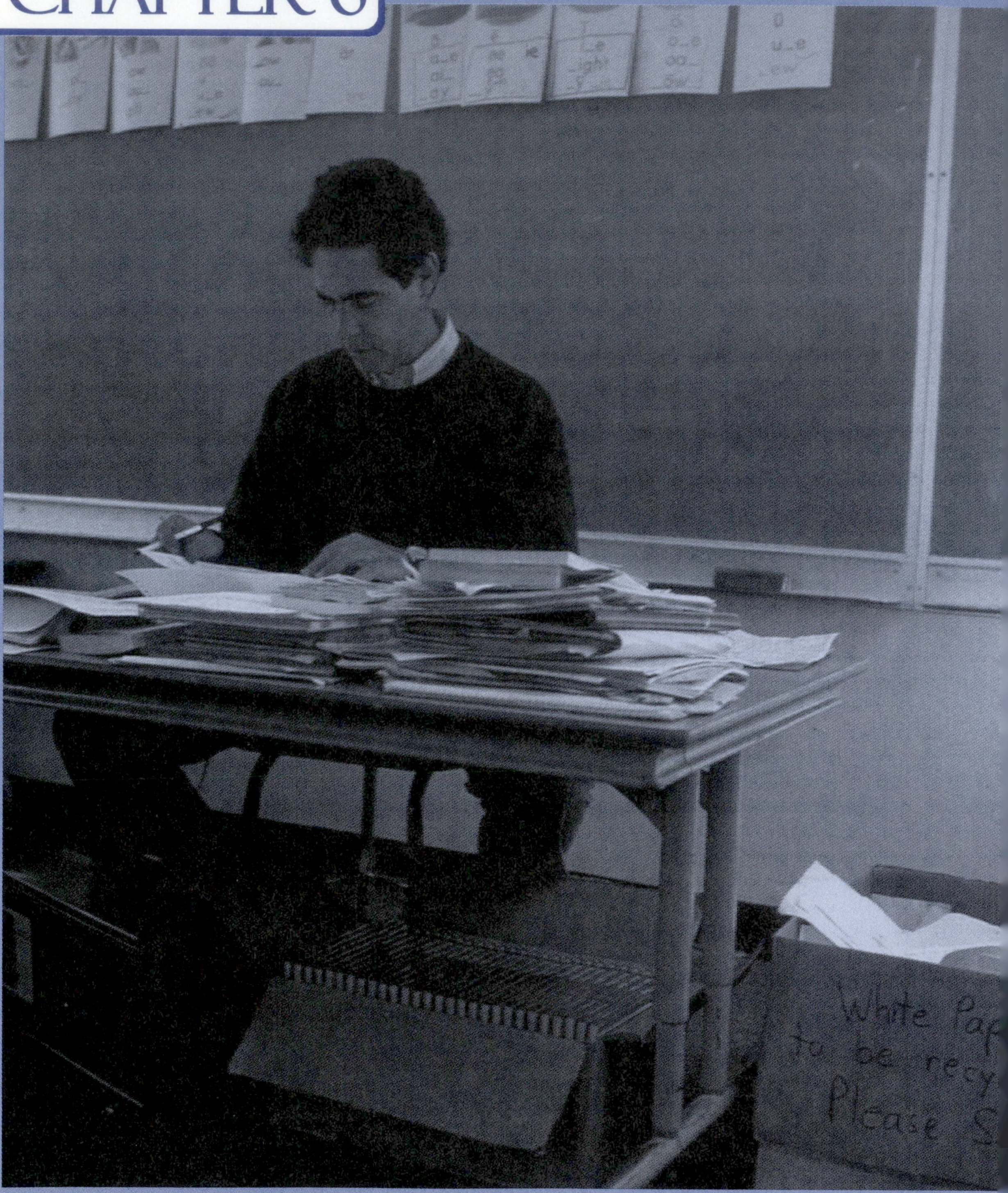

GRADING PUPIL PERFORMANCE

CHAPTER OBJECTIVES

After reading this chapter, the student will be able to:

1. define basic terms: for example, norm-referenced grading, criterion-referenced grading, and grading curve.
2. identify general principles of grading and explain why each is important.
3. develop, critique, and defend a grading scheme from given information about pupil performance.
4. describe other, nongrading strategies for providing information about pupils' classroom performance.

As discussed in previous chapters, teachers use a variety of techniques to gather information about their pupils' learning. Classroom teachers must do more than just describe pupils' performances, however; they must also make judgments about them. The process of judging the quality of a pupil's performance is called grading. It is the process by which scores and descriptive assessment information are translated into marks or letters that indicate the quality of each pupil's performance and learning. Assigning **grades** to pupils is an important professional responsibility, one a teacher carries out many times during the school year and one which has important consequences for pupils.

Grading is the process of judging the quality of a pupil's performance by comparing it to some standard of good performance.

Teachers assign grades both to individual assessments and to groups of individual assessments. When a pupil says I got a B on my book report or I got an A on my chemistry test, the pupil is talking about a grade on an individual assessment. Report card grades, on the other hand, represent a pupil's performance across all the individual subject area assessments completed during a term or grading period. Some people refer to the former process as assigning grades and to the latter as assigning marks, but the basic processes are similar, so here the term *grading* is used. Grading means making a judgment about the quality of either a single assessment or multiple assessments produced over time.

To judge the quality of a pupil's performance, it must be compared to something. Thus, when a teacher grades, he or she is making a judgment about the quality of each pupil's performance by comparing it to some standard of good performance. Suppose that Jamal got a score of 95 on a test. His score *describes* his performance, 95 points. But does 95 mean excellent, average, or poor achievement? This is the grading question. In order to answer this question, more than just Jamal's test score is needed. For example, the number of items that were on Jamal's test and how much each item counted provide important information. A score of 95 does not provide this information. It undoubtedly makes a difference in the way Jamal's performance is judged if he got 95 out of 200 items right as opposed to 95 out of 100 items right. Similarly, it would be helpful to know how Jamal did in relation to the other pupils in the class. A score of

95 does not tell us this. It makes a difference to know whether Jamal's score was the highest or the lowest in the class. Finally, one might like to know whether Jamal's 95 represents an improvement or a decline compared to his previous test scores. A score of 95 does not tell us this.

GRADING: ITS RATIONALE AND DIFFICULTIES

The purpose of this chapter is to outline the questions teachers face when grading and to provide guidelines to help answer these questions. There are many different ways to assign grades, many issues to consider when grading, and many ways to convey performance to pupils and parents. While the main focus is on the process of assigning report card grades in academic subjects, the principles discussed are also appropriate to grading single tests or performance assessments. A logical place to begin discussion is with the question Why grade?

Why Grade?

The simplest and perhaps most compelling reason that teachers grade their pupils is because they have to. Grading is one kind of official assessment that teachers are required to carry out. Nearly all school systems demand that classroom teachers make periodic written judgments about their pupils' performance.

Grading is an official assessment required of teachers.

The form of these written judgments varies from one school system to another and from one grade level to another. Some school systems require teachers to record pupil performance in the form of letter grades (e.g., A, A–, B+, B, B–, C+. . .); some in the form of achievement categories (e.g., excellent, good, fair, poor); some in the form of numerical grades (e.g., 90–100, 80–89, . . .); some in the form of pass/fail; some in the form of a rubric or checklist of specific skills; and some in the form of teachers' written narratives about a pupil's performance. The two most widely used systems are letter grades, which are the main grading system in upper elementary, middle, and high schools, and skill-based or objective-based ratings, which are the most prevalent in kindergarten and the primary grades (Friedman & Frisbie, 1993).

Some school systems also require teachers to write comments about each pupil's performance on the report card, while others require teachers to grade performance in both academic subject areas and social adjustment areas. Generally, subject matter grades appear in a different section of the report card in an attempt to differentiate academic performance from social adjustment. There are many different varieties of grade reporting forms, and Figures 6.1, 6.2, and 6.3 show three examples.

Regardless of the grading system or reporting form used, grades are always based on teacher judgments.

STOUGHTON PUBLIC SCHOOLS
Pupil Progress Report - Grades 1, 2 and 3
Anthony L. Sarno, Jr., Superintendent of Schools

NAME_____ GRADE_____ SCHOOL YEAR_____

SCHOOL _____ HOMEROOM TEACHER_____

KEY

C Commendable	✓ denotes an area of weakness
S Satisfactory	M denotes modified program
N Needs Improvement	+ or - may be used to modify S

ATTENDANCE RECORD

TERM	I	II	III	IV	TOTAL
ABSENT					
TARDY					
DISMISSED					

READING GRADE	1	2	3	4	SCIENCE (grade 3 only) GRADE	1	2	3	4
Effort					Effort				
Connects literature with other experiences					Uses science process skills				
Learns and applies vocabulary					Understands concepts and ideas				
Comprehends teacher read selections					**ART** GRADE				
Understands story structure					Effort				
Uses word attack skills					Conduct				
Applies appropriate reading strategies and skills					Understands concepts and ideas				
Reads with fluency					**COMPUTERS** GRADE				
Reads with understanding					Effort				
Makes good use of independent reading time					Conduct				
LANGUAGE GRADE					Understands concepts and ideas				
Effort					**MUSIC** GRADE				
Organizes and expresses ideas orally					Effort				
Expresses ideas through writing					Conduct				
Develops and organizes ideas in written work					Understands concepts and ideas				
Writes with correct usage and mechanics					**PHYSICAL EDUCATION** GRADE				
Edits and revises as necessary					Effort				
SPELLING GRADE					Conduct				
Effort					Understands concepts and ideas				
Masters assigned spelling words					**WORK HABITS** GRADE				
Spells correctly in written work					Listens attentively				
HANDWRITING GRADE					Works cooperatively in a group				
Effort					Participates in class				
Forms letters correctly					Completes homework				
Writes neatly and legibly					Completes work independently				
MATHEMATICS GRADE					Uses time efficiently				
Effort					Has a positive attitude toward learning				
Understands concepts					Follows directions				
Masters basic facts					Seeks help when needed				
Works with accuracy					Organizes work and materials				
Interprets information to solve problems					Uses study skills				
SOCIAL STUDIES (grade 3 only) GRADE					**CONDUCT** GRADE				
Effort					Follows classroom rules				
Demonstrates geographic awareness					Follows school rules				
Understands cultural similarities and differences					Demonstrates self control				
Understands historical concepts and ideas					Accepts responsibility				
					Respects rights, opinions and property of others				

FIGURE 6.1
Example of an Elementary School Report Card

SOURCE: Pupil Progress Report from the Stoughton Public Schools System, Stoughton, MA. Reprinted by permission of the Stoughton Public Schools.

COMMENTS

TERM 1	TERM 2

TERM 3	TERM 4

Assignment for September 19____ School _____ Grade_____ Room _____

FIGURE 6.1
Continued

Regardless of the particular system or report form used, grades are always based on teacher judgments.

Figure 6.1 shows a report card for an early elementary school in which pupils are graded in academic and social adjustment areas using a grading system based on commendable, satisfactory (with options for + or –), and need for improvement. Figure 6.2 shows a high school report card based solely on academic performance and based on the letter grade A through F system. Figure 6.3 shows a kindergarten report card in which a grade is given to each item in a set of objectives pupils are expected to master.

The purpose of grades is to communicate information about a pupil's academic achievement (Friedman & Frisbie, 1995). Within this general purpose are four more specific purposes: administrative, informational, motivational, and guidance. *Administratively,* schools need grades to determine such things as a pupil's rank in class, credits for graduation, and suitability for promotion to the next grade.

Informationally, grades are used to tell parents, pupils, and others about a pupil's academic performance. Grades represent the teacher's summary judgment about how well pupils have mastered the content and behaviors taught in a subject during a particular term or grading period. Because report card grades are given only four or five times a year, the information they convey is limited to summary judgments, rarely providing detailed diagnostic information about pupil performance. Teachers recognize this limitation (Hubelbank, 1994). However, lack of detail does not diminish the importance of grades for pupils and parents. Remember, grades are only one means of communicating with pupils and parents. Other

The general purpose of grades is to communicate information about a pupil's academic achievement.

Administrative reasons for grading include determining a pupil's rank in class, credits for graduation, and readiness for promotion.

STUDENT NAME			YEAR OF GRAD 1991	STUDENT I.D.	TELEPHONE	HOME ROOM	PREV. CREDITS 62.00

SEMESTER SCHOLARSHIP REPORT

NO.	COURSE	TEACHER	1ST GRADE	1ST MISSED	2ND GRADE	2ND MISSED	EXAM	FINAL GRADE	CREDITS EARNED
11	HEALTH	Mr. Fleagle	A	1	A–		B	A–	1.00
133	ENGLISH	Mr. Turcotte	B	2	B+		B	B+	2.50
221	AP EUR HIS	Mrs. Golden	B	1	B+		B	B	2.50
321	GEOMETRY	Ms. Franklin	B	2	C+	1	C+	B–	2.50
433	PHYSICS	Mr. Wind	B–		B	2	B–	B	3.00
737	INTRO LAW	Mr. Tarot	B+	1	A–		B+	A–	2.50
	MERITS		100		100				

CREDITS TO DATE   76.00

ATTENDANCE	THIS GRADING PER.	TOTAL THIS YEAR
DAYS ABSENT	0	0
TIMES TARDY	0	0
TIMES DISMISSED	1	1

ATTENDANCE IS RECORDED AS OF 01-19-90

GUIDANCE COUNSELOR

TELEPHONE

NATICK HIGH SCHOOL
15 WEST STREET
NATICK, MASS. 01760

PARENT / STUDENT

PLEASE SEE REVERSE SIDE FOR EXPLANATION OF GRADES

FIGURE 6.2
Example of a High School Report Card

SOURCE: Natick High School Report Card Form. Reprinted by permission of Natick Public Schools.

KINDERGARTEN PROGRESS REPORT

Our Lady of Lourdes School
54 Brookside Avenue
Jamaica Plain, MA 02130
542-6136

Student's Name

Teacher's Name

ATTENDANCE

	D	M	J
Absent			
Tardy			

School Year 19___ - 19___

EVALUATION KEY
G - Good   S - Satisfactory
I - Needs Improvement
N - Not expected at this time

READING READINESS

	D	M	J
Recognizes own name			
Knows alphabet in sequence			
Recognizes upper case letters			
Recognizes lower case letters			
Associates sounds with letters			
Is able to blend sounds into words			
Works from left to right			
Shows interest in books/stories			

LANGUAGE DEVELOPMENT

ORAL

	D	M	J
Speaks clearly			
Expresses ideas and feelings well			
Shares ideas and feelings well			
Uses adequate vocabulary			
Speaks in complete sentences			
Tells story in sequence			

WRITTEN

	D	M	J
Can print full name			
Prints alphabet			

MATH READINESS

	D	M	J
Can count in order			
Recognizes numbers to 10			
Recognizes numbers above 10			
Writes numbers clearly			
Applies knowledge of numbers			
Identifies basic shapes			
Understands math items			
Visually discriminates among likenesses and differences			

PHYSICAL DEVELOPMENT

SMALL MUSCLE

	D	M	J
Dresses self			
Buttons			
Zips			
Laces			
Controls pencil well			
Can cut well			
Colors neatly			
Pastes neatly			

LARGE MUSCLE

	D	M	J
Runs and jumps well			
Can catch, bounce, and throw ball			
Shows partiality to left or right			

DEVELOPMENT IN ART AND MUSIC

	D	M	J
Is eager to explore art materials			
Is imaginative with art materials			
Identifies colors, shapes and sizes			
Shows enthusiasm for music			
Enjoys singing			

RELIGIOUS DEVELOPMENT

	D	M	J
Is learning to pray and talk to God			
Is learning about God and His creation			

SOCIAL DEVELOPMENT

	D	M	J
Accepts responsibility			
Respects others' property			
Respects others' feelings			
Respects authority			
Works well with others			
Plays well with others			
Listens when others talk			

WORK HABITS

	D	M	J
Observes rules and regulations			
Listens carefully			
Follows directions			
Has good attention span			
Completes activities promptly			
Works well independently			
Uses materials correctly			
Takes care of materials			
Cleans up after work period			
Finishes what has been started			
Values own work			
Is observant			

PERSONAL

	D	M	J
Knows full name			
Knows address			
Knows phone number			
Knows age and birthday			

FIGURE 6.3
Kindergarten Report Form

SOURCE: Kindergarten Progress Report from Our Lady of Lourdes School, Jamaica Plain, MA. Reprinted by permission of the Our Lady of Lourdes School, Jamaica Plain, MA.

Grades are used to motivate pupils to study and to guide them toward appropriate courses, course levels, colleges, and special services.

methods such as parent-teacher conferences can provide more detailed information about school progress; these are described later in this chapter.

Grades are also used to *motivate* pupils to study. A high grade can be a reward for studying and learning. This motivational aspect of grading is, however, a two-edged sword. Motivation may be enhanced when grades are high, but diminished when grades are lower than expected. Also, it is not desirable to have students study solely to get a good grade. Teachers should try to balance grading rewards with other kinds of rewards.

Lastly, grades are used for *guidance.* They help the pupil, parent, and counselor choose appropriate courses and course levels for the pupil. They help identify pupils who may be in need of special services, and they provide information to colleges about the pupil's academic performance in high school.

Thus, grades are used in schools for many reasons. And while there are periodic calls to abolish grades, it is difficult to envision schools in which judgments about pupils' performance were not made by teachers and communicated to various interested parties. The basis on which teacher grades are derived might change, the format in which the grades are reported might be altered, and the judgments might no longer be called grades, but the basic process of teachers' judging and communicating information about pupil performance, that is, grading, would still be going on.

Because grades can affect students' chances in life, teachers are ethically bound to be as fair and objective as possible when grading pupils.

In any form, grades are potent symbols in our society, symbols that are taken very seriously by pupils, parents, and the public at large. Communicating pupil performance to pupils and parents is an integral part of teaching (Brookhart, 1998; Friedman & Frisbie, 1995). Some people object to grading because grades can influence pupils' motivation and self-esteem and encourage cheating. There is some truth to these arguments—grades are not perfect. But because grading is supported by parents and most teachers, it is necessary to take the process seriously and to devise a grading system that (1) is fair to pupils and (2) conveys the intended message about pupil performance. Teachers have a responsibility to be objective and fair in assigning grades and should never use grades to punish or reward pupils they like or dislike.

The Difficulty of Grading

Grading is often a difficult task for teachers for four main reasons: (1) few teachers have had formal instruction in how to grade pupils (Airasian, 1991; Slavin, 1994); (2) school districts and principals provide little guidance to teachers regarding grading policies and expectations (Hubelbank, 1994); (3) teachers know that grades are taken seriously by parents and pupils and that the grades a pupil gets will be scrutinized and often challenged; and (4) there is a fundamental ambiguity in the teacher's classroom role (Brookhart, 1991), in which the knowledge of pupils' needs and characteristics is difficult to ignore when the teacher is called upon to be a dispassionate, objective dispenser of grades.

Teachers inevitably face the dilemma of what constitutes fairness in grading. Must a teacher always be fair to the institution that expects dispassionate grading, or can fairness include consideration of a pupil's unique needs, disabilities, and problems? Which is the greater misuse of power: to ignore or to take into account individual circumstances when grading? The special helping relationship that teachers have with their pupils makes it difficult for teachers to judge them on a totally objective basis (Brookhart, 1992; Hubelbank, 1994). This is especially so for grading because the judgments are public, perceived to be very important, have real consequences for pupils, and can influence the pupil's educational, occupational, or home status.

The helping relationship that teachers have with their pupils makes it difficult to judge them on a completely objective basis.

The following remarks indicate some of the ambivalence teachers feel about grading.

> Report card time is always difficult for me. My pupils take grades seriously and talk about them with each other, even though I warn them not to. They're young (fourth graders) and some let their grades define their self-images, so grades can have a negative effect on some. Still, I guess it doesn't do a kid much good to let him think everything's great in his schoolwork when it really isn't . . . but putting it down on a report card makes it final and permanent. You know you can't make everyone happy when you grade and that some hopes will be dashed. One thing's for sure. I agonize over the grades I give.

> The first report card of the year is always the toughest because it sets up future expectations for the child and his or her parents.

> At the high school level where I teach, grades are given more by the book than I think they are in the elementary school. Here we don't get to know our students as well as elementary school teachers and so we can be more objective and give grades based almost exclusively on the students' academic performance. For many teachers at this level, the rank book average defines the grade a student gets, plain and simple. I have to admit that I do recognize differences in pupil interest, effort, and politeness that probably influence my grades a little bit.

These comments indicate that grading is a difficult, time-consuming process that demands considerable mental and emotional energy from teachers and that has important consequences for pupils. Grading is further complicated by the fact that there are no uniformly accepted strategies for assigning grades. Instead, each teacher must find his or her own answer to questions about the grading process.

There are no uniformly accepted strategies for assigning grades.

Table 6.1 summarizes both the purposes of grading and some of the more difficult considerations teachers face when assigning grades to their pupils.

GRADING AS JUDGMENT

The most important aspect of the grading process is its dependence on teacher judgments.

The single most important characteristic of the grading process is its dependence upon teacher judgments. Although there are general guidelines to help develop a classroom grading system, all such systems depend on teacher judgment because the teacher knows the pupils and their accomplishments better than anyone else. Consequently, in assigning grades, teachers are granted considerable discretion and autonomy; no one else can or should make grading judgments for a teacher.

Teacher judgments are dependent upon two characteristics: (1) information about the person being judged (e.g., test scores, book reports, performance assessments) and (2) a basis of comparison that can be used to translate the information into grading judgments (e.g., the level of performance that is worth an A, a C, or an F). Since information provides the basis for judgment, judging is different from mere guessing. Guessing is the recourse when there is no information or evidence to help make a judgment: I have no information, so I'll just have to guess. To *judge* implies that some evidence is considered in making the judgment. Thus, a teacher gathers assessment evidence of various kinds to help make judgments and decisions about instruction and pupil learning. Without this evidence, the teacher's decisions are guesses, not judgments.

A judgment is neither a guess nor a certainty but is based upon evidence the teacher deems valid and reliable.

Judgment also implies uncertainty, however, especially in the classroom setting. When there is complete certainty, there is no need for a teacher to judge. For example, when teachers state John is a boy, Mary's parents are divorced, or Sigmund got the highest score on the math test, they are stating facts about pupils, not making judgments about them. Judgment, then, is somewhere between guessing and certainty. It is based on evidence, but the evidence is rarely conclusive or complete. This uncertainty requires that a teacher judge. Increasing amounts of information reduce, but rarely eliminate, the need for judgment. It is because assessment evidence is always incomplete that teachers must be concerned about the validity and reliability of judgments made from assessment evidence.

To summarize, the goal in grading is to obtain enough valid evidence about pupil accomplishments to make a grading judgment that is fair and can be supported. Since grades are important, they should be based mainly on formal evidence such as tests and performance assessments. The concreteness of these types of information not only helps the teacher to be objective in awarding grades, but also can help explain or defend a grade that is challenged. Bearing this in mind, there are three main teacher judgments that make up a **grading system** that provides answers to the following questions:

♦ Against what standard shall I compare my pupils' performance?
♦ What aspects of performance shall I include in my grades?
♦ How should different kinds of evidence be weighted in assigning grades?

Few school districts have explicit grading policies that provide teachers with answers to these questions. Most districts have particular grading formats teachers must use (A, B, C, . . . ; good, satisfactory, poor; etc.), but teachers must work out for themselves the specific details of their grading system by determining such criteria as the level of performance that is A work and that which is D work, the difference between good and satisfactory performance, and whether pupils will be failed if they're trying. Even if a teacher does not consciously address such issues when grading, he or she must implicitly do so because grades cannot be assigned otherwise.

STANDARDS OF COMPARISON

A grade is a judgment about the quality of a pupil's performance. It is impossible, however, to judge performance in the abstract. Recall how difficult it was to judge how good Jamal's test score of 95 was when that was the only piece of information. Additional information that facilitated comparison of Jamal's performance to some standard of goodness or quality was needed. Thus, without comparison, there can be no grading.

Many bases of comparisons can be used to assign grades to pupils (Borich, 1996; Frisbie & Waltman, 1992; Guskey, 1996). Those most commonly used in classrooms compare a pupil's performance to

♦ the performance of other pupils;
♦ predefined standards of good and poor performance;

♦ the pupil's own ability level;

♦ the pupil's prior performance (improvement).

The vast majority of teachers use one of the first two comparisons in assigning grades to their pupils (Friedman & Frisbie, 1993). This is just as well, since for technical and substantive reasons, the latter two types of comparison are not recommended.

Comparisons with Other Pupils

Assigning grades to a pupil based on his or her performance compared to other pupils' performance is referred to as **norm-referenced grading.** Other names for this type of grading are relative grading and grading on the curve. A high grade means a pupil did better than most of his or her classmates, while a low grade means the opposite. When a teacher says things like Jim is smarter than Julie, Rowanda works harder in social studies than Mike and Pat, and Maria completes her math worksheets faster than anyone else in the class, the teacher is making norm-referenced comparisons. The quality of a pupil's performance is determined by how that pupil compares to others in the class.

In the norm-referenced system, not all pupils can get the top grade no matter how well they perform. The system is designed to ensure that there is a range of grades across the various grading categories. Notice that in the norm-referenced system, a grade contains no indication of how well a pupil did in terms of actually mastering what was taught; a pupil gets an A grade for being higher than his or her classmates. If a pupil answered only 40 out of 100 test questions correctly, but was the highest scorer in the class, he or she would receive an A grade in norm-referenced grading, even though he or she had low mastery of what was tested and taught. The opposite is true at the other end of the scoring range: a pupil may answer 97 out of 100 questions but still get a C because most other pupils in the class got a 98, 99, or 100.

In practice, teachers set up a norm-referenced grading system by establishing a **grading curve.** This curve, which varies from teacher to teacher and class to class, establishes quotas for each grade. The following is an example of a grading curve.

Top 20% of pupils	A grade
Next 30% of pupils	B grade
Next 30% of pupils	C grade
Next 10% of pupils	D grade
Last 10% of pupils	F grade

In using this grading curve to grade a chapter or unit test, the teacher administers the test, scores it, and arranges the pupils in order of their scores from highest to lowest. The highest scoring 20% of the pupils (including ties) get an A grade, the next 30% get a B grade, the next 30% get a C grade, and so on. If the same curve is applied to report card grading, the teacher first has to summarize the varied information about pupil performance that has been gathered over the entire term. The summary score for each pupil is arranged in order from highest to lowest, and the percentages in the curve are applied to allocate grades.

There is no single best grading curving. Teachers construct their grading curves by considering the pupils, the subject studied, and their own beliefs about grading. Some teachers give mostly A's and B's, while others give mainly C's. Some teachers do not believe in giving pupils F's while others give many F's. However, if the curve gives too many high grades to mediocre pupils, pupils will not respect it. If it is too difficult to get an A even for bright, hardworking pupils, they will give up. In the end, the goal is a grading curve that is fair to the pupils and represents academic standards that the teacher feels are appropriate and realistic for the pupils.

A grading curve that represents appropriate and realistic academic standards is fair.

The comparison chosen to assign grades can influence pupils' effort and attitude. Norm-referenced grading, for example, tends to undermine the achievement and effort of pupils who continually score near the bottom of the class, since they continually receive poor grades. Norm-referenced grading poses a lesser threat to the top pupils in the class. Competitive, norm-referenced approaches that make a pupil's success or failure dependent on the performance of classmates can also reduce pupil cooperation and interdependence, because success for one pupil reduces the chance of success for others.

Norm-referenced grading makes a pupil's grade dependent on the performance of classmates, which can reduce student cooperation.

Comparison to Predefined Standards

Instead of grading by comparing pupils to each other, a teacher can compare a pupil's performance to preestablished performance standards. These **performance standards** define the performance level a pupil must attain to receive a particular grade. The test for a driver's license is a simple, pass-fail example of a performance standard. In many states, the driver's test contains two parts, a written section covering knowledge of the rules of the road and a performance section in which the applicant must actually drive an automobile around local roads. (Notice how paper-and-pencil tests *and* performance assessment are combined in the driver's tests to make certain all important behaviors related to safe driving are assessed. This is a good model for teaching.)

An applicant must pass the written portion of the driver's test before the performance portion is attempted, and the written part is usually made up of 10 or 20 multiple-choice items. The test is administered to groups of applicants in much the same way paper-and-pencil tests are administered in classrooms. In most states, passing the test depends upon getting 70 percent of the items correct. In this case, 70 percent is the performance standard. Whether any single applicant passes or fails depends only on how he or she does compared to the performance standard of 70 percent. Passing has nothing whatsoever to do with how the other applicants do on the test because applicants' scores are not compared to one another. Note that in this system it is possible for all or none of the applicants to pass.

Grading that compares a pupil's achievement to preestablished performance standards rather than to other pupils' achievement is called criterion-referenced grading.

Grading that compares a pupil's achievement to a predefined performance standard is called **criterion-referenced grading.** As in the driver's test, each pupil is graded on the basis of his or her own performance. Since pupils are not compared to one another and do not compete for a limited percentage of high grades, it is possible for all applicants to get high or low grades on a test. Criterion-referenced, or absolute, grading is the most commonly used grading system in schools.

Performance-Based Criteria

Criterion-referenced grading is the most commonly used grading system in schools.

There are two types of performance standards that are used in criterion-referenced grading. One type spells out in detail the specific behaviors pupils must perform in order to receive a particular grade. This is rubric scoring. For example, suppose a teacher wants to use a rubric to provide performance standards for each pupil who gives an oral speech. The teacher devises and explains to the pupils the following four levels of the scoring rubric.

A grade   Pupil consistently faces audience, stands straight and maintains eye contact; voice projects well and clearly; pacing and tone variation appropriate; well-organized points logically and completely presented; brief summary at end.

B grade   Pupil usually faces audience, stands straight and makes eye contact; voice projection good, but pace and clarity vary during talk; well-organized but repetitive; occasional poor choice of words and incomplete summary.

C grade   Pupil fidgety; some eye contact and facial expression change; uneven voice projection, not heard by all in room, some words slurred; loosely organized, repetitive, contains many incomplete thoughts; little summarization.

D grade   Pupil's body movements distracting, little eye contact or voice change; words slurred, speaks in monotone, does not project voice beyond first few rows, no consistent or logical pacing; rambling presentation, little organization with no differentiation between major and minor points; no summary.

The teacher observes each speech, concentrating on the specific behaviors listed in the performance standards. On the basis of comparing the observation to the preceding performance standard or rubric, the teacher assigns a grade to each pupil. Again, notice that each pupil's grade depends upon how he or she performs in comparison to the standard, not in comparison to other pupils.

Rubrics are useful for grading complex performance-based achievements.

Percentage-Based Criteria

The second, more common type of criterion-referenced standard uses cutoff scores based on the percent of items answered correctly. In the case of report card grading, an overall percentage of mastery across many individual assessments is used. Perhaps the most widely used standard of this type is one that has the following cutoff percents.

A grade	90 percent to 100 percent of items correct
B grade	80 percent to 89 percent of items correct
C grade	70 percent to 79 percent of items correct
D grade	60 percent to 69 percent of items correct
F grade	less than 60 percent of items correct

Any pupil who scores within one of these performance standards receives the corresponding grade. There is no limit on the number of pupils who can receive a particular grade, and the teacher does not know the distribution of grades until after the tests are scored and graded. Note that this is not the case in the norm-referenced approach.

Many teachers use different cutoff scores than these; some use 85 percent and higher as the cutoff for an A grade and readjust the cutoffs for the remaining grades accordingly. Others refuse to flunk a pupil unless he or she gets less than half (50 percent) of the items incorrect. Like the curve in norm-referenced grading, the grading standards that are used in criterion-referenced grading are based upon a teacher's judgment about what is suitable and fair for his or her class. Standards should be reasonable given the ability of the class and the nature of the subject matter, and they should be academically honest and challenging for the pupils.

In criterion-referenced grading, there is no limit to the number of pupils who can receive a particular grade.

In recent years, a number of states have developed statewide assessment programs. Schools in the state are expected to employ the same specific objectives or standards in various subject areas. These objectives form the basis for instruction and assessment, with pupils being graded on the number of objectives they have achieved (*Education Week*, 1999). Results of these statewide assessments are scored using criterion-referenced grading. Performance standards based on rubrics or on the proportion of tasks pupils get correct determine the pupil's grade. If the standard has only two levels, say mastery or nonmastery, scoring specifies a single cutoff score that will be used to differentiate pupils who mastered from those who did not. For a standard that has more than two levels, for example, commendable, satisfactory, limited,

In recent years students are being graded not only by their teachers, but also by statewide assessments.

or unsatisfactory, a rubric to differentiate among pupils who belong at each level is used.

Interpreting and Adjusting Grades

A criterion-referenced grading system is intended to indicate how much a pupil has learned of the things that were taught. Grades based on invalid assessments or on assessments that fail to cover the full range of what pupils were taught convey an incorrect message about pupil learning. Of course, valid assessment instruments, those that fully assess what pupils have been taught, should always be used, regardless of the grading approach. However, the content-mastery focus of criterion-referenced grades makes it especially crucial that teachers using this grading system develop assessments that cover the full range of behaviors and skills taught.

Regardless of whether a norm- or a criterion-referenced grading system is employed, the grading curve or performance standards should be defined before assessment is carried out. This leads teachers to think about expected performance early and allows them to inform pupils of what is needed to get high grades. When properly defined, a grading system tells pupils what constitutes high and low achievement. However, established performance standards and grading curves sometime turn out to be inappropriate when tried out. Consequently, performance standards and grading curves need not be set in stone. If a standard or curve turns out to be inappropriate or unfair for some reason, it can and should be changed before grades are assigned. If, for example, a teacher found that many of the items on a test were not taught or were worded in a confusing manner, he or she might decide to discount these items when grades are assigned. In this case, the criterion-referenced standard should be changed to take into account untaught or poorly worded items.

If a grading standard or curve proves to be inappropriate or unfair, it should be changed before grades are assigned.

While changes in performance standards or grading curves should not be made frivolously, it is better to make occasional changes than to continue to award grades based on unfair and incorrect criteria. Usually, increased experience with a class helps a teacher arrive at a set of standards or a grading curve that is appropriate and fair.

Having made this point, it must also be emphasized that fairness to pupils does not mean selecting standards or grading curves to ensure that everyone gets high grades. Lowering standards or grading curves to guarantee high grades discourages pupil effort and dedication and diminishes the validity of the grades. Fairness means fully assessing what pupils were taught, using assessment procedures appropriate to the grade level and type of instruction used, and establishing performance standards or grading curves that can be reached if pupils work hard. These are the teacher's responsibilities in integrating instruction, assessment, and grading.

Fairness means assessing what pupils were taught, using appropriate assessment procedures, and establishing realistic performance standards or grading curves.

Table 6.2 compares the main features of norm- and criterion-referenced grading.

TABLE 6.2	COMPARISON OF NORM-REFERENCED AND CRITERION-REFERENCED GRADING	
	Norm-Referenced	**Criterion-Referenced**
Comparison made	Pupil to other pupils	Pupil to predefined criteria
Method of comparison	Grading curve; percent of pupils who can get each grade	Standard of performance; scores pupils must achieve to get a given grade
What grade describes	Pupil's performance compared to others in the class	Pupil's percentage mastery of course objectives
Availability of a particular grade	Limited by grading curve	No limit on grade availability

Comparison to a Pupil's Ability

Teachers frequently make such remarks as Ralph is not working up to his ability, Maurice is not doing as well as he can, or Rose continues to achieve much higher than I expected she would. When teachers make such statements, they are comparing a pupil's actual performance to the performance they expected based on their judgment of the pupil's ability. The terms *overachiever* and *underachiever* are used to describe pupils who do better or worse than judgments of their ability suggest they should. Many teachers assign grades by comparing a pupil's actual performance to their perception of that pupil's ability level (Hubelbank, 1994).

In this grading approach, pupils with high ability who do excellent work receive high grades, as do pupils with low ability who the teacher believes are achieving up to their potential. Even though the actual performance of the low-ability pupils is well below that of the high-ability, high-achieving pupils, each group receives the same grade if each is perceived to be achieving up to their ability. Conversely, pupils with high ability who are perceived by their teacher to be underachieving receive lower grades than low-ability pupils who are achieving up to expectations. One of the main arguments that is advanced in defense of this grading approach is that it motivates pupils to do their best and get the most from their ability. Further, it punishes the lazy pupils who do not work up to their perceived ability.

This approach to grading is not recommended for a number of reasons (Frisbie & Waltman, 1992). First, it depends on the teacher's having an accurate perception of each pupil's ability. In reality, teachers rarely know enough about their pupils to permit valid and reliable assessment of ability. Teachers do have a general sense of pupils' abilities from their

Teachers should not assign grades by comparing a pupil's actual performance to their perception of the pupil's ability level.

sizing-up assessments and the pupils' classroom performance, but this information is too imprecise to use as a baseline for grading.

Second, teachers often have a difficult time separating their perception of a pupil's ability from other pupil characteristics such as self-assurance, motivation, or responsiveness. Even formal tests designed to measure ability are rarely precise enough to accurately predict a pupil's capacity for learning. Experts find it all but impossible to make valid predictions about what a pupil of a certain general ability level is capable of achieving in any specific subject area.

Third, grades that compare actual performance to expected performance are confusing to people in and out of the classroom (Friedman & Frisbie, 1995; Azwell & Gulseth, 1995). For example, a high-ability pupil who attained 80 percent mastery of instruction might receive a C grade if perceived to be underachieving, while a low-ability pupil who attained 60 percent mastery might receive an A grade for exceeding expectations. An outsider viewing these two grades would probably think that the low-ability pupil mastered more of the course because that pupil got the higher grade. In short, there is little correlation between grades and student mastery of course content in ability-based grading systems.

All of these reasons argue strongly against the use of a grading system that compares actual to predicted achievement. However, some report cards do allow separate judgments about pupil achievement and ability. The teacher can record a subject matter grade based on the pupil's actual achievement, and then in a separate place on the report card indicate if the pupil is working up to expectations. Usually, the teacher writes comments or checks boxes to show whether the pupil needs improvement, is improving, or is doing best, relative to his or her ability. Even in this approach, teachers must be cautious about putting too much faith in their estimates of pupils' abilities and potential.

Comparison to Pupil Improvement

Basing grades on the improvement a pupil has made over time creates problems similar to those encountered when comparing actual to predicted achievement. Improvement is typically determined by comparing a pupil's performance early in the grading period to later in that same period. Pupils who show the most progress or growth get the high grades, and those who show little progress or growth get the low grades. An obvious difficulty with this approach is that pupils who do well early in the term have little opportunity to improve and thus have little chance to get good grades. Low scorers at the start of the term have the best chance for improvement and therefore high grades. It is not surprising that students graded on improvement quickly realize that it is in their best interest to do poorly on the early tests. There is an incentive to play dumb so early performance is low and improvement can be easily shown.

Like comparing actual to predicted performance, grading on the basis of improvement also makes grades difficult to interpret. A pupil who improves from very low achievement to moderate achievement may get an A, while a pupil who had high achievement initially and had little room for improvement may get a B or a C, even though the latter pupil mastered considerably more of the subject matter than the pupil who got the A grade.

Some teachers recognize this difficulty and propose the following solution: Give the pupils who achieve highly throughout the term an A grade for their high performance, but also give A grades to those pupils who improve their performance a great deal. Certainly this suggestion overcomes the problem noted previously. However, it creates a new problem. In essence, what these teachers are proposing to do is use two very different grading systems. The one for high-achieving pupils is based on content mastery while the one for low-achieving pupils is based on improvement. This approach provides rewards for both groups of pupils, but confuses the meaning of the grades.

When the same grade means different things, pupils and parents can misinterpret the teacher's meaning of the grade. The only way that grades can convey a consistent, understandable message is to apply the same grading system to all pupils in the class. Thus, neither a grading system based on improvement nor a grading system based on different approaches for different groups of pupils is recommended.

There is little correlation between grades and student mastery of course content in ability-based grading systems.

The same grading system must be applied to all pupils in the class in order to convey a consistent and understandable message about classroom standards.

Grading in Cooperative Learning

Classrooms at all levels of education are increasingly emphasizing group-based, or cooperative, learning strategies. In **cooperative learning,** small groups of two to six pupils are presented with a task or problem situation that they must solve together. While the problem itself can be posed in virtually any subject area, the main purpose of cooperative learning is to have pupils learn to work together to arrive at a single, group-generated solution.

In cooperative learning, teachers are usually concerned with assessing three important outcomes: (1) the interactive, cooperative processes that go on within the group, (2) the quality of the group's solution, and (3) each member's contribution to and understanding of that solution. Chapter 5 presented how group cooperation can be observed and rated using checklists and rating scales (see Table 5.5). While assessing such group processes is important, assessment of subject matter learning is equally important. However, assessing the subject matter learning of individual group members is quite difficult because in most cases, the group provides only a single cooperatively reached solution or product. At issue is how to assign individual pupil grades on the basis of a single group production.

The most common grading practice is to assign a single grade to the group's solution or product and to give that grade to each group member. The difficulty with such a strategy is that it assumes equal contribution and understanding on the part of each group member. Both the pupil who contributed and learned greatly and the pupil who contributed and learned minimally receive the same grade. On the other hand, to push too hard for individual pupil solutions and contributions destroys many of the benefits of cooperative problem solving. Thus, for many teachers, grading in cooperative learning situations creates problems not encountered in grading individual pupil performance.

There is no single acceptable solution to these problems. Many teachers see no difficulty in assuming equal contribution and learning by each group member and giving identical grades to all of them. Other teachers mingle assessment of the group process with assessment of the group product, relying on their observations and interactions with pupils to provide them with a sense of the contribution and comprehension of each group member. Teachers then adjust individual grades according to their observation of pupil participation, contribution, and understanding. Still other teachers let the pupils self-assess their contribution and understanding. This approach is less than ideal because pupils' self-assessments often are based as much on their self-perceptions and confidence as on their actual contribution and learning.

Teachers can use follow-up activities with individual students to determine how well they understand the processes used in a group-based solution.

Another strategy that has some advantages over the preceding ones combines group and individual grades. All members of the group get the same grade for their single, group-based solution or product. Subsequently, the teacher requires each pupil to individually answer or perform follow-up activities related to the group problem or task. The purpose of these follow-up activities is to determine how well individual pupils understand and can apply the group solution when solving similar types of problems. This approach blends group participation and contribution with subject matter learning.

SELECTING PUPIL PERFORMANCES

Once the comparative basis for assigning grades is decided, it is necessary to select the particular performances that will be considered in awarding the grades. When grading a single test or a project, there is obviously only one performance to be considered. When assigning report card grades, many formal and informal performances could be considered.

The quantity and the nature of the assessment information available to a teacher varies depending on the grade level and subject area. For example, assigning a term grade in spelling simply involves combining the results of each pupil's performance on the Friday spelling tests. In American history or social studies, however, a teacher may have information from quizzes, tests, homework, projects, reports, portfolios, and work-sheets. High school math teachers have homework papers, quizzes, and test results to consider in assigning grades, while English teachers have tests, reports, homework, quizzes, portfolios, projects, and class discussion to take into account. In addition to these formal assessments of achievement, teachers also have informal perceptions of pupils' effort, interest, motivation, helpfulness, and behavior. Each teacher must decide which of these available information sources to use in determining report card grades. This decision is critical because the sources included in the grade define what the grade really means. In many cases it is not necessary or even desirable to include all available information about pupils when assigning grades.

Each teacher must decide which of the many formal and informal information sources available to use in determining a report card grade.

Academic Achievement

Most people interpret subject matter grades as an indication of a pupil's mastery of the topics and behaviors that were taught in the course. Hence, grades should be based on achievement data gathered over the course of the grading period. The more valid the achievement performances obtained from pupils are, the more representative they are of the pupil's achievement. Formal indicators of pupils' achievement of course objectives should be a major component of subject matter grades. Conversely, effort, behavior, interest, motivation, and the like should not be major components of subject matter grades. To give an A grade to a pupil who is academically marginal but very industrious and congenial is misleading to the pupil, parents, and others who will likely interpret the grade as indicating high subject matter mastery. Pupils who work hard, are cooperative, and show greater motivation and interest than their classmates deserve to be rewarded, but subject matter grades are not the proper arena for such rewards. Also, grades should not be heavily dependent upon behavior, interest, and attendance and should not be used to punish pupils for behavior problems. Pupils' affective and citizenship characteristics should be separated from subject matter grades as much as possible.

Subject matter grades should reflect a pupil's academic achievement rather than such things as motivation, cooperation, and attendance.

Formal assessments of subject matter, such as teacher-made and textbook tests, papers, quizzes, homework, projects, worksheets, portfolios, and the like, are the best types of evidence to use in assigning report card grades. They are suitable in two respects. First, they provide information about pupils' academic performance, which is what grades are intended to describe. Second, being tangible products of pupils' work, they can be used to defend or explain a grade if the need arises. It is defensible to say to a pupil or parent I gave a C grade because when I compared your test scores, projects, and homework assignments in this marking period to my grading standards, you performed at a C level. It is not defensible to say I gave a C grade because I *had a strong sense* that you were not working as hard as you could and because I *have a negative general perception* of your daily class performance. This description would be difficult to explain and defend.

Formal subject matter assessments such as teacher-made tests and homework provide the hard evidence to explain or defend a grade.

Since formal assessments of pupil achievement ought to be accorded major weight in assigning grades, it is important to stress that the grades awarded are only as good as the formal assessment information on which they are based (Brookhart, 1998). The meaningfulness of grades is dependent upon the meaningfulness of the assessments on which they are based. Grading as a process cannot be separated from the quality of the assessment information teachers collect prior to grading. Just as good instruction can be undermined by invalid assessment, so too can good and meaningful grading be undermined by invalid achievement assessments. Irrelevant, invalid pupil assessments produce irrelevant, invalid grades.

Pupils are given greater opportunity to demonstrate achievement when grades are based on several types of assessment information.

As the culminating step in the process of assessing pupils' academic achievement, grading ought to be based on a varied assortment of valid and reliable evidence. A general rule of grading is to draw on several different types of information rather than a single type because this gives pupils more opportunity to show what they can do.

If subject matter grades were assigned by machines, it would be easy to base them solely upon formal assessments of pupil achievement. However, teachers are not machines and teachers know a great deal more about their pupils than any grading machine ever could. They know them as whole persons, not one-dimensional achievers. They understand the home background and different effects grades have on particular pupils. Because of this, teachers rarely can be completely objective, dispassionate dispensers of report card grades, as the following excerpts illustrate.

> Jerome works harder than any student in my class, but he cannot seem to overcome his lack of ability. No one tries harder yet his tests and projects are all failures. But I just can't in good conscience give Jerome a failing grade because he tries so hard and an F would destroy him.

> Melissa had a terrible term. Her test scores dropped off, her attention during instruction was poor, and she failed to complete many homework assignments. The reason for these behaviors is in her home situation. Her father left the home, her mother had to find a job, and Melissa had to assume most of the household and babysitting responsibilities because she is the oldest child. How can I not take this into account when I grade her this term?

> Joe is the ultimate itch: constant motion, inattentive, socializing around the classroom at inappropriate times. He drives me crazy. However, his classwork is well done and on time. When I sit down to grade him, I have to refrain from saying OK Joe, now I'm going to get you for being such a distraction. I have a hard time separating his academic performance from his classroom behavior.

Affective Considerations

One common instance in which pupil motivation, interest, effort, or behavior enters into grades is when they are used to give borderline pupils the benefit of the doubt. When a teacher awards a B+ to a pupil whose academic performance places her between a B and a B+ grade but who is motivated, participates in class, and works diligently, the teacher is taking into account more than assessments of formal achievement. Teachers often nudge upwards the grades given to conscientious, participating pupils in order to keep them motivated. Strictly speaking, such adjustments distort the intended meaning of a grade, but most teachers do make them based upon their knowledge of particular pupil characteristics and needs. Grading is a human judgmental process, and it is virtually inevitable that such adjustments will occur (Brookhart, 1992).

Pupil effort and participation can be used to adjust a grade but should not be the main determiner of the grade.

These borderline adjustments usually operate to the benefit of the pupil and the psychic comfort of the teacher. However, a teacher should guard against allowing effort, motivation, interest, behavior, or personality to become the dominant basis for grades. If this happens, grades are distorted, providing little useful information about the pupil's academic achievement. Although few teachers can totally ignore nonacademic evidence like pupils' ability, effort, and improvement when they grade, most correctly use such evidence as a basis for adjustments in pupils' grades, not as the central determiner of grades (Brookhart, 1992; Griswold & Griswold, 1992; Nava & Loyd, 1992).

To summarize, we have seen that teachers must decide what standards of comparison to use in assigning grades. This means deciding upon either a norm-referenced or a criterion-referenced standard. Once this decision has been made, the teacher must establish a grading curve in the norm-referenced approach or performance standards in the criterion-referenced approach. Next, the teacher must determine what performances to include in the grade. Since grades are mainly intended to convey information about pupils' subject matter mastery rather than their personal qualities, grades should be based primarily upon formal assessments of pupil achievement. Teachers' subjective perceptions and insights inevitably influence the grading process to some extent, but they should not be allowed to greatly distort the subject matter grade.

SUMMARIZING DIFFERENT TYPES OF ASSESSMENT

Report card grades require teachers to summarize pupils' performance on the many individual assessments gathered during the marking period (Brookhart, 1998). In some subject areas, summarization across a term is easy and straightforward. Suppose a teacher is getting ready to assign report card grades in spelling. The teacher simply refers to his or her marking or grade book for the pupils' scores on each of the weekly spelling tests given during the grading period. It is very important that teachers maintain such grade books and that they be carefully guarded to ensure confidentiality.

Report card grades summarize each pupil's performance on the many individual assessments gathered during the marking period.

Suppose there were 11 tests for each pupil, each scored on the basis of 100 points. The teacher's task is to summarize the scores for each pupil and use the results to assign a report card grade. This is a relatively easy task, since each test was scored on the basis of 100 total points and each test was equivalent in terms of importance. The teacher sums each pupil's score on the 11 tests and finds the mean, or average, score.

Assume that a teacher has decided to assign spelling grades using a criterion-referenced approach with the following performance standards: 100 to 90 is an A, 89 to 80 is a B, 79 to 70 is a C, and below 70 is a D. The teacher decides not to flunk any pupils in the first term, so D is the lowest grade she will give. She also decides not to award plusses and minuses, using only A, B, C, and D as possible grades. (It is important to recognize that not all teachers would have made these same decisions. Some might have used a norm-referenced grading system, selected different performance standards, and made adjustments based on effort and motivation.) In this example, the teacher simply compares each pupil's average across the spelling tests to the performance standards and then awards the corresponding letter grade.

This example provides a basic frame of reference for understanding the grading process. It shows how standards come into play in allocating grades, how formal assessment evidence is recorded in a marking book, and how individual scores can be summarized to provide an overall indication of pupil performance for report card purposes. However, most grading situations are not as simple as this example. Consider the more typical example of Ms. Fogarty's marking book for social studies, shown in Figure 6.4.

Notice two important differences between the information available to Ms. Fogarty for grading social studies and the information available in the spelling example. In the spelling example, the only formal assessments were the weekly spelling tests. On the other hand, Ms. Fogarty has collected many different kinds of social studies assessment information: four homework assignments, two quiz results, four unit test results, and two projects. In the spelling example, all test results were expressed numerically on a scale of 0 to 100. In social studies, Ms. Fogarty has used different grading formats for different activities: homework assignments were rated ✔+, ✔, ✔–; quizzes and tests were recorded on a scale of 0 to 100 in percents; and the two projects were recorded as letter grades. Ms. Fogarty's grading task is a more complicated process than grading spelling.

Despite their differences, both grading processes start out with the same concerns. First, what standard of comparison will be used to award grades? Second, what specific performances will be included in the grade? Let us assume that in social studies, Ms. Fogarty wishes to use a criterion-referenced grading approach and plusses and minuses in her grades. With this decision made, she must next determine which of the four different kinds of assessment information available to her to include in the grade. She must not only decide which of these to include, but how much each kind of information will count in determining the grades. For example,

SOCIAL STUD.

TERM # 1

	HW #1	HW #2	HW #3	HW #4	quiz	quiz	test unit 1	test unit 2	test unit 3	test unit 4	proj. explor Amer	proj. colon.
Aston, J.	✓	✓	✓	✓−	85	90	80	85	50	80	B+	B
Babcock, W.	✓	✓	✓	✓−	90	90	85	80	60	80	B	B
Cannata, T.	✓	✓−	✓	✓	80	75	70	70	45	75	C−	C
Farmer, P.	✓+	✓+	✓+	✓	100	95	90	85	70	95	A−	A−
Foster, C.	✓+	✓+	✓	✓	90	80	85	90	65	80	B	B+
Gonzales, E.	✓	✓−	✓−	✓−	70	75	60	70	55	70	C	B−
Grodsky, F.	✓−	✓−	✓−	✓−	65	65	65	60	35	60	C	C
Martin, J.	✓	✓	✓	✓	80	90	70	85	65	85	C	B
Picardi, O.	✓	✓	✓	✓	75	80	85	75	65	80	B	B−
Ross, O.	✓+	✓	✓	✓	85	80	90	90	75	95	A	A−
Sachar, S.	✓−	✓	✓	✓+	80	85	75	80	40	80	B+	B
Saja, J.	✓	✓	✓	✓	75	80	85	85	50	80	B	B+
Stamos, G.	✓	✓+	✓+	✓	70	60	75	85	50	70	B−	B
Whalem, W.	✓	✓	✓	✓	70	70	50	60	60	70	B−	B−
Yeh, T.	✓+	✓+	✓+	✓+	95	100	95	95	75	95	A	A−

FIGURE 6.4

Marking Book Assessments in Social Studies

should a project count as much as a unit test? Should two quizzes count as much as one unit test or four homework assignments? These are questions all teachers face when they try to combine different kinds of assessment information into a single indicator.

What Should Be Included in a Grade?

Figure 6.4 shows a marking book page with four different indicators of academic performance: homework, quizzes, unit tests, and projects. In addition to these formal indicators, Ms. Fogarty has many informal, unrecorded perceptions of each pupil's effort, participation in class, interest, and behavior. Should all of these formal and informal kinds of information be included in the grades?

Almost all teachers would include the unit test and the project results in determining their pupils' grades. These are major, summative indicators of pupil achievement that should be reflected in the grade a pupil receives. Most teachers also include quiz results and homework, although with less unanimity than for tests and projects. Some teachers regard quizzes and homework as practice activities that are more closely tied to

Some teachers view quizzes and homework as more closely tied to the instructional process than to the grading process.

instruction than to assessment. Other teachers view homework and quizzes as indicators of how well pupils have learned their daily lessons and thus include them as part of the pupil's grade. As with most grading issues, the final decision belongs to the classroom teacher.

Let us assume that Ms. Fogarty has decided to include three types of formal assessment information in her pupils' social studies grades: tests, projects, and quizzes. Let us also assume that she has decided not to include formal ratings of her pupils' effort, participation, interest, and behavior. She now must determine whether each kind of information counts equally or whether some kinds are weighted more heavily than others.

Selecting Weights for Assessment Information

An immediate concern in summarizing pupil performance on different kinds of evidence is how each should be weighted. In general, teachers should give the more important types of pupil performance, such as tests, projects, and portfolios, more weight than short quizzes or homework assignments, since the former provide a more complete and integrated view of learning. Ms. Fogarty has looked over the information in her marking book and has decided that unit tests and projects should count equally and that both should count more than quiz results. She is fairly certain that she has used valid tests—they reflected the important aspects of her instruction—and that the projects assigned required pupils to integrate their knowledge about the topic in the way she desired. Thus, she is confident in using tests and projects as the main components of her social studies grade. Finally, she has decided that the two quizzes count as much as one unit test.

Although many teachers do not count homework directly in determining grades, they often warn pupils that if more than three or four homework assignments are not turned in, their report card grade will be affected. Used this way, homework is more an indicator of effort or cooperation than of subject matter mastery. Other teachers do not actually compute pupil homework averages, but rely instead on an informal sense or intuition of how a pupil has performed. Although timesaving, this practice allows subjective factors such as the pupil's behavior or interest in the subject matter to influence the teacher's judgment. Neither lowering pupil grades for missed homework assignments nor determining grades on the basis of an informal sense of pupil performance is recommended.

Methods for weighting the various types of assessment information should be kept simple.

Regardless of how a teacher weights each kind of assessment information, it is strongly suggested that the weightings be simple. It is better to weight some things twice as much as others than to weight some five times as much and others seven times as much. In most instances, the final grades arrived at using a simple weighting scheme do not differ greatly from those arrived at using a more complex weighting scheme.

After deciding on her weightings for quizzes, unit tests, and projects, Ms. Fogarty identifies seven pieces of information that she will combine to determine her pupils' report card grades in social studies. The seven pieces are:

- ◆ one overall assessment of quiz results
- ◆ four scores from the unit tests
- ◆ two project grades

In the final weightings, quiz results count one-seventh of the grade, unit tests count four-sevenths of the grade, and projects count two-sevenths of the grade. Ms. Fogarty next has to combine the available information according to the selected weights.

Combining Different Assessment Information

Figure 6.4 shows that pupil performance on different assessments often is represented in different ways. Somehow Ms. Fogarty must combine the selected scoring formats into a single summary score that includes performance on tests, projects, and quizzes. Some of the information shown in Figure 6.4 will have to be changed into another format, preferably a numerical one. This means that the project letter grades will have to be converted into numerical scores on a scale of 0 percent to 100 percent so that they correspond to the scores for the quizzes and unit tests.

It is important to express all performance indicators in terms of the same scale so that they can be combined meaningfully. For example, suppose a teacher gave two tests, one with 50 items and one with 100 items, and that the teacher wanted each test to count equally in determining a pupil's grade. Now suppose that two pupils, Martin and Izumi, each got a perfect score on one of the tests and a zero score on the other: Martin got his perfect score on the 50-item test and Izumi got his on the 100-item test. Since the tests counted equally, it seems that Martin and Izumi's grades should be the same regardless of the number of items on a test. However, if the teacher calculated the average performance for Martin and Izumi using the *number* of items they got right across both tests, the result would be quite different averages (Martin's average = (50 + 0)/2 = 25; Izumi's average = (0 + 100)/2 = 50). Izumi would get a higher grade than Martin, even though they each attained a perfect score on one test and a zero score on another and the tests counted equally. Clearly, combining raw scores across both tests and finding their average does not give equal weight to each test.

The problem in the preceding example is that the teacher did not take into account the difference in the number of items on the two tests; the teacher did not put the two tests on the same scale before computing an average. If the teacher had changed the scores from number of items correct to *percentage* of items correct *before* averaging, Martin and Izumi would have had the same overall performance (Martin = (100 + 0)/2 = 50; Izumi = (0 + 100)/2 = 50). Similarly, if the teacher had expressed

Each type of assessment information should be expressed in terms of the same scale so that all can be combined into a composite score.

TABLE 6.3 SOCIAL STUDIES ASSESSMENTS PLACED ON THE SAME SCALE

Social Studies, Term 1

	Quiz 1	Quiz 2	Test 1	Test 2	Test 3	Test 4	Proj. 1	Proj. 2
Aston, J.	85	90	80	85	50	80	88	85
Babcock, W.	90	90	85	80	60	80	85	85
Cannata, T.	80	75	70	70	45	70	72	70
Farmer, P.	100	95	90	85	70	95	92	92
Foster, C.	90	80	85	90	65	80	85	88
Gonzales, E.	70	75	60	70	55	70	75	82
Grodsky, F.	65	65	65	60	35	60	75	75
Martin, J.	80	90	70	85	65	85	75	85
Picardi, O.	75	80	85	75	65	80	85	82
Ross, O.	85	80	90	90	75	95	95	92
Sachar, S.	80	85	75	80	40	80	88	85
Saja, J.	75	80	85	85	50	80	85	88
Stamos, G.	70	60	75	85	50	70	82	85
Whalem, W.	70	70	50	60	60	70	82	82
Yeh, T.	95	100	95	95	75	95	95	92

performance on both tests in terms of the 100-point test, the averages would have been the same, since Martin's perfect score on a 50-item test would be worth 100 points on a 100-point scale. Once again, if scores are not expressed in a common scale, pupil performance is distorted and grades do not reflect actual achievement.

Returning to Ms. Fogarty's example, a way must be found to express project performance on a scale that corresponds to the 0 percent to 100 percent scale used for quizzes and unit tests. She decides that for project grades, she will use the following scale to give numerical scores to the projects: 95 = A, 92 = A–, 88 = B+, 85 = B, 82 = B–, 78 = C+, 75 = C, 72 = C–, 68 = D+, 65 = D, 62 = D–, less than 60 = F. If, for example, a pupil got a B– on one of the projects, that pupil's numerical score on the project is 82. When Ms. Fogarty applies these values to the projects, she ends up with the information shown in Table 6.3. (It is important to note that Ms. Fogarty's is not the only way that the different scores could be put on the same scale, nor is it without limitations. It is, however, one way she can accomplish her task with a method she feels comfortable using.) With this task completed, Ms. Fogarty must confront one additional issue prior to computing grades.

Validity of Assessment Information

Before combining assessment information into a grade, the quality of that information must be considered. Grades are only as meaningful as the information on which they are based. If the project grades were assigned subjectively, with no clear criteria in mind and with shifting teacher attention during scoring, they do not accurately reflect pupil achievement. If the unit tests were unfair to pupils or did not test a representative sample of what was taught, the scores pupils attained are not valid indications of their achievement. In this regard, Ms. Fogarty ought to examine the results of the unit 3 test, since these scores were much lower than on the other unit tests. Do these scores indicate a problem with the test or a problem with the effort pupils put into preparing for the test? How should this result be handled in grading? These questions have to be answered before information can be combined and used to grade.

Grades are only as meaningful (valid) as the information upon which they are based.

Ms. Fogarty noticed the poor performance on the unit 3 test when she scored it, and she no doubt asked herself why the scores were so low. Normally, questions about the match between an assessment instrument and the things pupils were taught occur *before* an assessment instrument is used. Sometimes, however, mismatches are overlooked or do not become apparent until after the instrument is administered and scored. Typically, it is unexpectedly low scores that provoke teachers' concern and attention; rarely do unexpectedly high scores provoke the same reaction. The reason for this discrepancy in reaction is that most teachers probably assume that unexpectedly low scores are the result of a faulty assessment instrument, while unexpectedly high scores are the result of superior teaching.

Most teachers assume that unexpectedly low test scores are the result of a faulty assessment instrument, while unexpectedly high scores are the result of superior teaching.

Ms. Fogarty looked over the items in the unit 3 test, which was a textbook test, and compared the items to the topics and skills she had taught in that unit. She found that one section of the unit that she had decided not to teach contributed a large number of test items that she had not removed. The match between the unit test and classroom instruction was not good, and pupils were being penalized because her instruction had failed to cover many concepts included in the test. Thus, these unit 3 scores provide a distorted picture of her pupils' actual achievement, and this, in turn, reduces the validity of their grades.

To avoid this, Ms. Fogarty decides to change the pupils' scores on the unit 3 test to better reflect their achievement. She estimates that about 20 percent to 25 percent of the items on the test were from the section she had not taught. She checks and sees that most pupils had done poorly on these items, so she decides to increase each pupil's unit 3 score by 20 percentage points. She correctly reasons that the increased scores provide a better indication of what pupils had learned *from the instruction provided* than the original scores. All of the assessment information in Figure 6.4, including the adjusted unit 3 score, reflects a common scale, which ranges from 0 to 100 and indicates the percentage of mastery by each pupil on each assessment.

If unexpectedly low scores on some part of a test indicate a mismatch with instruction, then grading adjustments should be made.

It is important to point out that Ms. Fogarty adjusted the low scores on the unit 3 test only after reexamining both the test and her instruction. She did not raise the scores to make the pupils feel better about themselves, to have them like her more, or for other reasons. The test scores were raised so that they would provide a more valid indication of how well pupils learned from instruction; her grades now better reflect her pupils' subject matter mastery. Low assessment scores should not be raised simply because they are low or because the teacher is disappointed with them.

Computing Pupils' Overall Scores

Having decided on score equivalents for the project assessments and having adjusted scores on the unit 3 test to correct the partial mismatch between instruction and the test items, Ms. Fogarty is ready to compute her pupils' social studies grades. To do this, she must: (1) give each kind of assessment information the weight she decided on; (2) sum the scores; and (3) divide by 7, which is the number of assessment items she is using to grade (1 overall quiz score, 4 unit test scores, and 2 project scores). This computation provides an average social studies score for each pupil during the marking period. Table 6.4 shows the seven components Ms. Fogarty will include in each pupil's grade, their total, and their average. To make her task simpler, Ms. Fogarty decides that all fractions will be rounded off to the nearest whole number.

Strictly speaking, the actual weight that a particular assessment carries in determining a grade depends on the spread of scores on that assessment compared to the spread of scores on other assessments (Frisbie & Waltman, 1992). The greater the spread of scores on an assessment, the greater the influence that assessment has on the final grade when averaged with other assessments. Fairly simple and straightforward techniques are available for equalizing the influence of assessments whose scores are widely spread (Oosterhof, 1987). However, this is not a major problem with most classroom assessments, which generally are given in a similar format to the same group of pupils, cover the topics taught in instruction, and are scored in the same way. Under these conditions, the spread of scores on different assessments is usually close enough so that adjustments need not be made. Table 6.4 shows that the difference between the highest and lowest score on each of the seven assessments is 33 for the quiz score; 35, 35, 40, and 25 for the four unit tests; and 23 and 18 for the two projects. These ranges are similar enough to permit the seven components to be added and averaged to determine an overall pupil score.

Table 6.4 shows each pupil's final average after each piece of assessment information is weighted. Consider J. Aston's scores in Table 6.4. This pupil received a quiz score of 88, based upon the average of two quizzes rounded off to a whole number. The four test scores with 20 points added to the unit 3 test, as Ms. Fogarty decided, are shown. The two project grades are expressed in terms of the numerical equivalents

TABLE 6.4   COMPUTATION OF PUPILS' SOCIAL STUDIES GRADES

Social Studies, Term 1

	Quizzes	Test 1	Test 2	Test 3	Test 4	Proj. 1	Proj. 2	Total Score	Average
Aston, J.	88	80	85	70	80	88	85	576	82
Babcock, W.	90	85	80	80	80	85	85	585	84
Cannata, T.	78	70	70	65	70	72	70	495	71
Farmer, P.	98	90	85	90	95	92	92	642	92
Foster, C.	85	85	90	85	80	85	88	598	85
Gonzales, E.	73	60	70	75	70	75	82	505	72
Grodsky, F.	65	65	60	55	60	75	75	455	65
Martin, J.	85	70	85	85	85	75	85	570	81
Picardi, O.	78	85	75	85	80	85	82	570	81
Ross, O.	83	90	90	95	95	95	92	640	91
Sachar, S.	83	75	80	60	80	88	85	551	79
Saja, J.	78	85	85	70	80	85	88	571	82
Stamos, G.	65	75	85	70	70	82	85	532	76
Whalem, W.	70	50	60	80	70	82	82	494	71
Yeh, T.	98	95	95	95	95	95	92	665	95

Ms. Fogarty selected. Adding these scores gives a total score of 576, which, when divided by 7 (for the seven pieces of information that were combined), gives an average performance of 82. The average for each pupil provides an indication of the proportion of social studies objectives each pupil achieved in the marking period. Notice that this interpretation is only appropriate if Ms. Fogarty's various assessments are scored in terms of *percentage* mastery and if they are fair and representative samples of the things that were taught. Ms. Fogarty now can apply her performance standards to award pupils grades.

Combining all assessments into a numerical average estimates the proportion of objectives each pupil achieved during the period.

ASSIGNING GRADES

A Criterion-Referenced Example

Ms. Fogarty decides to assign grades based upon a criterion-referenced approach because she feels that this approach gives each pupil a chance to get a good grade if he or she mastered what was taught. The performance standards Ms. Fogarty adopts for her social study grades are:

A = 94 or higher	C− = 70 to 73
A− = 90 to 93	D+ = 67 to 69
B+ = 87 to 89	D = 64 to 66
B = 84 to 86	D− = 60 to 63
B− = 80 to 83	F = less than 60
C+ = 77 to 79	
C = 74 to 76	

This is a common criterion-referenced grading standard.

Looking at the overall semester averages as shown in Table 6.4, Ms. Fogarty can apply her performance standards to award grades. It is at this juncture that she is likely to consider pupils' nonacademic characteristics. For example, she may say to herself this child has worked so hard this term despite an unsettled home situation that it's amazing she was able to focus on her schoolwork at all or there is so little positive reinforcement in this kid's life right now that a failing grade would absolutely crush him, even though his performance has been very poor. In short, Ms. Fogarty, like most teachers, is aware of her responsibility to grade pupils primarily on their academic performance, but allows herself some room for small individual adjustments. Opinions will always differ about making such grading adjustments, as the following excerpts show.

> I grade strictly by the numbers. I calculate each pupil's average and assign grades based strictly on that average. A 79.4 average is not an 80 average, and thus will get a C+. This is the only way I can be fair to all pupils.

> I calculate the averages based on tests and assignments just like the books say to. But when it comes time to assign the grade, I know I'm not grading an average, I'm grading a kid I know and spend time with every day. I know how the kid has behaved, how much effort has been put into my class, and what effect a high or low grade will have on him or her. I know about the pressure the kid gets from parents and what reaction they will have to a particular grade. If I didn't know about these things, grading would be much easier.

When Ms. Fogarty applies her performance standards to her class averages, her grades will be as follows.

Name	Average	Grade	Name	Average	Grade
Aston, J.	82	B−	Picardi, O.	81	B−
Babcock, W.	84	B	Ross, O.	91	A−
Cannata, T.	71	C−	Sachar, S.	79	C+
Farmer, P.	92	A−	Saja, J.	82	B−
Foster, C.	85	B	Stamos, G.	76	C
Gonzales, E.	72	C−	Whalem, W.	71	C−
Grodsky, F.	65	D	Yeh, T.	95	A
Martin, J.	81	B−			

Notice that some pupils, such as J. Aston and E. Gonzales, are within one point of the performance standard for the next higher grade. It is for pupils who are close to reaching the next higher grade that teachers' judgments about nonacademic characteristics usually enter into grading.

To summarize, Ms. Fogarty had to make many decisions to arrive at these grades. She had to decide whether to use a norm-referenced or a criterion-referenced grading approach. Having selected the criterion-referenced approach, she had to decide on performance standards for awarding grades. Next she had to decide upon the kinds of assessment information that would be included in her grades and how to weight each one. Since some of the information she wished to include was expressed as percentage scores out of 100 and some was expressed as project grades, Ms. Fogarty had to decide how to put the project grades on the same scale as the test scores. Then she had to decide whether to adjust any scores because of faulty instruments. Finally, she had to decide whether to base her grades solely on the pupil's average academic performance or to alter them slightly because of affective or personal characteristics. Different teachers with different classes and in different schools would likely have made different decisions than Ms. Fogarty, but they all would have had to confront the same issues.

Table 6.5 summarizes the steps in the grading process (Borich, 1996).

Teachers' judgments about nonacademic characteristics often enter into grading when the student is close to reaching the next higher grade level.

A Norm-Referenced Example

To complete this example, consider how Ms. Fogarty would have assigned grades if she had chosen a norm-referenced grading approach. In this case, she would have decided in advance upon a grading curve that identified the percentage of pupils whom she wanted to receive each grade.

In norm-referenced grading, a teacher decides in advance the percentage of pupils receiving each grade.

TABLE 6.5   STEPS IN THE GRADING PROCESS

- ◆ Select a standard of comparison (norm or criterion).
- ◆ Select types of performances (tests, projects, etc.).
- ◆ Assign weights for each type of performance.
- ◆ Record the number of points earned out of the total possible points for *each individual performance* graded.
- ◆ Total the points earned for *each type of performance* and divide this by the total number of possible points. This gives a percentage for each type of performance.
- ◆ Mutliply each of these percentages by the weights assigned.
- ◆ Sum the totals and apply the chosen standard of comparison to the totals.
- ◆ Review the grades and make adjustments if necessary.

Suppose she used a norm-referenced grading curve that gave the top 20 percent of the pupils an A, the next 20 percent a B, the next 40 percent a C, and the last 20 percent a D.

To assign grades using this curve, Ms. Fogarty must first arrange the pupils from highest to lowest in terms of their average score over the marking period. Since a norm-referenced approach is based on how a pupil's performance compares to that of the rest of the class, the best way to compare performance is to rank pupils from highest to lowest in terms of their overall average. This ordering for Ms. Fogarty's class is shown here.

Name	Score	Name	Score
Yeh, T.	95	Saja, J.	82
Farmer, P.	92	Sachar, S.	79
Ross, O.	91	Stamos, G.	76
Foster, C.	85	Gonzales, E.	72
Babcock, W.	84	Cannata, T.	71
Aston, J.	82	Whalem, W.	71
Martin, J.	81	Grodsky, F.	65
Picardi, O.	81		

Since there are 15 pupils in the class, 20 percent of the class is three pupils. Thus, T. Yeh, P. Farmer, and O. Ross, the three highest scoring pupils, received A grades. The next 20 percent of her pupils—C. Foster, W. Babcock, and J. Aston—received B grades. The next 40 percent of the class (six pupils) got C grades. Finally, the last 20 percent of the class, T. Cannata, W. Whalem, and F. Grodsky, received D grades.

In norm-referenced grading, two pupils who achieve the same score must receive the same grade, regardless of the curve used.

In assigning grades by the norm-referenced approach it is important to bear in mind that two pupils who attain the same score must receive the same grade, regardless of the curve being used. Notice the differences in the grade distributions under the norm-referenced and the criterion-referenced approaches. Remember that these differences are mainly the result of decisions made about the grading curve or performance standards used.

Table 6.6 summarizes guidelines for grading.

Software can help teachers keep rank books, calculate grades, and store and organize test items.

Increasingly, teachers are applying technology to their teaching. One area where technology is particularly helpful is in grading. Many teachers use spreadsheets to keep records of pupils' test scores, quizzes, and other academic performances. Other teachers use software programs that maintain banks of test items, making it easy to develop tests. There also is software aimed specifically at helping teachers carry out grading. These programs can store records of pupil performances, apply different weights to different types of performances, and calculate a total score for each pupil. Most computer catalogs and computer stores can provide information on these types of software. If possible, teachers should become familiar with a program before it is purchased.

TABLE 6.6 GUIDELINES FOR GRADING

- ◆ The chosen grading system is consistent with the purpose of grading.
- ◆ Data for grading is gathered throughout the grading period.
- ◆ Varied pieces of data are collected (tests, projects, quizzes, etc.).
- ◆ Students are informed about the system used to grade them.
- ◆ The grading system separates subject matter achievements from nonacademic performance (effort, motivation, etc.). Nonacademic performance is presented in a different place than subject matter performance.
- ◆ Grading is based on valid and reliable assessment evidence.
- ◆ Important evidence of achievement is weighted more than less-important evidence (e.g., tests weighted more than quizzes).
- ◆ The grading system is applied consistently across all pupils.

OTHER METHODS OF REPORTING PUPIL PROGRESS

Grades, whether on individual classroom assignments or on report cards, are the most common way that pupils and their parents find out how things are going in the classroom. But grades are limited in the information they convey: they are given infrequently; they provide little *specific* information about how a pupil is performing; and they rarely include information about the teacher's perceptions of a pupil's effort, motivation, cooperation, and classroom demeanor. Moreover, since report card grades usually reflect pupil performance on a variety of assessment tasks, it is quite possible for two pupils to receive the same grade but to have performed very differently on the assessments used to determine the grade. Because of these limitations, other approaches for reporting pupils' school progress also are needed and used by teachers (Azwell & Gulseth, 1995; Guskey, 1996). Table 6.7 lists the many ways teachers can communicate and interact with parents. Each of these forms of communication can provide important supplementary information that rounds out the picture of a pupil's life at school.

Grades are the most common device by which students and parents are kept informed about how things are going in the classroom.

To have a complete and specific picture of their child's school performance, parents must receive more than the report card.

Parent-Teacher Conferences

Parent-teacher conferences allow flexible, two-way communication, unlike the one-way communication that grades provide. The nature of the communication differs as well. Conferences permit discussion, elaboration, and explanation of pupil performance. The teacher can get information from the parents about their concerns and perceptions of their child's

Unlike grades, parent-teacher conferences provide flexible, two-way communication.

> ### TABLE 6.7   OPTIONS FOR PARENT-TEACHER COMMUNICATION
>
> ♦ Report cards
> ♦ Weekly or monthly progress reports
> ♦ Parents' nights
> ♦ School visitation days
> ♦ Parent-teacher conferences
> ♦ Phone calls
> ♦ Letters
> ♦ Class or school newsletter
> ♦ Papers and work products

school experience. Information can also be obtained about special problems the pupil is having, from physical and emotional problems to difficulties with classroom adjustment. Parents can inform the teacher of their concerns and ask questions about the pupil's classroom behavior and about the curriculum being followed. Teachers who are in nursery school or at the last grade of elementary school or middle school are often asked by parents to recommend the type of school, teacher, or academic program that is most suitable for their child. Certainly a parent-teacher conference addresses a broader range of issues and concerns than a report card grade does.

It is natural for teachers to feel somewhat uneasy at the prospect of a conference with parents. The teacher wants to be respected by the parents, does not want a confrontational experience, and may have to tell parents some unpleasant things about their child. Because the teacher has certain things he or she wants the parents to know and because there is always an element of uncertainty about the way the conference will go, it is recommended that the teacher develop an agenda of the things he or she wants to cover. For example, most teachers provide a description of the pupil's academic and social classroom performance. The teacher also asks the parents questions such as does Robert act this way at home? or what does he say about the work load in school? Certainly the teacher wants to give parents the opportunity to ask questions. Finally, the teacher, in conjunction with the parents, often plans a course of action to help the pupil.

Planning is necessary to accomplish such agendas. The teacher gathers samples of the pupil's work, perhaps in a portfolio, and identifies (with examples) particular behavioral or attitudinal issues that should be raised. If there is a major existing or potential problem, the teacher ought to look over the pupil's permanent record file in the school office to see whether the problem surfaced in other grades. All this needs to be done before the conference.

Finally, the teacher should locate a comfortable, private spot to hold the conference. Usually this means before or after school in the teacher's classroom, when pupils are not present. If this is the case, the teacher should provide suitable, adult-sized chairs for the parents. Conferences work better when they are private and undisturbed and when all parties are comfortably situated.

The following tips can help the actual parent-teacher conference proceed successfully. The teacher should set a proper tone. This means making parents feel welcome, maintaining a positive attitude, and remembering that a pupil is not their concern or the teacher's concern, but a mutual concern. If possible, teachers should find out what parents want to know before the conference so as to prepare for their questions. The teacher should not do all the talking; he or she should be a good listener and use the conference to find out about parents' perceptions and concerns. Teachers should also talk in terms parents will understand, avoiding educational jargon, which often confuses rather than clarifies. Concrete examples, perhaps from pupil portfolios, help when explaining things to parents. Parents deserve frankness, but it is important to convey both the pupil's strengths and weaknesses. The aim of parent-teacher conferences is to understand and help the pupil, so even unpleasant information that may provoke a confrontation must be delivered. It is the teacher's responsibility to raise issues with parents that will help the pupil, even though discussion of those issues might be unpleasant. Teachers should admit to not knowing an answer and attempt to locate that answer following the conference.

Conferences should be private, undisturbed, and well planned.

There are many things a teacher should *not* say during a conference. They should not talk about other pupils or colleagues by name or by implication. They should not belittle colleagues or the principal in front of parents, no matter what. Statements like last year's teacher did not prepare Rosalie well in math or teachers get so little support for their ideas from the principal should be left unsaid. Regardless of whether the statements are true, it is not professional to discuss such issues with parents. One child's work should not be compared to other pupils' by name, and parents should not see other pupils' work, test scores, or grades. Teachers are professionals and they have an obligation to act professionally. This means being truthful with parents, not demeaning colleagues in front of parents, concentrating discussion only on the parents' child, and not discussing information from the conference with other teachers. These guidelines are appropriate for all forms of parent-teacher interaction.

Teachers must maintain their professional demeanor during parent-teacher conferences.

A course of remedial action for the pupil, if appropriate, should be determined jointly with the parents. Both parties should be responsible for implementing the plan: I will try to do these things with Charles in class, and you will try to do these other things with him at home. Finally, the teacher should summarize the conference before the parents leave, reviewing the main points and any decisions or courses of action that have been agreed upon.

Parent-teacher conferences can be very useful to both teachers and parents if planned and conducted successfully. They allow the teacher to supplement his or her information about the pupil while giving the parents a

TABLE 6.8   GUIDELINES FOR PARENT-TEACHER CONFERENCES

1. Plan in advance of the conference by gathering samples of pupil's work and identifying issues to discuss with parents; find out what parents want to know before the conference, if possible.

2. Identify a private, comfortable place for the conference.

3. Set a proper tone by
   a. Remembering that the pupil is of mutual concern to you and the parents;
   b. Listening to the parents' perspectives and concerns;
   c. Avoiding educational jargon and giving concrete examples; and
   d. Being frank with parents when conveying pupil's strengths and weaknesses.

4. Admit to not knowing the answer to a question and be willing to find out; do not try to bluff parents.

5. Do not talk about or belittle other colleagues or pupils by name or implication; do not compare one pupil to another by name.

6. If a remedial action is agreed to, plan the action jointly with parents and make each party responsible for part of the plan.

7. Orally review and summarize decisions and planned actions at the end of the conference.

8. Write summary notes of the conference.

broader understanding of their child's school performance. The main drawback to parent-teacher conferences is that they are time-consuming, although many school districts are beginning to set aside a day or two in the school calendar specifically for parent conferencing.

Table 6.8 summarizes the preceding guidelines for holding an effective parent-teacher conference.

Other Reporting Methods

Other, less commonly used methods of conveying information about a pupil's school performance are letters or phone calls to parents and pupil-teacher conferences. Letters and phone calls to parents are used mainly to inform parents of a special problem that has occurred and, as such, are used quite infrequently by teachers. Regular written or phone communication between a teacher and a parent is very rare and occurs only if the parent specifically requests frequent progress reports and the teacher agrees to provide them. Certainly from a time efficiency viewpoint, phone calls are better than writing letters to parents. If a teacher does write to parents, it is extremely important that the letter is free of spelling and grammatical errors. Few things can create a poorer impression in a parent's mind than a misspelled, grammatically incorrect letter from his or her child's teacher.

CHAPTER SUMMARY

♦ The process of judging the quality of a pupil's performance is called grading. The single most important characteristic of the grading process is its dependence on teacher judgment, which is always subjective to some degree.

♦ Grading is a difficult task for teachers because they have had little formal instruction in grading; they have to make judgments based on incomplete evidence; they have conflicting classroom roles; they must not allow pupils' personal characteristics and circumstances to distort subject matter judgments; and there is no single, universally accepted grading strategy.

♦ In grading, the teacher's primary aims are to be fair to all pupils and reflect pupils' subject matter learning.

♦ The main purpose of report card grades is to communicate information about pupil achievement. Grades have administrative, informational, motivational, and guidance functions.

♦ All grades represent a comparison of pupil performance to some standard of excellence or quality.

♦ Norm-referenced grades compare a pupil's performance to that of other pupils in the class. Pupils with the highest scores get the designated number of high grades as defined by the grading curve.

♦ Criterion-referenced grades compare a pupil's performance to a predefined standard of mastery. There is no limit on the number of pupils who can receive a particular grade.

♦ Basing grades on comparisons of a pupil's performance to the pupil's ability or record of improvement is not recommended.

♦ After selecting the comparative basis for grading, the teacher next must decide what pupil performances will be considered in awarding grades. For subject matter grades it is recommended that pupil performances that demonstrate subject matter mastery be included in the grade. Effort, motivation, participation, and behavior should not be major parts of subject grades.

♦ Grading requires teachers to summarize many different types of information into a single score. More important types of pupil performance such as tests and projects should be weighted most heavily in arriving at a grade.

♦ In order to summarize various types of information, each one must be expressed in the same way and on the same scale, usually a percentage scale.

♦ Before combining information into a grade, the quality of each piece of selected assessment information should be reviewed and adjustments made if invalid assessments are found. Grades will only be as valid as the assessment information on which they are based.

♦ Grading information should be expanded and supplemented by other means of parent-teacher communication such as conferences, parents' nights, progress reports, and papers and projects sent home.

QUESTIONS FOR DISCUSSION

1. What are the purposes of giving grades to pupils? How well do different grading formats meet these purposes?

2. What are a teacher's responsibilities to pupils when assigning grades on a paper, test, or project? What additional responsibilities to pupils do teachers have when they assign report card grades?

3. Is the task of assigning report card grades the same for elementary and high school teachers? How might the process of assigning grades differ at the two levels?

4. How can the information on report cards be made more informative for parents and pupils?

5. What are possible ways, both good and bad, that grades can impact pupils? What can be done to lessen the detrimental impact of grades?

REFLECTION EXERCISES

♦ Suppose that you are asked to develop the ideal report card for a school. What does the report card look like? What are its major strengths and major weaknesses?

♦ It was argued in this chapter that many teachers dislike report card grading and find it difficult to do. List as many reasons as you can to explain why this is so.

♦ (To be done after the following activity is completed.) What are the strengths and weaknesses of the grading system you have developed?

TABLE 6.9   GRADING ACTIVITY

Students	Test 1	Test 2	Test 3	Test 4	Project
Malcolm	40	60	55	100	A–
Gretchen	90	95	45	85	A
Charles	70	65	20	30	C
Thomas	85	80	50	85	B–
Jack	70	70	15	65	D
Susan	45	75	45	100	C
Maya	75	80	45	75	B–
Maria	70	75	30	70	A
Oscar	80	90	45	85	C
Angelina	30	40	10	40	D–
James	60	60	15	45	D

ACTIVITIES

1. Table 6.9 contains information that a teacher has accumulated about her students during a marking period. Use this information to assign a report card grade to each student. These questions will guide your task.

♦ Will you use a norm-referenced or a criterion-referenced grading approach? Why?

♦ Will you include all the information in the table in determining a grade or only some of the information? State what you will and will not include and explain why.

♦ Will all the pieces of information you have decided to include count equally, or will some things count more than others?

♦ How will you take into account the fact that students' performance on different pieces of information is represented differently (e.g., percentages, letter grades, excellent-good-poor, high-middle-low)?

♦ What, if anything, will you do about test 3?

♦ How will you summarize the different pieces of information into a single score or rating?

♦ What will be your grading curve (norm-referenced) or performance standards (criterion-referenced) for awarding grades?

♦ What grade will each student receive?

♦ In what ways is this exercise artificial? That is, would there be a difference between the way you graded these students and the way a teacher who has actually taught them for the marking period would grade them?

♦ If you graded the students in a norm-referenced way, go back and regrade using a criterion-referenced approach. If you graded the students in a criterion-referenced approach, go back and regrade using a norm-referenced approach.

♦ Complete Reflection Exercise 3.

TABLE 6.9 CONTINUED

Class Participation	General Effort	Quizzes and Homework	Behavior	Teacher's Ability (Estimate)
Good	G	G	G	M
Excellent	Ex	Ex	Ex	H
Excellent	G	P	P	M
Poor	P	G	P	H
Good	Ex	P	Ex	L
Excellent	Ex	G	G	M
Good	G	G	G	M
Excellent	G	G	G	M
Poor	P	P	P	M
Poor	Ex	P	Ex	L
Poor	P	P	P	H

2. Should pupils be held back if their school grades are very poor? What are the pros and cons of using grades to hold pupils back? If you had to choose whether to promote or hold back a very low-achieving pupil, what would you do? Why?

REVIEW QUESTIONS

1. What are grades and why are they important? Why do schools give grades?

2. What questions must a teacher answer in order to carry out the grading process? What teacher judgments must be made in the grading process? Why is there no single best way to assign grades to students?

3. In what way is all grading based on comparison? What are common methods of comparison used in grading and how do they differ? What is the difference between norm- and criterion-referenced grading? Which method would you use and why?

4. What are advantages and disadvantages of different grading methods?

5. Why should grades be determined mostly by the academic performances of students, rather than other information a teacher has about students?

6. What information should a teacher provide students about the grading process?

REFERENCES

Airasian, P. W. (1991). Perspectives on measurement instruction. *Educational Measurement: Issues and Practice, 10* (1), 13–16.

Azwell, T., and Gulseth, G. (1995). *Report card on report cards: Alternatives to consider.* Portsmouth, NH: Heinemann.

Borich, G. D. (1996). *Effective teaching methods.* Englewood Cliffs, NJ: Prentice Hall.

Brookhart, S. M. (1991). Grading practices and validity. *Educational Measurement: Issues and Practice, 10* (1), 35–36.

———. (1992). Teachers' grading practices: Meaning and values. Paper presented at the annual meeting of the American Educational Research Association, April, San Francisco.

Brookhart, S. M. (1998). Teaching about grading and communicating results. Paper presented at the annual meeting of the National Council on Measurement in Education, April, San Diego.

Quality counts '99. (January 11, 1999). Rewarding results, punishing failure. *Education Week, 18,* 17.

Friedman, S. J., and Frisbie, D. A. (1993). The validity of report cards as indicators of student performance. Paper presented at the annual meeting of the National Council on Measurement in Education, April, Atlanta.

———. (1995). The influence of report cards on the validity of grades reported to parents. *Educational and Psychological Measurement, 55* (1), 5–26.

Frisbie, D. A., and Waltman, K. K. (1992). Developing a personal grading plan. *Educational Measurement: Issues and Practice, 11* (3), 35–42.

Griswold, P. A., and Griswold, M. M. (1992). The grading contingency: Graders' beliefs and expectations and the assessment ingredients. Paper presented at the annual meeting of the American Educational Research Association, April, San Francisco.

Guskey, T. R. (1996). *ASCD Yearbook 1996, Communicating student learning.* Alexandria, VA: ASCD.

Hubelbank, J. H. (1994). *Meaning of elementary school teachers' grades.* Unpublished Ph.D. diss., Boston College, Chestnut Hill, MA.

Nava, F. J., and Loyd, B. (1992). The effect of student characteristics on the grading process. Paper presented at the annual meeting of the National Council on Measurement in Education, April, San Francisco.

Oosterhof, A. C. (1987). Obtaining intended weights when combining students' scores. *Educational Measurement: Issues and Practice, 6* (4), 29–37.

Slavin, R. E. (1994). *Educational Psychology.* 4th ed. Boston: Allyn and Bacon.

STANDARDIZED ACHIEVEMENT TESTS

CHAPTER OBJECTIVES

After reading this chapter, the student will be able to:

1. define basic terms: for example, standardized, stanine, percentile rank, test battery, norm group, standards, and cut-score.
2. state differences between teacher-made, commercial, and state-mandated achievement tests in terms of objectives, construction, scoring, and use.
3. interpret commercial standardized test score reports.
4. cite factors that influence the validity and reliability of standardized and state-mandated achievement tests.
5. describe the different forms and consequences of statewide assessments.
6. explain how statewide assessments are scored.

The types of classroom assessment discussed so far are those that are initiated and controlled by the classroom teacher. The teacher decides who to assess, when to assess, what to assess, how to assess, how to score and grade, and how to use the results. These teacher-produced assessments are fundamental ingredients in the teaching-learning process.

However, two types of external, standardized assessments are also administered in most classrooms. A **standardized assessment** is one that (1) is designed to be used in many different classrooms and schools and (2) is administered, scored, and interpreted the same way no matter when or where it is given. These assessments, which rarely are under the direct control of the classroom teacher, include commercially published national achievement tests and state-mandated achievement tests. In this chapter the development, scoring, and use of two types of standardized tests, commercial standardized achievement tests and statewide assessments, are examined and contrasted.

Standardized tests are designed for use across many different classrooms and schools and therefore are administered, scored, and interpreted the same way no matter where or when given.

Commercially published, national standardized achievement tests are constructed and sold to school systems by private testing companies. Among the most widely used are the California Achievement Tests, Comprehensive Tests of Basic Skills, Iowa Tests of Basic Skills, Metropolitan Achievement Tests, Sequential Tests of Educational Progress, SRA Achievement Series, and Stanford Achievement Tests.

Commercial achievement tests are usually given each year. They provide information about pupil performance over time and identify strengths and weaknesses.

Most school systems administer at least one commercial test each year to pupils in most grades. Their three main purposes are (1) to compare the performance of local pupils to that of similar pupils from across the nation, (2) to provide developmental information about pupils' performance over time, and (3) to identify pupils' strengths and weaknesses.

State-mandated tests are a more recent phenomenon and, as their name suggests, are mandated by a state legislature or board of education for use within that state (Airasian, 1993). Pupils' performance is compared to statewide performance standards to inform decisions such as whether pupils will be (1) allowed to graduate, (2) promoted to the next grade, or

TABLE 7.1   COMPARISON OF TEACHER-MADE, COMMERCIAL, AND STATE-MANDATED ACHIEVEMENT TESTS

	Teacher-Made	Commercial	State-Mandated
Content and/or objectives	Specific to class instruction; picked or developed by the teacher; narrow range of content tested, usually one unit or chapter of instruction in a subject	Topics commonly taught in many schools across the nation; broad range of content covering a year of instruction in a subject	Topics commonly taught or desired to be taught in schools of a state or district; broad range of content covered in a subject area, often covering many years of instruction in a subject
Item construction	Written or selected by the classroom teacher	Professional item writers	Professional item writers
Item type	Various types	Mainly multiple-choice items	Multiple-choice items and performance
Item selection	Teacher picks or writes items as needed for test	Many items written and then screened and tried out on pupils before few best items chosen for test	Many items written and then screened; best items chosen for test
Scoring	Teacher	Machine	Machine and scorers
Scores reported	Number correct, percent correct	Percentile rank, stanine, grade-equivalent scores	Usually pass-fail for individuals; percent or proportion of mastery for groups
Interpreting scores	Norm- or criterion-referenced, depending on classroom teacher's preference	Norm-referenced and developmental	Criterion-referenced

(3) assigned to remedial instruction. Other state-mandated tests are used to assess schoolwide achievement and to certify teachers.

Commercial and state-mandated achievement tests are similar in that both are standardized, intended for use across many different classrooms, assess content that is not selected by classroom teachers, and administered infrequently during the school year. They also differ from each other in many ways. Commercial achievement tests are given at the discretion of the local school system, whereas local systems are mandated to give the statewide achievement tests. Their purposes also differ. National commercial achievement tests are usually intended to compare the performance of pupils in a particular classroom, school, or district to the performance of similar pupils nationwide. State-mandated tests are intended to determine whether an individual pupil or group of pupils has achieved a minimum level of competence as defined by state educational authorities.

Commercial achievement tests compare the performance of local pupils to that of similar pupils from across the nation.

Table 7.1 compares teacher-made, commercially published, and state-mandated achievement tests.

Table 7.1 shows that teacher-made tests focus more on instructional objectives specific to a particular classroom than commercial or state-mandated tests, which focus on objectives common to most classrooms nationally or within a state. The type of items found on teacher-made tests vary at the teacher's discretion, while most commercial tests are composed largely of multiple-choice items and statewide tests combine various combinations of multiple-choice and performance-based items. Teacher-made tests provide information about the number or percentage of items a pupil gets right; commercial tests provide information about how a pupil compares to his or her peers nationwide; and state-mandated tests indicate pupil and group mastery of basic skills defined by state authorities.

This chapter is about commercial and state-mandated standardized achievement tests. It describes their construction, administration, scoring, and interpretation, as well as important cautions that should be exercised in their use. Before beginning that discussion, however, it is instructive to consider how teachers view these tests.

TEACHERS' PERCEPTIONS OF STANDARDIZED TESTS

Teachers have mixed reactions about both commercial and state-mandated achievement tests. The following comments provide a sense of the main issues that concern them.

The tests are inappropriate for my class because our curriculum doesn't cover some of the test content. I vary my instruction from the textbook, introducing enrichment material and omitting certain text sections. A lot of what I teach is on the tests, but the match between the test content and what I teach is by no means exact.

If a test has a separate answer sheet it's taken much more seriously by kids and their parents than if it doesn't. Parents put so much emphasis on the commercial achievement tests. They're so concerned about how their child compares to kids across the country. I dread sitting down with parents during a conference and trying to explain why Mary or Mark was above or, especially, below their expectations.

Many parents put more faith in a 50-item standardized test than in my judgment based upon months of observing their child in school. These tests are treated like the *Good Housekeeping* Seal of Approval of a kid's learning. Too much emphasis is placed on these short, general, one-shot tests.

My principal puts a great deal of emphasis on our school's performance on the state-mandated tests. He's very concerned about how we do compared to neighboring schools when the results are published in the local paper. There is pressure to include test topics in our curriculum and to give those topics more instructional time.

It's hard to know what to do with the commercial test results. They give a sense of how pupils are doing, but they mainly corroborate what I already know about the pupils. Occasionally a pupil will perform very differently than I expected and this forces me to look more carefully at my initial impression of the pupil. But for the most part, I don't need a standardized test to tell me how pupils are doing.

Two years ago we started testing students in the spring. I like this much better than testing them in the fall. I now look forward to seeing the results so I can compare them to my students' results from last year to see if they've improved. It's sort of like my report card for the year. I can also use the results in making suggestions to next year's teacher about the class.

These comments illustrate a number of points regarding the role that external, standardized tests play in classrooms. First, neither commercial nor state-mandated tests are viewed by teachers as being important in the day-to-day functioning of their classrooms. Second, teachers do not gain much formative information from the test results, although they do use them in parent conferences to corroborate their initial perceptions of pupils as well as to judge the success of their instruction at the end of the year. The main uses of standardized tests reside outside the classroom, although there is some pressure, particularly in the case of state-mandated tests, to alter classroom instruction to fit the tests. The primary reason for this pressure is that the consequences of poor performance on state-mandated tests are more immediate and severe than for commercial tests. With these teacher perceptions in mind, consideration now turns to commercial, standardized, norm-referenced achievement tests, which, for simplicity, are called commercial achievement tests.

Most teachers do not think standardized tests are important to the day-to-day functioning of their classrooms, but parents often view the results with great seriousness.

COMMERCIAL ACHIEVEMENT TESTS

There are two key points to remember about commercial achievement tests: (1) they are usually norm referenced and (2) their main function is to compare a pupil's performance to that of a national group of similar pupils. Statements such as John scored higher than 87 percent of seventh graders nationwide in math; Maria is in the third grade, but her grade equivalent score on the standardized test was sixth grade, third month; Kerry scored above average in science compared to eighth graders in the United States; and compared to second graders across the country, Sam was in the bottom quarter in reading refer to the results of commercial achievement tests. In each of these descriptions, a pupil's test performance was obtained by comparing it to a group of similar pupils across the country. Commercial achievement tests are used in schools mainly

Commercial achievement tests are usually norm referenced.

because they provide comparisons of pupil achievement beyond the confines of their classroom. Such comparisons are not available from teacher-made tests.

A test battery is a collection of tests in many different subject areas that are administered together.

The most commonly used commercial achievement tests are published in the form of test batteries. A **test battery** is a collection of tests in many different subject areas that are administered together. Rather than constructing one test for math, a totally separate test for reading, and yet another for science, most commercial test publishers construct a single test battery that contains many different subject area tests. For example, the Iowa Tests of Basic Skills battery for the fifth grade is made up of the following 13 subject tests, or, as they are commonly called, **subtests:** vocabulary, reading comprehension, spelling, capitalization, punctuation, usage and expression, maps and diagrams, reference materials, math concepts and estimation, math problem solving and data interpretation, math computation, social studies, and science. A pupil gets a separate score on each subtest. The entire battery consists of 458 items that take over 5 hours to complete. The main advantages of a test battery are (1) that its broad content coverage provides a general picture of a pupil's school performance and (2) that a pupil's score on one subtest can be compared to his or her score on other subtests.

A test battery provides a general picture of a pupil's school performance and compares performance across subject areas.

Test Construction

Since the information obtained from a commercial achievement test differs from that obtained from a teacher-made or textbook test, it should not be surprising to learn that the commercial test is constructed differently as well. A well-constructed commercial achievement test has three characteristics: (1) it is carefully constructed, with item tryouts, analysis, and revision occurring before the final version of the test is completed; (2) there are written directions and procedures for administering and scoring the test; and (3) score interpretation is based on the test having been administered to a carefully selected sample of pupils from across the nation. The performance of this national sample, or **norm group,** is what local pupils are compared to when they take the test. Figure 7.1 compares the steps in constructing a teacher-made achievement test with the steps in constructing a commercial achievement test.

Choosing Objectives

Commercial tests try to assess objectives that are taught nationally in classrooms at a particular grade level.

A teacher-made test and a national commercial standardized achievement test both start with educational objectives. In the teacher-made test, the objectives that have been emphasized during instruction are assessed. The commercial test constructor, on the other hand, seeks to assess only objectives that are commonly taught across the nation in all classrooms at a particular grade level. These objectives are found by examining widely used textbooks and state curriculum guidelines. The objectives and skills

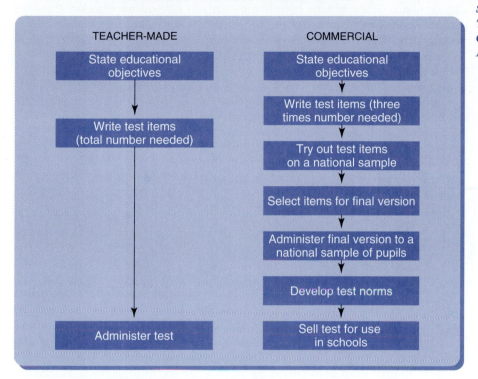

CONSTRUCTING ACHIEVEMENT TESTS

TEACHER-MADE

- State educational objectives
- Write test items (total number needed)
- Administer test

COMMERCIAL

- State educational objectives
- Write test items (three times number needed)
- Try out test items on a national sample
- Select items for final version
- Administer final version to a national sample of pupils
- Develop test norms
- Sell test for use in schools

FIGURE 7.1

Steps in Constructing Teacher-Made and Commercial Achievement Tests

that are *common* across textbooks and guidelines are selected for inclusion in the test. This means that some objectives a particular classroom teacher emphasizes may not be assessed by a commercial achievement test.

Writing and Reviewing Items

Once the objectives are identified, the commercial test publisher, like the classroom teacher, must construct or select test items. Unlike the classroom teacher, who writes just as many items as are needed for a test, the commercial test publisher writes two or three times more items than are needed on the final test.

> To provide a large pool of items for final test selection, one-and-one-half to two times as many items as would be needed were developed. A staff of professional item writers, most of them experienced teachers, researched and wrote items and passages to be tried out (CTB/McGraw-Hill, 1985, 5).

The mostly multiple-choice items go through several cycles of review and revision before being accepted for use. Curriculum specialists study the items to be sure they assess the intended objectives. Test construction

Commercial test items are reviewed and edited for content, style, and validity, as well as for ethnic, cultural, racial, and gender bias.

specialists review them to be sure they are well written, without ambiguity or clues. Other groups review the items to determine whether they are biased in favor of particular pupil groups. At the end of this stage of test construction, a large group of items that have been screened by many groups are available to the test publisher.

> Each item and subtest was reviewed and edited for content, style, and appropriateness for measuring the stated objective, as well as for ethnic, cultural, racial, and sex bias (The Psychological Corporation, 1984, 1-1).

Trying Out Items

All the test items are tried out and the more valid and reliable ones are selected for the final version of the test. Since no test constructor, whether a classroom teacher or a commercial test publisher, knows how well any item will work until it actually is tried on a group of pupils, the publisher tries out the items on a sample of pupils similar to those for whom the final test is intended. The communities chosen for these tryouts represent different sizes, geographical locations, and socioeconomic levels. The trial test forms look like the final test form and are administered by classroom teachers so that the administrative situation during the tryout is as similar as possible to the way that the final, published test will be administered.

After tests are tried out, commercial test items are statistically analyzed to ensure that they provide the spread among scores that are needed on norm-referenced tests.

There are two reasons for trying out test items before finalizing the test. First, the test constructor wants to make sure that all the items are clearly written and understood by pupils. By examining pupil responses after the tryout, unclear items can be identified, revised, or discarded. Second, test items that ensure a spread of test scores among the test takers must be selected. After the tryout, the statistical properties of each item are analyzed to make certain the final test contains items that differentiate among test takers. This permits the desired norm-referenced comparisons in the commercial achievement tests.

Item difficulty indicates the proportion of test takers who answered the item correctly.

Item discrimination compares overall test scores on a particular item.

Two important indices for judging test items are difficulty and discrimination. The **difficulty** of a test item indicates the proportion of test takers who answered the item correctly. Thus, a difficulty of 90 means that 90 percent of the pupils answered the item correctly, while an item with a difficulty of 15 was answered correctly by only 15 percent of the test takers. The **discrimination** of an item indicates how well pupils who scored high on the test as a whole scored on a particular item. An item that discriminates well among test takers is one that high test scorers get correct, but low test scorers get incorrect. That is, the item discriminates between pupils in the same way as the whole test.

The test constructor's purpose is to differentiate among pupils according to their levels of achievement. The test constructor is not likely to select final items for the test that all pupils got right or wrong in the tryout, because these items do not help differentiate high from low achievers. To accomplish the desired norm referencing among test takers, the test must consist of items that about half the pupils get correct and half get incorrect and that discriminate among pupils in the same way as the test as a whole. Only then does the test differentiate pupils across the possible scoring range and permit the desired norm-referenced comparisons among test takers. The item tryout provides the information needed to select items for the final test version.

The preceding steps accomplish three important aims: (1) they identify test objectives that reflect what most teachers across the nation are teaching; (2) they produce test items that assess these objectives; and (3) they identify a final group of items that will produce the desired norm-referenced comparisons among test takers. The final version of the test, including the selected test items, directions for administration, separate answer sheets, and established time limits, must then be "normed."

To differentiate among students, commercial tests contain many items that approximately one-half of the test takers get right and one-half get wrong.

Norming the Test

In order to provide information that allows comparison of an individual pupil's performance to that of a national sample of similar pupils, the final version of the test must be given to a sample of pupils from across the nation. This process is called norming the test. **Norms** describe how a national sample of pupils who took the test actually performed on it.

Suppose that a commercial test publisher wishes to norm the final version of an achievement test for fifth graders. To do this, the publisher needs to obtain information about how fifth graders across the nation perform on the test. The publisher (1) selects a representative sample of fifth graders from across the country, (2) administers the test to this sample, (3) scores the test, and (4) uses the scores of the sample to represent the performance of all fifth graders across the country. Assuming the sample of fifth graders was well chosen, the scores made by the sample are a good indication of how all fifth graders would perform on the test.

Obviously, the representativeness of the sample determines how much confidence a teacher can have in the comparisons made between individual pupils and the "national average." The development of norms is a critical aspect of constructing these tests. Commercial test publishers recognize this fact and strive to select samples that are representative of the group for whom a test is intended.

Test norms describe how a national sample of students who are representative of the general population perform on the test.

> A test is standardized nationally by administering it under the same conditions to a national sample of students. The students tested become a norm or comparison group against which future individual scores can be compared. . . . The sample should be carefully selected to be representative of the national population with respect to ability and achievement. The sample should be large enough to represent the many diverse elements in the population (Riverside Publishing Company, 1986, 11).

Four criteria are used to judge the adequacy of standardized test norms: sample size, representativeness, recentness, and description of procedures (Popham, 1990). In general, a large sample of pupils in the norm

If we assume a norming sample is representative of the general population, a large sample is preferred to a small one.

group is preferable to a small sample; other things being equal, we would prefer a norming sample of 10,000 fifth graders to one of 1,000 fifth graders. But size alone does not guarantee representativeness. If the 10,000 pupils in the norming sample were all from private schools in the same state, the sample would not provide a good representation of the performance of pupils nationwide. There must be evidence that the norming sample is representative of the national group for whom the test is intended.

School curricula change over time. New topics are added and others are dropped. Thus, it is important to renorm commercial norm-referenced tests about every 7 to 9 years in order to keep up with these changes. It is unfair to compare today's pupils to a norm group that was taught a different curriculum.

The final criterion for judging the adequacy of standardized test norms is the clarity of the procedures used to produce them. The clearer and more detailed the description of the procedures followed in test construction, the better the test user can judge the appropriateness of the test for his or her needs. Publishers provide different kinds of manuals outlining procedures to accompany their tests. A *technical manual,* for example, provides information about the construction of the test, including objective selection, item writing and review, item tryout, and norming. A *teacher's manual* provides a description of the areas tested, as well as guidelines for interpreting and using the results of the test. These manuals ought to be accessible to classroom teachers to help them understand and use the test results. Another source of information about published tests is the *Mental Measurement Yearbooks,* which provide reviews written by experts in the field.

Commercial test manuals provide information about test construction and interpretation.

ADMINISTERING COMMERCIAL STANDARDIZED ACHIEVEMENT TESTS

Once a test is normed, it is ready to be sold to local school systems. School systems usually base their selection of a particular test on the judgment of a district administrator or a joint administrator-teacher committee. Once the testing program is selected, other decisions have to be made. In what grades will pupils be tested? Will all subtests of the achievement battery be administered? What types of score reports are needed? Should pupils be tested at the start of the school year or at the end of the year? Different school systems answer these questions differently. Whatever the ultimate decisions, it is usually the classroom teacher who is given the task of administering the tests.

A standardized test is meant to be administered to all pupils under the same conditions whenever and wherever it is given. The reason for standardizing administrative conditions is to allow valid comparisons between local scores and those of the national norm group. If a pupil takes the test under conditions different than the national norm group, then comparisons of the pupil's performance to the norm group are misleading. It is not fair to compare the performance of a pupil who was given 40 minutes to complete a test to others who were given only 30 minutes. It is not fair to compare a pupil who received coaching during testing to pupils who did not. Thus, every national standardized test comes with very specific and detailed directions to follow during test administration.

The directions spell out in great detail how a teacher should prepare for testing, how the room should be set up, what to do while the pupils are taking the test, how to distribute the tests and answer sheets, and how to time the tests. In addition, the directions suggest ways to prepare pupils for taking the test. Finally, the directions provide a script for the teacher to read when administering the test.

Commercial tests must always be administered under the same conditions in order for there to be valid comparisons between local scores and those of the national norm group.

Every teacher who administers a commercial standardized test is expected to use its accompanying script and not deviate from it. If the conditions of administration vary from the directions provided by the test publisher, comparisons with the norming sample and interpretations of pupils' performances may be invalid.

INTERPRETING COMMERCIAL ACHIEVEMENT TEST SCORES

Four to 8 weeks after test administration, results are returned to the school. It is important to remember that the tests usually are norm-referenced and compare a pupil's performance to those of a reference group of pupils. The most common comparisons are of a pupil against a national sample of pupils in the same grade or of a pupil against his or her own performance in different subtest areas. However, these are not the only comparisons that can be made from a commercial achievement test.

A school system may also compare its pupils to a narrower sample than pupils in the same grade nationwide. For example, suppose a school district is an urban sector and serves a large, multi-racial, multi-ethnic population. The information sought for this school is likely to be how pupils compare to a national sample drawn from similar urban sector school districts. Most commercial test publishers can provide such a comparison.

Suppose that a school district is in an affluent suburban area. Past experience has shown that when pupils in the district are compared to a representative national sample, they generally do very well. Here the information sought is likely to be how pupils in the district do in comparison to similar pupils in other affluent suburban districts. Once again, commercial test publishers can usually provide such a comparison.

Sometimes school districts are interested in comparing pupil performance within that district. Test publishers can provide this information.

Norms that compare pupils in a single school district are called **local norms.** Although national norms are the most commonly reported and used, most commercial test publishers can provide more specific standardized test norms according to geographic location, type of community (rural, suburban, urban), type of school (public, private), and particular school system. Note that a pupil's test performance may appear quite different depending on the choice of norm group to which he or she is compared: a representative national sample, a sample of pupils in urban schools, a sample of pupils in suburban schools, or a sample of pupils from his or her own school district.

Commercial achievement tests provide the classroom teacher with many different kinds of scores. In interpreting these tests, the number of items a pupil got correct, called the **raw score,** is not useful in itself. The teacher needs to know how that raw score compares to the chosen norm group, and special types of scores provide this information. Since there are so many types of scores available, discussion here is confined to the three most common types: percentile rank, stanine, and grade equivalent score. If there is a question about the meaning and interpretation of scores not discussed here, the teacher or class guide manual that accompanies a test contains the desired explanation.

Percentile Rank Scores

Probably the most commonly used score is the **percentile rank.** Percentile ranks range from 1 to 99 and indicate what percentage of the norm group the pupil scored above. If Tawon, a seventh grader, has a percentile rank of 91 on a standardized science test, she scored higher on the test than 91 percent of the national sample of seventh grade pupils who made up the norm group. If Josh has a percentile rank of 23 in reading, he scored higher on the reading test than 23 percent of the pupils in the norm group. Percentiles do not refer to the percentage of items a pupil answered correctly; they refer to the percentage of pupils in the norm group who scored *below* a given pupil.

The composition of the norm group defines the comparison that can be made. Thus, Tawon's percentile rank of 91 based upon local norms means that she did better than 91 percent of the seventh graders in her own school district. This does not necessarily mean that she would have a percentile rank of 91 if compared to seventh graders nationally. A pupil's percentile rank can vary depending on the group to which he or she is compared.

One of the main advantages of commercial achievement test batteries is that they are normed on a single group. This allows the teacher to compare a pupil's performance across the many subtests and to identify strengths and weaknesses. Thus, a teacher can make statements about how a given pupil performs in math as compared to science, reading, vocabulary, and other tested areas.

TABLE 7.2	APPROXIMATE PERCENTILE RANKS CORRESPONDING TO STANINE SCORES

Stanine Score	Approximate Percentile Rank
9	96 or higher
8	89–95
7	77–88
6	60–76
5	40–59
4	23–39
3	11–22
2	4–10
1	below 4

Stanine Scores

The **stanine** is a second type of standardized test score. Stanines are a nine-point scale, with a stanine of 1 representing the lowest performance and a stanine of 9 the highest. These nine numbers are the only possible stanine scores a pupil can receive. Like a percentile rank, stanines are designed to indicate a pupil's performance in comparison to a larger norming sample.

Stanines are a nine-point scale with 1 representing the lowest category and 9 the highest.

Table 7.2 shows the approximate relationship between percentile ranks and stanines.

Although there is comparability between stanine scores and percentile rank scores, most teachers use stanines to represent general achievement categories, with stanine scores of 1, 2, and 3 considered below average, 4, 5, and 6 considered average, and 7, 8, and 9 considered above average. While stanines are not as precise as percentile ranks, they are easy to work with and interpret, which is a major reason for their popularity among teachers and test publishers. As with the percentile rank, a pupil's stanine score in one subject can be compared to his or her stanine performance in another subject on the same test battery to identify strong and weak areas of the pupil's achievement.

Grade Equivalent Scores

While stanines and percentile ranks provide information about a pupil's performance compared to the norm group, other types of standardized test scores seek to identify a pupil's development across grade levels. They are intended to compare pupil performance to a series of reference groups that vary developmentally. The most common developmental scale is the **grade equivalent score,** which is intended to represent pupils' achievement in terms of a scale based upon grade and month in school. A grade equivalent score of 7.5 stands for seventh grade, fifth month of school. A grade equivalent score of 11.0 stands for the beginning of the eleventh grade. On some tests, the decimal point is omitted in grade equivalent scores, in which case a grade equivalent score of 43 stands for fourth grade, third month and a score of 108 stands for tenth grade, eighth month.

Grade equivalent scores are easily misinterpreted. A scoring scale that is organized in terms of grade and month in school is so familiar to most test users that it can seduce them into making incorrect interpretations regarding pupil performance. Consider Audrey, who took a standardized achievement test battery at the start of the fifth grade. When her teacher received the results, he saw that Audrey's grade equivalent score in mathematics was 7.5. What does this score indicate about Audrey's mathematics achievement?

If we were to ask 100 teachers what Audrey's grade equivalent score in math means, the great majority of them would say that Audrey does as well in mathematics as a seventh grader in the fifth month of school or that she can succeed in a seventh grade mathematics curriculum or that she is working at a seventh grade level in mathematics. In fact, except under very rare conditions, each of these interpretations is incorrect or unsubstantiated.

The grade equivalent provides an estimate of a pupil's developmental level, but it is not a prescription for the grade in which a pupil should be placed. Remember, Audrey took a *fifth* grade mathematics test, which assessed mathematics objectives commonly taught in the fifth grade. Audrey did not take a seventh grade mathematics test, so there is no way of knowing how Audrey would do on seventh grade math material. Certainly she would not have had the benefit of what is normally taught in the sixth grade. All that is known is how Audrey performed on a fifth grade test, and this tells nothing about how she might perform on higher grade level tests. If a common test had been given to both fifth and seventh grade pupils, a comparison of how Audrey performed to seventh graders is possible, but this is rarely done.

If all of the preceding interpretations are inappropriate, what is the correct interpretation of Audrey's grade equivalent score of 7.5? The most appropriate interpretation is that compared to other fifth graders, Audrey is well above the national average in *fifth* grade mathematics. Her score was higher than expected of the average fifth grader who took the test at the start of the fifth grade. Developmentally, she is ahead of the "typical" fifth grader in mathematics achievement.

Another use of the grade equivalent score is to assess a pupil's academic development over time. That is, the change in a grade equivalent score over time is used as an indication of whether the pupil is making "normal progress" in his or her learning. For example, if a pupil's grade equivalent score is 8.2 when tested in the eighth grade, one might expect the pupil's grade equivalent to be around 9.2 if tested at the same time in

	Percentile Rank	**Stanine**	**Grade Equivalent Score**
TABLE 7.3 COMPARISON OF THREE COMMON STANDARDIZED TEST SCORES			
Format of score	Percentage	Whole number	Grade and month in school
Possible scores	1 to 99 in whole numbers	1 to 9 in whole numbers	Prekindergarten to 12.9 in monthly increments
Interpretation	Percent of pupils a given pupil did better than	1 to 3 below average; 4 to 6 average; 7 to 9 above average	Above average, average, below average compared to pupils in the same grade
Special issues	Small differences often overinterpreted	General index of pupil achievement	Frequently misinterpreted and misunderstood

the ninth grade. However, teachers must be careful when assessing pupils' growth across different grades because development is an irregular process; it may jump ahead greatly at certain times, but remain static at others. Thus, small deviations from "normal" growth should not be interpreted as a problem. Table 7.3 compares the characteristics of percentile rank, stanine, and grade equivalent scores.

Three Examples of Commercial Test Interpretation

Although many types of standardized commercial test scores can be provided by test publishers, the percentile rank, stanine, and grade equivalent are most often used. Given the preceding discussion, here are specific examples of how standardized commercial achievement tests are reported to classroom teachers.

Standardized commercial tests usually report percentile rank, stanine, and grade equivalent scores.

Example 1: Pupil Performance Report

Figure 7.2 shows Brian Elliott's test results on the Metropolitan Achievement Test battery. The extreme top of the report tells us that Brian was administered both the Metropolitan Achievement Test and the Otis-Lennon School Ability Test, which is a test of general ability, not of achievement in specific school subjects. The top of the form tells us also that Brian's teacher is Ms. or Mr. Smith, his school is Lakeside Elementary School, and the school is part of the Newtown school system.

INDIVIDUAL REPORT
FOR
Brian Elliott

TEACHER: SMITH

SCHOOL: LAKESIDE ELEMENTARY GRADE: 04

DISTRICT: NEWTOWN

MAT/ OLSAT

1992 NORMS: SPRING

NATIONAL NATIONAL
ELEM 2   E
S   2

TEST DATE: 05/93

LEVEL: NATIONAL
FORM: ELEM 2

AGE 09 YRS 10 MOS

TESTS	NO. OF ITEMS	RAW SCORE	SCALED SCORE	NATL PR-S	NATL NCE	GRADE EQUIV	ACC RANGE
Total Reading	85	66	632	68–6	59.9	5.9	MIDDLE
Vocabulary	30	27	667	90–8	77.0	8.4	HIGH
Reading Comp.	55	39	618	53–5	51.6	5.0	MIDDLE
Total Mathematics	64	43	602	55–5	52.6	5.1	MIDDLE
Concepts & Problem Solving	40	29	617	68–6	59.9	6.0	MIDDLE
Procedures	24	14	579	37–4	43.0	4.3	LOW
Language	54	33	609	51–5	50.5	4.8	MIDDLE
Prewriting	15	10	606	47–5	48.4	4.7	MIDDLE
Composing	15	8	602	43–5	46.3	4.5	LOW
Editing	24	15	614	56–5	53.2	5.3	LOW
Science	35	25	628	65–6	58.1	5.9	MIDDLE
Social Studies	35	25	630	69–6	60.4	6.0	MIDDLE
Research Skills	36	29	635	73–6	62.9	6.5	MIDDLE
Thinking Skills	83	56	615	61–6	55.9	5.7	LOW
Basic Battery	203	142	617	60–6	55.3	5.4	MIDDLE
Complete Battery	273	192	619	62–6	56.4	5.5	MIDDLE

OTIS-LENNON SCHOOL ABILITY TEST	RAW SCORE	SAI	AGE PR-S	AGE NCE	SCALED SCORE	NATL GRADE PR-S	NATL GRADE NCE
Total	72	49	112	77–7	65.6	632	81–7	68.5
Verbal	36	25	114	81–7	68.5	637	85–7	71.8
Nonverbal	36	24	109	71–6	61.7	627	76–6	64.9

FIGURE 7.2

Standardized Test Report for an Individual Pupil

The top middle portion of the form tells us that Brian is in the fourth grade and that he took the Metropolitan in May, 1993. This is near the end of the school year, which has an important bearing on the national norming group against whom Brian's performance is compared. Suppose that Brian took the test in October, at the beginning of the school year. How would his performance in October probably compare to his performance in May? In October, Brian was just starting the fourth grade and had not had much instruction on fourth grade objectives. By May, Brian had 9 months of instruction on fourth grade objectives, so it is likely that he would test better in May than in October. The time of year when a pupil takes a standardized achievement test makes a considerable difference in his or her performance level; the more instruction the pupil has had, the higher his or her scores should be.

Commercial achievement test constructors recognize this fact and take it into account when they norm their tests. Most standardized test constructors norm their tests in both the fall and the spring, so that pupils who are tested in the fall can be compared to the fall norming group and pupils who take the test in the spring can be compared to the spring norming group. At the top of the report form under Norms is the entry Spring, which means that Brian's scores were compared to a national sample of fourth graders who were tested in the spring.

Because pupils tested in the spring have received more instruction than those tested in the fall, commercial tests contain both fall and spring norms.

Finally, the top of the form describes the **level** and **form** of the test Brian took. This information usually is not critical to interpreting the test results. The level of a test describes the grade level for which the test is intended. On the Metropolitan Achievement Test the level called Elem 2 is intended for the fourth grade. The form of the test refers to the version of the test administered. Often standardized test constructors produce two interchangeable versions of a test to allow schools that wish to test more than once a year to use a different but equivalent version of the test each time.

Below this general information are Brian's actual test results. First, marked by the circled A is a list of all the subtests that make up the Metropolitan Achievement Test battery and the number of items in each. These subtests start with total reading and end with thinking skills. Each of these subtests assesses Brian's performance in a distinct curriculum area. Subtest results can be grouped to provide additional scores. Thus, the total reading score is made up of the combined performance on the vocabulary and reading comprehension subtests. What three subtests are combined to make the total language score? The basic battery includes all subtests except science and social studies, while the complete battery total includes these two subtests. Finally, below the Metropolitan scores are the scores on the Otis-Lennon School Ability Test.

Subtests assess pupil performance in a specific curriculum area.

What kind of information is provided about Brian's performance on the Metropolitan subtests? Scores included in the section marked with a circled B are raw scores, scaled scores (a developmental score used to measure year-to-year growth in pupil performance), national percentile ranks and national stanines (NATL PR-S), national normal curve equivalents

(NATL NCE, a score similar to the percentile rank but with equal differences between adjacent percentile ranks), grade equivalent scores, and an achievement-ability comparison. The raw score tells how many items Brian got correct on each subtest. He got 27 of the 30 items on the vocabulary subtest and 29 of the 40 items on the concepts and problem solving subtest correct. Because there are different numbers of test items on the subtests, raw scores are not useful for interpreting a pupil's performance or comparing performance on different subtests. Also, since scaled scores are difficult to interpret and normal curve equivalents replaceable by percentile ranks in most cases, these are not described here. (More detailed information about these and other standardized test scores can be found in the interpretive guides for teachers that are available for most commercial achievement tests.)

The score column labeled NATL PR-S shows Brian's national percentile rank and corresponding stanine score on each subtest. How should Brian's performance of 56-5 on the editing subtest be interpreted? Brian's percentile rank of 56 means that he scored higher than 56 percent of the fourth grade national norm group on the editing subtest. His stanine score of 5 places him in the middle of the stanine scores and indicates that his performance is average for fourth graders nationwide. How would Brian's national percentile rank and stanine on the vocabulary test be interpreted?

Fairly large differences in percentile rank, especially near the middle of the percentile rank, may produce no difference when scores are expressed as stanines.

Compare Brian's performance in reading comprehension and composing. In terms of percentile rank, Brian did better in reading comprehension (53rd percentile rank) than in composing (43rd percentile rank), but in terms of stanines, Brian's performance on the two subtests was the same (stanine 5). The apparent difference in the percentile rank and stanine scores illustrates two points. First, the stanine score provides a more stable indication of performance than the percentile rank. Second, and more important, fairly large differences in percentile ranks, especially near the middle of the percentile rank scale, are not different when expressed as stanines.

Many teachers and parents forget that no test scores are perfectly reliable. No test score, not even one from a published standardized test, can be assumed to provide an exact, error-free assessment of a pupil's performance. Unfortunately, people who ignore this fact mistakenly treat small differences in percentile ranks (up to eight or so percentile ranks) as indicating a meaningful difference in performance. The stanine score, though more inclusive than the percentile rank, is a reminder that although Brian's percentile ranks differed on the two subtests, his performance did not differ when expressed in terms of stanines. Sometimes answering only one or two more items correctly can change a pupil's score by eight to 10 percentile ranks, yet not alter a pupil's stanine score. This reality should act as a caution for all teachers, including Brian's, not to read too much into the percentile rank differences in these two areas.

Note that standardized test batteries such as the one Brian took are not only useful for comparing a pupil's performance to that of similar pupils nationwide, but also for identifying a given pupil's strengths and weaknesses.

Thus, Brian's teacher can see that Brian is average in most subtests (stanines of 4, 5, or 6), and he is weaker in math procedures (37–4) than he is in vocabulary (90–8). The use of standardized tests to identify pupils' strengths and weaknesses is more important from an instructional view-point than is information about how pupils' rank compared to a national sample of pupils in the same grade.

Brian is a fourth grader who took the Metropolitan Achievement Test in the ninth month of the school year. If he had performed the same as the average of fourth graders from across the country who took the test in May, his grade equivalent scores on each subtest would have been 4.9, since that is the score given to average performance for fourth graders who take the test in May. Examination of Brian's grade equivalent scores in Figure 7.2 shows that in most areas, his score is at the fourth, fifth, or sixth grade level. Compared to the national sample of fourth graders in the norm group, Brian is average to a bit above average. He got more an-swers correct on the fourth grade tests than did the average fourth grader in the norm sample. This is basically the same information provided by Brian's percentile ranks and stanines. As with percentile ranks, small dif-ferences in grade equivalent scores (4 to 6 months) should not be overin-terpreted or used as the primary basis for decision making about pupils.

The achievement-ability comparison shown in Figure 7.2 is provided by many test publishers when the school testing program includes both a standardized achievement test and a standardized ability test. In essence, the comparison tries to provide information about how a pupil performs on the achievement test compared to a national sample of pupils who have a similar ability level. The issues associated with interpreting and using the ability-achievement comparison meaningfully are similar to those raised in the discussion of grading pupils based on their ability in Chapter 6: (1) there are problems in assessing ability; (2) the error in each test used in the comparison compounds the imprecision of the informa-tion; (3) the information is difficult to translate into meaningful, instruc-tionally related practices; and (4) the information may label a pupil or in-fluence a teacher's expectations for the pupil. For these reasons, achievement-ability comparisons can be misleading and should be used with extreme caution.

The area of Figure 7.2 marked with a circled C shows the national per-centile bands for Brian's performance on each subtest. Presenting Brian's performance in this way is useful, not only because it provides a graphic contrast to numerical scores, but because it reminds the test user about the error in all test scores. In essence, the **percentile bands** indicate that no score is error-free, so it is wrong to treat a score as if it were precise and infallible. It is best to think of a score not as a single number, but as a range of numbers, any one of which could be the pupil's true performance on an error-free test. Thus, because all tests have some degree of unrelia-bility, it is more appropriate to say that Brian's performance on the total reading subtest is somewhere between about the 62nd and 80th percentile rank than it is to say it is exactly and precisely at the 68th percentile. His

Percentile bands are provided on commercial tests as a reminder that no test scores are error-free.

performance on the math procedures subtest is better interpreted to be between a percentile rank of about 22 and 45 than exactly 37. In most cases, the percentile bands indicate the range of scores we can expect a pupil to fall in about 70 percent of the time. That is, about 70 percent of the time the pupil's score would be expected to be within the percentile bands. Thinking of performance in terms of a range of scores prevents overinterpretation of test results based on small score differences. Even if percentile bands are not provided as a reminder of the error in test scores, it is important to think of all types of test scores as representing a range of performance, not a single point.

Commercial achievement tests do not always tell how well students perform within their own classroom.

What does all of this information tell about how Brian performs in his fourth grade classroom? In itself, it tells very little. However, in conjunction with the teacher's own classroom observations and assessments, commercial achievement test results can be useful. Commercial achievement tests usually provide information about (1) how a pupil compares to a national sample of pupils in the same grade, (2) the pupil's strengths and weaknesses in important subject areas, and (3) the pupil's development level. The tests do not tell how the pupil does in the day-to-day activities of his or her own classroom. If Brian is in a class of low achievers, he may perform very well in class, much better than would be expected on the basis of his standardized test scores. If he is in a class of high achievers, he may perform much lower than his standardized test scores would suggest. In either case, commercial achievement tests scores should *not* be interpreted without also considering information about the pupil's daily classroom performance.

In addition to that shown in Figure 7.2, commercial test publishers often provide information on pupils' performance on specific topics and skills that make up each subtest. For example, the vocabulary subtest of the Metropolitan is made up of test items covering synonyms, antonyms, and multiple meaning words. The science subtest contains items covering life science, physical science, earth science, science process skills, and research skills. Commercial test publishers can provide information about each pupil's performance on each of the more specific skill areas that make up a subtest. Similar information about the performance of the class as a whole can also be obtained. Performance on each specific skill area is usually reported as being below average, average, or above average in comparison to the national norm group. The classroom teacher can use this information to identify more specific areas where a pupil or the class as a whole has difficulty.

One caution should be noted in using this skill-level information. In most cases, any single skill is assessed by a small number of items, so teachers should not undertake substantial curriculum review or change on the basis of a few test items. Small numbers of items cannot provide reliable enough information for curriculum planning or decision making. Rather, teachers should follow up the commercial test information with additional information collected on their own.

Example 2: Class Performance Report

Figure 7.3 shows the overall class performance for Mr. or Ms. Ness' fourth grade on the Iowa Tests of Basic Skills. The subtests of the test are listed across the top of the figure, beginning with vocabulary and ending with math computation. The scores reported are the average scale or standard score (SS), the average grade equivalent score, the average normal curve equivalent, and the average national percentile rank. This information can provide the teacher with a general picture of the performance of the class as a whole.

The percentile ranks indicate the average of the class as a whole on each of the subtests of the Iowa Tests of Basic Skills in comparison to a national sample of fourth grade pupils. The composite score, which describes class performance across all the subtests in the battery, is a percentile rank of 82, indicating that the typical pupil in the class did better than 82 percent of similar students across the nation. Overall, on the various subtests, the average percentile ranks and average grade equivalents indicate that the class is somewhat above the national average in most areas. However, note that the figure also shows that compared to most other subject areas, the class is relatively weak in vocabulary. This is something the teacher may wish to investigate further.

Class performance reports help teachers identify subject areas in which their class is doing well and those in which they need additional work.

Example 3: Summary Report for Parents

Figure 7.4 shows a report that is sent home to parents after testing with the California Achievement Test. All commercial achievement test publishers have similar forms, intended to help parents understand their child's performance. The section of the figure marked with a boxed A provides parents with a general introduction to the test and its purposes. The section marked B shows Ken Allen's percentile ranks on the total reading, total language, and total math tests, as well as his performance on the total battery. Note the areas labeled below average, average, and above average to give parents a general indication of how Ken did compared to his national fifth grade peers.

The right third of the figure (C and D) provides more detailed information about Ken's performance. The four boxes contain, respectively, percentile ranks for the subtests that made up the total reading, total language, total math, and remaining battery subtests. Thus, for example, Ken's percentile ranks in vocabulary and comprehension, the two subtests that make up total reading, were 47 and 68. The boxes also show Ken's strengths and weaknesses on the skills that make up the reading, language, and math tests. This information is similar to the skill-level information described during the discussion of Figure 7.2. Teachers should be prepared to answer parents' questions about the information contained in such home reports.

Commercial test publishers can provide scores and information in addition to those described in the preceding sections, but Figures 7.2, 7.3, and

Teachers should be prepared to answer parents' questions about standardized test results.

Iowa Tests of Basic Skills

Service 9:
Report of Class Averages

Class/Group:	NESS
Building:	WEBER
Building Code:	304
System:	DALEN COMMUNITY
Norms:	SPRING 1992
Order No.	000-A33-76044-00-001

Grade:	4
Form:	K
Test Date:	03/93
Page:	40

AVERAGES — ITBS:

N TESTED= 27

Subtest	N	SS	GE OF AVG SS	NCE	PR OF AVG SS: NATL STUDENT NORMS
READING					
VOCABULARY	24	203.0	5.0	54.2	58
COMPREHENSION	24	224.3	6.5	67.1	78
TOTAL	24	213.6	5.8	62.5	72
LANGUAGE					
SPELLING	24	214.5	5.9	62.8	74
CAPITALIZATION	24	255.7	9.3	78.7	91
PUNCTUATION	24	249.2	8.7	76.6	88
USAGE/EXPRESS	24	227.8	6.9	65.4	77
TOTAL	24	236.9	7.6	75.4	88
MATHEMATICS					
CONCEPTS/ESTIM.	24	214.5	6.1	65.5	77
PROBS/DATA INTERP.	24	216.4	6.0	61.8	72
TOTAL	24	215.5	6.0	63.8	74
CORE TOTAL	24	221.9	6.4	68.8	81
SOCIAL STUDIES	24	221.3	6.2	66.4	78
SCIENCE	24	228.5	6.9	69.2	81
SOURCES OF INFO.					
MAPS & DIAGRAMS	24	219.0	6.1	61.8	74
REF. MATLS	24	227.0	6.8	71.2	84
TOTAL	24	223.0	6.3	67.1	79
COMPOSITE	24	223.0	6.4	69.8	82
MATH COMPUTATION	24	213.9	5.9	66.0	78

SS=Standard Score, GE=Grade Equivalent, NCE=Normal Curve Equivalent, NPR=Nat'l%ile Rank

FIGURE 7.3
Standardized Test Report for a Class

CAT/5 Home Report

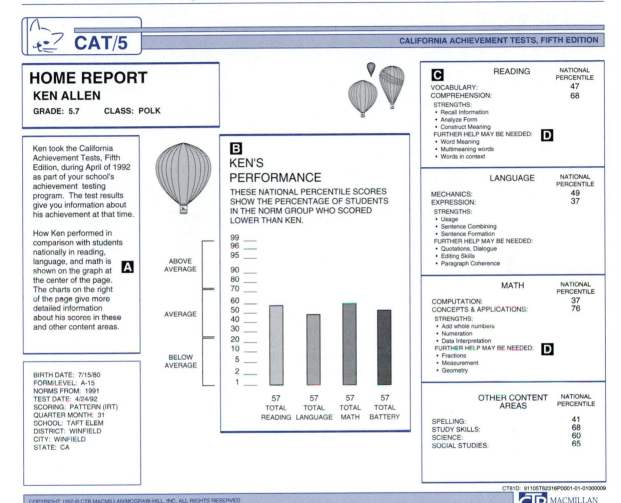

CAT/5

CALIFORNIA ACHIEVEMENT TESTS, FIFTH EDITION

HOME REPORT

KEN ALLEN

GRADE: 5.7   CLASS: POLK

Ken took the California Achievement Tests, Fifth Edition, during April of 1992 as part of your school's achievement testing program. The test results give you information about his achievement at that time.

How Ken performed in comparison with students nationally in reading, language, and math is **A** shown on the graph at the center of the page. The charts on the right of the page give more detailed information about his scores in these and other content areas.

BIRTH DATE: 7/15/80
FORM/LEVEL: A-15
NORMS FROM: 1991
TEST DATE: 4/24/92
SCORING: PATTERN (IRT)
QUARTER MONTH: 31
SCHOOL: TAFT ELEM
DISTRICT: WINFIELD
CITY: WINFIELD
STATE: CA

B
KEN'S PERFORMANCE

THESE NATIONAL PERCENTILE SCORES SHOW THE PERCENTAGE OF STUDENTS IN THE NORM GROUP WHO SCORED LOWER THAN KEN.

ABOVE AVERAGE

AVERAGE

BELOW AVERAGE

99
96
95
90
80
70
60
50
40
30
20
10
5
2
1

| 57 TOTAL READING | 57 TOTAL LANGUAGE | 57 TOTAL MATH | 57 TOTAL BATTERY |

C READING — NATIONAL PERCENTILE

VOCABULARY: 47
COMPREHENSION: 68
STRENGTHS:
• Recall Information
• Analyze Form
• Construct Meaning
FURTHER HELP MAY BE NEEDED: **D**
• Word Meaning
• Multimeaning words
• Words in context

LANGUAGE — NATIONAL PERCENTILE

MECHANICS: 49
EXPRESSION: 37
STRENGTHS:
• Usage
• Sentence Combining
• Sentence Formation
FURTHER HELP MAY BE NEEDED:
• Quotations, Dialogue
• Editing Skills
• Paragraph Coherence

MATH — NATIONAL PERCENTILE

COMPUTATION: 37
CONCEPTS & APPLICATIONS: 76
STRENGTHS:
• Add whole numbers
• Numeration
• Data Interpretation
FURTHER HELP MAY BE NEEDED: **D**
• Fractions
• Measurement
• Geometry

OTHER CONTENT AREAS — NATIONAL PERCENTILE

SPELLING: 41
STUDY SKILLS: 68
SCIENCE: 60
SOCIAL STUDIES: 65

CT81D: 91105T62316P0001-01-01000009

CB MACMILLAN/MCGRAW-HILL

FIGURE 7.4
Parent Report Form

Source: Reproduced from the California Achievement Tests, 5th Edition, by permission of the publisher, CTB/McGraw-Hill, a division of McGraw-Hill School Publishing Company. Copyright © 1992 by McGraw-Hill School Publishing Company. All rights reserved.

7.4 show the basic types of information that are returned to classroom teachers and parents as part of a school district's commercial achievement testing program. Each test publisher presents the results in slightly different formats, but the basic information and its interpretation do not vary much from publisher to publisher. The variety of forms and pupil analyses that are available from a commercial test publisher can be found in the teacher or class information manual that accompanies the test.

THE VALIDITY OF COMMERCIAL ACHIEVEMENT TESTS

A great deal of time, expertise, and expense are put into the construction of commercial achievement tests. The most widely used tests are technically strong, with well-written items, an attractive format, statistically sophisticated norms, and reliable, consistent pupil scores. More care, concern, and expertise are put into producing a standardized commercial achievement test than are typically put into constructing a teacher-made or textbook test.

It is still appropriate, however, to raise the question of whether a commercial achievement test provides the information needed to make valid decisions about pupil achievement. Teacher-made and textbook tests are judged mainly in terms of whether they provide a fair assessment of how well pupils have learned the things they were taught. Commercial achievement tests are judged on this basis too, but also on other bases as well. Regardless of the test, if it does not provide the desired information about pupil achievement it is not valid and therefore not useful for decision making. For commercial achievement tests, four factors influence validity and reliability: (1) the appropriateness of the content and objectives tested; (2) the representativeness of the norming sample; (3) the conditions under which the test is administered; and (4) misinterpretations of test results. This section examines these issues and their potential effect on the validity of standardized achievement tests.

Coverage of Objectives

Commercial tests are designed to assess the core objectives that most classroom teachers at that grade level cover in their instruction.

Standardized tests are not constructed to assess every classroom teacher's unique instructional objectives. Rather they are designed to assess the core objectives that *most* classroom teachers cover in their instruction. By selecting a common set of objectives, commercial test constructors seek to ensure that most pupils have had exposure to the objectives tested. Of course, this does not mean that every commercial test is equally relevant to the curriculum in a given classroom. Some of the topics taught in a given classroom are not included on standardized tests.

A commercial test cannot be valid for a particular class if it does not match the instruction given in that class.

While most classroom teachers find that the objectives tested on commercial achievement tests reflect their own instruction, few teachers find *all* of the topics they included in commercial tests. Teachers whose classroom instruction deviates greatly from the text or who consistently introduce unusual materials and concepts often find that the topics covered by the national tests are different from those they have been teaching. The time of year when testing takes place and the teacher's sequencing of topics also influence pupils' opportunities to learn the objectives being assessed.

Finally, virtually all commercial achievement tests rely heavily on multiple-choice test items. Restricting items to the multiple-choice format means that some topics or objectives may be tested differently than they were taught or tested in the classroom. For example, to assess spelling, most teachers give a weekly spelling test in which pupils have to spell each word correctly. In commercial achievement tests, spelling is assessed by presenting pupils with four or five words and asking them to identify the one that is spelled incorrectly. This is not the way most pupils are taught spelling. This and the preceding factors discussed can reduce the match between the content of a standardized achievement test and the content of classroom instruction, thus lowering validity.

It is the responsibility of each local school district to determine if the content of a commercial achievement test is valid for pupils in that system or classroom. If, after inspecting the test items and the publisher's description of what is tested, the test content appears to be different from what pupils were taught, judgments about pupils' achievement may not be valid and should be made with caution.

Each school or district must decide if the content of a commercial achievement test matches its own objectives.

Test Norms

Commercial test publishers strive to obtain norming samples that are representative of national groups of pupils. However, there are some important factors that can undermine the appropriateness of test norms and thereby test validity: (1) norms go out of date; (2) the curriculum in a subject area changes; (3) textbooks are revised and new instructional materials appear; and (4) the same test is often administered in a school district over a number of years so teachers and pupils become familiar with its content and items. Inappropriate or out-of-date test norms reduce the validity of comparisons and decisions made from standardized achievement tests. While there is no hard-and-fast period within which standardized achievement test norms should be revised, 7 to 9 years is a generally accepted time period used by the publishers of the most widely used standardized tests. Obviously, the older the test norms, the less representative they are of instructional content and national pupil performance. Specific information about test norming procedures and the age of the norms should be provided in the publisher's test manual.

When commercial test norms do not match the characteristics of the local students, valid decisions cannot be made from the test results.

Test Administration

It was emphasized earlier that valid interpretations of pupils' standardized test performance depend on pupils taking the test under the conditions recommended by the test publisher. Deviations from the test administration directions such as allowing pupils more time than specified, helping pupils while they are taking the test, coaching pupils before the test on the specific items they will be asked, and generally not following the

Deviating from test administration directions reduces the validity of test results.

directions provided all reduce the validity of the test results and the decisions based on those results.

Of course, pupils who require accommodations in testing should be provided with the appropriate resources (see Chapter 4). Typically, when the scores of pupils who receive accommodations are reported, they are flagged to indicate the test was not taken under standard conditions. While this is generally an appropriate practice, the mere flagging of a pupil's score may lead to bias or discounting performance on the part of the test interpreter or user (Heaney & Pullin, 1998).

Interpreting Commercial Test Results

There are two common problems in interpreting standardized test scores: misinterpretation and overinterpretation. Because the types of scores that are used to describe pupil performance on standardized achievement tests are different from those teachers commonly use, the likelihood of misinterpretation is heightened. The most common misinterpretations involve the percentile rank, which is mistaken for the percentage of items a pupil answered correctly, and the grade equivalent score, which is mistakenly thought to indicate the curriculum level at which a pupil is performing in a subject area. Percentile ranks indicate the percentage of pupils in the norm group that a pupil scored above. Grade equivalent scores indicate how well a pupil performs on grade-level objectives compared to other pupils in his or her grade.

The main problem in interpreting commercial test scores is overinterpretation.

Information gained from commercial tests may not be as revealing as information gathered through daily instruction and assessment by the classroom teacher.

The main problem in interpreting commercial test scores is *over*interpretation, not misinterpretation. Because standardized tests are constructed by professionals, tried out on nationwide samples of pupils, and provide numerical indices that describe a pupil's performance compared to pupils nationwide, there is a widespread belief that they give precise, accurate descriptions of pupils' achievement. Certainly parents and the public at large put more faith in standardized test results than in teacher-made assessments gathered over time in the day-to-day classroom setting. While the information provided by the 40 or so multiple-choice items found in a typical commercial subtest is useful, it can never match the information a teacher accumulates through daily instruction and assessment of pupils.

> . . . test scores represent achievement in basic skills areas at only one particular time and must be reviewed together with the student's actual classroom work and other factors. Parents [and others: author] should also understand that the test measures the basic content skills that are most common to curricula throughout the country. It cannot possibly measure, nor should it attempt to measure, the full curriculum of a particular classroom, school, or district (CTB/McGraw-Hill, 1986, 100).

Even when there are no problems with test content, norms, and administration, standardized test scores still are overinterpreted. For example, it is common for teachers and parents to treat small differences in standardized test scores as if they are significant and indicate real performance differences. A percentile rank difference of 6 to 8 points or a 2- to 5-month grade equivalent difference between pupils rarely indicates important or meaningful differences in their achievement or development. There is sufficient unreliability in any test score, whether standardized or teacher-made, to make small scoring differences indicators of true differences among pupils. Standardized test constructors try to defeat overinterpretation of small score differences by warning against them in their test manuals and by presenting scores as percentile or stanine bands (see Fig. 7.2), but they are not always successful. In short, teachers should guard against treating small score differences as if they are meaningful.

Teachers should guard against treating small differences in commercial test scores as if they are reliable indicators of real differences among pupils.

Overinterpretation also occurs when teachers put too much faith in achievement-ability comparisons. These comparisons provide at best a general indication of how a pupil compares to other pupils of similar ability. Before a teacher acts on standardized test information of this type, he or she should reflect on personal knowledge of the pupil's work habits, personality, and achievement gained by daily exposure to the pupil in the classroom.

Finally, the smaller the number of items that make up a test, the less reliable its results and the less trustworthy its score. This can be a particular problem in commercial standardized achievement tests that include a few performance-based, open-ended items. While performance-based items can assess areas not tested by multiple-choice items, one must interpret performance-based items cautiously because there are relatively few such items. Normally, the subtest scores on standardized test batteries are quite reliable and consistent. However, when a subtest is further broken down into specific topics, skills, or objectives, and separate scores given for each, caution about reading too much into the scores must be exercised. Often such information is used to diagnose a pupil's strengths and weaknesses, and while such information may provide a basis for further exploration of pupil performance, it should be reviewed critically because of the very few items on which it is typically based.

While standardized achievement tests can give teachers useful assessment information that they cannot gather for themselves, such information should be used in conjunction with information gathered from their own assessments. For the most part, the information from standardized achievement tests corroborates perceptions the teacher has already formed about pupils. When the two types of evidence do not corroborate each other, the teacher should look again at his or her perceptions to be sure the pupil is not being misjudged.

Information from commercial achievement tests usually corroborates a teacher's perceptions of pupils.

STATE-MANDATED ACHIEVEMENT ASSESSMENTS

The use of statewide tests has been common in the United States for many years. In prior decades, statewide testing stood alone, largely divorced from the teaching-learning process carried out in classrooms. The main purpose of the tests was to provide a general indication of how pupils across a state were performing in particular subject areas. Typically, data were aggregated to the state level, and little information about the performance of individual schools or pupils was reported. Further, in most cases, the state-based tests were not linked to a single, statewide set of standards or curriculum objectives that state authorities required to be taught in all classrooms.

However, in the past 15 or so years, the focus and emphasis of statewide testing has changed greatly. There has been a much more active and concerted effort to link statewide testing (now commonly called statewide assessment) to specific, state-endorsed subject matter objectives. States have identified objectives (more commonly called content standards or curriculum frameworks) in various subject areas that pupils statewide are expected to achieve. These standards are at the heart of current statewide educational reform. They are used to guide activities such as teacher education and improvement, textbook selection, and statewide assessments. Teaching and assessment are coordinated to reflect the statewide subject matter standards. Teachers are strongly encouraged to incorporate these standards into their curriculum, and statewide assessments based on the statewide standards are administered to pupils.

State-mandated standards are used to assess pupils, teachers, and schools in a particular state. The standards are intended to guide statewide learning and assessments.

At present, 40 states have defined statewide standards in core subject areas such as reading, math, and English/language arts. Forty-eight states now have statewide assessment programs, most linked to the statewide standards (Olson, 1999). Thus, most states have defined statewide learning standards, encouraged teachers to teach the statewide standards, developed statewide assessment programs, and linked the standards and instruction to the statewide assessments.

Figures 7.5 and 7.6 illustrate two sets of statewide standards. Figure 7.5 shows a portion of Virginia's statewide standards for seventh grade mathematics. The standards are the numbered statements. All pupils in Virginia who are taking seventh grade mathematics are taught these standards and are expected to demonstrate their mastery of them on statewide assessments. Figure 7.6 shows one of the five areas that Colorado has identified for students to learn in reading, writing, and speaking: students write and speak using conventional grammar, usage, sentence structure, punctuation, capitalization, and spelling. Notice that unlike the Virginia standards, which are stated for each grade, the Colorado standards focus on groups of grades, K to 4, 5 to 8, and 9 to 12. In most cases, standards that encompass more than one grade, as in Colorado, are linked to statewide assessments

Different states produce different standards, but most states do have achievement standards.

Mathematics Standards of Learning

Grade Seven

The seventh-grade standards place emphasis on solving problems involving consumer applications and proportional reasoning. The student will gain an understanding of the properties of real numbers, solve linear equations and inequalities, and use data analysis techniques to make inferences and predictions. While learning mathematics, students will be actively engaged, using concrete materials and appropriate technologies such as fraction calculators, computers, laser discs, and videos. However, facility in the use of technology shall not be regarded as a substitute for a student's understanding of quantitative concepts and relationships or for proficiency in basic computations. Students also will identify real-life applications of the mathematical principles they are learning that can be applied to science and other disciplines they are studying.

Mathematics has its own language, and the acquisition of specialized vocabulary and language patterns is crucial to a student's understanding and appreciation of the subject. Students should be encouraged to use correctly the concepts, skills, symbols, and vocabulary identified in the following set of standards.

Problem solving has been integrated throughout the six content strands. The development of problem-solving skills should be a major goal of the mathematics program at every grade level. Instruction in the process of problem solving will need to be integrated early and continuously into each student's mathematics education. Students must be helped to develop a wide range of skills and strategies for solving a variety of problem types.

Number and Number Sense

7.1   The student will compare, order, and determine equivalent relationships between fractions, decimals, and percents, including scientific notation.

7.2   The student will find common multiples and factors, including least common multiple and greatest common factor.

7.3   The student will simplify expressions by using order of operations, mental mathematics, and appropriate tools. Exponents will be included.

7.4   The student will explain orally and in writing the following properties of operations with real numbers:
  • the commutative and associative properties for addition and multiplication;
  • the distributive property;
  • the additive and multiplicative identity properties;
  • the additive and multiplicative inverse properties; and
  • the multiplicative property of zero.

Computation and Estimation

7.5   The student will solve consumer application problems involving tips, discounts, sales tax, and simple interest, using whole numbers, fractions, decimals, and percents.

7.6   The student will
  • solve practical problems involving basic operations with integers by formulating rules for operating with integers and using a number line to compute; and
  • explain the need for integers, using examples from real-life situations.

7.7   The student will use proportions to solve practical problems, including scale drawings that contain whole numbers, fractions, decimals, and percents.

Measurement

7.8   The student, given appropriate dimensions, will estimate and find the area of polygons by subdividing them into rectangles and right triangles.

7.9   The student will investigate and solve problems involving the volume and surface area of rectangular prisms and cylinders, using concrete materials and practical situations to develop formulas.

Geometry

7.10   The student will compare and contrast the following quadrilaterals: a parallelogram, rectangle, square, rhombus, and trapezoid. Deductive reasoning and inference will be used to classify quadrilaterals.

7.11   The student will identify and draw the following polygons: pentagon, hexagon, heptagon, octagon, nonagon, and decagon.

7.12   The student will determine if geometric figures (quadrilaterals and triangles) are similar and write proportions to express the relationships between corresponding parts of similar figures.

7.13   The student will construct a three-dimensional model using cubes, given the top, side, and/or bottom views, and determine the volume and the surface area of the model.

FIGURE 7.5

State of Virgina Grade Seven Mathematics Standards
SOURCE: Mathematics Standards of Learning Copyright © 1997 by the Commonwealth of Virginia Department of Education. Reprinted with Permission.

Mathematics Standards of Learning

7.14   The students will inscribe equilateral triangles, squares, and hexagons in circles, using a compass and straightedge.

Probability and Statistics

7.15   The student will investigate and describe the difference between the probability of an event found through simulation versus the theoretical probability of that same event.

7.16   The student will make a sample space for selected experiments and represent it in the form of a list, chart, picture, or tree diagram.

7.17   The student will determine the probability of a given simple event and express that probability as a ratio, decimal, or a percent as appropriate for the given situation.

7.18   The student will identify and describe the number of possible arrangements of several objects using a tree diagram or the Basic Counting Principle.

7.19   The student will create and solve problems involving the mean, median, mode, and range of a set of data.

7.20   The student will display data, using frequency distributions, line plots, stem-and-leaf plots, box-and-whisker plots, and scattergrams.

7.21   The students will make inferences and predictions based on the analysis of a set of data that the student(s) collect.

Patterns, Functions, and Algebra

7.22   The student will investigate and describe functional relationships, including the number of sides of a regular polygon and the sum of the measures of the interior angles.

7.23   The student will write verbal expressions/sentences as algebraic expressions/equations.

7.24   The student will use the following algebraic terms appropriately in written and/or oral expression: equation, inequality, variable, expression, term, coefficient, domain, and range.

7.25   The student will
- solve two-step linear equations and inequalities in one variable, using strategies involving inverse operations and integers; and
- solve practical problems requiring the solution of a two-step linear equation.

7.26   The student will identify and graph ordered pairs in the four quadrants of a coordinate plane.

FIGURE 7.5
Continued

Various uses of statewide assessment include awarding or withholding a diploma, promotion decisions, and evaluation of teachers and schools.

administered at the end of the fourth, eighth, and eleven or twelfth grades. Different states present, organize, and assess their standards in different ways. However, what is common across most states is the intent to identify important standards for pupils to learn, making the standards public, encouraging teachers to teach the standards, and developing statewide assessments based on the standards to determine progress.

In many states, the results of the state-based assessments have important consequences for teachers, schools, and pupils. Presently in 19 states and in an additional seven others by 2003, pupils who fail to pass a statewide exit exam will be denied a high school diploma; they will receive a certificate of attendance instead. Six states link pupil's promotion to the next grade to statewide assessments; failure to pass the assessment results in being held back. In 14 states teachers can receive monetary rewards if student performances on the statewide assessments improve over time. In two states, teachers are evaluated in terms of how their pupils do on performance of statewide assessments.

Not only do statewide standards and assessments influence pupils and teachers, they can also influence what happens to schools. Sixteen states have the power to close, take over, or overhaul schools whose students chronically do poorly on the statewide assessments (*Education Week,* 1999). Two states, Virginia and North Carolina, are introducing statewide end-of-course exams. Clearly, statewide standards and assessments have become powerful and consequential instruments for pupils, teachers, and

Students write and speak using conventional grammar, usage, sentence structure, punctuation, capitalization, and spelling.

In order to meet this standard, students will

- know and use correct grammar in speaking and writing;
- apply correct usage in speaking and writing;
- use correct sentence structure in writing; and
- demonstrate correct punctuation, capitalization, and spelling.

In grades K–4, what students know and are able to do includes

- knowing and using subject/verb agreement;
- knowing and using correct modifiers;
- knowing and using correct capitalization, punctuation, and abbreviations; and
- spelling frequently used words correctly using phonics rules and exceptions.

In grades 5–8, what students know and are able to do includes

- identifying the parts of speech such as nouns, pronouns, verbs, adverbs, adjectives, conjunctions, prepositions, and interjections;
- using correct pronoun case, regular and irregular noun and verb forms, and subject-verb agreement involving comparisions in writing and speaking;
- using modifiers, homonyms, and homophones in writing and speaking;
- using simple, compound, complex, and compound/complex sentences in writing and speaking;
- punctuating and capitalizing titles and direct quotations, using progressives, and correct paragraphing in writing;
- using prefixes, root words, and suffixes correctly in writing and speaking;
- expanding spelling skills to include more complex words;
- demonstrating use of conventional spelling in their published works; and
- using resources such as spell checkers, dictionaries, and charts to monitor the spelling accuracy.

In grades 9–12, what students know and are able to do includes

- using pronoun reference correctly in writing and speaking;
- using phrases and clauses for purposes of modification and parallel structure in writing and speaking;
- using internal capitalization and punctuation of secondary quotations in writing;
- using manuscript forms specified in various style manuals for writing (for example, indenting for extended quotations, precise placement and form of page numbers, appropriate line spacing); and
- refining spelling and grammatical skills and becoming a self-evaluator of their writing and speaking.

FIGURE 7.6
State of Colorado Reading, Writing, and Speaking Standards

school accountability. The varied consequences associated with performance on the statewide assessments create pressure to emphasize the defined standards in instruction.

Construction of Statewide Assessments

Most statewide assessments are based on criterion-referenced scoring and are constructed in the following way. First, the standards for the different subject areas are determined by statewide curriculum committees made up of teachers, administrators, parents, businesspeople, and other concerned citizens. Figures 7.5 and 7.6 are examples of such standards, although as noted, standard-based formats and coverage vary from state to state. The identified standards are often not confined to ones presently taught in schools. Usually the standards include new curriculum areas not previously emphasized by all teachers.

The format of statewide assessments differs considerably from that of commercial standardized achievement tests. As noted previously, the main format of commercial achievement tests is multiple-choice items. State-based assessments use a broader mix of item types. Once the standards are identified, items are written to assess them. Of the 48 states that assess their students statewide, 42 include items requiring writing in some form, 34 include other performance-type assessments, 13 rely exclusively on multiple-choice items, and two states require portfolios (Olson, 1999). Thus, a large portion of the items produced for statewide assessments are performance assessments of various kinds. The constructed items are then reviewed to determine whether they actually do assess the intended standard or objective, are culturally unbiased, and are at an appropriate language level for pupils in that grade. Items are then assembled into tests. Often the items are tried out on some pupils to determine how well they will work, though not on pupils in the grades to be assessed.

Most statewide assessment programs use performance-based items and tasks, although some states also include multiple-choice items.

When the purpose of statewide assessments is to provide information about achievement at the school or school district level, it is not necessary for every pupil in a school or district to answer every test question. For school or district reporting purposes, the amount of information gathered can be maximized and the amount of assessment time minimized by having each pupil answer only some of all the items developed. Suppose a curriculum committee identified 12 science standards that it felt seventh graders statewide ought to learn. Suppose also that 10 items were written to assess each of the 12 standards, thus producing a total of 120 seventh grade science items. Rather than giving each seventh grade pupil a 120-item test, the items could be divided into four tests of 30 items each. All four tests would then be administered at random to seventh graders in each school or district in the state, but each pupil would be required to take only one of the tests. Summing the results of all four tests across pupils would give a very good estimate of school or district performance on all 12 of the seventh grade science standards. It is important to recognize,

Statewide assessments can include all pupils or schools if scoring is based on individual schools and pupils or samples of schools and pupils if overall statewide information is desired.

however, that if the purpose of a statewide test is to make a decision about an individual pupil's performance, promotion, graduation, or placement, it is necessary to give all pupils the same assessment. That is the only fair way to make pupil by pupil decisions.

Scoring Statewide Assessments

Scoring statewide assessments is usually carried out using a criterion-referenced approach: 42 of the 48 states that employ statewide assessments use a criterion-referenced scoring approach. Twenty-nine states supplement their criterion-referenced scoring with norm-referenced information obtained from commercial standardized tests. In general, criterion-referenced scoring is used to make decisions about individual pupil performance and grouped norm-referenced results are used to compare state performance to that of other states. Since each state has its own, unique statewide assessment, the only way comparisons across states can be obtained is with commercial standardized tests that are used nationally.

For criterion-referenced scoring, predetermined performance levels are established and pupil performance is compared to the levels. Two types of criterion-referenced standards are used in statewide scoring: percentage and performance scoring (see Chapter 5). In percentage scoring, passing the assessment is based on obtaining a given percentage of the items correct. The percentage selected is often called a **cut score** or a cutoff score. For example, if a state defines mastery as a cut score of 70 percent or above on a statewide assessment, pupils who correctly answer 70 percent or more of the items pass. Pupils answering fewer than 70 percent of the items correctly do not pass the assessment. Percentage scoring is not limited to pass-fail decisions. The statewide assessment in Massachusetts, for example, uses the cut score approach to place pupils into one of four scoring categories: fail, needs improvement, proficient, and advanced.

Performance scoring is used to score assessments that require pupils to write essays, perform a process, or present a portfolio. Percentage scoring is often difficult and cumbersome to implement for complex performances such as writing an essay, oral reading, performing a science experiment, or judging a portfolio. Instead, performances and portfolios are typically scored using rubrics. Figure 7.7 shows a rubric that could be used to score the quality of third graders' writing for personal expression in a state-based assessment program. There are four criteria associated with writing for personal expression: development, organization, focus on audience, and language. The rubric contains four levels of performance, labeled 3 to 0. Scorers read a third grader's essay and assign it to one of the categories, depending on which category best describes the quality of the pupil's writing. A class, school, or district with many 1's and 0's would be alerted to the need to reexamine its curriculum to determine why many pupils did poorly. Note that the state-based results do

Statewide assessments are scored by criterion-referencing using a cut score or a rubric.

SCORING RUBRIC: WRITING TO EXPRESS PERSONAL IDEAS

3 points
- *Development:* consistently develops ideas into a complete, well-developed whole.
- *Organization:* sequences in a logical and effective manner.
- *Focus on Audience:* anticipates and answers the audience's needs and questions.
- *Language:* consistently uses language that enhances the writing.

2 points
- *Development:* partially develops the ideasand does not provide a complete, well-developed whole.
- *Organization:* purposely orders ideas for reader to follow.
- *Focus on Audience:* usually anticipates and answers the audience's needs and questions.
- *Language:* frequently uses language to enhance the writing.

1 point
- *Development:* rarely develops ideas produces poorly-developed and incomplete ideas.
- *Organization:* usually orders ideas but some interruptions in the flow.
- *Focus on Audience:* occasionally anticipates and answers the audience's needs and questions.
- *Language:* sometimes uses language that enhances the writing.

0 points
- *Development:* no development of ideas into a complete whole.
- *Organization:* rarely evidences logical ordering of ideas.
- *Focus on Audience:* does not anticipate and answer the audience's needs and questions.
- *Language:* fails to use language that enhances the writing.

Blank—no written response

Focus—did not answer the stated question

Unreadable—writing is illegible, writing not comprehensible

FIGURE 7.7
Scoring Rubric for Expressing Personal Ideas

not *dictate* changes in curriculum, but they do provide information that can help in deciding whether or not instruction in an area needs to be revised.

An Example of Statewide Assessment

One of the most highly developed and pervasive statewide assessment programs is that proposed in North Carolina (North Carolina Department of Public Instruction, 1992). It provides an example of how states are trying to use assessment to focus and improve teaching and learning. The North Carolina assessment program is linked to the North Carolina statewide standard course of study, which is the state-adopted curriculum that defines what pupils are to know and do in school subjects at all grade levels. All statewide assessments are constructed to match closely the standard course of study. Note that in addition to the assessments mandated by the state, local school districts may also administer additional commercial achievement test batteries of their choice to pupils.

The features of the North Carolina statewide assessment program are outlined here.

- ◆ Grades 1 and 2: Assessment in the first two grades will be by portfolios of pupils' work. The samples of pupils' work can be reviewed by parents and teachers to determine pupil progress towards the designated goals.
- ◆ Grades 3 through 8: Three different mandated assessments are administered in these grades.

1. The North Carolina End-of-Grade (EOG) Tests will be administered at the end of each school year to assess mastery of grade-level knowledge and skills. Pupils will be assessed annually in five subject areas: reading, writing, mathematics, science, and social studies.

2. The Minimum Skills Diagnostic Tests (MSDT) will be given at the end of the year in grades 3, 6, and 8 to pupils who score below the state-designated passing score on the End of Grade Tests and who show other forms of difficulty with schoolwork. The primary purpose of the Minimum Skills Diagnostic Tests is to identify a pupil's strengths and weaknesses so proper instruction and remediation can be planned. The MSDT is administered in reading, mathematics, and language.

3. North Carolina Competency Tests (NCCT) are administered to pupils in grade 8 in the subjects of reading, mathematics, and writing. Pupils in grade 8 who score below the cutoff score on these tests will be retested every year until they reach the minimum passing score in all three subjects. Obtaining a passing score on all three tests is necessary to receive a high school diploma.

♦ Grades 9 through 12: Two types of mandated assessment are carried out in these grades.

1. The North Carolina Competency Tests (NCCT) are administered yearly to those pupils who failed to attain the minimum passing score in reading, mathematics, and writing in grade 8.

2. The North Carolina End-of-Course (EOC) Tests are administered at the end of each course in the following subject areas: algebra I and II, geometry, biology, physical science, physics, chemistry, U.S. history, economic/legal/political systems, English I and II, and others.

The North Carolina state assessment program is more extensive than most other statewide assessments, mainly because very few other states have specific end-of-course or end-of-grade tests to determine pupil and schoolwide progress. North Carolina is, however, one of a growing number of states that link statewide standards in subject areas to the state-based assessment program. In other respects, the North Carolina assessments are different to those in other states.

Figure 7.8 presents a sample of four different state-based assessment programs, including one state that does not carry out state-based assessment. The four programs give an idea of the differences among states. All of the states shown have defined standards for pupils in the state, although different states call their standards different names—academic expectations, state curriculum guides, etc. The grade levels and the subject areas assessed vary across states, as does the type of item or performance used to collect evidence of pupil learning. Some of the states have a fully developed statewide assessment program, while others are still in the process of constructing theirs. All of the states except Nebraska tie assessment to statewide standards and use state-based assessment to make important decisions about pupils or schools. Maryland relies on their assessment program to help identify schools and districts that are not performing well. Louisiana and Nevada use statewide assessment results to decide which pupils will receive a high school diploma.

Features of statewide assessment programs that are common to most programs include the following:

♦ a sizable amount of assessment is required
♦ part of the assessment includes performance-portfolio-based information
♦ decisions about performance are made by comparing a pupil's score to a predetermined, statewide passing score
♦ the assessments have important implications for pupils and schools
♦ because poor performance on the assessment can affect pupils' opportunities, teachers must decide how much time they will devote to preparing pupils for the assessments

State	Name of Standards	Assessment
Louisiana	state curriculum guides	State curriculum guides apply to all grades, but are usually grouped by elementary, secondary, and high school levels. The state curriculum guides are mandatory. State-based assessment is focused on the curriculum guides. Grades 3, 5, and 7 pupils take criterion-referenced tests. High school pupils take tests in math, language arts, writing, science, and social studies. Material for all the tests comes from the state curriculum guides. Pupils must pass the high school subject tests to graduate.
Maryland	Maryland learning outcomes	Learning outcomes describe pupil learning in grades 3, 5, 8, and high school. Learning outcomes are mandatory and tied to state-based assessments. Criterion-referenced tests in grades 3, 5, and 8 in math, reading, science, social studies, and writing/language usage are administered. High school tests are being developed. Schools that do not make adequate progress toward state performance standards face possible reconstitution. The standards may be tied to high school graduation in the future.
Nevada	courses of study	The courses of study identify what pupils are to learn in grades K, 3, 6, 8, 9, 10, 11, and 12. The courses of study are mandatory. A state-based writing assessment and a norm-referenced commercial test are administered to pupils. A state-based high school graduation test in reading, writing, and math is given.
Nebraska	curriculum frameworks	The state department of education is developing curriculum standards for student learning in grades pre-K to 5, 6 to 8, and 9 to 12. Nebraska is a strong local control state so the frameworks are voluntary for schools and districts. There is no state-based assessment.

SOURCE: Adapted from Olson. Setting the standards from state to state. *Education Week,* April 12, 1995, 23–35.

FIGURE 7.8
*State-Based Testing
in Four States*

◆ combining performance across pupils provides information that can be used for district, school, or teacher accountability

Although teachers have little influence over statewide standards and assessment programs, the programs can and do influence teachers considerably. Statewide assessments, especially those with important consequences for schools, teachers, or pupils, increase the pressure on school districts and teachers to revise their curricula to better match the state standards and assessments. Teachers tend to increase the amount of instructional time devoted to the standards because the better their pupils learn them, the more the district and its teachers and pupils are rewarded. In fact, one of the main reasons for statewide standards and aligned statewide assessments is to define and standardize the instructional emphases across a state.

The consequences associated with most statewide standards and assessments put pressure on teachers, students, and administrators to obtain high scores.

Additional pressure is put on teachers because performance on statewide assessments is usually reported in newspapers. Parents and school administrators follow state-based assessment scores with the same intensity that they follow baseball pennant races and the Dow Jones averages. This interest produces pressure on schools and districts to "look good" relative to other schools and districts in the state. In Massachusetts, for example, state-based assessment results have been reported not only on a district-by-district basis, but also in smaller groupings composed of districts of similar size, location, and socioeconomic status. A district's results are reported along with the results of similar districts in its group.

The publication of these results creates pressure on the low-scoring districts to improve their performance. This message is echoed in districts across the nation when statewide assessment results are made public. Parents pressure administrators, who then pressure teachers to respond to the low performance, usually by rearranging the curriculum to spend more time on assessed topics. This pressure is magnified when comparisons are also made among the individual schools within a given school district. A general rule describing the impact of statewide assessment on instruction is whenever the results of an assessment have important consequences for pupils, teachers, or school districts, the assessment will be taken seriously and there will be pressure to incorporate the assessed objectives into the school curriculum.

State-based assessment is a fact of teaching life in most states. While teachers cannot ignore such assessments, they also must find a viable balance between the demands of the state-based assessments and the needs of their pupils.

CHAPTER SUMMARY

◆ Two important types of standardized achievement tests are commercial, norm-referenced tests and state-mandated, criterion-referenced tests. Commercial, norm-referenced tests provide information about how a pupil's achievement compares to that of similar pupils nationwide. State-mandated tests usually provide criterion-referenced information about a pupil's or school's performance in relation to statewide achievement standards.

◆ Standardized assessment instruments must be administered, scored, and interpreted in the same way no matter where or when they are used. Otherwise, valid interpretations of their scores are difficult.

◆ Although teachers have little voice in the selection and scoring of either type of standardized test, pressures are often exerted on them to ensure that their pupils do well on such tests.

◆ Commercial, norm-referenced tests are constructed and scored differently than teacher-made classroom assessments. The steps in construction are (1) identifying objectives that are common to most classrooms at a given grade level, (2) trying out many items to find ones that will spread out the scores of test takers for the final version of the test, (3) administering the final version to a large, national norm group of pupils, and (4) using the performance of the norm group as a basis for comparing the performance of pupils who subsequently take the test.

◆ Four criteria are used to judge the adequacy of commercial standardized test norms: sample size, representativeness, recency, and description of procedures.

◆ Commercial standardized achievement tests usually come in the form of a test battery containing subtests in a variety of subject areas. Scores are provided for each subtest and a composite score is provided for the overall test. The scores for a pupil or a class can be compared across subtests to identify strengths and weaknesses.

◆ In order to make valid interpretations from a commercial achievement test, its directions must be strictly followed.

◆ Special comparative and developmental scores are used to represent pupil performance on commercial achievement tests. The most commonly used scores are (1) the percentile rank, which indicates the percentage of similar pupils nationwide a given pupil scored above, (2) the stanine, which uses the scores 1 to 9 to indicate whether a pupil is below average (stanines 1, 2, and 3), average (stanines 4, 5, and 6), or above average (stanines 7, 8, and 9) compared to similar pupils nationwide, and (3) grade equivalent score, which is a developmental score that indicates whether a pupil is above, below, or at the level of similar pupils in his or her grade nationwide.

◆ A pupil's test performance may appear quite different depending on the norm group (national, state, local, high or low achieving, etc.) to which he or she is being compared.

◆ Caution should be exercised when interpreting small differences in norm-referenced test scores, especially percentile ranks and grade equivalent scores. Since all tests have some degree of error in them, it is best to think of a score not as a single number, but as a range of numbers, any one of which indicates the pupil's true performance. Small differences in test scores are not usually significant.

◆ Interpretation and use of commercial, norm-referenced achievement tests should be guided by a number of concerns: how well the tested content matches classroom instruction, how the information agrees or disagrees with the teacher's own perceptions of pupils, the recency of the test norms, the extent to which administrative directions were followed, and the understanding that no score is exact or infallible.

◆ Commercial achievement tests provide useful comparative and developmental information that teachers cannot get for themselves. However, teachers should always use such information in conjunction with their own assessments when making decisions about pupils. Usually, the two types of information corroborate each other. At present, 48 states have defined standards.

◆ In the past 15 years, there has been a concerted effort to link statewide assessments to specific, state-endorsed subject matter standards. The state standards are used to guide activities such as teacher education, textbook selection, and statewide assessments. Teaching and assessment are coordinated with the standards.

◆ The results of statewide assessments can have important consequences for teachers, pupils, and schools. Performance on the assessments can influence high school graduation, promotion to the next grade, teacher evaluation, and school closure.

◆ Subject matter standards are developed by committees. Once the standards are developed, items are written to reflect them. The items vary in form, but large numbers of statewide assessments are focused on performance-based items, including writing and other open-ended forms. Relatively few states rely solely on multiple-choice items.

♦ When statewide assessments are used to provide information about the achievement of a school or school district, it is not necessary to assess each pupil with the same items. However, when assessments are to provide information about individual pupils, all pupils should take the same assessment.

♦ The most common statewide assessments are based on criterion-referenced scoring. If commercial standardized tests are used, the norm-referenced feature allows comparison of performance among states. When the intent is to score individual pupils, criterion-referenced scoring methods are used. Scoring can be based either on a percentage cut score or a scoring rubric.

QUESTIONS FOR DISCUSSION

1. Are standardized tests fair to all students? Why or why not? What personal characteristics could influence how a student does on a standardized test? Would these same characteristics influence how he or she performs on a teacher-made test? Why?

2. What can a teacher do to help make students less anxious about taking standardized tests? Would the same actions help students when they take teacher-made tests?

3. If you could select only one scoring format from a norm-referenced standardized test to explain to parents, which would you choose? Why? What are the limitations of your choice?

4. What factors should influence the use of standardized test results by classroom teachers?

5. What are the differences in the information provided by a norm-referenced and a criterion-referenced standardized test?

6. What are some of the reasons many states have adopted state-mandated standardized testing programs for all schools in the state?

REFLECTION EXERCISES

♦ Why do students, parents, and school administrators put so much emphasis on standardized test results?

♦ How does a state-mandated testing program such as that in North Carolina influence classroom instruction for the better and for the worse?

♦ Make a list of the words and thoughts that come to mind when you think about all the standardized tests you have taken. What does your list tell you about your perceptions and feelings about standardized tests?

♦ How influential have standardized tests been in your life? Do you think your life would have been much different if you never had taken a standardized test?

ACTIVITY

Read the standardized test report for Nicole Kovitz, a fourth grade student, in Figure 7.9. Your task is to write a **one-page letter to Nicole's parent explaining the results of her standardized test performance.** The following suggestions should guide your letter.

1. Nicole's parent will receive a copy of the test report sheet.
2. Nicole's parent is not a standardized testing expert and basically wants to know how his/her daughter performed.
3. You should start with some information about the test and its purpose.
4. You should describe the information in the test report sheet.
5. You should interpret the information about Nicole's performance.
6. What are Nicole's overall strengths and weaknesses? How can the parent see these on the test report form?
7. Describe Nicole's overall performance to the parent.
8. Indicate what the parent should do if she/he has questions.

Your letter will be judged on the accuracy of the information about Nicole's performance you convey to the parent **and** the extent to which you make the information understandable to the parent. You do not have to convey every bit of information in the test report. You must identify the most important information and convey that in a way that a parent can understand. A letter full of technical terms will not do. Remember, the parent can always arrange to visit you in school if more information is desired.

REVIEW QUESTIONS

1. What is a standardized test? What information can a standardized test provide a teacher that a teacher-made or textbook test cannot? What is a test battery? What are subtests? How does the construction of a standardized achievement test differ from that of a teacher-made achievement test? Why are there these differences?
2. What are test norms? What information do they provide a teacher about a pupil's performance? How are the following norms interpreted: percentile rank, stanine, and grade equivalent score? How do test norms differ from raw scores? Why are norms used instead of raw scores?
3. What are fall and spring norms? Why do standardized tests provide them?
4. What factors should teachers consider when they try to interpret their pupils' standardized test scores? That is, what factors influence the results of standardized tests and thus should be thought about when interpreting scores?
5. What are the differences in construction and use of district-focused and individual pupil-focused state-mandated tests?

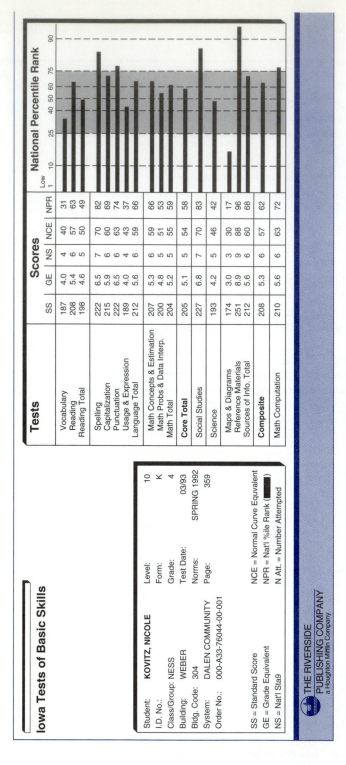

Iowa Tests of Basic Skills

Student:	**KOVITZ, NICOLE**	Level:	10
I.D. No.:		Form:	K
Class/Group:	NESS	Grade:	4
Building:	WEBER	Test Date:	03/93
Bldg. Code:	304	Norms:	SPRING 1992
System:	DALEN COMMUNITY	Page:	359
Order No.:	000-A33-76044-00-001		

SS = Standard Score
GE = Grade Equivalent
NS = Nat'l Sta9
NCE = Normal Curve Equivalent
NPR = Nat'l %ile Rank (■■■)
N Att. = Number Attempted

Tests	SS	GE	NS	NCE	NPR
Vocabulary	187	4.0	4	40	31
Reading	208	5.4	6	57	63
Reading Total	198	4.6	5	50	49
Spelling	222	6.5	7	70	82
Capitalization	215	5.9	6	60	69
Punctuation	222	6.5	6	63	74
Usage & Expression	189	4.0	4	43	37
Language Total	212	5.6	6	59	66
Math Concepts & Estimation	207	5.3	6	59	66
Math Probs & Data Interp.	200	4.8	5	51	53
Math Total	204	5.2	5	55	59
Core Total	205	5.1	5	54	58
Social Studies	227	6.8	7	70	83
Science	193	4.2	5	46	42
Maps & Diagrams	174	3.0	3	30	17
Reference Materials	251	8.9	9	88	96
Sources of Info. Total	212	5.6	6	60	68
Composite	208	5.3	6	57	62
Math Computation	210	5.6	6	63	72

FIGURE 7.9

Standardized Test Report for an Individual.

REFERENCES

Airasian, P. W. (1993). Policy-driven assessment or assessment-driven policy? *Measurement and Evaluation in Guidance and Counseling, 26,* (April): 22–30.

CTB/McGraw-Hill. (1985). *California Achievement Tests forms E and F: Technical bulletin 1.* Montery, CA: CTB/McGraw-Hill.

CTB/McGraw-Hill. (1986). *California Achievement Tests forms E and F: Class management guide.* Montery, CA: CTB/McGraw-Hill.

Quality Counts '99: Demanding Results. Education Week, January 11, 1999, p. 5.

Heaney, K. J., and Pullin, D. C. (1998). Accommodations and flags: Admission testing and the rights of individuals with disabilities. *Educational Assessment, 5* (2), 71–93.

North Carolina Department of Public Instruction. (1992). Quick reference for parents and teachers: Testing at various grade levels. *Parent Involvement,* September–October.

Olson, L. (1999). In search of better assessments. *Quality Counts '99, Education Week,* January 11, pp. 17–20.

Popham, W. J. (1990). *Modern educational measurement.* Englewood Cliffs, NJ: Prentice Hall.

The Psychological Corporation. (1984). *Stanford Achievement Test technical review manual.* New York: The Psychological Corporation.

Riverside Publishing Co. (1986). *Iowa Tests of Basic Skills: Preliminary technical summary.* Chicago: Riverside.

APPENDIX A

STANDARDS FOR TEACHER COMPETENCE IN EDUCATIONAL ASSESSMENT OF STUDENTS

The professional education associations began working in 1987 to develop standards for teacher competence in student assessment out of concern that the potential educational benefits of student assessments be fully realized. The Committee[1] appointed to this project completed its work in 1990 following reviews of earlier drafts by members of the measurement, teaching, and teacher preparation and certification communities. Parallel committees of affected associations are encouraged to develop similar statements of qualifications for school administrators, counselors, testing directors, supervisors, and other educators in the near future. These statements are intended to guide the preservice and in-service preparation of educators, the accreditation of preparation programs, and the future certification of all educators.[2]

A standard is defined here as a principle generally accepted by the professional associations responsible for this document. Assessment is defined as the process of obtaining information that is used to make educational decisions about students, to give feedback to the student about his or her progress, strengths, and weaknesses, to judge instructional effectiveness and curricular adequacy, and to inform policy. The various assessment techniques include, but are not limited to, formal and informal observation, qualitative analysis of pupil performance and products, paper-and-pencil tests, oral questioning, and analysis of student records. The assessment competencies included here are the knowledge and skills critical to a teacher's role as educator. It is understood that there are many competencies beyond assessment competencies which teachers must possess.

By establishing standards for teacher competence in student assessment, the associations subscribe to the view that student assessment is an essential part of teaching and that good teaching cannot exist without good student assessment. Training to develop the competencies covered in the standards should be an integral part of preservice preparation. Further, such assessment training should be widely available to practicing teachers through staff development programs at the district and building levels.

The standards are intended for use as:

- ◆ A guide for teacher educators as they design and approve programs for teacher preparation
- ◆ A self-assessment guide for teachers in identifying their needs for professional development in student assessment
- ◆ A guide for workshop instructors as they design professional development experiences for in-service teachers
- ◆ An impetus for educational measurement specialists and teacher trainers to conceptualize student assessment and teacher training in student assessment more broadly than has been the case in the past

The standards should be incorporated into future teacher training and certification programs. Teachers who have not had the preparation these standards imply should have the opportunity and support to develop these competencies before the standards enter into the evaluation of these teachers.

Approach Used to Develop the Standards

The members of the associations that supported this work are professional educators involved in teaching, teacher education, and student assessment. Members of these associations are concerned about the inadequacy with which teachers are prepared for assessing the educational progress of their students, and thus sought to address this concern effectively. A committee named by the associations first met in September 1987 and affirmed its commitment to defining standards for teacher preparation in student assessment. The committee then undertook a review of the research literature to identify needs in student assessment, current levels of teacher training in student assessment, areas of teacher activities requiring competence in using student assessments, and current levels of teacher competence in student assessment.

The members of the committee used their collective experience and expertise to formulate and then revise statements of important assessment competencies. Drafts of these competencies went through several revisions by the committee before the standards were released for public review. Comments by reviewers from each of the associations were then used to prepare a final statement.

Scope of a Teacher's Professional Role and Responsibilities for Student Assessment

There are seven standards in this document. In recognizing the critical need to revitalize classroom assessment, some standards focus on classroom-based competencies. Because of teachers' growing roles in education and policy decisions beyond the classroom, other standards address assessment competencies underlying teacher participation in decisions related to assessment at the school, district, state, and national levels.

The scope of a teacher's professional role and responsibilities for student assessment may be described in terms of the following activities. These activities imply that teachers need competence in student assessment and sufficient time and resources to complete them in a professional manner:

- ♦ **Activities Occurring prior to Instruction.** (a) Understanding students' cultural backgrounds, interests, skills, and abilities as they apply across a range of learning domains and/or subject areas; (b) understanding students' motivations and their interests in specific class content; (c) clarifying and articulating the performance outcomes expected of pupils; and (d) planning instruction for individuals or groups of students

- ♦ **Activities Occurring during Instruction.** (a) Monitoring pupil progress toward instructional goals; (b) identifying gains and difficulties pupils are experiencing in learning and performing; (c) adjusting instruction; (d) giving contingent, specific, and credible praise and feedback; (e) motivating students to learn; and (f) judging the extent of pupil attainment of instructional outcomes

- ♦ **Activities Occurring after the Appropriate Instructional Segment (e.g., Lesson, Class, Semester, Grade).** (a) Describing the extent to which each pupil has attained both short- and long-term instructional goals; (b) communicating strengths and weaknesses based on assessment results to students and parents or guardians; (c) recording and reporting assessment results for school-level analysis, evaluation, and decision making; (d) analyzing assessment information gathered before and during instruction to understand each student's progress to date and to inform future instructional planning; (e) evaluating the effectiveness of instruction; and (f) evaluating the effectiveness of the curriculum and materials in use

- ♦ **Activities Associated with a Teacher's Involvement in School Building and School District Decision Making.** (a) Serving on a school or district committee examining the school's and district's strengths and weaknesses in the development of its students; (b) working on the development or selection of assessment methods for school building or school district use; (c) evaluating school district curriculum; and (d) other related activities

◆ **Activities Associated with a Teacher's Involvement in a Wider Community of Educators.** (a) Serving on a state committee asked to develop learning goals and associated assessment methods; (b) participating in reviews of the appropriateness of district, state, or national student goals and associated assessment methods; and (c) interpreting the results of state and national student assessment programs

Each standard that follows is an expectation for assessment knowledge or skill that a teacher should possess in order to perform well in the five areas just described. As a set, the standards call on teachers to demonstrate skill at selecting, developing, applying, using, communicating, and evaluating student assessment information and student assessment practices. A brief rationale and illustrative behaviors follow each standard.

The standards represent a conceptual framework or scaffolding from which specific skills can be derived. Work to make these standards operational will be needed even after they have been published. It is also expected that experience in the application of these standards should lead to their improvement and further development.

1. **Teachers should be skilled in choosing assessment methods appropriate for instructional decisions.** Skills in choosing appropriate, useful, administratively convenient, technically adequate, and fair assessment methods are prerequisite to good use of information to support instructional decisions. Teachers need to be well-acquainted with the kinds of information provided by a broad range of assessment alternatives and their strengths and weaknesses. In particular, they should be familiar with criteria for evaluating and selecting assessment methods in light of instructional plans.

    Teachers who meet this standard will have the conceptual and application skills that follow. They will be able to use the concepts of assessment error and validity when developing or selecting their approaches to classroom assessment of students. They will understand how valid assessment data can support instructional activities such as providing appropriate feedback to students, diagnosing group and individual learning needs, planning for individualized educational programs, motivating students, and evaluating instructional procedures. They will understand how invalid information can affect instructional decisions about students. They will also be able to use and evaluate assessment options available to them, considering among other things, the cultural, social, economic, and language backgrounds of students. They will be aware that different assessment approaches can be incompatible with certain instructional goals and may impact quite differently on their teaching.

Teachers will know, for each assessment approach they use, its appropriateness for making decisions about their pupils. Moreover, teachers will know where to find information about and/or reviews of various assessment methods. Assessment options are diverse and include text- and curriculum-embedded questions and tests, standardized criterion-referenced and norm-referenced tests, oral questioning, spontaneous and structured performance assessments, portfolios, exhibitions, demonstrations, rating scales, writing samples, paper-and-pencil tests, seatwork and homework, peer- and self-assessments, student records, observations, questionnaires, interviews, projects, products, and others' opinions.

2. **Teachers should be skilled in developing assessment methods appropriate for instructional decisions.** While teachers often use published or other external assessment tools, the bulk of the assessment information they use for decision making comes from approaches they create and implement. Indeed, the assessment demands of the classroom go well beyond readily available instruments.

Teachers who meet this standard will have the conceptual and application skills that follow. Teachers will be skilled in planning the collection of information that facilitates the decisions they will make. They will know and follow appropriate principles for developing and using assessment methods in their teaching, avoiding common pitfalls in student assessment. Such techniques may include several of the options listed at the end of the first standard. The teacher will select the techniques which are appropriate to the intent of the teacher's instruction.

Teachers meeting this standard will also be skilled in using student data to analyze the quality of each assessment technique they use. Since most teachers do not have access to assessment specialists, they must be prepared to do these analyses themselves.

3. **Teachers should be skilled in administering, scoring, and interpreting the results of both externally-produced and teacher-produced assessment methods.** It is not enough that teachers are able to select and develop good assessment methods; they must also be able to apply them properly. Teachers should be skilled in administering, scoring, and interpreting results from diverse assessment methods.

Teachers who meet this standard will have the conceptual and application skills that follow. They will be skilled in interpreting informal and formal teacher-produced assessment results, including pupils' performances in class and on homework assignments. Teachers will be able to use guides for scoring essay questions and projects, stencils for scoring response-choice questions, and scales for rating performance assessments. They will be able to use these in ways that produce consistent results.

Teachers will be able to administer standardized achievement tests and be able to interpret the commonly reported scores: percentile ranks, percentile band scores, standard scores, and grade equivalents. They will have a conceptual understanding of the summary indexes commonly reported with assessment results: measures of central tendency, dispersion, relationships, reliability, and errors of measurement.

Teachers will be able to apply these concepts of score and summary indexes in ways that enhance their use of the assessments that they develop. They will be able to analyze assessment results to identify pupils' strengths and errors. If they get inconsistent results, they will seek other explanations for the discrepancy or other data to attempt to resolve the uncertainty before arriving at a decision. They will be able to use assessment methods in ways that encourage students' educational development and that do not inappropriately increase students' anxiety levels.

4. **Teachers should be skilled in using assessment results when making decisions about individual students, planning teaching, developing curriculum, and school improvements.** Assessment results are used to make educational decisions at several levels: in the classroom about students, in the community about a school and a school district, and in society, generally, about the purposes and outcomes of the educational enterprise. Teachers play a vital role when participating in decision making at each of these levels and must be able to use assessment results effectively.

Teachers who meet this standard will have the conceptual and application skills that follow. They will be able to use accumulated assessment information to organize a sound instructional plan for facilitating students' educational development. When using assessment results to plan and/or evaluate instruction and curriculum, teachers will interpret the results correctly and avoid common misinterpretations, such as basing decisions on scores that lack curriculum validity. They will be informed about the results of local, regional, state, and national assessment and about their appropriate use for pupil, classroom, school, district, state, and national educational improvement.

5. **Teachers should be skilled in developing valid pupil grading procedures which use pupil assessments.** Grading students is an important part of professional practice for teachers. Grading is defined as indicating both a student's level of performance and a teacher's valuing of that performance. The principles for using assessments to obtain valid grades are known and teachers should employ them.

Teachers who meet this standard will have the conceptual and application skills that follow. They will be able to devise, implement, and explain a procedure for developing grades composed of marks from various assignments, projects, in-class activities, quizzes, tests, and/or other assessments that they may use. Teachers will understand and be able to articulate why the grades they assign are rational, justified, and fair, acknowledging that such grades reflect their preferences and judgments. Teachers will be able to recognize and to avoid faulty grading procedures such as using grades as punishment. They will be able to evaluate and to modify their grading procedures in order to improve the validity of the interpretations made from them about students' attainments.

6. **Teachers should be skilled in communicating assessment results to students, parents, other lay audiences, and other educators.** Teachers must routinely report assessment results to students and to parents or guardians. In addition, they are frequently asked to report or to discuss assessment results with other educators and with diverse lay audiences. If the results are not communicated effectively, they may be misused or not used. To communicate effectively with others on matters of student assessment, teachers must be able to use assessment terminology appropriately and must be able to articulate the meaning, limitations, and implications of assessment results. Furthermore, teachers will sometimes be in a position that will require them to defend their own assessment procedures and their interpretations of them. At other times, teachers may need to help the public to interpret assessment results appropriately.

Teachers who meet this standard will have the conceptual and application skills that follow. Teachers will understand and be able to give appropriate explanations of how the interpretation of student assessments must be moderated by the student's socioeconomic, cultural, language, and other background factors. Teachers will be able to explain that assessment results do not imply that such background factors limit a student's ultimate educational development. They will be able to communicate to students and to their parents or guardians how they may assess the student's educational progress. Teachers will understand and be able to explain the importance of taking measurement errors into account when using assessments to make decisions about individual students. Teachers will be able to explain the limitations of different informal and formal assessment methods. They will be able to explain printed reports of the results of pupil assessments at the classroom, school district, state, and national levels.

7. **Teachers should be skilled in recognizing unethical, illegal, and otherwise inappropriate assessment methods and uses of assessment information.** Fairness, the rights of all concerned, and professional ethical behavior must undergird all student assessment activities from the initial planning for and gathering of information to the interpretation, use, and communication of the results.

Teachers must be well-versed in their own ethical and legal responsibilities in assessment. In addition, they should also attempt to have the inappropriate assessment practices of others discontinued whenever they are encountered. Teachers should also participate with the wider educational community in defining the limits of appropriate professional behavior in assessment.

Teachers who meet this standard will have the conceptual and application skills that follow. They will know those laws and case decisions which affect their classroom, school district, and state assessment practices. Teachers will be aware that various assessment procedures can be misused or overused resulting in harmful consequences such as embarrassing students, violating a student's right to confidentiality, and inappropriately using students' standardized achievement test scores to measure teaching effectiveness.

Notes

[1]The Committee that developed this statement was appointed by the collaborating professional associations. James R. Sanders (Western Michigan University) chaired the Committee and represented NCME along with John R. Hills (Florida State University) and Anthony J. Nitki (University of Pittsburgh). Jack C. Merwin (University of Minnesota) represented the American Association of Colleges for Teacher Education, Carolyn Trice represented the American Federation of Teachers, and Marcella Dianda and Jeffrey Schneider represented the National Education Association.

[2]The associations invite comments that may be used for improvement of this document. Comments may be sent to: Teacher Standards in Student Assessment, American Federation of Teachers, 555 New Jersey Avenue, NW, Washington, DC 20001; Teacher Standards in Student Assessment, National Council on Measurement in Education, 1230 Seventeenth Street, NW, Washington, DC 20036; or Teacher Standards in Student Assessment, Instruction and Professional Development, National Education Association, 1201 Sixteenth Street, NW, Washington, DC 20036.

Please note that this document is not copyrighted material and that reproduction and dissemination are encouraged.

APPENDIX B

WEB SITES

Eric Clearinghouse on Assessment

http://ericae.net/

The Eric Clearinghouse on Assessment seeks to provide 1) balanced information concerning educational assessment and 2) resources to encourage responsible test use. It contains links to numerous assessment and evaluation sites on the Internet, as well as full on-line assessment articles and digests and a test collection database with records on over 10,000 tests and research instruments covering a wide range of subjects and fields.

U.S. Department of Education

http://www.ed.gov/

This site provides current information on educational issues, as well as the latest research findings, statistics, and information on education and links to other Department of Education-funded on-line educational resources. It is also the place to learn about the current administration's education priorities, educational funding opportunities, and department of education programs and services.

Measurement and Evaluation

http://galaxy.tradewave.com/galaxy/Social-Sciences/Education/Measurement-and-Evaluation.html

This site contains links to academic organizations, research methods resources, and periodicals that deal with measurement and evaluation.

CRESST

http://cresst96.cse.ucla.edu/index.htm

The site of the National Center for Research on Evaluation, Standards, and Student Testing (CRESST), which conducts research on important topics related to K–12 educational testing, contains an on-line library with full text research reports and newsletters, assessment samples, guidebooks, and databases, and a listserve for discussion on relevant topics.

Massachusetts Department of Education

http://info.doe.mass.edu/
This website contains information for administrators, teachers, students, parents, and communities regarding the MA curriculum frameworks, state tests, teacher certification, school reform, educational technology, and more.

National Association of Test Directors

http://www.natd.org
The NATD web site contains full-text symposium papers, news about national achievement tests and other issues, and links to Internet assessment and evaluation resources, including general K–12 assessment resources, curriculum standards, the regional education laboratory network, US government resources, professional organizations related to assessment and evaluation, and grant seeker information available on the Internet.

CSTEEP

http://www.csteep.bc.edu.ctest
The Center for the Study of Testing, Evaluation, and Educational Policy (CSTEEP) is an educational research organization with the goals of conducting research on testing and evaluation and public policy studies to improve school assessment practices. The CSTEEP site contains information on current CSTEEP projects and links to useful education sites on the Internet.

National Education Goals

http://www.ed.gov/legislation/ESEA/Guidance/app-c.html
This site lists National Education Goals from the September 1996 Elementary and Secondary Education Act.

National Council for Teachers of English

http://www.ncte.org
This site contains useful resources on teaching ideas, teacher talk, standards, public policy, professional development, teacher preparation, journals, grants and awards, jobs, research, NCTE meetings and membership, and various NCTE organizations.

National Council for Social Studies

http://www.ncss.org

This site contains information of interest to social studies teachers, including the NCSS annual conference and membership information, social studies journals and publications, teaching resources, news for educators, and standards and curriculum, as well as Internet links and resources, discussion groups, a bookstore, and local and state organizations.

National Council for Teachers of Mathematics

http://www.nctm.org

This site provides information about NCTM membership and meetings, full-text articles and abstracts of articles in NCTM publications, a fax-on-demand service, a means for ordering NCTM products, full-text NCTM principles and standards, and on-line classified job listings and math announcements.

International Reading Association

http://www.reading.org

This site provides information related to the International Reading Association: conferences, publications, projects, research, and news, as well as an on-line bookstore and an on-line membership directory.

Berliner/Biddle study

http://olam.ed/asu.edu/epaa/

Volume 4 of the on-line scholarly journal, Educational Policy Analysis Archives, contains a full-text review of Berliner and Biddle's book, *The Manufactured Crisis,* as well as a reply to this review by Berliner and Biddle themselves.

Children's Defense Fund

http://www.childrensdefense.org

This site contains news and reports, job information, Internet links, and other publications related to the Children's Defense Fund's mission of ensuring every child a healthy start, a head start, a fair start, a safe start, and a moral start in life and a successful passage to adulthood.

National Alliance for Safe Schools

http://www.safeschools.org

Dedicated to the promotion of an orderly educational environment, this site contains NASS news and publications, information on NASS workshops, school security assessments, and links to related sites on the Web.

National School Safety Center

http://nssc1.org/
This site presents information related to research on school crime and violence, as well as NSSC services, training programs, school safety studies, resources for parents, and links to other resources.

National Center for Education Statistics

http://nces.ed.gov/pubs98/violence/index.html
This site contains the full research report, "Violence and Discipline Problems in US Public Schools: 1996–97," which was published in March 1998 by the National Center for Education Statistics. The report can be downloaded or viewed as a PDF file.

Eric Clearinghouse on Urban Education

http://eric-web.tc.columbia.edu/
This clearinghouse contains digests, bibliographies, parent guides, abstracts, and other publications on such subjects as equity and cultural diversity, urban teachers, curriculum and instruction, compensatory education, administration and finance, and other subjects that are of interest in urban education. It also contains links to other urban education and Historically Black Colleges and Universities resources on the Web, as well as links to the entire ERIC database.

Teachers Connecting Through the Web

http://www.teachnet.com
This website presents "smart ideas for busy teachers" in the form of lesson ideas, how-to information, teaching activities, teacher discussion groups, and resources and links.

Creating Lesson Plans

http://www.ericsp.org/lesson.html
This site of the ERIC Clearinghouse on Teaching and Teacher Education contains an extensive collection of lesson plans for every subject, ideas to help manage and access information for the classroom, and extensive K–12 educational resources.

American Federation of Teachers

http://www.aft.org
This site provides the latest AFT union information, conference information policy briefs and other publications, and news and information for

K–12 teachers, public employees, higher education staff, nurses and health professionals, and paraprofessionals and school-related personnel.

Education Week

http://www.edweek.org

This site contains the full text of the current week's *Education Week,* American Education's Newspaper of Record, as well as links to past issues. It also provides In Context, or background pages on key education issues, lists of terms, organizations, and Web sites. The full text of *Teacher Magazine* is on this site, as well as the *Daily News,* a resource containing newspaper articles about schools from all over the US.

New Teachers Page

http://www.newteacher.com

This site is a resource site for education students, student teachers, first-year teachers, teacher certification candidates, and those who are considering teaching as a profession. It contains information about professional development opportunities, major books and authors in education, practically- and theoretically-oriented articles for new teachers, and teaching advice.

Developing Educational Standards

http://www.putwest.boces.org/standards.html#section2

This site contains links to full-text versions of standards by state and subject area, as well as US government standards and standards from other nations. It also provides links to centers, clearinghouses, labs, state-focused groups, newspapers, magazines, and other organizations that deal with or focus on standards.

Ask ERIC

http://ericir.syr.edu/

This site contains an ERIC Question & Answer Service, links to the ERIC Virtual Library and the ERIC database, and information on new and noteworthy recent contributions to the ERIC database.

GLOSSARY

Ability   What one has learned over a period of time from both school and nonschool sources; one's general capability for performing tasks.

Achievement   What one has learned from formal instruction, usually in school.

Affective behaviors   Behaviors related to feelings, emotions, values, attitudes, interests, and personality; nonintellective behaviors.

Analytic scoring   Essay scoring method in which separate scores are given for specific aspects of the essay (e.g., organization, factual accuracy, spelling).

Anecdotal record   A short, written report of an individual's behavior in a specific situation or circumstance.

Aptitude   One's capability for performing a particular task or skill; usually involves a narrower skill than ability (e.g., mathematics aptitude or foreign language aptitude).

Assessment   The process of collecting, synthesizing, and interpreting information to aid classroom decision making; includes information gathered about pupils, instruction, and classroom climate.

Assessment error   Inconsistencies in scores, ratings, or observations that result from systematic factors such as faulty test items and a poor testing environment as well as from nonsystematic, uncontrollable factors such as guessing success and physical or emotional state at the time of assessment; all assessments have some degree of error.

Behavioral objective   *See* Educational objective.

Bias   A situation in which assessment information produces results that give one group an advantage or disadvantage over other groups because of problems in the content, procedures, or interpretation of the assessment information; a distortion or misrepresentation of performance.

Checklist   A written list of performance criteria associated with a particular activity or product in which an observer marks the pupil's performance on each criterion using a scale that has only two choices.

Cognitive behaviors   Behaviors related to intellective processes like thinking, reasoning, memorizing, problem solving, analyzing, and applying.

Cooperative learning   Groups of pupils working together to perform a task or solve a problem.

Criterion-referenced grading   Determining the quality of a pupil's performance by comparing it to preestablished standards of mastery.

Curriculum   The skills, performances, attitudes, and values pupils are expected to learn from schooling; includes statements of desired pupil outcomes, descriptions of materials, and the planned sequence that will be used to help pupils attain the outcomes.

Cut score   A predetermined score used to differentiate levels of pupil performance, usually in statewide assessment.

Descriptive summarization   See rubric.

Diagnose   Identify specific strengths and weaknesses in pupils' past and present learning.

Difficulty   Indicates the proportion of pupils who answered a test item correctly.

Discrimination   Indicates the extent to which pupils who get a particular test item correct are also likely to get a high score on the entire test.

Distractor   A wrong choice in a selection test item.

Educate   To change the behavior of pupils; to teach pupils to do things they could not previously do.

Education   The process designed to change pupils' behaviors in particular ways.

Educational objectives   Statements that describe a pupil accomplishment that will result from instruction; the statement describes the behavior the pupil will learn to perform and the content on which it will be performed.

Evaluation   Judging the quality or goodness of a performance or a course of action.

Form   The particular version of a commercial test that has more than one equivalent versions.

Formative assessment   Assessment carried out for the purpose of improving learning or teaching while it is still going on; assessment for improvement, not grading.

Goals   Broad objectives that define comprehensive, visionary objectives.

Grade   The symbol or number used by a teacher to represent a pupil's achievement in a subject area.

Grade equivalent score   A standardized test score that describes a pupil's performance on a scale based upon grade in school and month in grade; most commonly misinterpreted score; indicates pupil's level of performance relative to pupils in his/her own grade.

Grading curve   The proportion of pupils who can receive each grade in a norm-referenced grading system.

Grading system   The process by which a teacher arrives at the symbol or number that is used to represent a pupil's achievement in a subject area.

Group assessment   Assessing many pupils at the same time.

Higher level cognitive behavior   Intellectual processes that are more complicated than simple memorization; e.g., problem solving, interpretation, analysis, and comprehension.

Holistic scoring   Essay scoring method in which a single score is given to represent the overall quality of the essay across all dimensions.

Individual assessment   Assessing one pupil at a time.

Instruction   The methods and processes by which pupils' behaviors are changed.

Instructional assessments   Collection, synthesis, and interpretation of information needed to make decisions about planning or carrying out instruction.

Instructional objectives   Specific objectives used to plan daily lessons.

Interpretive exercise   Test situation that contains a chart, passage, poem, or other material that the pupil must interpret in order to answer the questions posed.

Items   Questions or problems on an assessment instrument.

Key   A list of correct answers for a test.

Level   The grade level(s) at which a particular commercial test should be administered to pupils.

Local norms   Test norms that describe a pupil's performance in comparison to pupils in his/her class, school, or city.

Logical error   The use of invalid or irrelevant assessment information to judge a pupil's characteristics or performance.

Lower level cognitive behavior   Intellectual processes that involve only memorization (e.g., reciting number facts, writing spelling words, stating a poem from memory).

Measurement   The process of quantifying or assigning numbers or categories to performance according to rules and standards.

Norm group   The group of pupils who were tested to produce the norms for a test.

Norm-referenced grading   Determining the quality of a pupil's performance by comparing it to the performance of other pupils.

Norms   A set of scores that describes the performance of a specific group of pupils, usually a national sample at a particular grade level, on a task or test; these scores are used to interpret scores of other pupils who perform the same task or take the same test.

Numerical summarization   Use of numbers to describe performance on an assessment.

Objectives   Statements that describe what pupils are expected to learn from instruction.

Objective score   Different scorers or raters will independently arrive at the same scores or rating for a pupil's performance.

Observation   Watching or listening to pupils performing an activity or producing a product.

Observer prejudgment   The use of prior information or beliefs that leads a teacher to label a pupil prematurely.

Official assessments   Assessments teachers are required to carry out to fulfill their official, bureaucratic decision-making responsibilities, such as grading, grouping, placing, and promoting pupils.

Options   Choices available to select from in answering a multiple-choice test item.

Peer review   Pupils discuss and rate each other's work based on clear performance criteria.

Percentile band   The range of percentile ranks in which a pupil is expected to fall on repeated testing; a way to indicate the error in scores to avoid overinterpretation of results.

Percentile rank   A standardized test score that describes the percentage of pupils a given pupil scored higher than; 89th percentile rank means that a pupil scored higher than 89 percent of the pupils in the norm group.

Performance assessments Observing and judging a pupil's skill in actually carrying out a physical activity (e.g., giving a speech) or producing a product (e.g., building a birdhouse).

Performance criteria The aspects of a performance or product that are observed and judged in performance assessment.

Performance standards The levels of achievement pupils must reach to receive particular grades in a criterion-referenced grading system (e.g., higher than 90 receives an A, between 80 and 90 receives a B, etc.).

Portfolio A well-defined collection of pupils' products or performances that shows achievement of particular skills over time.

Practical knowledge The beliefs, prior experiences, and strategies that enable a teacher to carry out classroom duties and activities.

Prejudgment Situations in which a person's prior knowledge, first impression, or stereotypes interfere with the ability to make a fair and objective assessment of another person.

Premise The stem or question part of a selection item.

Psychomotor behaviors Behaviors related to the performance of physical and manipulative activities such as holding a pencil, buttoning buttons, serving a tennis ball, playing the piano, and cutting with scissors.

Rating scale A written list of performance criteria associated with a particular activity or product in which an observer marks the pupil's performance on each criterion in terms of its quality using a scale that has more than two choices.

Raw score The number of items or total score a pupil obtained on an assessment.

Reliability How consistent the results of an assessment procedure are; if an assessment is reliable, it will yield nearly the same performance information about a pupil on retesting.

Response A pupil's answer to a test item.

Rubric A scoring guide that describes varied levels of quality of student performance or product assessments.

Scoring rubric A rating scale based upon written descriptions of varied levels of achievement in a performance assessment.

Selection questions Test items in which the pupil responds by selecting the answer from choices given; multiple-choice, true-false, and matching items are examples.

Self-assessment Making a pupil responsible for judging and critiquing his or her performance or product according to clear performance criteria.

Self-fulfilling prophecy Process in which teachers form perceptions about pupil characteristics, treat pupils as if the perceptions are correct, and pupils respond as if they actually have the characteristics, even though they might not have originally had them; an expectation becomes a reality.

Sizing-up assessments Assessments used by teachers in the first weeks of school to get to know pupils so that they can be organized into a classroom society with rules, communication, and control.

Specific determiners Words that give clues to true-false items: *all, always, never, none* (choose false); *some, sometimes, may* (choose true).

Standardized assessment An assessment that is administered, scored, and interpreted the same for all pupils taking the test.

Stanine A standardized test score that describes pupil performance on a nine-point scale ranging from 1 to 9; scores of 1, 2, and 3 are often interpreted as being below average; 4, 5, and 6 as being average; and 7, 8, and 9 as being above average.

State-mandated test Test required of all pupils at certain grade levels in a state; intended to assess individual pupil competence or school-level performance.

Stem The part of a multiple-choice item that states the question to be answered.

Subjective score Different scorers or raters will not agree on a pupil's score or rating; independent scorers produce different scores or ratings for a pupil.

Subtests Sets of items administered and scored as a separate portion of a longer, more comprehensive test.

Summative assessment Assessment carried out at the end of instruction to determine pupil learning and to assign grades; different from formative assessment, which is intended to improve a process while it is still going on.

Supply questions Test items in which the pupil responds by writing or constructing his/her own answer; short-answer, completion, and essay items are examples.

Taxonomy A classification system.

Teacher comment Any formal or informal verbal interaction between the teacher and pupil(s).

Test A formal, systematic procedure for obtaining a sample of pupils' behavior; the results of a test are used to make generalizations about how pupils would have performed on similar but untested behaviors.

Test battery A group of subtests, each assessing a different subject area but all normed on the same sample; designed to be administered to the same group of test takers.

Test norms *See* Norms.

Test wiseness skills The test taker's ability to identify flaws in items that give away the correct answers; used during tests to outwit poor item writers.

Validity The extent to which assessment information is appropriate for making the desired decision about pupils, instruction, or classroom climate; the degree to which assessment information permits correct interpretations of the desired kind; the most important characteristic of assessment information.

NAME INDEX

SUBJECT INDEX

Note: Page numbers in *italics* indicate illustrations; those followed by a "t" indicate tables.